The Imaginary Puritan

The New Historicism: Studies in Cultural Poetics
Stephen Greenblatt, General Editor

The Imaginary Puritan

Literature, Intellectual Labor, and the Origins of Personal Life

Nancy Armstrong
Leonard Tennenhouse

UNIVERSITY OF CALIFORNIA PRESS
Berkeley · Los Angeles · London

University of California Press
Berkeley and Los Angeles, California

University of California Press, Ltd.
London, England

© 1992 by
The Regents of the University of California

First Paperback Printing 1994

Library of Congress Cataloging-in-Publication Data

Armstrong, Nancy.
    The imaginary puritan : literature, intellectual labor, and the
origins of personal life / Nancy Armstrong, Leonard Tennenhouse.
        p.   cm. – (The New historicism ; 21)
    Includes bibliographical references and index.
    ISBN 0-520-08643-0
    1. English literature—Early modern, 1500-1700—History and
criticism—Theory, etc. 2. English literature—18th century—
History and criticism—Theory, etc. 3. American literature—
History and criticism—Theory, etc. 4. Great Britain—Intellectual
life—17th century. 5. Literature and history—Great Britain.
6. Literature and history—United States. 7. United States—
Intellectual life. 8. Imagination—History. 9. Authorship—
History. 10. Self in literature. I. Tennenhouse, Leonard, 1942-
II. Title. III. Series.
PR431.A76   1992
820.9'004—dc20   91-40263
                                                                    CIP

Printed in the United States of America

9 8 7 6 5 4 3 2 1

For Henry, George, and Rey

Contents

Acknowledgments

This project was supported by two grants from the Rockefeller Foundation which allowed each of us to be part of the multiyear project on narrative conducted at the Center for the Humanities, Wesleyan University. Armstrong was a fellow at the center in 1987–88, and Tennenhouse in 1989–90. While a fellow at the Huntington Library in the winter of 1987, Tennenhouse began the research on chapters 2 and 4. A section of chapter 4 appeared as "Gender and the Work of Words," *Cultural Critique* 13 (1989): 229–78, and a portion of chapter 7 as "The Interior Difference: A Brief Genealogy of Dreams, 1650–1717," *Eighteenth-Century Studies* 23 (1990): 458–78. For permission to reprint a revised version of the first essay, we wish to thank the editor, Donna Przybylowicz. For permission to reprint a version of the second, we thank the editors of *Eighteenth-Century Studies*. Our special thanks go to Doris Kretschmer and Tony Hicks for the care they took with the manuscript of this book.

The Imaginary Puritan could not have been conceptualized and written without the enabling fantasy of the very kind of community it elaborates. The book exists for us as the instrument and record of a sequence of scholarly exchanges that took place across the United States and in Portugal over a three-year period. For this community, we are indebted to the Center for the Humanities at Wesleyan University; to Richard Vann and Richard Ohmann, respectively, who directed the Center while we were fellows there; and to those members of the Wesleyan faculty who provided the center of the Center. We thank you for creating a milieu where ideas could be tried out, passed around, tinkered with, and regarded with still more affection for the experience. During the alternate school years, 1988–89 and 1990–91, we lived with the intellectual pressure and generosity of a second community—again largely imagined because hardly the norm—as members of the Department of Comparative Literature at the University of Minnesota. Our appreciation extends to Susan McClary and to Paula Rabinowitz as well. Our summers were spent in Solana Beach, where it was possible both to synthesize the pieces of research and writing of the previous year as we walked along the beach and to produce each of several drafts while looking out over the Pacific.

An early draft went out to yet another group of friends and colleagues who were as generous with their time and criticism as the first. We cannot imagine having proceeded further with the project without Joseph Wittreich's suggestions for chapter 1; the readings Paul Christianson, Richard Vann, and Henry Abelove gave of chapter 2; Mark Poster's and Henry Abelove's advice on the historians of the family, discussed in chapters 3 and 6; suggestions by Thomas Laqueur, John Frow, Michael Denning, and Joan Scott for chapter 4; Richard Ohmann's insights concerning the subject matter of chapter 5 as well as Bruce Robbins's response to an early version of that chapter; Richard Vann's advice on research and Felicity Nussbaum's comments on chapter 7; and the help of Carroll Smith-Rosenberg, Doris Sommer, and Page duBois in conceptualizing chapter 8. After these responses and suggestions found their way into the manuscript, it went on the road. It grew both sharper and more mellow as it encountered an unanticipated range of objections, questions, and suggestions. Though we cannot possibly acknowledge these contributions individually, we count on those who offered them to recognize their handiwork in the finished product. We must thank Marjorie Garber for providing a forum for an earlier version of chapter 4 at Harvard University; John Carlos Rowe for devoting a seminar to our draft of chapter 5 at the University of California Humanities Research Institute; Irene and Boaventura Santos for organizing a challenging debate over chapter 5 at the University of Coimbra; Kathleen Woodward for arranging a very helpful discussion of chapter 7 at the Center for Twentieth-Century Studies at the University of Wisconsin-Milwaukee; Sharon Salinger for making chapter 8 the focus of a Women's Studies colloquium at the University of California-Riverside, sponsored by the University of California Humanities Research Institute; and Carroll Smith-Rosenberg and Peter Stallybrass for organizing a seminar around this chapter at the University of Pennsylvania.

Once all these exchanges had made their mark on the manuscript, it had the good fortune to fall into the hands of several readers who were as good-humored as they were honest, informed, shrewd, and practical. For putting this kind of effort into our manuscript, we want to thank George Mariscal, Josué Harrari, Homer Brown, J. Paul Hunter, and Michael Davidson. We owe a special debt to Stephen Greenblatt. With his expert and unwavering support from beginning to end, we were able to pursue our research and assemble our argument with a sense of intellectual freedom that perhaps few scholars enjoy.

Another kind of gratitude is reserved for Henry Abelove, George Mariscal, and Rey Chow, who were willing to entertain any idea—no matter how pedestrian, how grandiose, how speculative, or how crudely constructed—during the entire period it took to complete this book. Where do the best ideas come from if not from such friends?

Introduction:
The Imaginary Puritan

In passing from history to nature, myth acts economically:
it abolishes the complexity of human acts, it gives them the
simplicity of essences, it does away with all dialectics, with
any going back beyond what is immediately visible, it organizes a world which is without contradictions because it is
without depth, a world wide open and wallowing in the evident, it establishes a blissful clarity: things appear to mean
something by themselves.

Roland Barthes, "Myth Today"

This is a book about the appearance of "the author" during the late
seventeenth and early eighteenth centuries and what happens to traditional historical narratives once one grants central importance to this
event. Indeed, for purposes of argument we have equated the appearance
of the author with nothing less than the onset of modernity itself. It
might be argued that there were writers before this moment—Ben Jonson
or Cervantes, perhaps—who imagined having much the same kind of
power as writers that modern readers now attribute to authors, but we
are not interested in arguing for the anomalous figure or the lone prototype. By the appearance of "the author" we mean the emergence of
the group who first gave the term its modern meaning, the class of people
on whom writing conferred authority by placing them in a new and
distinctive relationship with themselves, with other people, and with a
world of objects.

We gladly concede that neither the subject matter nor the theoretical
issues this book addresses are all that new. Even the most conventional
histories of seventeenth- and eighteenth-century England note the si-
multaneous lifting of censorship, the emergence of the popular press,
the growth of a mass readership, and the increasing importance of popular
media in determining the outcome of political conflict. Each of these

events, furthermore, has been the focus of any number of specialized studies. While such scholarship has proved invaluable to our project, it is grounded on historiographical assumptions that critical theory challenged some time ago. With nearly flawless consistency, accounts of the modern period assume that events occurring to, through, or within writing belong in a secondary or derivative relationship to economic, political, and social history.[1] To compose a history of such events, we therefore turned away from the very materials that history most often uses to explain the relationship between past and present-day Western culture. We have focused instead on materials that usually testify to effects rather than causes, and we have privileged what are generally thought to be contingent rather than necessary relations among them. In granting such phenomena a central role in our account of modernity, we have given them causality, and thus, one might say, a kind of necessity. In doing so, we will be questioning the basic categories of modern historiography.

We should perhaps begin to lay out our argument by saying that in identifying the problem we have with traditional literary criticism and British historiography, we found it advantageous to downplay the schism that developed within poststructuralism more than two decades ago over the question of history.[2] In *Of Grammatology*, Derrida asks his readers to relinquish the hierarchical relationship between speech and writing that literate members of modern European cultures pretty much take for granted. He invites them to invert the commonsense assumption that writing necessarily presupposes speech, which in turn presupposes human thought and feeling. This chain of assumptions makes truth depend on tracing the printed word back to an origin within an individuated consciousness—what is meant by an "author." Indeed, he argues, this commonsense epistemology perpetuates the belief that where there is writing there must once have been someone thinking those thoughts and putting them into words. Despite the rhetorical battle he waged with Derrida almost thirty years ago, Foucault's work proceeds from this same proposition.[3] He questions only its universality. Derrida exposes the ahistoricity of any history that anchors language to a world of referents outside and prior to the act of inscription. Foucault uses another tactic. He turns history against itself by historicizing the very classification system that makes history possible, which includes the distinction between that which originates outside the individual consciousness and that which comes from within it, as well as the distinction between words and things. He does this by giving the Derridean inversion a specific location in space and time.

At some time in the late seventeenth century, according to this deliberately strange retelling of the story, certain people in France, England, Germany, and presumably elsewhere in western Europe undertook a project whose enormity could be understood only in retrospect. For Foucault, the thoroughgoing, irreversible effects of the venture rested not so much on the classification system they managed to put in place as on a twofold fact of its semiotic character: the tendency to individuate things and people by assigning them a place and function, and the tendency to do this first of all in writing. It was when a whole new group of people began to write—and to write, we might add, for a wholly different purpose than ever before—that the inversion which empowered writing must have taken place. As words began to master things through various and subtle procedures of classification, writing began to imply a source in individual thought, and that source consequently became the means of mastering both objects and other people. If Derrida calls attention to the ahistoricity of traditional historiography, then Foucault historicizes the symbolic behavior that simultaneously produces an origin for meaning outside and prior to language at the same time that it declares one can know anything—a person, an idea, a disease—by determining where it came from. He historicizes the moment when histories in this general sense began to provide the explanatory logic of Western culture.

By writing his off-centered histories—of madness, of the reclassification of nature, of the clinic, of sexuality, of the modern penitentiary—Foucault argues that modern history has heretofore been turned backward, so that it can specify where something that presently exists "came from." That is to say, history by its very nature is a kind of just-so story that gives the operative categories of industrial cultures a location well in the past, thus allowing the present order of things to emerge as so many facts of human nature. For Foucault, however, history also offers the only way out of the dilemma posed by history. One must give up the whole pretense of knowing the past (which only conceals the effects of writing about it); one must show precisely when and how the most basic categories of modern culture developed and how they related to one another. Rather than explain how a particular sequence of humane reforms transformed the scaffold into the modern penal institution, for example, *Discipline and Punish* offers the reader a snarl of contingencies—theories, procedures, architectural drawings—that worked together to produce an entirely new understanding of crime. Foucault assembles the remains of particular practices from various local sites to show how, when viewed retrospectively, these practices attributed crime to asocial tendencies within the individual or, more precisely, to aspects of human nature that had not been properly managed.

His account pursues the principle of overdetermination orchestrating the development of an institutional culture with the production of people who require its managerial procedures. In providing us with such an account, his point is never to make one see the past as it really was. His concern is wholly for the present. He submits to literary analysis precisely those statements that seem literally true. Then, having turned fact into metaphor, he can establish what kind of ideological work such metaphors do. Foucault's histories no more presume to say what things, people, words, thoughts, or feelings are now than they do to say what these things used to be. He simply wants to demonstrate how they were written into existence in one way rather than some other. The only true history is the history of discourse, or how an entire field of symbolic practices became meaningful in relation to specific kinds of writing that could be called knowledge.

Foucault begins from the assumption that history actually authorizes certain power relations in the here and now by giving them a source in earlier periods of time. As it establishes narrative continuity between modern phenomena and their earlier counterparts, history also establishes an unbreachable distinction between the subject and object of writing. To overturn history, one simply has to demonstrate that words come chronologically as well as ontologically before the things they are presumed to represent and the differences that already exist among those things. Those of us who are willing to entertain this possibility have had little difficulty finding evidence to substantiate the inversion of traditional historical priorities.[4] Such a claim can be made with unwavering confidence, however, only until one tries to historicize the moment when writing and writers changed places and words began to create a new source for themselves in the kind of individual they named as their author. At that point, one must address the question of who authored the author.

It is all well and good to argue, as poststructuralism has done, that writing produces its author rather than the other way around. It is just as important to understand that writing did not always imply such a source. For only by dispelling the universality of "the author" can one understand the significance of writing that called authors—countless varieties of them—into being. But there is still a trade-off involved in demystifying the author, as there is, no doubt, in any act of demystification. The magic simply gets relocated, and theory tends to mystify writing instead of authors. In Foucault's accounts of modernity, for example, writing ceases to operate as an effect of other causes, located mainly in the church and the nobility, and becomes a cause in its own right. To give writing this priority, he grants it the capacity to authorize itself, and the will to do so, at some point in the late seventeenth or the eighteenth century. Before relying on Foucault, then, one has to consider what is gained—theoretically, historically, or otherwise—by deciding to place all the emphasis where he did. To what advantage does one substitute "discourse" not only for "authors" but also for "money," "Parliament," nationalism, man's relentless will to dominate, his unquenchable thirst for freedom, or any of the other causes traditionally thought to have ushered in the modern age? If this attribution of causality produces only another mystification, why undertake such a project at all?

We have fixed on writing because it is on this point that poststructuralism inadvertently collaborates with traditional historiography in refusing to grant writing much causality, if any at all. Poststructuralism charges writing with the mysterious power to create what it presumes to represent, while historiography unselfconsciously exploits that power whenever it claims to be putting us in touch with things that no longer exist and the people who used to know them. Some investigators use the idea of textuality as a way of closing this gap between literature and history. Let us think of history itself as a text composed of various bits of cultural material, symbolic systems, and social practices, they say. Indeed, they add, let us assume further that descriptions or theories of that text add something to the object of analysis and can therefore transform the very nature of its being. All well and good, we say—until one finds that the old opposition between philosophical "text" and historical "narrative" has been put back in place.

To be historical, others insist, a text must have a narrative that connects it to the larger narrative of history. Thus, for example, after demonstrating the literary element in nineteenth-century historiography, Hayden White connects the figurative behavior of specific historical texts to "deep" narrative structures that are somehow universal to human cultures, and yet historical in that they can enter into play in a specific field through one of several protocols that fix the field to its moment in time. As he says of "Michelet, Ranke, Tocqueville, and Burckhardt among the historians, and of Hegel, Marx, Nietzsche, and Croce among the philosophers" of nineteenth-century history: "through the disclosure of the linguistic ground on which a given idea of history was constituted, I have attempted to establish the ineluctably poetic nature of the historical work and to specify the prefigurative element in a historical account by which its theoretical concepts were tacitly sanctioned."[5] The influence of this residual structuralism, or layered model of textual production, is still very much with us and could indeed be said to linger in Fredric Jameson's idea that the master narrative of a given age offers one way of getting at the political unconscious of the people who actually lived during that time.[6] If not human nature, then a peculiar residue of the folktale, and thus a sense of the archaic, clings to the concept of narrative whenever it provides a quasi-somatic bond between the text and the people.

But it is not only the humanistic side of the debate that recognizes the power of narrative. Whereas White and Jameson identify it as a "deep," or prewritten, dimension of collective human experience, Foucault and Derrida assume that the story is all on the surface; narrative is what produces the illusion of depth. For Foucault, narrative is more specifically what creates a cause-and-effect relationship among people and things that leaves words out of the picture. The superficial aspect of human experience is really all there is, since it produces the language of the nonself, the underclass, the non-Western, the otherwise gendered, and thus the unconscious. This being the case, why can't one simply look at narrative as a function of the surface? Because narrative form, no matter how formal, tends to drag one back into the ahistorical quagmire of deep meaning. Thus to reject narrative is in a sense to acknowledge its peculiar ability to locate meaning outside of words themselves.

Poststructuralism may have identified the problem, but it has not found a way to resolve it. Even Foucault leaves the opposition between text and narrative alone, and this makes him vulnerable on two counts. He has committed what traditional humanism regards as "the sin" of poststructuralism, that of having focused on the text rather than on the experiences of real people. At the same time, poststructuralism suspects Foucault of telling stories without explaining exactly why and how he is doing so. His work somehow embodies both sides of the question of history; it is at once too concerned with the text and not concerned enough. But whether narrative constitutes an a priori and more material, because collective, reality or whether it is a function of the text to create the illusion that its words have come to life in a kind of motion picture, the verdict for narrative is virtually the same. It is assigned to a realm of sub- or pretextuality.

We want to question the distinction between text and narrative, if for no other reason than that such an interrogation is long overdue. It is probably true, as Geoff Bennington protests, that narrative ultimately introduces an element of self-deception into critical discourse. "The claim to be able to discern the real continuities and thus to ground those fantasies at least partially in 'truth' depends simply on the illusion of an intelligentsia as subject of science to stand outside and above that reality and those fantasies. This," he asserts, "is on its own terms not at all a historical or historicising position" (25). But what if one were to consider the narrative as purely a function of the surface? What if it were nothing else but the traces of the labor that went into organizing various materials, representations, representations of representations, into a reproducible and consumable body of knowledge that could be converted into speech—that could indeed produce a speech community? Then narrative could not be distinguished from writing in a fully historicized material sense. Narrative would have to be seen as the principle by which a modern scientific culture "works."[7] If such a definition of narrative bears a residue of nineteenth-century idealism, this cannot be helped; that residue is part of the history of the concept of intellectual labor itself. But concealing that labor has not at all curtailed its historical effects, as we will explain in subsequent chapters. Its disappearing act only mystifies the way intellectual labor works and the power it wields in modern cultures. Such labor disappears into writing, which in turn melts either into things or else into thin air, where it seems to refer to nothing at all. Indeed, if history is the story that scientific cultures tell about themselves, then the story apparently does its work by simultaneously empowering writing and rendering it transparent. The story of intellectual labor consequently remains to be told.

To privilege writing among the various changes that are said to have inaugurated our age is therefore to question historiography at several points at once: on the material terrain of social history, where labor and money make things happen; on the epic battlefields of political history, where armies and parliaments determine the course of the events; and on the loftier plateaus of intellectual history, where one set of ruling ideas inevitably gives way to another. We will argue that late-seventeenth-century England saw certain changes in intellectual and artistic practice that were both startling and profound. These changes simultaneously called into being an author with a personal life and transformed irreversibly what writing was, because they changed forever what writing did and could henceforth do. Writing could make demands in the name of the author on behalf of others. Thus, one can imagine, it created a sense among certain people that the so-called author—no longer to be understood as the spokesperson of God, king, or some lesser patron—exemplified the English people themselves.

Each of Foucault's histories identifies a strategic location where discourse can be observed at work, producing the cultural ground in which capital could take seed and flourish. He organizes these accounts by overturning the two presuppositions common to virtually all other histories of the modern period. He uses the strategies of history to show that changes in ruling ideas preceded changes in economic production and consumption. He also makes history argue that changes in the production and consumption of "ruling ideas," the emergence of "discourse," a certain form of "literacy," and distribution of "power" or "cultural capital" preceded the appearance of "the author," a vernacular "literature," and a horizontal affiliation among those people whom eighteenth-century scholarship considers part of a "readership."[8] In this way, Foucault demonstrates how words produced an object world precisely when they presumed to do no more than accurately describe and classify one. He also demonstrates that words produced a historically new form of individual as they began to reveal that, for centuries presumably, secrets had been repressed within each mind concerning the relationship between that mind and the body in which it was enclosed; these were the secrets of such an individual's desire. Two meanings of the word "subject" can consequently be—and often have been—used to describe the modern subject. He is, as Foucault explains, "subject to someone else by control and dependence, and tied to his own identity by a conscience or self-knowledge."[9] What Foucault does not explain is how the two inversions are related: how did those people who possessed the new "self-knowledge" acquire power over those who were simply subjects in the first sense, and what does that have to do with the process by which words gained ascendance over things? Both of these inversions are required to place rational man in a position of cultural authority. This omission in Foucault's account—*how* it happened—is what our book attempts to elaborate.

The phrase "Imaginary Puritan" refers to a logical, ontological, and historical gap shared by historicisms old and new, as well as to the theoretical and rhetorical sutures that insist one has received a whole picture of the seventeenth century, despite the time shift form early modern to modern that in fact severs one side of this cultural territory from the other.[10] To the gap and the continuity concealing it we have assigned the name "puritan," because the word invokes the generic intellectual ancestor that British and American scholars identify as the source of the power that makes individuals into subjects and vice versa. The puritan in question is "imaginary" because the term does not come from or refer to anybody in particular. As far as we know, it never did.[11] It came along and endowed an ensemble of cultural practices with a purely discursive body that made them vividly—indeed, powerfully—graspable as an originary moment, a moment that at once sowed the seeds of the Enlightenment, motivated the rise of the new middle classes, and enabled the onset of capitalism. Such an image does not arise from events but gives them meaning, places them in relation to us, and, in a word, makes them real.[12] Before laying out this argument in more detail, however, it is only fair to explain the reasons why we have used Milton to launch such an investigation.

When he described Milton as "the poet, the statesman, the philosopher, the glory of English literature, the champion and martyr of English liberty" as well as the embodiment of "the noblest qualities of every party," Lord Macaulay was not asserting an obvious truth; he was launching a spirited partisan defense.[13] Using the occasion of the publication of Milton's recently discovered *De Doctrina Christiana*, Macaulay turned Milton into a figure suitable for Whig celebration. While modern historians have generally understood Macaulay's use of Milton as a response to David Hume's equally partisan rendering of the seventeenth century, literary critics have tended to see it as an answer to Samuel Johnson's harshly critical "Life of Milton." In either case, with this statement Macaulay joined an argument about Milton that had begun decades before the publication of Hume's *History of Great Britain* and Johnson's essay on the poet.[14] The argument continues to this day.

Successive generations of cultural historians and literary critics have fought over Milton as over perhaps no other author, but they all tend to invoke features of the poet's life and works as if his mind alone could be said to contain the poles of modern humanism. Some, as Macaulay said of Johnson and his kind, "contrive in the same breath to extol the poems and to decry the poet"; others, T. S. Eliot prominent among them, attack Milton for writing poetry that could not be read "without our theological and political dispositions ... making an unlawful entry."[15] The debate over which—politician or poet—defines the true Milton has set the political inflexibility of the puritan moralist against the extraordinary learning and artistic virtuosity of the Renaissance humanist. It has also placed the regicidal pamphleteer in contention with the poet of Christian forgiveness. More recently, Milton's celebration of the common man, long thought to express a boldly progressive political stance, has come to be seen as evidence of a deep-seated conservatism on gender issues because of its relative exclusion of women.[16] And thus the argu-

ment proceeds as if Milton himself were capable of generating the differences among intellectual positions so diverse as those of William
Blake, Samuel Johnson, Lord Macaulay, T. S. Eliot, Christopher Hill,
Harold Bloom, and Sandra Gilbert and Susan Gubar. It is no doubt
because his "mind" seems capable of authorizing all these positions and
yet satisfying none that Milton continues to appear to each succeeding
generation as both extraordinarily capacious and significantly lacking—
for modern readers, the kind of mind that exemplifies human nature
itself. Regular unmaskings only perpetuate his status in this respect, and
he remains curiously unchanged through all the twists and turnings of
literary fashion, more so perhaps than any other author. Two centuries
of debate have made him into something on the order of what Roland
Barthes calls a mythology, namely, something "at the same time imperfectible and unquestionable."[17]

These terms first call to mind, perhaps, the Milton of the high aesthetic
tradition to whom the late eighteenth century gave credit for anticipating
the epistemological questions that coalesced around the concept of the
sublime.[18] Since then, Milton has served as the model of the Anglo-
American poet; he defines the contours of the discipline of English literature and anchors the canon of English letters. Literary criticism celebrates him as both the great exemplar of Renaissance humanism and
its last true embodiment in English cultural history. In practically the
same breath, however, the critical tradition routinely declares Milton the
first modern poet. Alienated from the political world after the failure of
the English Revolution, he is said to have withdrawn into a world of
pure imagination. With nothing but the resources of his own milieu to
depend upon, he inaugurated a poetic tradition that rolls through the
Enlightenment to inform Romanticism on both sides of the Atlantic and
from there worms its way into the heart of high modernism. One consequently finds him likened to William Blake, on the one hand, and to
Henry James and Wallace Stevens on the other.[19]

It is no doubt because his career includes the period of the English
Revolution that Milton provides such a convenient bridge between Renaissance humanism and the kind of humanism that came into fashion
with the Enlightenment in England. In sealing over what social and political historians regard as a definitive rupture, he also becomes the means
of drawing a natural line between the materials that can be called literature and those of history. Biographical accounts expand upon the
claim that he wrote prose on behalf of the revolutionary government at
the expense of his poetry and then returned to poetry only after he lost

his eyesight and retired from public life. In this way, the historical contradictions contained within the body of writing that bears his signature have broken apart along disciplinary lines (i.e., separating the politician and the poet) and then bonded together to compose the self-conflict of a single individual (i.e., the author). As a result, no one has found it necessary to deal with the fact that what it meant to write poetry as well as political prose changed drastically at least twice during Milton's lifetime.

But Milton is equally important for our purposes because he has been used in American high school and college literature courses to establish the continuity between English and American culture. Often represented as the quintessential puritan poet, he was the most widely read author in eighteenth-century America. Accounts of American literature generally mention his poetry as providing some of the soil in which an American republic of letters could take root and flourish. If a home in the American colonies possessed any books besides the Bible, they were likely to be *The Pilgrim's Progress* and *Paradise Lost.* George Sensabaugh has described Milton's stature in colonial America as so great that until the early nineteenth century "his shadow eclipsed even Homer and Virgil."[20] In the nineteenth century he continued to be an important source for an indigenous American imagination. And because such writers as Emerson, Thoreau, Hawthorne, and Melville saw fit to acknowledge a debt to Milton, F. O. Matthiessen identified him as a major force behind the American Renaissance. For quite a long time, according to Matthiessen, "Milton remained the archetype of the poet for New England."[21] For American literary criticism, then, he provides the cultural conduit between English and American literature by providing an English prototype for American poetry and fiction.

Serving in this capacity, Milton has almost single-handedly perpetuated the twin beliefs that English literature is *our* national literature and that Britishness is a distinctive feature of our national culture.[22] What else if not such convictions can explain Margaret Fuller's pronouncement that Milton was "more emphatically American than any author who has lived in the United States?"[23] Like other nineteenth-century American writers, Fuller appears to have been not only quite self-conscious about her struggle to invent a literary past but also acutely aware of what was at stake in that struggle. Yet our purpose is neither to argue for national autonomy vis-à-vis literature nor to imply continuity in the discursive fact of this bridge. We are ultimately interested in how each side of the Atlantic depended on the other for its sense of national identity. The uses of English in North American culture have certainly changed over time, and each generation that perpetuates this continuity does so for its own political reasons.[24]

These rather basic observations (convictions, really) prompted us to address the following questions: What was it about Milton's mind and world that enabled him to straddle the fault line between early modern and modern culture? Why does his position in literary criticism set his poetry in conflict with his politics? How did scholars and critics come to defend certain features of this author at the expense of others? Why perpetuate this conflict? What notion of human identity compels modern readers to do so? What truth is produced by representing Milton as the author of authors? How have we as modern intellectuals used Milton to deny our position as American subjects of English literature?

To address these questions we have constructed something called "the mind of Milton." If this phrase has a familiar ring to it, that is perhaps because we have tried to think of Milton much as Barthes thought of Einstein in "The Brain of Einstein," Garbo in "The Face of Garbo," or humankind in "The Great Family of Man." That is to say, we have assumed the object of our analysis to exist, in Barthes's words, as "a kind of nebula, more or less hazy, of a certain knowledge. Its elements are linked by associative relations; it is supported not by an extension but by a depth" (122). The Milton that we are after is one that indeed links a self-evident character with a cloud of associations whose principle of coherence resists analysis. This construction has nothing transcendental about it even though it always tries and usually manages to create the impression of transcendence. In contrast with those who wish to mystify art or any other aspect of a culture, Barthes pokes among the images, objects, or signs of industrial cultures for the ones that display the essential properties of the commodity fetish.

The nineteenth century was only half underway when Marx described much the same kind of inversion as the one with which poststructuralism has attempted to come to terms. He foresaw a situation where men would no longer determine what things they themselves produced and consumed, and instead things would tell people what to desire in one another as well as in the world of things. He described an object that not only inverts what he presumes to be the natural relationship between people and things; it simultaneously overturns the relationship between signs and their users. The commodity fetish is an object that has acquired the power to determine its own meaning and value. Barthes's "mythologies" behave in much the same way. They are complex images, objects, or signs that seem to exist free of any known form of human control for the simple reason that they have been cut off from the history of their production. Indeed, there can be no historical explanation for this kind of object since it appears to be iconic by nature. It seems to contain the source of its own meaning and value.

Though he was certainly not the only author to have acquired the properties of such an object while England developed a national literature, we believe we are on safe ground in saying that no one else has revealed quite so many flaws as Milton and still retained such unquestionable authority.[25] There is something about his very name, as we have tried to suggest, that makes him both impossible for literary scholars of any subsequent period to ignore and extremely difficult for them to wrest free of a particular historical moment and beatify. This unique position in English cultural history obviously has something to do with Milton's double foothold in the disciplines of literature and history. If the richness of the poetry seems to call into question the politics of the puritan, then his work in Cromwell's government somehow challenges the integrity of the poet. And so any defense of Milton on one of these bases necessarily renews the other, which produces new grounds for attack and in turn calls forth another defense. A corrective reading of such a figure, as Barthes explains, "will in no way increase its power or its ineffectiveness: a myth is at the same time imperfectible and unquestionable; time or knowledge will not make it better or worse" (130). It is, in a word, the perpetual need for such a defense that matters in making mythologies. Much like those congealed bits of information that operate as "mythologies" in the Barthean sense of the term, Milton incorporates some of the important contradictions of our culture. These take the form of a compensatory set of shortfalls and surpluses, invariably reproducing a gap between the Milton historical scholars discover and the model author whom literary critics try to make him measure up to.

After a decade and a half of critical demand for a new literary history, it may well strike our readers as somewhat odd for us to pass by so much of the work that goes by the name of new historicism, postmarxism, and cultural studies in favor of the Barthes of the *Mythologies*. However, we regard this way of defining our object of analysis as no more or less peculiar than borrowing Foucault's argument with modern historiography to define our historical method. We turned to both Barthes and Foucault after extensive research on Milton and the period during which he wrote had convinced us that academic discourse has yet to deal adequately with the insights offered in that unassuming book on "mythologies" written more than three decades ago. Even as theory was rapidly imported during the 1970s and certain critical practices acquired both prominence and sophistication in the United States, the political justification for the theory revolution and the motive for a new literary history—often called "demystification"—were well on their way to being ignored or simply forgotten.

Our examination of the scholarly constructions we call "the mind of Milton," "the English Revolution," "family history," and "the work of literature" led inevitably to the conclusion that no one can really distinguish the past from what subsequent critics and historians have made of it. Our own work has therefore concentrated on the intellectual gap that remains in these accounts of modernity, on the means of transformation from one cultural frame of reference to the other, on the people responsible for this profound change, and on the political consequences that ensued from their efforts. To explain this transformation, we have gathered information from various historical accounts—of the English Revolution, of the rise of the modern family, and of the emergence of a vernacular literature, for example—where changes in the production, dissemination, and political effects of information are thought to have played a minor though instrumental role in bringing about the industrialized world we presently inhabit. We have used Milton both to identify the logical tautologies in traditional historical narratives and to propose another narrative. But we have neither looked for the continuities between the two halves of his career nor taken the other way around the problem and closed the chapter on the Caroline Milton only to open another with his political writings or his great poetry written after the Restoration. Our argument abruptly turns away from Milton's life and work in order to focus on details related to the formation of what Foucault calls "discourse," a field of symbolic practices that exist in relation to writing. A standard of literacy that includes both reading and writing inevitably dominates such a field.

Having provided some sense of our motive, method, and object of analysis, let us provide a more detailed account of the steps in this argument and how our readers will encounter them on a chapter-by-chapter basis.

To launch an investigation into the origins of modernity, in chapter 1 we offer a brief discussion of the main trends in Milton scholarship. This may seem all too conventional for a book that aims to overturn a number of basic literary historical presuppositions. Nevertheless, it does allow us to integrate a Barthean notion of the author as a mythology with a Foucaultian notion of the modern moment as an inversion whereby words began to have their sources located in individual authors, and their meanings in those authors' relations to things. Milton scholarship reproduces one half of this process whenever it uses Milton's poetry to "discover" and then reproduce the kind of consciousness—self-conflicted and enclosed—that Milton's poetry called into being. In taking the mind of the author as its object of knowledge, criticism inadvertently provides direct access into the other half of the process by which "the mind" of the author became a mythology. By reading Milton criticism for purposes of observing this process at work, we demonstrate, further, why Milton is not just any old author but, in a very literal way, the author of authors.

One of the themes resounding throughout this criticism, and a large part of the reason Milton must be valued even where he is disliked, is the self-reflexivity of his later poetry, especially *Paradise Lost.* For a wide spectrum of readers, such self-reflexivity suggests that in a quite deliberate way he defined himself as an author—an author who, these readers assume, had to preexist that self-representation. In this way, the modern critical tradition naturalizes the solitary individual whom the poem designates as its source. We consider Milton among the first and best examples of those who had reason to think of writing rather than their relationship to God and king as the basis for their political identity. But we do not agree with the mainstream of Milton scholarship and criticism when it assumes that the individual so represented had to be there in order to represent himself as the source of those words. Indeed, writing takes on such power of self-definition only when it has inverted the historical priorities of author and individuated text.

In chapter 2 we turn to British social history in an effort to discover when writing eluded the control of a centralized monarchy and began to name its source in independent-minded individuals. Such decentralization of writing is recorded as one of the more short-lived effects of the English Revolution. Almost every historical narrative invites us to think that the revolution in writing ended when censorship was reimposed during the protectorate and that it did not pick up again until 1695, when Parliament failed to renew the Licensing Act of 1662. In turning to some of the best-known attempts to determine the revolutionary effects marking the onset of modernity, however, one finds no cause other than discursive events and a "revolution" constituted after the fact in writing. Thus, "the English Revolution" operates much as does an "author"—that is, as a magical first cause, or cause of all other causes—to fill the gaps that would otherwise appear in the accounts of the transition from early modern to modern. In these accounts, the English Revolution brings about a world based on productive labor, and therefore a whole new notion of historical causality. Yet the Revolution itself is not identified with the rise of such labor; it is a prior cause. Nor does the Revolution, as history describes it, fulfill any of the definitions of revolution formulated in the centuries to follow, definitions that characteristically use events during the 1640s in England as the very model of the changes that brought modern Europe into being. We are interested in how the mythology of an English Revolution—that is, an apocalyptic change and cause of causes—has operated as a cause in its own right and why it remains essential to the story that modern culture tells about itself.[26]

The modern notion of the "author" did far more than locate the source of writing inside the individual and so constitute the individual as such. It also located history outside rather than inside both the author and his writing. With a few notable exceptions, historians collaborate with literary criticism to extend this purely modern relationship of text to author back across the divide between early modern and modern England, even while the same historians proclaim that violent disruptions brought one epoch to an end and initiated another. During this period, a majority of them insist, everything changed. In this way, we contend, the mythology of the English Revolution takes up a relationship of mutual dependency with the mythology of the author. Without the Revolution there would be no way of explaining swift and radical changes in the means of publication, the status of writing, the identity of those who wrote, the kinds of feelings, thoughts, and speech they verbalized, and the object relations they consequently designated as real. Without the transcendental mind of an author, on the other hand, there would be nowhere to look for a revolutionary cause except to the ways and means of producing and disseminating information. And historians do look to such a mind, and specifically to the speech community it began to represent during the mid–seventeenth century, whenever they want to identify a first cause for this inaugural event. The English Revolution fulfills the logic of a mythology when it prevents historians from considering the possibility of a revolution that took place in writing. By standing in for the action, speech, thought, and feeling that historically preceded the words through which these became a narrative, the term "English Revolution" conceals the story of how writing first got out of hand some three and a half centuries ago. It also conceals the story of how the English Revolution came to represent this event for a much later readership.

Having thus defended itself against interrogation, however, history still has a problem. The Revolution itself requires a cause. To fend off a series of attempts at demystification, the Revolution has to be naturalized in a way that makes modern history appear unintelligible without it. According to the logic that insists one knows what an event is by knowing its origin, historians proceed to give the Revolution an origin, or prior cause, outside of history per se. As we discuss in chapter 2, contending schools within the discipline appear to be of one mind in locating that source in the very kind of individual to whom such authors as Locke and Defoe attributed typically English thoughts and speech. This individual was the same man who occupied the world of private property as it had been described in puritan autobiographies, books on domestic economy, handbooks on marriage, and educational treatises, as well as in a poem such as *Paradise Lost.* If historians find it reasonable to locate a first cause for the Revolution in the desire for self-government, it is because writing allows them to do so whenever it represents Englishmen as those individuals who possess such a desire. Past and present authors characteristically identify themselves as the source of representation in a second sense as well.

In presuming to "speak" on behalf of the individual, they not only locate the source of writing in themselves, they also imply that writing came from a much larger speech community. In writing his or her "mind," in other words, the author always speaks on behalf of such a community. He or she "represents" the members of that community and acquires authority by his or her exemplary status in this respect as much as they do.[27] Some common ground among individuals is therefore essential to the complex ideological package we are elaborating, so essential in fact that such ground has to exist logically prior to authors and revolutions, as the natural milieu that could have given rise to both. Otherwise, literary and social historians would be left with nothing more or less than an ensemble of discursive effects to account for the foundational categories of modern culture.

The family provides that milieu. In chapter 3, we show how it provides a cultural space where culture and nature collaborate to produce individuals. For this is where everyone is born of a more or less caring mother and understands himself or herself as occupying a more or less adequate position determined by a father's status in the world outside the family.

The family is the origin, in other words, of all the drives and impulses the social world either gratifies, sublimates, controls, or thwarts to the point where some kind of rebellion becomes necessary. That these supposedly indisputable facts of biological birth supply modern scholarship with the theoretical portals by which individuals enter history and change the course of events is nowhere so apparent as in the work of the British historians of the family, to whom other historians and literary critics turn with increasing frequency when they want to account for the personal lives of men and women in earlier times. On the one hand, we would insist, this will to historicize the family indicates a sincere attempt at self-understanding on the part of modern scholars. The move into this area of research implies that the family, long the sacred preserve of nature, has a history too. But the recent expansion of history into new territories is certainly not without its perils, as Derrida suggested almost two decades ago; and the downside of historicism is especially evident in British historical studies of the family. That so much of it has been written in defense of Peter Laslett's *The World We Have Lost,* a work that embodies all the themes of *Paradise Lost,* demonstrates that historians have never questioned the compulsion to establish origins for the modern middle-class individual in a timeless world of nature outside of history.

To be sure, British histories of the family do document certain changes in the internal organization of the family—Laslett arguing that industrialization tore asunder what nature had joined together at the dawn of English culture, and Lawrence Stone contending, to the contrary, that modern family feeling was stifled by the economic motivations and general lack of privacy that can be inferred from the evidence that remains regarding earlier sexual practices. But the Anglo-American tradition of the history of the family has in the main proved to be self-contradictory. The major historical accounts of British family life begin by assuming that the family *is* that intimate feeling of kinship attributed to the family in certain countries of western Europe during the nineteenth century.[28] Working from this assumption, these accounts assume, further, that any other kinship relations disrupt, stifle, or otherwise tamper with nature. If one turns to the literature that came off the presses in the years following the interregnum, however, a rather different story emerges. In chapter 4, which (along with chapters 5 and 6) provides the keystone of our argument, we read a range of these materials in relation to Milton's *Paradise Lost,* arguing that if the poem is both a product of its time and representative of English literature, then literature must have played an active role in modernizing English culture.[29]

In *Paradise Lost,* one household disintegrates and another must be formulated in its place. As we all know, the modern family depends upon the labor of a man and woman rather than the bounty of some patron. This is, according to the angel Michael in Books XI and XII, the reason why history begins. History, as he explains it, is what broke up the materials of an older theocentric patronage culture—much as Freud's notion of "dreamwork" does—so that these materials might be used to make a new world, a world at once anthropocentric and logocentric. In certain respects, however, the world that emerges in the poem is not all that heretical. For one thing, it is only the domestic world that changes— and, at that, a domestic world that only strives to reproduce the aristocratic culture it is in fact displacing. Indeed, *Paradise Lost* rather explicitly articulates the wish to return to an original state of plenitude from which the author and those he addresses have been forever detached. As the poem also illustrates, however, humanity moves farther away from this state of effortless luxury the more it tries to get back. The quest for origins—of self, nation, family, and language—displaces that past with an arduous set of textualizing practices that authorize a new class of authors and readers.

There is another paradox in this, which we examine in chapter 5. *Paradise Lost* demonstrates that the activity called intellectual labor represents itself as secondary and derivative—dependent on the world to which it refers—just when it acquires the power to revise the very nature of things. To produce a history of the mythologies that still organize much of everyday experience, intellectual production, and political policy, binding these various domains together despite their contradictions into a single culture, we have to foreground the very cultural activity that receded by its own devices into the background. We have to explain how the labor of representation disappeared into its product, the representation of labor. To this end, we try to isolate those places in critical theory where intellectual labor becomes the object of analysis. If theory characteristically mobilizes the distinctive tropes of modern culture, all of which make language point to something outside, prior to, and more real than itself, then this is especially true of theory that deals with cultural production and reception. As if responding to an invisible imperative of writing itself, both Marx and Gramsci represent intellectual labor as something outside of their critical analysis, something that refers in turn to something outside itself.

As we have already suggested, Foucault's model of "discourse" provides an important exception in this respect to the mainstream of social history and theory. He argues that the rise of "writing" cannot be distinguished from the rise of a class of people whose purpose in life was to reform both themselves and other people in compliance with abstract norms of humanity that were, by definition, impossible to meet. Informing the formation of institutional cultures is the logic of the same wish to return to origins that receives perhaps its most complete and explicit articulation in *Paradise Lost*. Even in his later work, Foucault seems to see the institutions most characteristic of modern culture as developing according to a will of their own, one that transcends individuals, the spaces they inhabit, and the textualizing procedures that fixed them there. Foucault makes intellectual labor into an object of knowledge—indeed, something one must know if one is to know anything at all, because it produces both subjects and objects. But he also removes intellectual labor from history—in much the same way that his predecessors removed the individual mind, nation, and family—by allowing that labor to provide its own cause. He deliberately avoids the question of why, or by what other cause, writing began to operate in an entirely new way and to constitute a form of power in its own right.

In an effort to avoid reproducing the tautology whereby authors appear to author themselves, in chapter 6 we turn to Benedict Anderson's account of what he calls "print capitalism." As writing extended across the ocean and formed a kind of umbilical cord that connected the monarch's agents in the New World back to the European metropolis, something apparently happened to the relationship between writing and speech. At first, one might imagine, only writing, and then writing that made it into print and was distributed on a mass basis, began to take on a life in the New World apart from the European metropolis, apart from speech, and in contradistinction to the European speech community—or so Anderson tells the story. In his account, the extension of writing to the New World gave words new importance as the means of cementing the Old World to the New. As print vernaculars acquired such importance, they empowered those people who controlled the means of producing information. This change in what writing *did* changed what writing *was*. Simply by indicating that people of a particular cultural and linguistic competency belonged to its readership, as Anderson claims, writing may well have provided the basis for a whole new class and nation.

One might regard his account of the extension of European languages to the colonies as the most literal unfolding of a fable in which intellectual labor brings a new world into being, a world that appears to be based solely on labor, were it not for the fact that Anderson neglects to complete the historical process encapsulated in *Paradise Lost*. He does not stress the fact that what was being written in Spanish, Portuguese, French, Dutch, and English was written so as to reproduce the very European cultures from which the emissaries to the New World had been exiled. Nor does he say what happened to the print-based bureaucracies that served the centralized monarchies back in Europe. As these bureaucracies were extended to include other worlds, information from those worlds began to circulate along with that from their own, and to become part of European culture. If *Paradise Lost* went virtually everywhere that English-speaking people did, then captivity narratives poured back just as consistently into Europe along with news from the colonies. Early modern colonialism was, in other words, far less one-sided than Anderson's narrative suggests; simply in terms of the information which people consume on a day-to-day basis, it changed western European culture profoundly. (At least, that is how it looks from a North American perspective.) The very attempt to maintain the "original" English might have destroyed the aristocratic monopoly on information back in Europe just as it displaced that language in the New World with a modern print vernacular.

But if Foucault's historical model requires Anderson's transnational narrative to carry it from one historical moment to another, then Anderson requires Foucault for a yet more basic reason. Anderson explains how print got out of hand and acquired priority over speech at the very moment when print appeared to detach itself from what had been the international language of power and to adhere instead to speech in the form of vernacular English. His model assumes that speech comes from individuals, and that they as authors produced the new language of power even though they as readers consequently understood themselves in relation to that language. Such a model can explain why but not how the new print vernacular that seemed to imitate speech also changed thought and feeling, specifically the people's sense of themselves as private individuals who never had to intermarry or even to meet in order to feel they belonged to the same community.

In the first six chapters of this book we work through the tautology of representation characterizing modern culture and propose a way out of the problem by taking that tautology as our object of analysis. The last two chapters demonstrate what a history of the inversion of speech and writing might look like. We began with the premise that the writing appearing during the late seventeenth century produced what is now called an "author" as the model of an educated English person. Accom-

panying the appearance of the "author" were any number of assurances
that he sought to reproduce the values of a fallen aristocracy in writing
alone, and only on a personal scale. In chapter 7 we read such canonical
texts as Locke's *Second Treatise of Government* and *Essay Concerning
Human Understanding* and Defoe's *Robinson Crusoe* as attempts to
articulate the logic of *Paradise Lost* for the purpose of showing how
the educated individual might reproduce those values for himself. In each
case, what begins as a question of how to legitimize the sovereign rights
of individual man through his labor ends up by legitimating the sovereign
rights of those who can perform a certain form of intellectual labor
associated with "rationality" in the case of the Lockean individual, and
with an intricate protoinstitutional form of prevarication that might be
called "fiction," in the case of Defoe's. For all their differences, all such
arguments begin with the question of how best to reproduce an original
England. But they invariably answer the question by transferring that
hierarchical order onto a purely interior plane, by implication producing
a nation of self-governed individuals.

Foucault requires one to think of the writing that established a basis
for individual rights across western Europe in terms of the discursive
technologies that produced that individual in the first place; we try to
stress the reproductive dimension of his productive hypothesis. We use
Locke and Defoe to shift attention away from what history has traditionally taken for events and onto the plane of discourse. There we use
these authors to argue that the very writing we identify with the advent
of modernity aimed at reforming monarchy rather than at producing
something new and hostile to the status quo. Unless it attends to the
nostalgia that infuses *Paradise Lost* and lends it moral force, no theory
can account for the success of those works which—like Milton's later
poetry—open out onto the modern age. Despite obvious differences in
the authors' social positions and in their genres and intended readers,
the works in question speak with a single voice and express the longing
to return to a speech community that was supposed to exist prior to the
reign of writing.

Our last chapter considers how such an inherently conservative fantasy
might have eliminated the possibility of returning to a culture of powerful
landowners simply by reproducing that fantasy in writing. In the process,
we surmise, writing itself began to operate according to what has been
called the principle of supplementarity; it added something that required
a thoroughgoing internal reorganization of the culture. To make this
move, we have borrowed Anderson's strategy of turning time into space.

We have shifted attention to North America in order to explain what happened in Europe during the historical gap we are investigating. We have regarded Mary Rowlandson's account of her captivity as the best demonstration of how supplementation works simultaneously to transfer the power of monarchy onto the written word, to substitute literacy for both labor and birth in determining individuals' identity, and thus to reconstitute the nation as a readership.

Although gender has not entered into our argument up to this point, we are nevertheless acutely aware of what is usually meant by gender; it is essential to our story. Our title suggests a relationship between the origins of personal life and the onset of modernity that would be impossible to imagine without a historical understanding of gender. In her now famous critique of Gareth Stedman Jones's *Languages of Class*, Joan Scott demonstrates that any model of the languages of class remains incomplete if it fails to account for the relationships such languages establish between the categories of class and gender.[30] To make her point, she turns to the collapse of Chartism in 1848, the cataclysmic event in English working-class history that Stedman Jones sought to explain by looking to "language." Scott shows how even that most language-sensitive social historian fails to understand this turning point in modern history because he fails to perceive gender as a linguistic instrument of class rather than a fact of nature. Acceding to the same notion of gender as their opponents, the workers did not see that in order for them to cut a deal with the factory owners, both sides had to agree to a notion of individual rights based on the gendered division of labor—a notion that, in Scott's analysis, goes back to the beginnings of Enlightenment thought as formulated in Locke's *Second Treatise of Government*. Accordingly, workers and owners agreed that only those men who possessed their own labor were men, and that only men should be enfranchised. Those who existed in a feminine relationship of dependency to such men were not so entitled. By accepting this gendered definition of rights, the working class clinched the deal and lost the struggle for some of their kind to own their labor. Other workers would identify their interests as the interests of the very class whose powers they were contesting.

Many modern historians reproduce the mistake of the Chartist negotiators when they accept the idea that the emergent middle class was made up of modern men. This one supposition makes it unlikely that those historians will see how such turning points in modern history accompanied sweeping changes in distinctions based on gender and the uses to which those distinctions were put. How, after all, can anyone be expected to tell where "gender" intersects with the histories of "class" and "writing" when none of the major accounts of the modern period bothers to isolate the revolutionary move that placed private life, personal emotions, family relations, domestic affairs, and the writing that deals with such things, outside of history and in the domain of women? To create a narrative explaining how writing might have gained ascendancy over authors, families, and nations and begun rewriting them, we have tried to make this move explicit. We have connected gender to the fate of writing.

It is what might be called feminine writing that declares itself by nature detached from politics and history so that it might change the status, behavior, and political objectives of writing. Scott's insights prompt us to add what we regard as a necessary step to any account of the rise of writing. She suggests that it is not enough to show, as Foucault does, how writing turns the tables on both authors and the things they are supposed to represent. Nor can one really solve the problem, as Anderson contends, by showing how print vernaculars became the basis of the New World nation, not if these moves neglect the formation of the modern woman-centered family. For it is out of such a matrix that important men emerge and carry on their business, just as it is of such households and the emotional glue that binds them that the new nation-state is made at once cohesive and coherent.

Because she is only a woman, Mary Rowlandson can do all this while seeking to return to the community from which she was forcibly removed. Unlike her fictional counterparts who were made, not born, men of property, the abducted woman can return and assume her rightful place within that community. In this respect, Rowlandson offers a solution that neither Locke nor Defoe could very well imagine. Once rescued from his island, Crusoe cannot find an appropriate place within English society for his self-forged identity. Nor can Locke imagine how the form of self-government that individuals might achieve within the sanctuary of the home would modify the political status quo. Only in America, where territory had not already been politically inscribed—a place, in other words, without a history—could private property provide the basis for an individuated kingdom where each individual reigned supreme. Locke limits his concept of self-government in England to the home and immediate family, where it in turn limits the absolutist definition of monarchy favored by the Stuart kings. In Rowlandson's account, however, the new individual can nest within the old society and never disturb its political order because she nests within a purely domestic space rather than camping on someone else's property. At the same time, she "adds on" a space that had never existed before.

By showing how closely Richardson's Pamela observes the same pattern of exile and return as Rowlandson's persona, we propose that the insertion of such private domestic spaces within an earlier landowning culture could just as well have transformed Europe too. The abduction and the return of these women perform a transformation that could not be accomplished in overtly political terms. They begin as wordless objects in an exchange among men, but both evolve into bodiless subjects of writing. In doing so, they distinguish an earlier, apparently more primitive aristocratic culture from one in which every literate individual matters. The community to which they belong changes accordingly, from one governed by a monopoly on violence to one in which mastery is exercised strictly through words. In returning to their mother cultures, then, they quietly and almost imperceptibly change those cultures forever. A speech community gives way to one for which writing not only establishes the model but also poses as speech, thought, or human nature itself.

In using American literature to write modern British history, we do not presume to be discovering the origins of that or any other culture. Convinced that a compulsion to determine where something comes from naturalizes what is most ideological about modern culture, we try to show how any narrative that fulfills the fantasy of *Paradise Lost* will transform the place to which that narrative longs to return. We would like to think that our own endeavor to discover the origins of modern culture offers something of an exception to the rule, because we have used *Paradise Lost* and other writing of the period to suggest how and why knowledge might have come to be equated with the search for origins. As Milton's attempt to reproduce a culture from which he had been irrevocably separated, the poem offers a paradigm for the operations of a peculiarly European brand of nostalgia. Separation from an originary speech community compels translation of English culture into the writing that subsequently became the basis for the existence of that culture. In looking forward to the new world that was supposed to emerge with the coming of Christ, the author has his eyes cast only backward. The "forward" movement of the narrative must be understood as an attempt to "return." The desire on the part of North American English men and women to return to an originary speech community required reproduction at once of that community and of the lack that cannot be filled by written words. Under these conditions, language loses its innocence—its Adamic character—and begins to behave as signs, writing, or the supplement. It displaces speech and relocates the preindustrial speech community still farther in the past with each successful written replication of the originary speech community. The logic that brings us from revolutionary England to prerevolutionary America to modern England is one that preserves the traces of intellectual labor from *Paradise Lost* into captivity narratives, then into fiction, and from there into what nineteenth-century intellectuals called history.

In going back to the origin of the myth of origins, we hope to provide some insight into the means of that myth's production. We hope to show that modern humanism began in writing and continues both to empower and to conceal the power of intellectuals. We hope to show, further, that through the humanities our culture not only reproduces the reigning concepts of self, family, and nation but also conceals the history of their production, allowing these same concepts to constitute and classify resources and to disperse those resources to individuals, long after the historical purpose and social efficacy of "self," "family," and "nation" have disappeared. If the work of feminism and cultural studies is going to dislodge what now exist as purely discursive entities, it cannot, we would argue, simply posit some new fantasy—even a fantasy of multiple origins—in place of the so-called Western tradition. If our study has anything to contribute to modern scholarship and critical theory, there is no question what we would like that contribution to be. We would like to make it just a little easier for others to abandon the whole concept of origins as the basis of identity politics and to study, in its place, the discursive practices by which we are made and remade into selves, families, and nations.

CHAPTER ONE

The Mind of Milton

Milton did not belong strictly to any of the classes which
we have described. He was not a Puritan. He was not a free-
thinker. He was not a Royalist. In his character the noblest
qualities of every party were combined in harmonious union.

Thomas Babington Macaulay, "Milton"

It has been said that nothing breathes new life into a dead poet so fast
as an attempted assassination. If the historical figure in question should
survive the attack, he or she is likely to come back to life, warts and all,
in a culturally more durable form. This is certainly what happened when
T. S. Eliot attacked Milton for setting up a model of English poetry that
stifled the poetic creativity of successive generations. But attacks on this
particular figure have effects far removed both from the object of the
attack and from the intentions of those who have exposed his feet of
clay. His very flaws give Milton a vitality in our time that he probably
lacked in his own. They become facts of his nature—a reality in their
own right, as well as the framework in which his work is subsequently
read. This being the case, the question arises: In defending Milton against
Eliot's charge, does one come closer to representing the true Milton or
does one reproduce the same mythology that Eliot was himself perpetuating? "Myth," Barthes reminds us, "can always, as a last resort, signify
the resistance which is brought to bear against it."[1] Any claim that the
object in question is really less exalted than was formerly thought, further
establishes the reality of that object outside and independent of its
representation.

Douglas Bush's magisterial account perhaps best describes the Milton
who comes down to us as the embodiment of the major English currents
of Renaissance humanism. The following passage illustrates how such
portrayals of the author of *Paradise Lost* reconcile certain features of
early modern culture with those characterizing the Enlightenment:

Our present view of Milton is not unanimous or final but, with a better understanding of his background, roots, and evolution, we have perhaps struck a juster balance between the Renaissance humanist and the Puritan. Milton may be called the last great exponent of Christian humanism in its historical continuity, the tradition of classical reason and culture fused with Christian faith which had been the main line of European development. His Christian humanism, intensified and somewhat altered by the conditions of his age and country and by his own temperament, becomes as he grows old a noble anachronism in an increasingly modern and mundane world.[2]

By anthropological and historical standards, Bush's description of the maturing Milton is rather muddled. Within the bounds of the author's personal history, the conflict between humanism and puritanism that tore apart Caroline culture, and indeed—it might be argued—led to the execution of the king, somehow turns into a conflict between what Bush identifies as "Christian humanism" and what he simply claims was "an increasingly modern and mundane world." Bush translates both the political conflicts that organized Milton's world and the cultural conflicts that consequently organized his work, into a story about the author's mind. By the end of the passage quoted above, the intense political conflict between an aristocratic tradition of letters and an emergent culture that was aggressively secular has dissolved into the psychology of internal conflict.

Milton provides the means of producing a continuity, precisely where historians locate a decisive political rupture within English culture. Just as the violent conflict between the values of humanism and of puritanism modulates into a conflict between one epoch and another in Bush's account, so too the clash between old and new fades into the melancholy of a mind that had outlived its age to become nothing more than a "noble anachronism." However radically the world in which Milton wrote may have changed, the mind that did the writing remained essentially the same.[3] By insisting on the constancy of the author's identity, Bush conceals the gap between a culture that warred almost continuously over what ought to be the proper relationship between God and the monarch and a new culture that sought to differentiate the individual's rights from those of both God and king. Thus Bush contains within Milton's mind the conflicts shaping early seventeenth-century English letters and sets that mind against the modern conditions (godlessness and anarchy) for writing. This use of Milton to incorporate the past within the present is hardly peculiar to Bush. We contend that it is a good part of his business, as a literary historian, to suppress any changes in human consciousness that might have occurred within Milton's career.[4] Maintaining the continuity of this author's mind is essential for an unbroken tradition of letters across the cultural fault line that divides seventeenth-century England.

Balachandra Rajan's *Paradise Lost and the Seventeenth Century Reader* affords a slightly different angle on the political operations of the paradox that puts literature outside of political and social history. True to his title, Rajan establishes a relationship between the kind of knowledge that became obsolete with the onset of modern culture and the fascination Milton holds for modern readers. According to Rajan, *Paradise Lost* was written before English culture rendered poetry a less than reliable source of knowledge about the world: "There is hardly a question which the seventeenth century could ask which it *[Paradise Lost]* does not directly or indirectly answer. So," Rajan concludes, "if we must think of Milton in connection with his poetry, it is perhaps best to think of him thus, within the impersonal requirements of his office, and as possibly the last person in history to hold all human knowledge for his province."[5] Even more baldly than Bush, then, Rajan explains why literary scholars tend to focus on Milton. For Rajan, as for many Miltonists, this poet allows them to define "the poet" as someone who personifies "all human knowledge." They can then abstract Renaissance literature from political history and confine it to a domain both personal and aesthetic. Once enclosed in the consciousness of an author, the history of the language bearing Milton's signature is submerged in the fate of his body, and its meaning becomes thoroughly personalized. Furthermore, once consciousness is assumed to be the source of literary language and a work of literature can be read as the very embodiment of an individual's consciousness, the text and the author can explain each other without reference to the historical conditions for their coexistence.

In what continues to be a very influential reading of Milton, Joseph Summers embraces what may at first appear to be a contrary position. Although he reads the poem as the embodiment of Renaissance humanism, he regards Milton as a man ahead of his time—a modern author. Thus, Summers suggests, the poem does incorporate the historical gulf between early modern and modern culture that we are trying to identify. But instead of placing its author in a world where he lacks a suitable readership, *Paradise Lost*

> demands of its readers, now and in the seventeenth century, qualities of attention and discrimination similar in some respects to those which many readers have only lately learned to bring to certain modern works of fiction: we must recognize and respond to the carefully delineated contexts and qual-

ifications; we must read *this* work and not confuse it with others. We must
recognize the natures of the speakers, the points of view behind the speeches,
and we must not confuse the dramatic participants with the voice of the
author.[6]

Unique in anticipating modernism, Milton made certain that readers
would distinguish his voice from those of other authors and from the
speech of characters within his poem; his voice is consequently everywhere and nowhere. Resembling no one so much as Henry James in this
respect, Milton makes visible the operations of his own highly individuated consciousness.[7] For Summers, the telling difference between an
ordinary consciousness and one like Milton's has nothing to do with the
gulf between the Renaissance and "an increasingly modern and mundane
world," as Bush suggested. That readers admire Milton and still find him
meaningful today, testifies, in Summers's account, both to the transcendence of great minds and to the fact that Milton had one. Thus history
drops out of the equation as contemporary readers reenact Milton's
relationship to the audience for whom he wrote whenever they recognize
the superiority of his authorial consciousness to their own. What Bush
and Rajan identified as a gulf between the kind of knowledge required
by Renaissance poetry and that possessed by modern readers, Summers
regards as the measure of poetic genius, a quality of individual consciousness that transcends an individual's moment in time.

Acknowledging his debt to Summers, Stanley Fish avoids the whole
problem of authorial intention. He does not see any point in trying to
figure out what the poem really meant in its time, not if Milton's poetry
educates readers today much as it originally did—indeed much as the
angel Michael instructs Adam in the last two books of *Paradise Lost*.
"I believe Milton's intention to differ little from that of so many devotional writers," claims Fish: " 'to discover to us our miserable and
wretched estate through corruption of nature' and to 'shew how a man
may come to a holy reformation and happily recover himself.' "[8] Fish
couples his claim for Milton's immortality as a poet with an assertion
of the reader's relative inferiority, when he describes the poem itself as
"Milton's programme of reader harassment" (4). The claim of immortality identifies the poet with a rhetorical component of the poem that
survives into the present day; the assertion of "reader harassment" defines
the poem as a set of activities that take place entirely in the mind of the
reader. Together, these moves make history vanish, along with the whole
problem of how Milton's poem might have changed over the centuries.[9]
For, as Fish explains, "if we transfer the emphasis from Milton's interests

and intentions which are available to us only from a distance, to our responses which are available directly, the disparity between intention and execution becomes a disparity between reader expectation and reading experience; and the resulting "pressures" can be seen as part of an intelligible pattern" (3). True, one can attribute the difficulty experienced in reading *Paradise Lost* to one's own (human) deficiency, and one can say something about what the poem was doing to seventeenth-century readers of devotional poetry. But, having done so, has the literary critic really eliminated the problem of history, or merely sidestepped it? Fish's proposition can be reversed.

It can also be true that in experiencing the difficulty of reading *Paradise Lost*, the modern reader experiences a conflict between the culture that dominated England centuries ago and the one that dominates the United States today. Students bring to their classroom encounters with Milton (and where else but in the classroom do most such encounters take place nowadays?) a knowledge of both poetry and human nature garnered from home, from peer groups, and from other classrooms. Reading Milton forces them, as it has forced most of us at one time or another, to recognize the limits of such homely knowledge. But few of us are ever encouraged to read the gap between high and low culture as a gap between two cultures, or even between two moments in a single culture. According to Fish's uniquely frank model of reading, the gap is and has always been one that distinguishes elite from popular culture. Milton authorizes specialized methods of interpretation designed to make his readers feel the inadequacy of the interpretive equipment they bring to the poem. But this inadequacy can hardly be the same for members of a theocentric culture as it is for present-day American students enrolled in an English literature course, nor are the relationships to authority the same, nor the consequences that ensue from success or failure at reading. The historical approach of Bush and Rajan suppresses the historical differences between the culture summed up in *Paradise Lost* and the milieu in which they themselves read that poem; but these very differences sneak back into the cultural picture as a qualitative difference between high and low. By placing the mind of Milton within a single framework alongside the modern reader, Fish makes the inherent conflict between author and reader impossible to ignore. His method is, in this sense, ultimately more historical than more traditional biographical criticism.

That the two critical methods—emphasizing textual production and reception, respectively—are ultimately compatible, however, becomes apparent once we turn to Louis Martz. If the Renaissance Milton of Bush and Rajan contained more learning than any later poet could, then the modern Milton described by Summers and Fish transcends his readers because his is a literary mind. The Renaissance Milton's body of knowledge is larger than that of his readers because it encompasses the coherent body of theology, politics, and science made available through humanist training; and the modern Milton's is superior insofar as it has been transformed into poetry capable of transcending history. Logically, these two bases for authorial power should contradict each other the moment we attach the name of Milton to both of them. Martz, like Bush, understands Milton as the consummate personification of high cultural knowledge and the author of "the last great poem of the European Renaissance, a poem that combines the cool objectivity of Homer, the sensitivity of Virgil, and the strong personal presence of Ovid and the Renaissance poets. Standing as it does on the very latest verge of the Renaissance— indeed beyond that verge—the poem," in Martz's view, "looks backward toward the traditional examples of epic narrative."[10] To become the poet whom Bush calls a "noble anachronism," Martz's Milton undergoes the very form of alienation that made possible the modernism of James, Eliot, Pound, Lawrence, Joyce, and Yeats; he is a "poet of exile." His poetry consequently supplies the vital link that connects ancient to modern literature in an unbroken tradition. According to Martz, *Paradise Lost* "looks backward towards the traditional examples of epic" and, at the same time, makes "a motion forward to the time when the figure of the poet, representing the individual consciousness of man, will become the only organizing center for the long poem, as in Wordsworth's *Prelude,* Whitman's *Song of Myself,* or Pound's *Cantos*" (79).

Forget that Milton was English and steeped in an aristocratic tradition of letters. Martz understands the contradiction between the consummate humanist and the modern genius as a conflict between the tradition in which Milton was trained and the one in which he was, as Eliot laments, largely received and lionized. In this, Martz agrees with Bush. At the same time, Martz seems to concede Summers's point that men who produce great literary works are more alike in their superiority to readers than different because they write at different moments of time. From the assumption that Homeric verse had its source in a similarly alienated individual, Martz infers that disillusionment with the English Revolution gave Milton the detachment required to write a poem of epic proportions; this detachment is what he shares with Wordsworth, Whitman, and Pound as well as with the Greek and Roman poets.

Another tradition of criticism challenges the idea of the poet as a self-contained mind. "No poet compares to Milton in his intensity of self-consciousness," contends Harold Bloom. This intense awareness of self as poet or poet as self—both assumptions seem to be at work in Bloom's description—"necessarily involved Milton in direct competition with Homer, Lucretius, Ovid, Dante, and Tasso, among other precursors."[11] His competition extended ultimately to God, whose word Milton reproduced as poetry; and this boundless desire to surpass all his "fathers" led Milton to place his own words instead of theirs at the origins of Western culture. "Precisely here," in the enormity of his oedipal crisis, according to Bloom, "is the center of Milton's own influence upon the Romantics, and here also is why he surpassed them in greatness, since what he (was able to do?) for himself was the cause of them becoming unable to do the same for themselves" (127). In this theoretical restatement of Eliot's complaint, Bloom clearly intends us to see the poet as a text rather than the other way around. Yet that text, as he describes it, still contains all of English culture, past and present. And, like more traditional scholars and critics, Bloom personifies the differences among historical epochs and translates those differences into a psychodrama that relocates the creative process within each author's mind.[12]

The last fifteen to twenty years have seen a feminist critique of this grandiose Milton produced by literary criticism take root and flourish.[13] Sandra Gilbert and Susan Gubar adapted Bloom's contention that Milton was "the great Inhibitor, the Sphinx who strangles even strong imaginations in their cradle" to formulate one of the most influential feminist representations of English literature in general and of Milton in particular.[14] Whereas Bloom's Milton embodied the various sources of authority at the heart of Western culture, Gilbert and Gubar reject the idea that the gap between author and readers is a function of either the superiority of his mind or the cultural distance created by his historical remove. Instead, they use Bloom's competitive model to argue against what was then the reigning literary tradition, in whose oedipal dynamic only male authors could acquire the status of genius.

If the capacities of Milton's mind oppressed his male successors, Gilbert and Gubar speculate, then imagine what it must have done to would-be women authors to think of themselves as excluded from the competition because of their gender. On the one hand, Gilbert and Gubar say, Milton conceptualized women "as at best a serviceable second" to men (214). At the same time, however, he represented the poetic imagination—"insofar as it [that imagination] was a *demonic* world"—as more often identified "with Eve, Satan, and femaleness than with any of the

'good' characters [of *Paradise Lost*] except the epic speaker himself"
(203). Thus Gilbert and Gubar argue that men could participate in a
tradition transmitted through the mind of Milton in a way that women
could not: "As a figure of the true artist, God's emissary and defender
on earth, Milton himself, as he appears in *Paradise Lost*, might well have
seemed to female readers to be as much akin to God as they themselves
were to Satan, Eve, or Sin" (210). For Gilbert and Gubar, the author's
maleness represents both the limitations and the exalted status of the
knowledge he embodies.

This move to identify the psycho-sexual limitations of the mind of
Milton inaugurated an important feminist critique of the literary tradition. Rather than equating the possession of classical learning with a
qualitatively superior form of consciousness, Gilbert and Gubar made
many readers aware that such learning was actually limited to men by
virtue of a circular process that identified it with masculinity. This critique,
launched against so central a figure, was quite compatible with others
that soon followed in identifying the class and ethnic biases of the English
literary canon: it was made not by authors but by white Europeans, and
beginning with the English Renaissance, by white Anglo-Saxon men.
However, in exposing the limitations of the literary tradition and of
Bloom's model as well, Gilbert and Gubar accepted Bloom's most fundamental assumption about literary production. They conceded that literature was produced by a struggle within and among individual minds.
They did not examine the cultural processes that allowed Milton to
transmit ancient knowledge and transform that knowledge into the kind
of poetry that would make sense to the readership of a much later age.
Instead they drained the historical character of Milton's writing of all
materiality, choosing instead to emphasize the biological fact that Milton
was a man. Despite its boldness of purpose, Gilbert and Gubar's position
came under attack on the grounds that it was exclusionary in its own
way. That is to say, feminism itself identified the assumption that people
are either men or women and always have been as the belief system of
an elite and timebound minority.[15]

More recent feminisms deem it highly unlikely that even in modern
cultures can writing take the form or exercise the authority it does simply
because of an author's sex. Though on quite different grounds, poststructuralism and the new historicism have also taken issue with the
tradition of reading that represents the author as an embodied consciousness, grandiose and unified, and so produces a continuous tradition
of high culture from antiquity to the present day. Prompted by these

developments in critical theory, another generation of Miltonists has reacted against traditional methods of textual interpretation and historicism.

The critical procedures associated with deconstruction aim at reducing the kind of transparency that encourages readers to assume that writing comes from an individual who preexists the text and continues to give it meaning and coherence. It is with a strong sense of self-irony, then, that Herman Rapaport takes sides with T. S. Eliot in order to produce a deliberately anachronistic Milton, one whose seventeenth-century poetry is allied with the project of twentieth-century poststructuralism: "Milton's transgression of what Eliot calls 'actual speech' by the 'auditory imagination' corrupted by book learning in general and rhetoric in particular, is very reminiscent of the kind of transgression that French poststructuralists address in terms of a writing that usurps or supplements voice."[16] If Milton's words do not strike us as so freighted with thought, feeling, or truth as Eliot wants them to be, it is, according to Rapaport, because Milton does not harbor the essentialist ambitions of Eliot. He is not trying to represent what is outside of language; he is an iconoclast who "incorporates important resistances within his texts to prevent the word from acceding to an idolatrous notion of the Word" (15). Rather than simulate either the word of God or the voice of a Romantic poet, Milton's poetry asks us to observe its rhetoric at work. In calling attention to the rhetorical surface of the text, Rapaport may seem to echo Summers and Fish. However, according to the logic of poststructuralism, the surface of the text does not give one access either to Milton's mind or to the minds of his readers, but only to the operations of the text itself—the procedures by which it distinguishes itself from language that comes from a source other than the author, and the measures it takes to make an "internal" world appear coherent. By forcing us to see the rhetorical operations that allow Milton's poetry to exist, poststructuralism detaches the text from the man, and the method should do away with the construct of "the author."

Despite his theoretical antagonism to traditional humanism, however, Rapaport assumes that Milton's poetry preserves intact the intricate game plan of a master mind. For Rapaport regards the rhetorical strategies of that poetry—no matter how belated, iconoclastic, stifling, or enabling—as deliberate moves in the great game of high culture where genius locks horns with others of its kind at the expense—but ultimately for the edification—of the reader. Capable of embracing contradictions, the poetry so described tends to resemble the mind that performs extraordinary feats of rhetoric and so, Fish claims, browbeats each and every reader. Indeed it might be said that in eluding history Rapaport's Milton becomes historical, much as Fish's Milton did. For neither critic is this author dead—as Barthes, Foucault, and Derrida have proclaimed he should be. At the same time, neither Fish nor Rapaport identifies Milton as the seventeenth-century Milton who was once adored by readers on both sides of the Atlantic—readers, we might add, who had no special literary education. If anything, Rapaport's Milton is more aloof than Fish's Milton; he is the very model of poetic consciousness and the forbear of a critical tradition connecting him to Rousseau and Derrida rather than to Blake and James.

The editors of the collection *Re-Membering Milton* are similarly conscious of their relationship to a tradition of reading that reproduces the powerful and unified consciousness we call "the author" by alternately idolizing and castigating Milton. In contrast with Rapaport, however, they embrace historicism as the means of demystifying authorial presence. The introduction begins by declaring "that the figure of Milton the author is itself the product of a certain self-construction; and that signs of motivated self-constitution can be seen even more clearly in the various critical and cultural traditions in which Milton enjoys an afterlife."[17] The editors promise that their collection will elaborate the relationship among the many different constructions that cling to Milton's name. It will accomplish this by looking at various self-constructions, determining the various contexts that gave rise to them, and specifying some of the interrelations between Milton's self-presentations and "the numerous representations of him to be found throughout the last three centuries" (xiii). To explain the historicist assumptions that inform the collection as a whole, they turn to Foucault's well-known essay, "What Is an Author?" They contend that "Foucault's comments suggest the possibility of locating the emergence of the author Milton in an historically specific conjunction of socio-economic and discursive practices, even though the exact character of that conjunction continues to be fiercely debated among historians of the Civil War period" (xiii). No matter how one feels about Milton, it is important to acknowledge that his state of mind was the product of an age different from ours. As the editors explain, "Milton's self-authorship both participates in his political and religious radicalism and reveals features of an emerging bourgeois class-consciousness in ways that have yet to be fully explored" (xiii).

That "the figure of Milton is itself the product of a certain self-construction" they make very clear. This figure is in fact a composite of

constructions, all of which came into being in "an historically specific
conjunction of socio-economic and discursive practices" (xii–xiii). Some
of these constructions are Milton's own doing and can be labeled "self-
construction," "self-constitution," "self-authorship," or "self-presentation." Such representations of the author are distinctive. They differ from
"the numerous representations of him to be found throughout the last
three centuries" (xiii). Much like older historicisms, then, the new historicism supposes that there was an authentic Milton whose construction,
constitution, authorship, and presentation differ in some essential way
from what people subsequently wrote about him. The editors of *Re-
Membering Milton* regard "the author" as purely a cultural construct;
but to locate Milton within the historical context where he became an
author, curiously enough, they posit an originary Milton who was already
there to author the author. That this one move reintroduces all the
problems of the old historicisms should become clear once we reconsider
the editors' statement of their thesis: "Milton's self-authorship both participates in his political and religious radicalism and reveals features of
an emerging bourgeois class-consciousness in ways that have yet to be
fully explored" (xiii). The statement implies that (1) a single consciousness
is capable of giving rise to another, ideologically conflicting one, and (2)
texts originate in "selves" rather than the other way around. Thus, while
they acknowledge that all they have to go by is representation, the editors
nevertheless promise readers a historicism capable of arriving at a human
reality beyond representation.

There is an obvious reason for the durability of the literary object we
have called "the mind of Milton." As we have already explained, the
supposition that literary language originates in a solitary and unified consciousness has allowed literary scholars to elide what social historians
regard as a deep and irreversible break between early modern England
and the modern nation-state. Few Milton scholars would dispute that a
new humanism, which would prove ideologically and philosophically at
odds with the preceding tradition of letters, began to emerge around
1660, seven years before the publication of *Paradise Lost*. Even so, as
we have tried to suggest, they persistently produce a modern authorial
consciousness from the cultural material that bears Milton's name and
identifies his position in history. We take issue with the critical procedures
described above in order to challenge the assumption that Milton did
in fact traverse the gap between Renaissance humanism and bourgeois
humanism as a consciousness single and entire. He offers a particularly
convenient focus for identifying the transformation of the one culture

into the other. Because he lived and wrote through the period that saw the end of one epoch and the beginning of another, most scholars have settled on Milton as the means of extending backward in time a purely modern definition of the author even as they acknowledge the political turbulence that he experienced.

By no stretch of the imagination can Terry Eagleton and Fredric Jameson be called Miltonists. They regard *Paradise Lost,* much as we do, as the product of a moment of profound historical transformation, and thus a document capable of explaining the advent of modern culture. To read the poem, both locate their object of analysis on a semiotic terrain that is neither individuated—in the sense that what bears the name of an author originates in the author's mind—nor lacking agency, in the sense that the text in question belongs to a rarefied domain of high cultural performances. They see the poem as part of a larger cultural process that broke down an older aristocratic culture into the categories we are calling "mind," "family," and "nation." So placed, it can be read as the record and instrument of change. Jameson and Eagleton distinguish the culture that produced *Paradise Lost* from the individualistic culture to which that poem gave shape and meaning. In this way, they invite us to question the prevailing critical assumption that it took a modern author to produce a modern author, while history provided the backdrop.

Eagleton accepts the traditional view that Milton was so positioned socially as to identify with the bourgeoisie and so placed within an aristocratic tradition of learning "as to revise, reject, assimilate, and appropriate its contents in the cause of his own people."[18] As we have seen, most literary criticism asks us to imagine Milton within an aesthetic tradition that authorized the very forms of power against which he turned his pen as Cromwell's Latin secretary. Eagleton goes along with tradition this far. But he diverges sharply from the critical consensus when he contends that Milton did not stop being political when he wrote his great poems. Eagleton holds to a view that the writing of Milton the poet, like that of Milton the politician, brought about change in its own right rather than simply reflecting changes that took place elsewhere in the culture. He identifies Milton as "the organic intellectual of the English Revolution" without translating that identity into the familiar codes of a modern industrialized culture (346). Eagleton subjects the genres used by the youthful Milton to a minimum of the psychologizing that might apply to the poetry written in a later period, when Milton's rhetorical mastery testified to the breadth of his knowledge and imagination rather than to his relationship with the church and the nobility.[19] Eagleton is one of the few who use the contradictions and discontinuities within Milton's poetry and within his career to understand how the culture's most basic requirements for meaning differ historically from those of modern culture. "What is most fascinating about *Paradise Lost*," according to Eagleton,

> is precisely its necessary lack of self-identity—the persistent mutual interferences of what is stated and what is shown. . . . The epic form of traditional intellectual culture at once magnifies and mystifies the prosaic realm of bourgeois revolution; and conversely, that discursive bourgeois realism is exposed in all its paucity by the epical splendour even as the realism appropriates and undercuts it. (346)

If Eagleton explains how *Paradise Lost* wrought a permanent change in the aristocratic tradition of letters, then Jameson's essay "Religion and Ideology" translates these changes into ideological events that ramify far beyond the poem, and even beyond literature.[20] Jameson contends that in preindustrial societies "religion is the cultural dominant; it is the master-code" (317). He identifies *Paradise Lost* with a change in that code.

It is instructive to compare the aspect of *Paradise Lost* that fascinates Jameson with the aspect that evokes a remarkably similar reaction from Eagleton in the passage quoted above. Both critics are struck by the way in which the poem changed the humanist tradition of letters. "What is astonishing about *Paradise Lost*," Jameson writes,

> is the utter silence and absence of all these great themes of church and collectivity. The narrative moves at once from the family—with its great evocation of married love and sexuality—to the fallen privatised world of individual belief and individual salvation; nor are the other collectives glimpsed in its course. . . . Milton's text thus anticipates the social impoverishment of the modern world, and as a narrative confronts the formal dilemma of relating the henceforth sundered and distant levels of the political and domestic. (333)

Jameson translates Renaissance humanism into "the great themes of church and collectivity." As he does so, Milton ceases to provide the site where one aesthetic code comes up against another and enters into mortal combat for cultural supremacy. His Milton is a politically active reclassifier of the cultural material that went into poetry: "Alongside the feudal world of God and his court, of Satan and his host, Adam is clearly of another species—the commoner, the first bourgeois, the extraordinary mutation which is middle-class man" (332). Thus what Jameson's reading might lose in its lack of attention to the artistry of *Paradise Lost*, it gains in historicity. He dissolves the poem into the historical circumstances that made it possible for someone like Milton to formulate a world more like the one we presently inhabit.

By comparing the features that strike Eagleton as "fascinating" with those things Jameson seems to find "astonishing" about *Paradise Lost,* we gain certain insights from both Eagleton and Jameson that are easy to overlook when their statements are read separately. Whereas Eagleton thinks "the lack of self-identity" is the truly fascinating quality of the poem, it is "the utter silence and absence of all these great themes of church and collectivity" that Jameson finds astonishing. The point is not to say whether the personal or the political element is lacking in the poem. It is more important to recognize that both of these readers are observing one and the same phenomenon—a noticeable lack of distinction between the subject and object worlds. A noticeable lack, we would argue, because the very distinction between the personal and the political comes into being during the course of the poem. Even when Milton opens books I, III, VII, and IX with the voice of the epic poet, he speaks with the voice produced by his particular education, the voice of culture transmitted down through the ages. There is little sense of a voice that came from the mind that dwelled within his body and used language to express itself. It is true enough that after the Fall, poetry has its source within a private world of consciousness remote from political affairs. But the poem represents this source as at once the lack and the only guarantee of political authority. Looking at the poem from the author's side, Eagleton feels the absence of personal authority as a lack. Considering the poem as a product of its age, on the other hand, Jameson listens in vain for its collective political themes. In this way, both acknowledge that a vast cultural transformation is necessary to turn a pre-Enlightenment author into one that is recognizably modern. The first division of the conceptual zygote, in both accounts, separates political information ("great themes of church and collectivity") from the material of personal life ("the privatised world of individual belief and salvation"). This is not to say that information "belonging to personal life" was already there in the poem, commingled with political information and waiting to be sorted into its proper category. All the evidence, including the poem itself, suggests that, to the contrary, in Milton's day personal life was yet to be set apart where it could either engage in a contractual relationship with the state or decide to oppose it.

Eagleton shows how *Paradise Lost* makes a permanent change in English literature; Jameson translates the literary themes of the poem into ideological conflicts that shaped the milieu in which Milton thought and wrote. The one critic grants the poem a certain historical agency, though only of a literary kind; the other appears to take such agency away. For Jameson, *Paradise Lost* is in large part the product of historical conditions that govern the author's use of the cultural materials available to him, conditions specific to his moment in time. From this perspective, one sees that larger processes of meaning that might be called history were in fact shaping Milton even though—and especially when—he seems to be shaping literary history. Together, then, Jameson and Eagleton inscribe *Paradise Lost* within a paradox that allows authors to shape culture on one level while culture shapes them on another and perhaps more basic level.

Yet can this be true if what they both say about the poem is accurate, namely, that it reduces the collective themes and epical splendors of Renaissance culture to the themes of a thoroughly prosaic domestic world? For such a world did not exist when Milton wrote his poem. He simply wrote an elegiac tribute to a culture from which divine authority had been withdrawn. The world represented in the poem was not supposed to be one in which people could feel at home. It was a world whose meaning had been depleted. More than a century after he wrote *Paradise Lost,* however, a readership who adored Milton above all other authors regarded that world as a perfectly reasonable place to be, and regarded the poem as a celebration of their values.

Eagleton and Jameson do suggest that by privatizing the family and setting domestic life apart from church and collectivity, *Paradise Lost* helped to bring about a revolutionary change in what people thought life was and how it ought to be lived. If the poem is thus engaged in history, however, it cannot be understood as a symbolic struggle from which bourgeois realism, in all its "paucity," emerges triumphant over the "epical splendour" of an earlier tradition of letters. The poem dramatizes neither the "social impoverishment of the modern world" nor the sundering of "the political and domestic," as Eagleton and Jameson have claimed. To imply that we are left with little else but aesthetic "paucity" and "social impoverishment" obscures the fact that a brand-new category, which might be called "personal life," emerges in the poem. And to that category belong all things holy to a modern culture. As we will argue in subsequent chapters, personal life constitutes the space in which modern consciousness discovers its first and only home. Many of the materials that had an overtly political meaning in early seventeenth-century England—especially kinship, art, and religion—would eventually be reclassified as manifestations of personal life. As such, they exerted authority from a position that appeared to be outside rather than squarely within the field of economic and political interests.

But if, as we are arguing, *Paradise Lost* demonstrates how personal life began to gain autonomy and cultural centrality, then why do Eagleton and Jameson close ranks with Douglas Bush and other Miltonists who greet the dawn of modernity with disparagement? We prefer to read *Paradise Lost* as one of the places in cultural history where an older language of power and privilege gave way to a new language of power and privilege, though one significantly less visible as such. David Norbrook comes to our aid by suggesting that Milton, early on in his career, wanted to produce what might be called a split in the sign.[21] In describing the poetry that was later published in Milton's 1645 collection, Norbrook claims that the masque conventions had already lost their iconic character in the poetry Milton wrote before the civil war, and that they had become sites where a mind akin to that of a modern poet strained against the poetic form in which he worked: "As Milton almost defiantly proclaimed by his title, the Ludlow 'Maske' adhered to the orthodox conventions of the genre. But only just that: the work keeps threatening to break out of its allotted boundaries" (263). We would certainly grant the possibility that, given who he was, Milton was dissatisfied with the rhetorical conventions that were then most likely to earn one recognition as a poet in his day. But we would also argue that no individual attempt to erode the authority of such conventions—which in a very material way "belonged" to the patron-king and thus represented his power—succeeded until that bond had been severed along with the head of Charles I, removing the traditional state iconography from state control.

If Milton happened to be in the position to do this by means of poetry, then he was certainly not alone. He belonged to a large and variegated group of professionals and divines: medical men and scientists who were redefining the biological body and how to extend its life; philosophers and political theorists who were revising the idea of the nation and how to manage it; entrepreneurs and colonizers who were revising the idea of labor and how to maximize it; and still others— writers and publishers—who were retailoring Renaissance materials in order to reach a Restoration audience and readership. Their combined efforts can be viewed in retrospect as an unwitting conspiracy. Together these people rewrote the old language of power that authorized monarchy. They made a language that individuated the subject and situated his body within the state and yet enclosed his mind in a personal world which limited the powers of the state.[22] As they positioned it outside and indeed above political power, they gave this mind a power of its own. More than any other single factor, we will argue, the emergence of an individuated mind, or "self," empowered the very people who accepted *Paradise Lost* as the model and centerpiece of their cultural tradition.

Given the fact that such people had everything to gain from the fall of aristocratic culture, how do we account for the strong sense of nostalgia with which the poem infuses that heritage? Milton wrote what modern readers consider his best poetry when he was politically and socially about as far from both court and government as a man of his position could ever be; yet those same readers bow to the logic of "the Fall." Eagleton and Jameson are not exempt from this charge. They talk about the splendid rituals that Milton relegates to the past, as if those rituals were somehow superior to the prosaic domestic practices that more nearly resemble our own. It does not require much imagination to think that Milton—old, tired, angry, and debilitated—was bitterly disappointed when Charles II returned to take the throne and it became clear that all recent political measures to change the course of English history were at an end. But why should so many of Milton's readers share his disappointment? Surely there would not have been much, if any, place for modern academics under the regimes of Charles I or Cromwell. Let us consider precisely what inducement the poem does extend to its readers across the gulfs of time and geography.

It has been said of England that it had no European-style bourgeoisie because each generation of shopkeepers, upon making its fortune, moved out into the country in search of aristocratic leisure.[23] The appeal of archaic aristocratic culture was used to lure people to the North American colonies. In 1652, in the wake of the English civil war, John Clarke seemed to be acknowledging this fact when he wrote that while "Olde England was becoming newe, Newe England was becoming old."[24] What he meant by this is probably what a number of historians have established since: the colonies held forth the promise that one could live a version of that aristocratic life which the patrimonial system placed out of the reach of most people, and which the civil war in England put forever in the past for the many members of the gentry and aristocracy whose fortunes were destroyed. Advertisements and travel accounts written during the first half of the seventeenth century described America as a land where one could enjoy the ease and abundance of an older and more authentically aristocratic existence. And once in America, seventeenth-century immigrants from England took these advertisements at their word, building homes, establishing social practices, and adopting work patterns that had passed out of fashion in England years before. Seen in relation to the economic inducements of the period, it is not so surprising that *Paradise Lost* should reproduce in its readers much the same desire to regain paradise with which God's emissary, the angel Michael, inspires Adam during the protracted history lesson that takes up most of books XI and XII.

The fantasy of returning to one's origins in an elite community (whether that community consisted of persons with noble blood or persons with pure souls) must be considered an inherently conservative one in 1667. As it was reproduced for a rapidly expanding readership, however, the same fantasy obviously organized collective ambitions and desires that Milton could not have anticipated. For one thing, the "great themes" and "epical splendour" of the first eight books of *Paradise Lost* were detached from the milieu in which they were written. They were reinflected within the text itself, where they lent majesty to the author who possessed such an expanse of knowledge and aesthetic virtuosity. In short, they exalted the activity of writing. The poem began to provide a standard of literacy that distinguished those who had acquired the cultural knowledge lost during the Revolution from those who had not.

One can also regard the appeal of *Paradise Lost* as an early version of what Renato Rosaldo calls "imperialist nostalgia"—the tendency of literate people to idealize precisely the cultural phenomena they have actively destroyed, simply by observing, recording, classifying, and analyzing those phenomena.[25] Just as the earlier way of life—celebrated, in inflated terms, as a perfect world, innocent and erotic, natural and opulent at once—was disappearing, the fantasy was set forth in print that could be distributed on a mass basis. Reproduction of the fantasy that one could return to a more authentic England helped to consolidate and empower a class of people who rather quickly displaced the older landowning culture as the symbolic center of English society.[26] When today's readers join Milton in lamenting the fact that the world has grown gray with the fall of aristocratic culture, they are not exalting the distant past of an England once ruled by men and women of noble blood. In the years following the Commonwealth period, the world of work imagined in the last two books of *Paradise Lost* provided a model for representing the world as it really was and improving one's position in it. This world, paradoxically, exalted neither monarchy nor manual labor but relocated authority in the literate mind. Thus when critics join the poet in lamenting their isolation within the world of work, they are actually positioning

themselves as authors and intellectuals outside and above that world—
from where, like Gabriel, they can tell people how to cope with it.

In taking Milton as the focal point of this study, we are less interested
in discovering who he really was or why *Paradise Lost* assumed the form
it did, than in examining the notion of the "self" and the role that writing
plays in making families and nations of such selves. Focusing on Milton
is simply a way of committing the individuated mind to historical analysis.
This "mind" incorporates what members of industrial cultures identify
as human nature—the needs, desires, and responsive capabilities that
come into being with the human body. Even though it may transcend,
repress, or grow alienated from its somatic origins, the mind produced
by modern industrial cultures remains fastened to those origins for life.
The skin surrounding the body also distinguishes what is essentially oneself from what is not.[27] Indeed, members of such cultures equate the
consciousness enclosed within the body with life itself. This is clear.
What requires explanation is how the symbolic use of the body to individuate the mind both distinguishes mind from body and subordinates
the physical body, just as it inevitably subordinates the laboring body to
its objectification in writing, money, and goods. No matter how bound
to a physical body one believes oneself to be, the modern body is an
eviscerated body that has delivered its insides over to X rays, sonograms,
statistics, and charts. This body is not a particular person's body but
"the body." Thus the body that we know as our own belongs to us only
to the degree it has been hollowed out and filled with consciousness. By
providing the boundary between the consciousness so embodied and
virtually everything else, the skin makes the difference that identifies all
members of industrial cultures—the difference between specific subject
and object worlds.

No one disputes that this is the difference on which modern thought—
both reason and its violations—depends. We cannot use our bodies to
think of ourselves as other than a self-enclosed consciousness and still
belong to this culture. That this is so becomes apparent whenever those
of us whose business it is to trace the operations of this self in its most
highly nuanced and well-preserved form—the literary text—find it nigh
on impossible to recognize historically earlier uses of the body. No doubt
literary criticism's failure to do so has something to do with the fact that
the modern body also connects the mind and text with the hand that
holds the pen or rests upon the keyboard, thus granting individuals a
sense that what they write comes from a source within their bodies. If
centuries of debate over the character of Milton's mind and the status

of his work have not shaken the belief that such work indeed originates within an author, then at least that indicates what task literary criticism performs for modern culture. It maintains the continuity of a particular kind of consciousness, the crucial element of modern culture, precisely where social historians claim that the definitive break between early modern and modern must have occurred.

CHAPTER TWO

The English Revolution

A good deal of history has been written on the assumption
that the bases of the society, its political, economic, and "social" arrangements, form the central core of facts, after
which the art and theory can be adduced, for marginal illus-
tration or "correlation." There has been a neat reversal of
this procedure in the histories of literature, art, science, and
philosophy, when these are described as developing by their
own laws, and then something called the "background" . . .
is sketched in.

Raymond Williams, *The Long Revolution*

By rights, Milton's position should be considered unique among English
poets. How many others have written their way through the death of
one historical moment and the birth of another? Yet within two or three
hundred years readers routinely characterized the uniqueness of his situation in terms that can only be called clichéd. He existed for them as
a unity amid discontinuities, a spot of stillness in a flux, the principle of
constancy in a field of change—a figure (if we may add one more cliché
to the catalogue) resembling the eye of a storm. In the face of such
commonplaces, the temptation is to recapture what was unique about
Milton. Yet in succumbing to precisely this temptation, literary critics
and scholars accept a modern definition of "the author" and reproduce
what we have called "the mind of Milton." Alternatively, if one attends
to the clichés that are applied to Milton, one will find that they go
straight to a paradox that is as essential to the discipline of history as it
is to literature: the sudden appearance in writing of an individual who
could claim that he had, in a sense, always been there because his particular nature was in fact universally human.

Those scholars who posit a continuous literary tradition also posit
some apocalyptic break between early modern and modern England.
How else, after all, can one explain the qualities peculiar to modern
literature, not to mention our present way of life? Literary scholars can

locate this change within the life and mind of an author—as dramatized
in Milton's poetry—and thus account for sweeping cultural changes that
obviously hit a collective nerve in their day. Without the sleight of hand
that simultaneously contains change within a unified consciousness and
exteriorizes history, there would be little more than individual whimsy
to account for the modern character of *Paradise Lost* and virtually all
the other canonical works of English and American literature. But it is
not nearly so evident why historians also embrace the idea of the author
as the continuous and unified source of language.

Once again, the commonplaces may prove instructive, especially those
that invite us to think of Milton as occupying a position something like
the eye of a storm. The surrounding violence makes the eye visible, and
it provides a location within the storm from which to grasp that storm's
organization and gauge its velocity and direction. In arguing that the
upheavals surrounding the English civil war did in fact amount to a
revolution, historians have grounded their observations on certain continuities of consciousness. Without the transhistorical body of human
responses that we have identified with the author, historians would be
at a loss to identify a motivation for the Revolution, and the advent of
modernity would suddenly dissolve into a web of contingencies to which
one can attribute a revolutionary purpose only in retrospect—that is to
say, by making a historical narrative. Without the ahistorical properties
of human nature, furthermore, these same historians would have nowhere
to turn for a revolutionary cause except to the ways and means of producing and disseminating information. Indeed, the effects of history and
literature are practically the same, in that both disciplines produce the
same narrative of timeless human nature against the ever-fluctuating,
often turbulent backdrop of history. The mythology of the English Revolution is essential to this narrative. It incorporates the literary notion
of "the self" to kick off the story of modernity. This narrative charts
the formation of the individual and his rise to power and insists, all the
while, that this same individual was also the cause and motivation of
that historical change.

Throughout the eighteenth century and well into the nineteenth, the
phrase "the Revolution," when used in reference to a political upheaval
in seventeenth-century England, most commonly meant the Glorious
Revolution of 1688.[1] After François Guizot published his *Histoire de la
révolution d'Angleterre* in 1826, the situation began to change. This is
not to say that English writers and politicians, particularly those of Tory
sympathies, readily agreed to Guizot's choice of terms when it came to

describing their country's history. At least one politician accused the Frenchman of confusing "the Great Rebellion" with "the Glorious Revolution."[2] Guizot's phrase nevertheless took hold. With revolutions in America and France still fresh in their minds, not to mention the revolutions that occurred throughout Latin America and the general threat of revolution haunting many of the capitals of Europe as well, nineteenth-century Englishmen were quite willing to say that they had already experienced a violent popular uprising. They were happy to put revolution behind them and to think in terms of reform. What is more, like Guizot, they tended to think that the events of the mid–seventeenth century could explain the revolutions that broke out during the late eighteenth and nineteenth centuries, as if these modern upheavals were nothing new. Revolution was already over and done and yet always about to happen.

Guizot's model defined revolution as an originary moment. As a politician, he wanted it understood that the English Revolution initiated a process that would eventually include the other western European nations as well. Though it took the form of violent upheavals two centuries before, according to this view, the Revolution had ended only recently; it had kicked off a long evolutionary process culminating in the form of representative democracy that spread from England to America and France. Such an idealized concept of revolution was clearly designed to authorize the status quo. After Guizot was forced out of political office in 1848, however, his views on the French Revolution naturally soured. In a pamphlet entitled *Pourquoi la révolution d'Angleterre a-t-elle réussi?* he used the English Revolution to elaborate a theory of what a revolution ought to be. Measured against this ideal, the French Revolution was found lacking:

> The Revolution of England succeeded. It succeeded twice. Its authors founded in England constitutional monarchy; its descendants founded in America the Republic of the United States. There is no longer any obscurity about these great events: . . . I seek to show the causes which have given, in England to constitutional monarchy, in English America to the republic, the solid success which France and Europe have hitherto been pursuing in vain, amid those mysterious experiments in revolution, which, as they are well or ill sustained, make nations great, or send them astray for ages.[3]

This statement assumes that once England had undergone revolution, steady peace and prosperity ensued. Everyone was better off.

Such a view of the English Revolution did not go unchallenged for long. In a review of this pamphlet, Marx attacked Guizot's theory that the English brought an end to political conflict by bringing an end to monarchy. "Where M. Guizot sees only placid tranquility and idyllic peace," he writes, "most violent conflicts and most thoroughgoing revolutions, were actually developing."[4] In true revolutions, Marx writes, "entire classes of the population disappear, and new ones with new conditions of existence and new requirements take their place" (94). From this point of view, Guizot's celebration of English history was entirely misplaced; it ignored the fact that "class antagonisms in English society have become more acute than in any other country" (94). Throughout the nineteenth century, these remained the terms in which people debated the question of the English Revolution. Did the Revolution initiate a gradual process of democratization, as Guizot had argued, or did it, by definition, bring a new class of people into power? Upon one's view of the past in this respect hinged one's view of the contemporary political scene. Had the Revolution succeeded, or was the fulfillment of its promise yet to come? And if so, how would change come—through reform or violent upheaval?

At the very time when Guizot was claiming that the events of the 1640s and 1650s had initiated two centuries of reform, English historians generally held to the position summarized by David Hume. In his *History of England from the Invasion of Julius Caesar to the Revolution in 1688,* "revolution" simply meant "change." The meaningful distinction in his day was that between change in the form of disorder and change in the form of a cyclical return or "restoration"; the "cyclical" meaning informs the title of his history of England.[5] Like many others before him, Hume felt that the events of 1688 restored authority to Parliament and placed limits on the king according to a principle established by an ancient constitution.[6] He described the revolution of 1688 as fulfilling a process that began with James I; in this view the events of the 1640s and 1650s were relatively insignificant. By the nineteenth century, Whig history had systematically incorporated all the upheavals after 1642 into a story about England's progress toward representative democracy—a story obviously designed, as Guizot's was, to legitimize the Whig view over and against that of the Tories.

Beginning in 1863, with the appearance of the first volume of S. R. Gardiner's monumental study of the period from 1603 to 1656, the question of the Revolution gradually disappeared from the arena of partisan politics. Like Gardiner himself, the debate surrounding the events of the 1640s found a place in the academy, where the terms of debate underwent the transformation that made the English Revolution one of the presiding mythologies of modern history.[7] Defining the English Revolution ceased to be a way of staking out a position on contemporary political issues and became a question of historical truth and what narrative strategies should be used to represent it.[8] In taking this discursive turn, however, the English Revolution did not cease to be a political issue. Scholars made that revolution the moment in modern history when the old world started to turn into a world that we, as literate members of one of the great Western imperial nation-states, can imagine ourselves inhabiting. A lot hung on this tale. It provided both a model of truth and a historical truth in its own right. As such, it determined which events could qualify as causes, what could be called political effects, and where historical agency resided.

Although Gardiner disliked the openly polemical character of the Whigs' accounts, he believed, as they did, that a revolution must "reveal more clearly than smaller changes the law of human progress."[9] His major contribution to the mythology of revolution might be summed up in his coinage of the term "Puritan Revolution." This term identified the upheavals of the mid–seventeenth century with Britain's emergence as a modern nation-state. By referring to the English Revolution as the Puritan Revolution, Gardiner also defined that conflict as a conflict between the monarch and the House of Commons, promoted by a conviction that grew in the hearts and minds of ordinary Englishmen. This yearning by each, no matter how humble, to become the master of his own individual fate incorporated all Englishmen in a new English nation.[10] Gardiner described the hero of his tale of gradual revolution in a way that made it less likely that later historians would ask exactly whose political interests were served by such a narrative. He located the ultimate cause of any revolution in what he called an "essence" that characterized a collective motive for action originating in the breasts of various individuals. Although it was always the same desire for freedom that motivated revolution, this desire could seek very different ends. For example, Gardiner considered that the "essence" of the catastrophic French Revolution was unsound from the beginning; that revolution was initiated so "that there should cease to be privileged orders."[11] In contrast, the English Revolution was intended only to make sure "that the authority of the King should be restricted."[12] The English Revolution had a positive essence because its aim was fundamentally conservative; it sought to reform the existing political order rather than to overthrow the state.

The period between the ascension of Charles I and the restoration of his son Charles II is one of the most thoroughly investigated periods in all English history. Although a minority opinion holds to the older view

that significant change did not occur until the time of the Glorious
Revolution, or even a century later with the introduction of the factory
system, the great majority of British historians agree that change—perhaps
the most profound change in English history—happened at some point
during the twenty-year period beginning with the civil war. Nor has
anyone managed to dislodge the long-abiding assumption that the human
desire for freedom inspired and propelled this change.

Having sketched the background for the contemporary debate about
the English Revolution, we will now map out the positions of this controversy.[13] As chapter 1 suggests, a consensus among historians as to
what happened during the period in question provides a terrain of fact
onto which literary criticism ultimately anchors meaning; such criticism
assumes, even if it does not openly declare, that the forces that went into
making the Revolution also shaped the mind of Milton the poet.

True to their Whig heritage, contemporary liberal historians represent
the period leading up to the 1640s as a time of conflict between two
cultures, one dying and the other powerless to be born. The English
Revolution itself was indeed revolutionary, according to this view, but
only in the sense that it inaugurated a long, slow process of social reform.
Or so Lawrence Stone tells the story:

> The mid–seventeenth century attack on almost all aspects of the social and
> political order was unsuccessful because it was premature.... Most of the
> schemes adumbrated at the time were peacefully implemented during the
> nineteenth and early twentieth century, since by then the social structure and
> ideological framework had evolved to the point where the reforms coincided
> with the aspirations and interests of the dominant classes.[14]

Liberal historians tend to maintain this double insistence on a revolution
that did occur but required the democratic reforms of the nineteenth
century to fulfill its revolutionary potential. Perez Zagorin, for one, writes
that "the revolution, for all its convulsion, wrought no lasting transformation" because the same aristocratic order that dominated English society before 1640 remained dominant after 1660.[15] "The revolution," he
concludes, "therefore did not bring about a displacement of the dominant class or produce any long-term effects on the fortunes of landed
society or the distribution of landed ownership" (185). While challenging
the irreversible transformation that Marx attributed to the English Revolution, Zagorin does not deny that something changed forever. He
simply psychologizes the change: "The most enduring consequence of
the revolution was the change it made in the beliefs and values ... [be-
cause] it embodied aspirations that clearly prefigured the liberal society

still far off in the future" (185–86).[16] The Revolution, in other words, produced the individual whose protoliberal "beliefs and values" are the ultimate if implicit cause of human progress.

The importance of this individual to narratives that represent the modern period as a period of progressive democratization is particularly evident in a well-known articulation of the liberal position. J. H. Hexter states that "beyond all contemporary and subsequent revolutions, the English Revolution was precipitated by a clash between a hereditary body and a representative body."[17] Liberal history—according to a logic that resembles Gardiner's theory of essences—creates an originary moment for a democratic future (and the ultimate triumph of Hexter's "representative body").[18] Such logic requires a psychological cause—the individual's desire for change and his determination to pursue that desire. The individual embodying that wish and that will has much the same rhetorical role that Milton, as author, has in literary histories. He establishes a continuity of consciousness, a single cause for democratic reform, where there might otherwise be several competing causes or else none at all.

Whereas liberal accounts of the English Revolution assume that the opponents of the king desired the very democratic institutions we have now, the marxist account presupposes a desire for freedom going back to the time of the Norman yoke—a desire that is yet to be fulfilled, according to the marxist view of Anglo-American culture.[19] Thus marxist accounts of the modern period also require an English Revolution, albeit an incomplete one. But the revolution in question cannot very well turn on a struggle between the class of people who dominated England before the interregnum and a class that came into being only after—and indeed because of—the Restoration. What distinguishes a true revolution from other upheavals is the appearance of new affiliations, new interest groups in contention, and new stories of struggle. Christopher Hill, most notably, has devoted his career to arguing that the anachronistic ideal of the state that Charles I sought to maintain was challenged by a "middle class" that had grown up within that state.[20] The disaffected individuals who belonged to this class were not the same people who established themselves in place of the exiled regime of Charles I, however. An entirely different class, a modern bourgeoisie, would eventually acquire power because British monarchy had been overthrown in 1642. According to Hill, the English Revolution was a revolution because it established "conditions far more favorable to the development of capitalism than those which prevailed before 1640."[21] Although it delayed the fulfillment of the formal requirements for revolution as described by Marx, the English civil war made it inevitable that the means of production would change hands, and that a new class would come into power as England began to industrialize and these people acquired the capital to purchase labor as well.

Whereas liberal historians read the records and parliamentary debates for the institutional changes brought about by those who opposed the autocratic power of the Crown, the marxist definition of "revolution" as an irreversible popular uprising prompts historians to read many of the same documents for signs indicating the emergence of a new class ethos around the ideal of individual freedom. Or so the terrain appeared until 1976, when a revisionist argument first intruded and began to collapse the contending views of liberal and marxist historians into one. In one of the first and most famous attacks of this kind, Conrad Russell claimed that no one could have predicted that relations between king and Parliament during the period from 1604 to 1629 would bring the country to civil war a decade later. There was nothing inevitable about those events, nor, therefore, about the emergence of representative democracy. To debunk the evolutionary and revolutionary narratives of liberals and marxists, respectively, Russell made this claim: "Before 1640, Parliament was not powerful, and it did not contain an 'opposition.' "[22] Following his lead, revisionist historians have reread documents for evidence of individuated responses, local concerns, and micropolitical practices that eluded the categories essential to narratives of continuous progress and class struggle alike.[23]

Revisionist historians may be characterized by their conscientious interrogation of the accounts which assume that the world we now occupy began back then and was therefore destined to take precisely the form that it has today. These historians try to read material from the past with an artificially induced naiveté, as if they were not modern readers but people who were actually involved in the events that history describes retrospectively—describes, according to the revisionists, in order to validate a particular outcome.[24] Testing the commonplace assumption that the Commons and the Lords were adamantly opposed to each other, Paul Christianson discovers extensive collaboration between the two Houses of Parliament.[25] His careful study of the first six months of the Long Parliament shows how regional interests and patronage ties enabled some members of the House of Lords to work closely with members of the House of Commons and to influence the decisions of the Commons on matters of mutual interest. John Morrill and Anthony Fletcher, examining local politics in select counties in the aftermath of the civil war, discovered that the counties maintained separate and cohesive political identities during the stormy period of the Revolution.[26] Morrill and Fletcher both conclude that counties could not have played the causal role in those upheavals that liberals claim they did. Mark Kishlansky's study of the New Model Army exemplifies the revisionist questioning of what has been taken for granted over the years. Kishlansky questions the assumption that ideology forged the army into a highly disciplined, radical fighting force united by a desire for religious freedom.[27] His second book, a close investigation of voting patterns, challenges what had previously been the conventional wisdom concerning the desire for representative democracy and the ideological motives for voting.[28] Even the term "puritan," so important to theories that rely on a clear polarization of political or economic interests, has gone under the revisionary microscope.[29]

In some respects, the assault on history launched a critique that was deeper and more lasting than any of the blows literary criticism received from poststructuralism. In striking at the fact of an English Revolution, revisionism attacked the long-accepted view of that revolution's historical causes. It is specifically to this attack on the idea of the English Revolution that Stone responds with biting irony:

> For those who like excitement, bliss has it been to be alive in the last thirty years as a Whig historian of early modern England. One vision of the past, the Marxist concept of a bourgeois revolution in the seventeenth century, has at last been laid to rest, and in retrospect it seems astonishing that it should last for so long. Another vision, the revisionist assault, based on philosophical and moral nihilism and an obstinate refusal to see the wood for the trees, tried to strip the story [of the Revolution] of all idealism or ideology or long-term causes.[30]

Though a long-standing opponent of Stone's, Christopher Hill shares the same antipathy toward the new work. Hill charges that

> revisionist historians have extended [G. R.] Elton's analysis to explain the origins of the English Revolution, though they eschew the word "revolution." They see the English civil war as an accident, the result of a series of coincidences. Again, the consequence is to minimize the ideological significance of that great turning point in English History.[31]

When put on the defensive, both Stone and Hill try to save "ideology." If stripped of ideology, Stone claims, the English Revolution loses its "idealism" along with its "long-term causes," and Hill is afraid that its "significance" will disappear. In order to explain what is at stake in the question of the Revolution, then, we must also figure out what is at stake in the challenge that revisionism has put to the narrative logic shared by Whig and marxist historians.

Liberal and left-leaning historians attribute their hostility toward revisionism to the fact that revisionist procedures are too easily misused. This claim is not entirely unfounded. The Tory historian J. D. C. Clark draws upon revisionist findings to show, for example, how public sentiment was individuated and localized during the years leading up to and through the interregnum. On this basis, he argues that there were no demonstrable causes for a revolution and therefore no permanent effects on England's national history.[32] He doubts that people felt particularly oppressed under the Stuart monarchy and insists that they were far more likely to be aroused to rebellion by the relationship between monarch and church, two inherently conservative institutions.[33] If Clark's argument represents the direction that revisionist logic can take, then it is fair to assume that the concept of a revolution was endangered when the revisionists applied the methods of historical research and found no evidence of the unified popular or Parliamentary opposition to royalist policies—no "essence" as Gardiner put it—that would cause a revolution.[34] But why does this matter? Why does such motivation have to be in place before a revolution can occur, and why is revolution so necessary to liberal and marxist accounts of modern history? Upon the answers to such questions hinges a clearer understanding of the political battle currently being waged around and through the question of the English Revolution.

Revisionists refute the claim that the Revolution was caused by a groundswell of support among the English people; these historians focus on local issues and personal responses to the events of the 1640s and 1650s in order to demonstrate that no such monolithic set of interests and motivations existed at that time. In what Barthes describes as the translation "from economic man to mental man," the political nature of a conflict and its outcome tends to disappear.[35] This is no doubt why Stone and Hill invoke "ideas" and "ideology" to stave off revisionist assaults on the English Revolution. Ideology allows them to explain how individuals coalesced into political factions or economic interest groups—for example, bourgeois, petit-bourgeois, capitalists, proletariat—that furthered their collective interests or goals. Both historians identify revolutionary change as a change in the relationship among such interest groups, though Stone avoids using a traditional marxist vocabulary to name them. More specifically, both understand modern history as the story of the emergence of what Stone describes as a new group of "elites" and Hill calls "the bourgeoisie," their domination of England, and their expansion into the colonies. In both views, the new class of people consisted of those Englishmen who opposed the old aristocracy either on their own behalf or on behalf of "the nation."[36] To participate in history, then, people either had to be members of the new class or had to be from some group that obstructed the rise of that class. Modern British history is, in this view, the story of the "true" people and how they gave the nation its modern character. The groups involved do not always have the same names, pursue the same course, or arrive in the same place in all versions of this story. The marxist, after all, has to see a new class of people come into dominance, and see the system of political relations change accordingly, before he can say there has been a revolution; whereas in order for the liberal or Whig to be satisfied that a revolution has occurred, all that is required is a shifting emphasis, a number of strategic reforms, and signs of inevitable and gradual progress. Despite these differences, the marxist and the liberal stories are about the same thing—how the identity of a relatively small social group became that of the nation.

The revisionists claim that a whole range of local and regional differences disappears whenever history identifies "the people" with those people who managed to tell their own story and identify their own self-image as that of England. Barthes provides the only explanation we know of how the name "bourgeois" lost its political edge and historical location. What he describes as "the haemorrhage" of its precise socio-historical meaning "is effected through the idea of the *nation*. This," he concedes, "was once a progressive idea, which has served to get rid of the aristocracy; today, the bourgeoisie merges into the nation, even if it has, in order to do so, to exclude from it the elements which it decides are allogenous (the Communists)" (138). In this way, according to Barthes, "the bourgeoisie is constantly absorbing into its ideology a whole section of humanity which does not have its basic status and cannot live up to it except in imagination" (141). It is no doubt in opposition to this tendency to accept the view of the few as that of the many that some literary and social historians have tried to write "unofficial" histories of the nation as well as histories from "the bottom up."[37] Such strategies certainly help to define English nationalism as the product and image of a relatively small group, but they do not explain what gave that image its extraordinary power—the power to expand across vast territories of cultural difference.

At issue in histories of the Revolution is the question of what was "there"—from our point of view, what existed outside Milton's mind and poetry. For historical scholars who formulate Milton as the consummate literary author, what is at stake is the myth of the "nation" that Barthes describes, a nation with a source within the individual that makes him, in turn, part of that collective. Milton personifies the revolution that failed to realize its immediate wish but succeeded later on in unexpected ways. "The English Revolution" and "Milton" compose a tautology, in which each provides the necessary precondition for the other. How the traditions of history and literature cooperate to produce and conceal this circular relationship between history and consciousness can be observed in criticism that works along the interstices of these disciplines.

Don M. Wolfe's *Milton in the Puritan Revolution* was published in 1941, a year after Christopher Hill's first extended account of the English Revolution. Wolfe made Milton into the embodiment of revolutionary consciousness—that paradoxical creature, the radical humanist.[38] The following excerpt joins together two Miltons produced by Wolfe's biographical procedures:

> Milton's background made him inevitably a partisan of the Parliamentary factions. A city home of Puritan inclinations, a neighborhood of wealthy merchants, a boyhood outlook of deep seriousness. . . . But it was inevitable, too, that Milton should dissent from Puritan orthodoxy. His imagination was too intense, his confidence in his intellectual powers too deep, to be bound by the Presbyterian creed. His prolonged reading of the Greek and Roman classics . . . emphasized his early love of liberty and mitigated the harshness of Calvinist discipline. Time after time he was to justify revolutionary opinions by the humanistic law of nature. But the most important factor in Milton's alliance with the Puritans was his belief in the individualistic interpretation of the Bible. Himself his own interpreter, he identified the law of nature with the law of God, unhesitatingly repudiating the religious and political teachings of his time. On Milton as on few other figures of the period, Protestant individualism stamped a revolutionary attitude. (2)

In Wolfe's analysis, Milton was first a man of his time, disposed to take up the puritan cause for economic as well as religious reasons: "Milton's background made him inevitably a partisan of the Parliamentary factions." This explains what would seem to be the historical Milton. And it is Milton's political prose that concerns Wolfe throughout the book. To make Milton into a radical in the marxist sense of the term, however, Wolfe obviously drew on the myth of the poet's mind. This allowed Milton to perform an about-face politically: "But it was inevitable Milton should dissent from Puritan orthodoxy." How, then, did Wolfe deal with this conflict between the puritan politics of Milton's career in government and the antipuritanism of his poetry in order to represent his life as a story of revolutionary consciousness? He constructed a first psychological principle—the essential Milton. By means of this construct, Wolfe created continuity where contradictions might otherwise exist. Ever the individualist, Milton's poetic identity is consistently opposed to the forces of political orthodoxy.

As a result, the contradiction between Milton the author and Milton the political figure disappears at the narrative level—only to reappear at the level of consciousness. In the passage just quoted from Wolfe, one can observe something on this order happening to humanism (the playground of the imagination and the means of aesthetic production) and puritanism (the locus of political belief). On the one hand, Milton is the creature of ideology and the product of his "background." As such, he responds in a typical fashion to external forces not of his making. But there is a counterforce within Milton that opposes historically determined ideas: "His imagination was too intense." His "imagination" is the suppressed agent of the statement, "it was inevitable that Milton should dissent from Puritan orthodoxy." Having endowed him with a mind that allowed the poet to transcend his moment in time, Wolfe attempts to reinsert Milton in history. To do so, he first redefines classical humanism. Rather than embodying the privileged knowledge of an aristocratic culture, according to Wolfe, the "Greek and Roman classics . . . emphasized [Milton's] early love of liberty and mitigated the harshness of Calvinistic discipline." Wolfe then does the same thing for puritanism: "On Milton as on few other figures of the period, Protestant individualism stamped a revolutionary attitude." Wolfe thus produces a new form of humanism that weds Renaissance poetry and prose to the spirit of democratic reform. In Wolfe's account, Milton's humanist training is reconciled with puritan orthodoxy through the poet's "belief in the individualistic interpretation of the Bible." An individual who could become "his own interpreter," as Milton reputedly did, presupposes a self prior to itself, a mind capable of liberating, authorizing, or constructing itself. In Wolfe's portrait of Milton, this tautology transforms whatever historical material comes within its reach.

Christopher Hill's study, *Milton and the English Revolution,* is dedicated to Wolfe.[39] Written almost forty years after Wolfe's *Milton in the Puritan Revolution,* it adopts Wolfe's basic method of intellectual biography, placing Milton the poet *in* a set of historical circumstances that

such a man would have experienced. As a historian, however, Hill does
not take historical events for granted. He describes the forces that shaped
Milton's experience with a precision lacking in other biographers. Indeed,
for him the whole point of studying Milton is to verify a marxist reading
of the English Revolution. Hence his insistence that the upheavals of the
mid–seventeenth century failed in the short run to democratize political
relationships. "The gentry were able to reunite in 1660," Hill explains,
"because the lines of civil-war division were drawn within a class which
had cultural ties and social prejudices in common despite differing political, religious, and economic aspirations."[40] Yet Hill insists that those
upheavals constituted the decisive event without which capitalism could
never have brought a new class into power and wealth later on:

> The English Revolution, like all revolutions, was caused by the breakdown
> of the old society; it was brought about neither by the wishes of the bourgeoi-
> sie, nor by the leaders of the Long Parliament. But its *outcome* was the
> establishment of conditions far more favorable to the development of capi-
> talism than those which prevailed before 1640. The hypothesis is that this
> outcome, and the Revolution itself, were made possible by the fact that there
> had already been a considerable development of capitalist relations in England,
> but that it was the structures, fractures, and pressures of the society, rather
> than the wishes of leaders, which dictated the outbreak of revolution and
> shaped the state which emerged from it.[41]

Hill does not suggest that "wishes" can start revolutions. That would
turn his explanation of the origin of modern England into a romance.

To deal with the problem of material cause, Hill locates the origins
of change in "conditions," "structures," "fractures," and "pressures"
external to the individuals who feel them. Although at this point in his
argument he implies that what we discern at the level of consciousness
was actually an effect of these structures and fractures, at another point
Hill describes the English Revolution as a revolution in thought:

> A great revolution in human thought dates from these decades ... that so-
> lutions to political problems might be reached by discussion and argument;
> that questions of utility and expediency were more important than theology
> or history; that neither antiquarian research nor searching the Scriptures was
> the best way to bring peace, order, and prosperity to the commonwealth....
> So although the Puritan revolution was defeated, the revolution in thought
> could not be unmade.[42]

The lag between "thought" and "the state which emerged from it" appears to solve the problem of how England could have experienced a
revolution during Milton's lifetime and felt the results only much later

on. It is the boldness of Hill's attempt to incorporate England's literary history within its political history that allows the flaws in such a resolution to surface. To make his theory work, he must accept some of the most ahistorical assumptions perpetuated by literary criticism. Thus his addition of the author "Milton" to the existing information concerning the events of 1630–50 changes that field of information, providing an excellent vantage point from which to see how "the Puritan revolution" can be transformed into "the English Revolution" of Hill's title.

Echoing Wolfe, Hill posits a Milton whom history made "more open than most of his peers to change, to novelty, to improvement, to heresy."[43] These tendencies made Milton "the steadfast propagandist of the English Revolution" as well as a man willing "to dedicate his life to becoming the English national poet" (348). With the failure of the Revolution, Milton found himself increasingly ambivalent about what Hill calls "the culture of the Protestant ethic" (465). "After the eclipse of the traditional culture of court and bishops," Hill, much like Wolfe, introduces a new element into the picture: "Milton found his allegiance divided between the culture of the Protestant ethic and the lower-class third culture, and . . . this may underlie many of the tensions revealed in his writings" (465). Let us pause for a moment and consider what this sudden introduction of a "third culture" does to the relationship between an authorial consciousness and a national history.

Hill begins by positing two ideological positions—he calls them "two cultures"—to characterize prerevolutionary England. "In speaking of two cultures," he informs the reader, "I refer to two bodies of ideas, not to groups of individuals. When we analyze the ultimate logic of these blocks of ideas, we can see that they are antagonistic" (77). These opposed logics are the familiar pair that Milton's biographers and literary scholars call "humanism" and "puritanism." In contrast with his literary predecessors, however, Hill's account of Milton smuggles another term into this opposition. Furthermore, this third term is not the compromise formation found in literary biographies whenever Milton's youthful extremism turns into the wisdom of a mature poet. In Hill's estimation, "the fact that individuals hedge, fudge, are inconsistent, seek a quiet life does not preclude the possibility of differentiating between the bodies of ideas which they muddle. . . . This consideration applies especially to what I have called the third culture" (77–78). He stresses the distinction between "blocks of ideas" and *either* individuals *or* social interest groups. And he assigns such ideas a kind of agency during the period of the English Revolution.

Relying on narrative logic much like Wolfe's, Hill argues that puritanism could be progressive, in that it opposed aristocratic power, and
yet regressive, in that it ultimately set limits on individual freedom. "Milton wanted this check to be internalized" (267), rather than imposed by
a Hobbesian state, and in this respect Milton's thought was opposed to
the thinking associated with a third culture. This claim allows Hill to
infer the emergence of a new and progressive body of thought from the
authoritarian thinking of an aristocracy that dallied with puritanism:

> Before 1640 authentic expressions of well-thought-out ideas of the third cul-
> ture are hard to come by. Intellectuals of lower-class origin, if they were to
> get on in the world, had to adopt (and mostly no doubt conscientiously did
> adopt) ruling-class ideas, or at least the "respectable" alternative ideas of
> Puritanism. Those intellectuals who played with the third culture were often
> arrogant and irresponsible aristocrats and their hangers-on."(78)[44]

The consequence of thus opening a space within early modern English
culture that allows some intellectual free play is a rather sophisticated
dialectic through which the present emerges from the past.

By virtue of this one move, Hill's is the only explanation which factors
anything like intellectual labor into an account of the English Revolution.
The occasional clunkiness of this explanation and its open manipulation
of facts identify the honest and stubborn adherence of narrative to the
logic of revolution. Hill even suggests that "ideas" provided the basis for
a class affiliation among various local and regional interest groups, one
that cut across an older system of status lines and so became a basis of
power in its own right. But he neither explores the implications of this
statement nor explains why ideas are so necessary to the resolution of
the puzzle confronting historians whenever they try to explain what was
revolutionary about the English Revolution. Behind the triadic configuration of "arrogant and irresponsible aristocrats and their hangers-on,"
"the 'respectable' alternative ideas of Puritanism," and "the third culture"
are the old class denominations that came into use during the first half
of the nineteenth century. Hill has simply introduced into an earlier epoch
the same categories of class that would emerge only later on, according
to his own account.[45]

What does he achieve by implanting these categories in English culture
two centuries before they actually organized popular thought? As we
have suggested, Hill is not so concerned with Milton as with the English
Revolution. Indeed, it is to validate his theory of revolution that he goes
to the poet. He uses Milton to represent the transition from past to
present, so as to position the modern individual at the beginning of the

modern period. To have a revolution that brings a modern bourgeoisie into dominance, he must have such an individual in place before the process begins. From this perspective, it is particularly interesting that Hill has revolutionary conflict begin in a struggle among what he calls "blocks of ideas." It is only in this form that class, as we now understand it, can be understood as the agent of that decisive revolutionary change. By reclassifying the political struggle in which Milton was embroiled at the turning point in his career as blocks of ideas, and then translating those ideas into anachronistically modern categories of class, Hill can insist that the "bourgeois aspects of Milton's thinking . . . were not of course peculiar to him"; "his heresies were the common currency of radical circles."[46] Milton's most individualistic impulses thus arose not from within himself but from ideas already in circulation. By thinking as an individual, he was thinking as part of a group. But then again, that group could not have existed when Milton wrote, not if it took a revolution to produce such a group.

In developing this relationship between the mind of Milton and the English Revolution, Hill tells us as much about the present as he does about the past. What he reveals by introducing a third "block of ideas" is the gap between the issues over which the civil war was fought and the interests and values—the very self-conception—of the group of people who would come into power as a result. He has to come up with something new in order to get from the factions that overthrew Charles I to those that consolidated to form a modern ruling class. Indeed, he occasionally comes close to adopting a Foucaultian hypothesis that the class in question began in literature (with only the properties and privileges we grant to a fiction) and, through its reproduction on various cultural terrains, eventually turned into the very things it represented, namely, a state of mind and a fact of life. Although the main drift of Hill's intellectual biography of Milton presupposes the same kind of individual as most modern histories do (that is, one already there and desiring his freedom), he sometimes turns the logic embodied in that subject on its ear. At such moments in *Milton and the English Revolution,* Hill's Milton loses all typicality. Like that of the literary Milton, this Milton's mind expands to contain what previously seemed to be outside, larger than, and prior to it, much as if the text were capable of transforming its context rather than the other way around. While contending that "his heresies were the common currency of radical circles," Hill also claims that Milton was "unique in his vast attempt to combine these heresies into a coherent system" (462). Although Milton's was a thoroughly "bourgeois conception of liberty," furthermore, this bourgeois "trend of thought came with the rise of a class" of people who, according to the preponderance of historical evidence, had not yet risen by the time Milton formulated his conception of liberty (263). Whenever his argument confronts this conflict between the terms of an earlier struggle and those defining social conflict after the so-called Revolution, Hill turns to Milton, the poet.

On occasion, Hill as much as admits that he uses the story of this author to transform revolutionary "blocks of ideas" into the materials of a modern historical narrative: "Milton, then, is the great eclectic, taking ideas from wherever he found them. He took more from the radical tradition than most 'Puritans' and evolved other ideas of his own in dialogue with the third culture" (336). In such statements as these, Milton embodies a formidable power uniquely capable of transforming "thought" into the blocks of ideas on which Hill can superimpose a modern narrative of class struggle. According to this narrative, certain members of Parliament contended with and overthrew an early modern monarchy, putting radical puritans of Milton's ilk in charge of the nation. Since these men did not represent an emergent class in the marxist sense of the term, Hill requires another element to satisfy his definition of revolution, which Milton conveniently provides. In addition to the puritanism that aligned him with Cromwell's party, Hill claims, Milton personally "evolved other ideas." These ideas had popular appeal. And without these "heresies . . . with their powerful emphasis on this world" (461–62), there can be no revolution; or so Hill indicates by insisting that ideas can exist only as "blocks," and then by connecting what is heretical in Milton's thought to a "third culture" that is at once residual and emergent. What came out of the period between the beheading of Charles I and the restoration of Charles II was, according to Hill, a new way of thinking that succeeded in permanently eroding both the monarchy and puritan orthodoxy.

However, rather than ask what group of people produced this new way of thinking and how they acquired the means to do so, in the end Hill circles around a self-contradiction. He fails to consider the possibility of a new basis and definition for class. He would rather grant transformative powers to a single poet, on the one hand, and attribute all that Milton thought to some preexisting "block of ideas" on the other, than consider what happened to the production and circulation of information during the period in question. Despite Milton's importance to his argument that an English Revolution occurred during the middle of the seventeenth century, Hill fails to acknowledge the degree to which writers and gatherers of information—including scientists and theologians—saw to it that England would never be an absolutist monarchy again. Much as he depends on the shifting relationship among "blocks of ideas" to produce a coherent account of the revolution, he grants to those who work with ideas only a passive role in his story. As he puts it, "ideas tend to be expressed by intellectuals: that is what intellectuals are for" (78), and this does not leave much room for the role of writers to change as they gained the means of producing what Marx calls "ruling ideas."

The temptation for literary people is to assign authors a place in history on the basis of what they wrote, and not on the basis of the conditions under which they lived and became writers. The relationship between writing and who an author is exercises a strange mirroring power, whereby the written text produces a historical identity rather than the other way around—"as if," one could say, "the signifier *gave a foundation* to the signified."[47] The fact that Milton wrote pamphlets on parliamentary matters and served as Latin secretary for the revolutionary government under Cromwell earned him only a relatively minor place in history. It is for his poetry that he is important to modern literary scholarship; and it is, significantly, to the literary Milton that Hill turns in order to identify the sources of revolution: "Milton is not merely rationally discussing and choosing between two sets of ideas . . . but in his poetry he reveals a personality which is also in some deeper way internally torn—between Adam's love for Eve and his orthodox theology" (337). Like his literary counterparts, then, Hill describes Milton as the first individual.[48] Resembling the Adam of *Paradise Lost,* Milton embodies a conflict between private needs and public obligations—between who he is and who, according to his time and place, he has to be. Like the postlapsarian Adam, the poet is his own maker. He and not God contains the magical agency of self-production. Ultimately, the question of the revolution and what was revolutionary about it boils down to the question of where this power came from and how one got it.

Everything we have read firsthand or encountered in secondary materials on the subject of the English Revolution indicates that something important happened during the period marked by Milton's career. Even revisionists admit that England was never the same again. Although the change in question is said to have been as permanent as it was profound, it has nevertheless eluded the very categories with which historians attempt to capture it. We are convinced that something happened, but both liberal and marxist historians are hard-pressed to show that any substantial institutional reforms or redistribution of power took place in England before 1688, even though these remain the criteria for revolutionary change. Nor do we find any economic evidence that a new class came into power until much later on. To be sure, most historians insist that what Gardiner called the Puritan Revolution was an English Revolution which did away with the principle of absolute monarchy.[49] But this fact is established by narratives demonstrating how the revolution initiated changes that allowed the modern state to take shape as it did—narratives, in other words, that seek legitimation for present policies in the past. Thus one comes away from reading accounts of the English Revolution with a clear sense that something happened, but with a very muddy sense of what in fact was revolutionary about those events. The revisionists simply expose a problem that Hill and Stone were already wrestling with, namely, that there is little evidence for permanent political change if one locates its cause either in popular resistance or in the demand for individual rights.

We have traced the main stream of Milton criticism as it maintains the internal coherence of Milton's thought in the face of what appear to have been gaping discontinuities in the construction of that thought. We then turned to history for verification of this literary critical representation of Milton's mind as a spot of sameness in a storm of categorical change; but we did not find what we were told was there. We did find an explanation for the changes that sent Milton from the margins of courtly life to the center of political power, before those changes cast him out of politics and into the role of an author. But no historian has demonstrated how similar things might have happened on a scale large enough to transform the thinking of literate people in general, much less that of the nation as a whole. And herein lies the problem. Historians frequently acknowledge that a veritable explosion of printed matter coincided with the abolition of the Star Chamber on 5 July 1641 and the consequent lifting of legal constraints on publication. Hill himself has noted, for example, that in 1640 twenty-two pamphlets were published; in 1642 the number increased to nearly two thousand.[50] A Licensing Order was subsequently issued by Parliament on 29 January 1642, and some restrictions were reinstated; this was followed by the more rigid order of June 1643, which Milton addressed in *Areopagitica*.[51] And further constraints were imposed over the following decade.[52] Indeed, from December 1649 to January 1653 one of Milton's own tasks was to serve as a government censor and inspect all printed matter. But after agreeing with Hill that nothing prior to 1640 or following 1660 can compare with the explosion of writing during the English Revolution, and after granting Stone's point that it was "an extraordinarily wordy revolution," one is left with no sense of the relationship between writing and other political activities.[53]

One is told there was a revolution in ideas, but one receives only the vaguest notion of what material changes were wrought by the amount of information produced: how did the momentary lifting of censorship alter what writing was, who produced it, and who read it? And when one turns to Raymond Williams, whose account of the "long revolution" deals specifically with these changes, one discovers that his account does not begin with the interregnum. It begins with Parliament's failure to renew the Licensing Act in 1695, leaving one to assume that no permanent changes in the production and distribution of information ensued from the English Revolution.[54] Williams proposes to show that the "creative" or cultural dimension of social experience led the way as, during the seventeenth and eighteenth centuries, a whole range of authors and intellectuals turned against the existing forms of political authority and won. The first section of *The Long Revolution* grants culture a historical priority over the official institutions of state. Williams says that cultural history "is more than a department, a special area of change. In this creative area the changes and conflicts of the whole way of life are necessarily involved" (122). But latent in his promise to extend the category of "the political" to include a "whole way of life" is the contradictory (and peculiarly modern) assumption that political practices are a specialized category of "the whole." This second notion of politics emerges in the second section of the book, where Williams describes the growth of the reading public, of the popular press, and of standard English, as a process through which the new middle classes converted the creative power of language into economic power. Here, political events are narrowly defined as those which take place in the houses of government, the courts, and the marketplace; and this definition assumes control over the "creative" or cultural dimension of social experience.[55] Williams, in maintaining that England underwent some kind of revolution during the course of Milton's career, does shift attention to the very personal and "creative" areas of culture that historians tend to ignore in favor of what they define as "political." But to work within the pale of British social historiography, he also has to think of things exactly the other way around.

In his influential study of Elizabethan culture, Stephen Greenblatt expands on the oft-rehearsed truth that literacy became a basis for political authority during the Protestant reformations of the sixteenth century. In a discussion of the impact of printing, he shifts the emphasis away from economics as the reason why Protestantism led to capitalism. "When Tyndale writes of arming oneself with the syllables of Scripture," Greenblatt explains, "or Bainham speaks of his fear that this word of God—pointing to the book in his hand—would damn him, we must take them at very close to the literal meaning: the printed English New Testament is, above all, *a form of power*. It is invested with the ability to control, guide, discipline, console, exalt, and punish that the Church had arrogated to itself for centuries."[56] Thus, although literacy empowered readers, it did not empower them to do anything they wanted. Reading the Bible afresh might reform the church, but, as Greenblatt stresses, it was also feared that democratizing reading might obscure the original meaning of that text.

Procedures for reading and interpreting the printed word had to be devised and disseminated in order to regulate the secular use of sacred material. From this perspective, one can see how the puritan emphasis on literacy might well have sown the seeds of an irreversible political change, even though this emphasis seemed to detach theology from partisan politics by making it an individual and, ultimately, a private matter. One can imagine the emphasis shifting from the idea that literacy was something that required regulation to the idea that literacy was a form of regulation. Once one has considered this possibility, it is only logical to insist that power itself must have changed—the sources, goals, and instruments of power as well as its effects.

CHAPTER THREE

Family History

What is the virtue of reduction either of scale or in the number of properties? It seems to result from a sort of reversal in the process of understanding. To understand a real object in its totality we always tend to work from its parts. The resistance it offers us is overcome by dividing it. Reduction in scale reverses this situation. Being smaller, the object as a whole seems less formidable. By being quantitatively diminished, it seems to us qualitatively simplified. More exactly, this quantitative transposition extends and diversifies our power over a homologue of the thing, and by means of it the latter can be grasped, assessed and apprehended at a glance. A child's doll is no longer an enemy, a rival or even an interlocutor. In it and through it a person is made into a subject. In the case of miniatures . . . knowledge of the whole precedes knowledge of the parts.

Claude Lévi-Strauss, *The Savage Mind*

Some common ground among individuals is absolutely essential to the complex ideological cluster we are elaborating. Otherwise, literary and social historians would be left with nothing more than an ensemble of discursive effects with which to account for the most basic categories of modern culture. There is no question that the family provides that common ground. It provides a conceptual space where nature and culture conspire to produce the individuals who write books and engineer revolutions. No matter how extraordinary some individuals turn out to be, they all have mothers and fathers, and they appear to enter into history in much the same way, pulsing with the most ordinary needs, drives, and passions.

The past two decades have seen not only a multifaceted theoretical critique that insists on the productive capability of texts, the agency of writing, and the historicity of precisely those areas where culture appears to be nature rather than culture, but also the explosion of a veritable industry in the history of the family. The development of such a specialized focus within social history might seem like a good idea. Indeed, one could argue that feminism, poststructuralism, and the new cultural history should converge around the effort to demystify the nuclear family. One might also expect these critical practices to show how and in whose interests the sexual distribution of labor and power has operated, what role writing played in producing the family's distinctively modern shape, and how the family has interacted with other institutions characteristic of cultures undergoing industrialization. But this has not occurred. Rather than seeing the sacred space of human reproduction as the soft but omnipotent center of modern culture, the place where science shakes hands with theology and literature, British historians of the family have settled for common sense and sentimentality. The result has been a burgeoning field within social history that demonstrates either that a particular family formation has always been with us or that any other living arrangement lacks love. In this chapter, we are interested in the political fantasy that is encapsulated and reproduced not only through popular representations of the family but also in the annals of historical scholarship.

Even the most sophisticated scholars and critics tend to assume that consciousness enters history and takes up a definitive relationship with the world by means of the family. Thus it is in the area of the history of the family that history rubs directly up against the very domain of human experience that literature places outside of history, in either the domain of nature or that of God.[1] It is in this area that historians join the nomenclature of class and status to that of emotion and moral character, hallmarks of the enclosed and individuated consciousness. Where then, if not here, might we find a historical description of the individual in whom literature and history locate the cause of revolutionary change? Such an individual, however, is the last thing the mainstream of Anglo-American social historians have been willing to historicize. Indeed, their whole mission has been to preserve the paradox of continuity (of consciousness) amid revolutionary change (in sociopolitical relations) that binds literature to history.

Even a casual glance at a few of these historical studies of the family shows how consistently they voice the conviction that family feeling has characterized English people and their culture since early modern times, if not well before. One is led to think that family feeling is endemically English. According to Keith Wrightson, the diaries of members of the gentry show that romantic love was alive and well in England even when marriages were arranged for largely economic and political reasons.[2] Ralph Houlbrooke finds that parish registers indicate relatively low infant mortality during the early seventeenth century, and he concludes from this evidence that most parents wanted their children and took care of them once they were born.[3] Michael McDonald, drawing on the records of an early seventeenth-century physician-astrologer, discovers that an early modern wife or parent could become so physically ill from bereavement as to require medical help.[4] From this evidence, McDonald concludes that early modern people enjoyed a close relationship with their spouses and children. Angus McLaren examines demographic statistics and medical tracts and concludes that from early modern to modern times "the rights of women to experience sexual pleasure were not enhanced, but eroded as an unexpected consequence of the elaboration of more sophisticated models of reproduction."[5] There are many more studies that share this view that family life is a constant of English culture.[6] We offer these examples from among the more respected scholarly efforts simply to suggest the kind of argument presently commanding the field of the history of the British family, and to pose the following questions: Against whom do historians feel compelled to defend a culture- and class-specific notion of the family? Why do so by arguing that the family, in contrast with every other institution and social alliance, is in some essential way exempt from history?

To find an answer, one must move backward two decades to one of the earliest and most influential examples of this kind of history. The current desire to rescue the family is first and most superficially an attempt to rescue Peter Laslett's version of the English family, set forth in what has become the foundational work of the history of the British family, *The World We Have Lost*.[7] This work began in the 1950s as a series of radio lectures, which were revised and published as a book in 1965; the book was subsequently revised twice more. It went through any number of printings and became one of the most frequently cited books written on the topic.[8] This pioneering effort to historicize the family married sociology to history in order to determine how ordinary people lived their lives in centuries past. The implications of this move cannot be overestimated. It provided the model for histories of the family. At the same time, it attracted attention to the Cambridge Group for the History of Populations and Social Structures, even though Laslett made it clear in subsequent editions of his book that he did not want his own argument

concerning the family in former times to be identified with the work of
the Cambridge Group. The later editions did, however, increasingly rely
on the Cambridge Group's demographic findings.

Laslett takes some of his evidence for the affective history of the family
from a standard source, the writing of the puritan clergy. He supports
his interpretation of what he describes as a "discussion of domestic,
economic and social relations by the men of the time" with data from
the Cambridge Group's file 3, the Listings File.[9] Elsewhere he identifies
the contents of this file as "every discoverable list of inhabitants which
gives evidence of being complete" and specifically as parish records from
one hundred communities.[10] These lists were compiled by "the miscel-
laneous body of persons living in our country between the years 1574
and 1821 who went to the trouble of counting and describing the inhabitants of the hundred communities whose figures we have recovered
and analysed."[11] Each subsequent edition of *The World We Have Lost*
includes more of these data. On the basis of this evidence, Laslett portrays
the family in former times as a small, relatively self-enclosed unit composed mostly of blood relatives with a biological father or his surrogate
at their head. In preindustrial societies, according to Laslett, "a man
usually lived and worked within the family, the circle of affection, [and]
released enough dissatisfaction to account for all the restlessness which
has marked the progress of the industrial world" (18).[12] The kind of
dissatisfaction that could be contained within a family exists for Laslett
in stark contrast with modern dissatisfaction. Our modern concept of
alienation, which he calls part of the "cant of the mid–twentieth century,"
"began as an attempt to describe the separation of the worker from his
world of work" (22). "Time was," as he tells it, "when the whole of life
went forward in the family, in a circle of loved, familiar faces, known
and fondled objects, all to human size. That time has gone forever," he
laments. "It makes us very different from our ancestors" (22).

Laslett applies his own brand of popular psychology to this statistically
reconstructed family. By an almost invisible logic of internalization, he
reasons that even "the head of the poorest family was at least the head
of something" (54). That each of them was on top of some little heap
of humanity apparently made it possible for heads of households to
identify with people higher up on the social scale in a way that became
impossible once the workplace was detached from the home. In an extension of the same logic, Laslett translates the old family feeling into
a collective consciousness that did not break down along class lines until
the nineteenth century. "The workers," according to Laslett, "did not

form a million *outs* facing a handful of *ins*. They were not in what might be called a mass situation. They could not feel the kind of affiliation we attribute to a class. "For this," by which he means the England of old, "was a one-class society" (54).[13] From time immemorial, then, Englishmen understood themselves in relation to the nuclear family (although he stops short of saying it in so many words, the family, for Laslett, is the nuclear family).[14] Englishmen either felt they were parts integrated into an organic whole or else they thought of themselves as parts broken off from that whole. Upon this concept of the family depends Laslett's idea that the loss of such wholeness of being gives human consciousness its modern shape.

The absence or presence of the family divides present from past. With the spread of the factory system, the family unit was no longer the work unit, and the worker-patriarch became mass man, that maelstrom of arbitrarily colliding atoms that Engels encountered in Manchester as the factory doors opened to disgorge their human contents.[15] On the grounds that no comparable change had previously torn men from their homes and villages or amassed them in factories and cities, Laslett concludes that the upheavals of the 1640s and 50s had very little impact at the level at which ordinary people lived:

> The truth is that changes in English society between the reign of Elizabeth and the reign of Anne were not revolutionary. The impression left by an attempt to survey the fundamental framework during these generations is of how little, not of how much, evolution seems to have taken place. Nothing in economic organization or in social arrangements seems to have come about which would have led of itself to political crisis, and the changes that did go on seem to have been gradual over the whole period rather than sudden.[16]

In an ingenious turn of argument, Laslett insists that the conflicts punctuating the period between the reigns of Elizabeth and Anne did not disrupt, but rather strengthened, affiliations at the local level of village and home. Conflicts at the center of power preserved life as it had been lived by the great majority of Englishmen until the industrial revolution. In thus establishing that English people lived in nuclear families much earlier than social historians had previously imagined, Laslett challenges the assumption that the events of the 1640s and 50s wrought a major change of some kind in the people's sense of who they were and how they were related to one another. Historians who want to identify the mid–seventeenth century as the revolutionary moment in England's political history must therefore deal with the claim that people did not change at the most personal level until much later on.

At first, most historians chose to ignore the implications of Laslett's theory. It was thought that, as one of the founding fathers of the British demographic approach, Laslett had simply established the family as a legitimate area of historical research. He had not made it necessary to integrate that research into political history, an area in which he was already a distinguished scholar. Whether or not Lawrence Stone began his equally influential study of personal life with the idea of defending the English Revolution against Laslett's argument, he was venturing into territory that had already been mapped out by that argument when he entered the debate on the origin of the nuclear family.[17] And the ahistorical character of Laslett's preindustrial family could not long remain unacknowledged. The thesis that the modern political order emerged as a result of the English Revolution was at stake. Chapter 2 tried to demonstrate that because they are unable to identify a social or economic cause for a revolution during the mid–seventeenth century, both Stone and Christopher Hill must resort to "blocks of ideas," "ideology," or, to use the terms Stone adopts in *The Family, Sex and Marriage, 1500–1800*, "values and behaviour" (10–11). Their arguments depend entirely on the supposition that a significant number of English people responded with the same emotion when government encroached upon their personal lives, since such emotion is the most important cause as well as a response to the events of the 1640s and 50s.

To challenge Laslett, Stone draws upon what he calls a "rag-bag of evidence," and from this material he tries "to create a coherent composite picture" (11):

> Every possible type of evidence has been examined to pick up hints about changes in values and behaviour at the personal level. The greatest reliance has been placed on personal documents, diaries, autobiographies, memoirs, domestic correspondence, and the correspondence columns of newspapers. Other sources which have been used are the more popular and most frequently reprinted handbooks of advice about domestic behaviour, before 1660 written mainly by moral theologians and after 1660 mainly by laymen . . . ; reports of foreign visitors; imaginative literature, concentrating on the most popular novels, plays and poems of the day; art . . . ; architectural house plans showing circulation patterns and space use; modes of address within families . . . ; folk customs such as bundling and wife-sale; legal documents such as wills, inventories, marriage contracts and litigation over divorce or sexual deviation; and finally, demographic statistics about birth, marriage, death, pre-nuptial conceptions and bastardy. (10–11)

Three points ought to be noted in this catalogue of sources. First, it appears that Stone thinks of "changes in values and behaviour at the personal level" primarily as changes in *sexual* values and behavior. Second, as Stone himself acknowledges, his research on the family in former times is limited to the families of a relatively small group of people; most of his evidence concerns the mating procedures and domestic practices of families of the gentry and nobility.[18] Finally, Stone's material overlaps that on which Laslett based *The World We Have Lost,* but he does not use the demographic findings of the Cambridge group; instead, he relies upon "imaginative literature," "art," and "architectural house plans." Stone uses this material to produce something less like paradise lost and more like paradise found, in order to refute Laslett's theory. To demonstrate that personal life underwent a profound change during the seventeenth century, Stone has to historicize what Laslett relegated to nature. He reworks the material he and Laslett share, to dismantle Laslett's idea that in early modern England there were fewer people in a social unit, that they spent more time together, and that as a result they enjoyed a closer emotional bonding than was the case during the modern period.

From the scant evidence available, Stone concludes that between 1450 and 1630, what he calls the Open Lineage Family was the dominant but not the only pattern. During the last fifty years of this period, affiliations among members of the immediate family apparently began to hold their own against allegiances to outside authorities, and to this intermediate formation he gives the name Restricted Patriarchal Nuclear Family. But it is only after 1640 that something like the values and behavior of the Closed Domesticated Nuclear Family actually organized people's thoughts and feelings as well as the way they lived. Although these different types of households represent a sequence of three time frames in the history of the family, in fact only two types—the biological family and a household that includes other people—organize Stone's historical narrative, and they boil down to a simple opposition. Laslett imagines that the world was significantly happier when household and workplace were one. What amounts to good company for Laslett is, for Stone, a crowd. Stone does not want extra children, servants, apprentices, aunts and uncles, or grandparents around his house, no matter how limited their numbers, constant their influence, or cohesive their presence in the group. He cannot imagine how a husband and wife could experience true intimacy while other people were looking on; he assumes that a powerful bond between parent and child could only be born out of a relationship that took place in the solitude of a private room. And he concludes that the privatization of the household, like the English Revolution itself, was a permanent change for the better.

Two kinds of relationships—"external" and "affective"—coexist as
contraries in Stone's account. Thus, regarding sixteenth-century kinship
relations, he writes: "This was a society where *neither* individual autonomy *nor* privacy were respected as desirable ideals" (4, Stone's italics).
"Relations within the nuclear family, between husband and wife and
parents and children, were *not* much closer than those with neighbors,
with relatives, or with 'friends,' " he continues, and marriage itself "was
not an intimate association based on personal choice" (5, our italics).
During the reign of the Restricted Patriarchal Nuclear Family the "total
amount of the affective feelings was limited" (7) by the authority of
church and state. By some natural principle, however, these feelings began
to flourish the moment a "series of changes in the state, the society and
the Church undermined this patriarchal emphasis, while continuing the
decline of external pressures on the increasingly nuclear family" (7). Affective individualism organized the household as soon as "external" in-
terventions in family life disappeared. As Stone explains, "this new type
of family was the product of the rise of *Affective* Individualism. It was
a family organized around the principle of personal autonomy, and bound
together by strong *affective* ties" (7, our italics). Our italics are meant to
point out Stone's tautological use of "affective."

Stone's account of the modern family suggests that it takes one to
make one, and *The Family, Sex and Marriage* consequently reproduces
the figure of the self-producing self whose operations we have been
tracing. If, as he claims, "this new type of family was the product of
Affective Individualism," then the new type of family structure was responsible for creating such individuals. Stone insists that people could
not feel close to one another in a world where "privacy was clearly a
rarity, which the rich lacked because of the architectural layout of the
houses and the prying ubiquity of their servants, and the poor lacked
because of confinement in a one-or-two room hovel" (6). He also insists
that restriction of the family to the genealogically related unit and the
elimination of "external" influences on its affairs automatically reproduced itself at the level of the individual. Privacy *of* the family created
privacy *within* the family, as demonstrated both by architectural spaces
where the individual body was out of other people's sight and by modes
of writing in which the individual mind appeared to constitute a world
unto itself.[19]

Where Laslett's argument proceeded by tropes of fusion or identifi-
cation, Stone's depends on tropes of enclosure and separation. And where
Laslett mobilized the concept of *Gemeinschaft* to associate the loss of

psychological closeness with the centrifugal force of industrialization, Stone's account is equally dependent on another familiar nineteenth-century theme, that which endorses rather than deplores the modern division of labor. Any reader of nineteenth-century fiction knows that no good can come of a relationship based on money rather than love. According to Stone's definition of the family, affective relations can flourish between man and woman, and between parent and child, only where marriage is not a matter of economic necessity. Only then can personal choice determine the composition of the family. And as for the world we have lost, he arrives at the conclusion that marriage then "was not an intimate association based on personal choice. Among the upper and middling ranks it was primarily a means of tying together two kinship groups. . . . Among peasants, artisans and labourers, it was an economic necessity" (5).

In Laslett's version, the family began as far back as men and women started living in houses together with their children and a few other people. On this basis, he argues that members of an ordinary English household in the past could experience the same kind of closeness that modern individuals can experience with their spouses and offspring, when not too preoccupied with work. In Stone's version, the family came into being only with the kind of privacy that allowed for sexual intimacy. At least at first, only those few who possessed space, time, and literacy evidently enjoyed such privacy. It is only now, after the separation of home and workplace, that ordinary people can enjoy it. Yet in reading each of these conflicting accounts, one has little doubt that the family is the historian's fantasy before it is anything else. For both Laslett and Stone, the early modern household embodies a feeling that people naturally feel for their spouses and biological offspring, the same feeling that these historians imagine parents and children experience now. Both assume that closeness among a small, enclosed group of people not only makes those people happy but also indicates they are decent, kind, and mature.

This is precisely the difficulty. In writing about personal life, neither Laslett nor Stone has historicized his own idea of what personal life is and should be. Having stressed the point on which they directly disagree with one another, we would now like to suggest that the Stone-Laslett debates are not nearly so important for their diverging positions, however fiercely held, as for the points on which they must concur in order to disagree. Rather than taking sides in the quarrel, we want to show how a single political fantasy—what we are calling a myth—provides a framework for these conflicting histories of the family and is therefore substantiated no matter which side ultimately wins.

To get at this fantasy, let us first work with Laslett. Having demonstrated to his satisfaction that most English households and villages were relatively small until well into the nineteenth century, he delivers up the following conclusion—or wish, or command, depending on how one reads it:

> We must imagine our ancestors, therefore, in the perpetual presence of their young offspring. A good 70 per cent of all households contained children. . . . In the pre-industrial world there were children everywhere. . . . The perpetual distraction of childish noise and talk must have affected everyone almost all the time, except of course the gentleman in his study or the lady in her boudoir; incessant interruptions to answer questions, quiet fears, rescue from danger or make peace between the quarreling. (109)

The world we have lost turns out to be an extended nursery of noisy needs and relatively undifferentiated individuals, a Munchkin land that could not survive the reality of the industrial cities that tore individuals apart from one another and then piled them together willy-nilly into monstrous slums. But this conception of the world was also the one with which Laslett began, and the one he sought to universalize.

Susan Stewart's wonderful analysis of miniaturization may seem worlds away from British historiography, but it describes precisely the logic that Laslett's description fulfills; a logic that equates smallness—small households, small villages, and small children—with emotional closeness.[20] As Stewart describes it, the logic of miniaturization begins with a world of things. Resembling the writing of history in this respect, the miniature promises to bring the past back to life. It erases the process of reproduction that presents objects to us, and allows consumers to lose themselves in representation. Although the world in miniature appears to be one of nature pure and simple when compared to present-day reality, it is anything but. Its immaculate precision marks "the inorganic body of the machine and its *repetition* of a death that is thereby not a death" (69). It is by triumphing over the natural forces of both time and space that the miniature offers its consumer a fantasy of control in which art (or history in this case) appears to master even death: "The miniature, linked to nostalgic versions of childhood and history, presents a diminutive, and thereby manipulatable, version of experience, a version which is domesticated and protected from contamination" (69). Another glance at Laslett's mode of description will reveal its involvement in the great game of cultural control.

Laslett's capacity to imagine the world as one big happy family depends upon his capacity to imagine his ancestors, through a historical inversion, as if from the position of their parent. Where Stone seems appalled by the very lack of privacy to which Laslett attributes the togetherness of premodern family life, Laslett is not the least bit concerned that the world we have lost must have been one in which people were constantly exposed to the prying eyes of their neighbors. The reason for this is clear. It is from the perspective of overseer of this brood that he imagines "the perpetual distraction of childish noise and talk . . . incessant interruptions to answer questions, quiet fears, rescue from danger or make peace among the quarreling" (109). By his own admission, Laslett's is a paternalistic view: "Immaturity implies authority," he confides, "and those who cannot look after themselves have to be commanded" (111).

Laslett offers us a past that was comparatively gratifying and harmonious, not because individualism flourished there, but because of the constraints placed upon individualism. The preindustrial family may appear to be one that empowered the ordinary individual, but in actuality the individual did not count for very much. Only the father mattered, and one was a father only to the degree that one had a family under his control. Laslett imagines the family as both a single body and one that exists in a feminized relationship to the father. In psychoanalytic terms, this particular configuration resembles the fantasy of the maternal body acted out in the game that Freud calls *fort-da,* a fantasy arguably specific to Western industrialized cultures and the social groups that dominate them.[21] The "family" allows Laslett to imagine political authority as analogous to the father's "natural" power over the mother's body. If an individual's identity as father depends upon controlling or manipulating the desires of women and children, then social order depends on subordinating the wish of a (feminine) population to the (masculine) will of the father. The political logic of the fantasy reveals itself early on in Laslett's argument, where he admits, "people came [i.e., existed] not as individuals, but as families" (20). Once the heterogeneous individuals within the preindustrial family unit can be boiled down to just one, then a similar process of reduction can repeat itself at the level of the nation. And so Laslett imagines England of old as

> an association between the heads of such families, but an association largely confined to those who were literate, who had wealth and status, those, in fact, who belonged with their families as part of them, to what we called the ruling minority. Almost no woman ever belonged to England as an individual, except it be a queen regnant—scarcely a woman in the ordinary sense—or a

noble widow and heiress or two, a scattering of widows of successful merchants and yeoman. No individual under the age of thirty was likely to be a
member, except in the very highest reaches of society, and very few men who
had never been married. (20)

The nursery requires an adult world. By miniaturizing the family, Laslett
rationalizes the use of marriage to settle economic and political obligations. When business mixed into marriage, it did not oppress children
so much as ensure their future. As he explains, "the authoritarianism of
traditional social life and educational practice becomes a little easier to
understand when the youthfulness of so much of the community is borne
in mind" (111). The fantasy of the world as a nursery requires an authoritarian father.

Where the old society greets Laslett with the undifferentiated babble
of children, it does not speak to Stone at all. It is strictly from the absence
of certain expressions of emotion in memoirs and diaries, as well as from
limited data concerning wet nursing, child rearing, and mortality during
the early years of childhood that he concludes: "There is no doubt
whatever that 'restraint of emotional outpouring characterized infant
departures as well as entries into the uncertain temporal scene', an observed psychological fact which stands in striking contrast with the evidence for the very late eighteenth and the nineteenth centuries" (105).
Should their offspring survive infancy, often in someone else's hands,
even those of a stranger, the first duty of parents was ruthlessly "to crush
the will of young children." Rather than a bustling and thriving nursery,
Stone contends, "England between 1500 and 1660 was relatively cold,
suspicious, and violence-prone" (102). On what grounds does he draw a
conclusion so much at odds with the extremely influential view that
Laslett, writing just twelve years before, had abstracted from some of
the very same evidence?

Stone infers a pervasive inhospitality toward children from the demonstrable "frequency with which infants at that period were deprived
of a single mothering and nurturing figure to whom they could relate
during the first eighteen or twenty years of life" (99). Obviously connected
to the lack of any domestic warmth in Stone's mind are the practices of
fostering out and of exchanging children. According to Stone, the children of the landed, upper bourgeois, and professional classes were generally fostered out to hired wet nurses for a year or two and then raised
by nurses, governesses, and tutors until about the age of ten, when they
were sent to boarding school. Lower down the social ladder, children
also left home at an early age. As Stone explains, "what one sees at these

middle- and lower middle-class levels is a vast system of exchange by which parents sent their own children away from home . . . and the richer families took in the children of others as servants and labourers. As a result of this custom, some very fragmentary census data suggest that from just before puberty until they married some ten years later, about two out of every three boys and three out of every four girls were living away from home" (107). Apparently, then, these practices were common in preindustrial societies, even though it hardly enters into Laslett's picture of that world at all. Children were kept at a distance from their parents at the upper levels of early modern society through the practice of fosterage, and the exchange of children was enough to prevent any family affection from developing at the lower. As a result of these practices, Stone explains, "members of the importing families lived, ate, and, at the lower social levels where rooms were few, even slept in the company of members of another family. Domestic relations must consequently have been more formal and more restrained than they need to be today because of the constant presence in the house of strangers, who were likely to gossip with the neighbors" (108). Stone admits that "it was only when bourgeois demand for privacy developed in the early eighteenth century that this [exportation of children] became a source of complaint" (108). He apparently cannot imagine, as Laslett does, that the presence of other children in the family might have extended the sense of closeness to a community beyond the biological family. Rather, he assumes that anyone coming into the family from outside it cannot be truly family and therefore contaminates it. A world that fails to grant autonomy to the biological family is, by Stone's definition, a world without love.

What appears to be a problem of fathers—the extent of their authority over other members of the family—turns out to be a problem of mothers: a world without love is for Stone a world without "a single mothering and nurturing figure." This world resembles the world Melanie Klein identifies with the "bad breast," a metaphor with which she explains why some people's gratification depends on the illusion of controlling its source, equivalent to an infant's illusion that it has the power to summon the maternal breast.[22] Laslett's description offers the fantasy of fully possessing the mother, as one might do prior to separation from her; Stone's offers a negative version of this world, a family in which the mother fails to nourish the infant-subject. Before the formation of the kind of family that provided maternal affection, the need was certainly there; "emotion," claims Stone, "was deflected into other channels, primarily into passionate religious enthusiasm. . . . Tempers were short, and both casual violence and venomous and mutually exhausting litigation against neighbors were extremely common" (99). The use of such terms as "violence," "venomous," and "mutually exhausting" is characteristic of the fantasy of the bad breast. Klein finds that this fantasy colors the world of individuals who felt that their mothers were unresponsive to their needs. Pursuing the logic of the "bad breast," Klein also discovered that these individuals achieve a sense of control over the desired object by regarding it as providing poison rather than milk.

In representing the early modern world as such a world, Stone speaks, not from the perspective of the father, as Laslett did, but from that of the child. However, the fantasy shaping this representation is the same as Laslett's, namely, a wish for control. We have already suggested similarities between Laslett's imagined world and the game of *fort-da,* by which Freud's grandson staved off fear of abandonment through imaginary control of his mother. And we can do the same with Stone's. In a psychoanalytic interpretation, for one to imagine a depleted world as Stone does is, symbolically, to send one's mother away. One thus fantasizes control of the withdrawal of the breast, much as the little boy did in making a bobbin-like toy disappear behind a piece of furniture in the *"fort"* part of the game his grandfather happened to observe. Such rejection of the beloved object is the other side of the fantasy that one can induce the mother's reappearance *("da")* simply by pulling the bobbin's string and bringing it back into view.

Let us return momentarily to the concept of miniaturization borrowed from Susan Stewart. In order to historicize the fantasy shared by Laslett and Stone, we must begin to repoliticize what we have just psychologized. It seems to us that something like miniaturization informs the logic on both sides of the argument. A theory that privileges the common household may seem logically at odds with one that makes private rooms the precondition for family feeling; but on a purely ideological level they are quite compatible. Both rely on tropes of miniaturization—smallness and enclosure. Whether it is a toy such as the bobbin or a scholarly description of the family, the miniature offers the promise of a special form of cultural control. Indeed, both Stone and Laslett use the family to perform a kind of embedding that Stewart associates with a dollhouse:

> Transcendence and the interiority of history and narrative are the dominant characteristics of the most consummate of miniatures—the dollhouse. A house within a house, the dollhouse not only presents the house's articulation of the tension between inner and outer spheres, of exteriority and interiority—

> it also represents the tension between two modes of interiority. Occupying a space within an enclosed space, the dollhouse's aptest analogy is the locket or the secret recesses of the heart: center within center, within within within. The dollhouse is a materialized secret; what we look for is the dollhouse within the dollhouse and its promise of an infinitely profound interiority. (61)

Although the two historians we have been discussing describe the family in mutually contradictory terms, they share a single object of analysis. Like the dollhouse, the family contains "the secret recesses of the heart" which in turn contain "the tension," as Stewart says, "between exteriority and interiority." The family provides the language whereby individuation, and thus the rift between consciousness and history, acquires its naturalizing metaphor, the individual's birth. It is also the place where the foundational metaphor of a body born that stands for an enclosed consciousness single and entire must be protected. This is accomplished whenever historians of the family translate a quantity of biologically related bodies into a quality of feeling.

We have described the argument between Laslett and Stone at some length in order to demonstrate that their positions on the family derive not so much from the historical material surviving from an earlier time as from a set of modern metaphors that are deeply ingrained in the thinking of both men, metaphors that shape their understanding of cultural material at the most basic level. Ecclesiastical court records; county histories; the exhaustive demographic studies by Wrigley and Schofield; diaries; autobiographies; medical tracts on obstetrics, conception, and human anatomy; the voluminous medical practice notes of a seventeenth-century astrological physician; supplemented by accounts of mental disorder and its treatment in coroner's inquests, court records, religious treatises, and popular literature—all are distilled down to signs of the presence or absence of the emotions that bind individuals voluntarily to their mates and to their immediate offspring.[23] One can arrive at this core of meaning only by pursuing a highly questionable string of assumptions.

The British histories of the family that we have read characteristically reduce a rich variety of kinship relations and domestic practices down to a sentimental discourse that reflects present-day common sense, or popular psychology. When not encrusted with the sociohistorical details of a place and time, definitions of the family have the properties of popular proverbs.[24] In rural cultures, Barthes explains, such statements "foresee more than they assert, they remain the speech of a humanity which is making itself, not one which is" (154). In modern bourgeois cultures, however, the same kind of statement is always directed downward as if from parent to child, using the power of knowledge to produce a paternal relationship. Thus translated into the bourgeois aphorism, or maxim, proverbial wisdom takes on many of the qualities Barthes attributes to a "mythology":

> Bourgeois aphorisms . . . belong to metalanguage; they are a second-order language which bears on objects already prepared. Their classical form is the maxim. Here the statement is no longer directed towards a world to be made; it must overlay one which is already made, bury the traces of this production under a self-evident appearance of eternity: it is a counter-explanation, the decorous equivalent of a tautology, of this peremptory *because* which parents in need of knowledge hang above the heads of their children. The foundation of the bourgeois statement of fact is *common sense,* that is, truth when it stops on the arbitrary order of him who speaks it. (154–55)

For our purposes, the family provides the clearest example of this behavior. To discover it in another culture or time is to reproduce what modern industrial cultures take to be the self-evident truths of human nature. For this reason, most modern scholarly representations of the family in former times can be reduced to a few aphorisms and maxims simply by stripping away a scant number of historically specific details.

Laslett, for example, claims that "time was when the whole of life went forward in the family, in a circle of loved, familiar faces, known and fondled objects, all to human size. That time has gone forever. It makes us very different from our ancestors" (22). Who is going to contest this truth, though it fleshes out the barest skeleton of demographic findings? To represent the modern family as a decided improvement, Stone represents the early modern family as one that was hostile to children: "In such a society relations with one's own children were not particularly close. Richer families put their infants out to wet-nurse, and when they returned, the advice of moralists, theologians and writers of domestic advice books was that the first duty of parents was ruthlessly to crush the wills of young children" (6). From there, it is fair to say, both Laslett and Stone proceed according to a logic of emotions that sounds as incontestable as it seems commonplace: a small number of individuals who are together for a long time without outside interference tend to care for one another as for themselves; they are attracted sexually to nonfamily members of the opposite sex; they need their mothers; they obey their fathers; and this is all to the good, for relationships within this unit magically reproduce themselves outside the family as well.[25] Although Laslett and Stone may disagree about what the family was in the sixteenth and seventeenth centuries, where it came from, how it changed, and what evidence counts most in formulating these answers, both unreflexively accept and transmit every one of these maxims.

Our first chapter argued that the project of literary criticism is to produce the kind of self or "mind" embodied in Milton, a self apart from and in many ways opposed to history per se. Our second chapter tried to illustrate the mutual dependency between self and world, text and context. Every attempt to fix an origin for either self or world sends scholars scurrying back and forth between the internal and external worlds, which consequently appear to be both juxtaposed and mutually embedded in each other. The "family" plays an important part in this collaboration between the disciplines. Historians who write about the family invariably produce a more extreme form of the problem that vexes accounts of either an author or his world. The "family" acts as the semiotic glue that lends coherence to a conceptual world made of such individuated minds and cohesive nations. It is also the mechanism for differentiating personal and psychological phenomena from events in the domain of political history. In other words, the family provides the means of conceptually nesting consciousness within history without tearing the membrane separating self from nonself. In this respect, the family provides the black box where ideology ceases to be an "external" force (e.g., the bourgeois ideas of liberty, affective individualism, or puritan orthodoxy) and becomes instead the "internal" stuff of human consciousness (i.e., sexual attraction and parental concern). For the family is where modern consciousness receives a body through the most natural process of all. It is born of two parents into a place in time where it resides until vanishing from history into the grave. The words and actions performed by the self so embodied—down to its smallest impact on others of its kind—can thus be considered relics of the vanished essence of that self.

Domestic behavior and sexual practices do not exist as historical objects in their own right, at least not yet; but they point to another order of events, which take place on a cultural terrain where the most private and primary emotions exist. This terrain is as close as one comes to sacred ground in a modern secular culture. It surrounds biological reproduction and ensures a place for the sexual practices of a white elite at the center of all its representations, scientific and sentimental alike.[26] It provides a natural body for the form of consciousness we have identified with the mind of Milton. The moment of embodiment is the utopic moment of a special form of freedom—for "man is," as Rousseau said, "born free." Biological reproduction allows one to imagine not only a society of free individuals but also the laws of nature that would limit them.[27] At the same time, the metaphor of tiny bubbles of human consciousness, each within its own skin and having its own distinctive features, makes all human bodies much the same by binding them to the natural facts of birth, desire, insemination, and death. As it naturalizes the difference between inside and outside, self and nonself, subject and object, text and context, however, the same metaphor also establishes hierarchies among them. It is here that God enters into scientific representations of man. As Barthes says of the American exhibition of photography entitled "The Family of Man": "The diversity of men proclaims his [God's] power, his richness; the unity of their gestures demonstrates his will."[28] For "his will" exerts itself in such facts of nature—birth, death, work, knowledge, play—as people, despite their diversity, invariably display for the camera.

In natural history, reproduction comes before production; and anthropology identifies the moment when history proper began as the moment when economic and political relations first gained ascendancy over the family and organized something like a state—the moment when, as Lévi-Strauss says, culture told nature it shall go no further.[29] From a literary critical perspective, however, one can see how its very name also places reproduction logically after and in a secondary or derivative relation to production. According to the disciplines of economics and political science, the practices relegated to the category of reproduction perpetuate social relations that are determined, first of all, by the practices classified as productive. If we have overstated the figurative properties of these familiar categories of literary and historical analysis, it is because we feel that reproduction is at once the less theorized and the more problematic concept of the two.

Although it appears to refer to the most self-evident of biological facts, "reproduction" includes a diverse field of practices. It links those activities having to do with information gathering, education, literacy, and the arts with those that surround sexuality—courtship, household management, the ordinary care of the body, childbirth and rearing, and the use of leisure time. "Reproduction" shapes the way middle-class people imagine intellectual life, on the one hand, and personal life, on the other. It also operates as a purely theoretical term to contain both arenas of cultural life without explaining the relationship between them. Anthropology, economics, political science, and history tend to identify mating rules and kinship practices as the first and most powerful orga-

nizing principle both for so-called primitive cultures and for earlier epochs in the history of most Western nations. In describing modern, industrialized cultures, however, these same social sciences privilege the
practices surrounding the production and distribution of goods and services over the practices surrounding biological reproduction. Laslett did
nothing to challenge this paradox when he demonstrated that the small,
self-enclosed family provided the basic module of English society until
industrialization put mothers in charge of households and sent fathers
off to work in factories.

By suggesting, to the contrary, that the modern household links
mother to father in a private heterosexual relationship, Lawrence Stone
also suggests that the organization of the family changed significantly
during the period immediately following the English Revolution. Indeed,
were it not for the fact that his findings apply to a very limited social
group, Stone's research would suggest that changes in the practices surrounding reproduction preceded those changes in the British government
and economy that indicate the onset of industrial capitalism. Aristocratic
kinship practices were "positively reinforced for over a century, from
1530 to 1660, as a buttress against anarchy," Stone contends (659). However, he also contends "that most of the features of the modern family
appeared before industrialization and among social groups unaffected by
it, and that even those exposed to it responded in different ways"(665).

If judged on the basis of sheer chronology, the tangible change in
"sentiment" that Stone identifies as occurring between 1660 and 1780
would have to be considered an effect of a change in family relations
following the English Revolution and a precondition for industrialization.
Yet Stone is unwilling to draw this conclusion from the chronology of
his data, and in the final pages of *The Family, Sex, and Marriage in
England, 1500–1800,* he reinserts a conflict among various class interests
and values, rather than family relations, as the cause for changes in
"sentiment" in England. Stone writes, "The key to family change in
middle- and upper-class circles is the ebb and flow of battle between
competing interests and values represented by various levels of social
organization, from the individual up to the nation state" (682). Where
it was once the very basis of political relationships, in other words, the
family now retires under the sign of secondariness—the "re" in "reproduction"—and reclaims all the innocence that modern cultures attribute
to primitive cultures as well as to nature.

The question of *when* the modern family began—whether during the
seventeenth or the nineteenth century—is at heart a controversy over

where it began: Did the kind of affection that modern cultures all but equate with humanity itself begin in the common households and villages of preindustrial England, or did it originate in the privacy of the bedrooms of the manor houses occupied by a social elite at the onset of the modern period? This is the most significant question that British historians of the family have addressed since Laslett began to consider the degree to which biological reproduction and child rearing were subject to history. Since then, the effort of British historians of the family has been to establish the origins of modern personal life in one of two groups, neither of which was a forbear of the modern middle class. In effect, this effort denies that the form of affection we now revere is specific to the modern ruling class, and represents it as a feeling inherited from the past.

To ground modern family feeling in a class of people who preexist the modern middle class is the project of historians of the family, whether like Stone they see modern consciousness as emerging in opposition to external authority among members of a social elite, or whether like Laslett they see that consciousness as the natural temperament of the common people when left to their own devices. Contending schools of British historians of the family set natural affiliations against those compelled by money and politics—though one school represents the opposition as one between rural and urban societies, and the other represents it as an opposition between private and public life. In arguing *for* the family, each school therefore positions itself outside the ruling class, outside the state. In this respect, their positions are exactly the same, namely, the position of the liberal intellectual—located outside the domain of production, one foot in the sanctuary of reproduction, the other poised in an unspecified relation to it. Stone and Laslett simply emphasize different components of a political fantasy wherein the intellectual imagines himself or herself to be speaking on behalf of the people, empowered to speak because he or she is the trustee and inheritor of a cultural tradition. Does it matter whether this is an elite tradition or a popular one, if each exercises much the same form of authority?

CHAPTER FOUR

The Work of Literature

If it is true that the leper gave rise to rituals of exclusion,
which to a certain extent provided the model for and general
form of the great Confinement, then the plague gave rise to
disciplinary projects. . . . The leper and his separation; the
plague and its segmentations. The first is marked; the second
analysed and distributed. The exile of the leper and the arrest
of the plague do not bring with them the same political
dream. The first is that of a pure community, the second that
of a disciplined society. Two ways of exercising power over
men, of controlling their relations, of separating out their
dangerous mixtures.

> Michel Foucault, *Discipline and Punish*

Though they existed at first largely in writing and were thus taken as
truth only by an elite minority of literate people, the modern concepts
of self, nation, and family soon became equated with nature itself—with
the skin surrounding the body, with the geographical limitations of the
island nation, and with the inviolable bonds of the biological unit. These
equations have made it nearly impossible for contemporary scholarship
and critical theory to historicize self, nation, and family. Indeed, historians
who try to trace these concepts back to some point of origin prior to
the dawn of modernity only produce versions of these mythologies that
are even more resistant to history. By underwriting this practice, literary
scholarship has conspired to make it difficult to imagine the early modern
period as truly premodern, as a time before the modern self, nation, and
family began to exist as facts of nature. Just by invoking their names,
one perpetuates the illusion that these distinctively modern cultural for-
mations were always there, albeit in various states of wholeness, mar-
ginalization, fragmentation, or repression. The moment one declares the
absence of the self, nation, or family in its full-blown natural state is
always the moment after his or her concept of self, nation, or family has
already begun to organize the field of investigation. And especially where

they are missing, the categories distinguishing modern cultures tend to live on. It is against the grain of both literary criticism and British historiography, then—and yet with a necessary reliance on each—that one must conceptualize the moment when these terms began to organize information across a whole range of cultural domains.

To examine the transition from one age to the next as the moment when these categories began to reorganize early modern culture, we will move back in time and then simulate the emergence of the classification system in question. To suggest what kind of agency accrued to certain kinds of writing during this transitional period, we are going to compare proposals for dealing with the plague after 1665 with the quarantine procedures that had been observed during the preceding two hundred years. This is an admittedly peculiar focus, but in treating contagion (as the government response to the present AIDS epidemic illustrates), society identifies what it thinks is essential to its self-preservation. The decision as to what has to be preserved and how to go about preserving it has not always been based on factors that modern scientific cultures would consider realistic or practical, of course. And that is precisely the point. The current critique of "AIDS discourse" insists that what we now call practical is no less symbolic than any of the preventive, quarantine, and therapeutic practices of prescientific cultures. In neither case is the problem of disease understood simply as a problem of disease. Each problem is also a solution to a problem that seems to require specific regulations for distinguishing between "us" and "them." Although such distinctions are produced at many different sites throughout the culture and on many different occasions, plague conditions automatically translate all other distinctions into the ultimate distinction between the living and the dead. From this point of view, plague is never a natural process. Indeed, it is probably only members of scientific cultures who imagine it is.

Given this description of plague, one might gather that the purpose of distinguishing "the people" is genocidal—to kill "others." It is possible to arrive at such a conclusion by examining the way Western cultures are dealing with AIDS, which might well eliminate certain ethnic groups in the United States and whole populations in Africa and southeast Asia. But that is not really the point of our argument. We are more concerned with the fact that in such massive life-and-death situations, virtually everyone agrees on the procedures in question, even though those who belong to high-risk groups would probably prefer to be in the position of those who are formulating and carrying out procedures for dealing with the disease. The plague victim agrees to his or her confinement within what Foucault describes as a cellular structure created by the quarantine procedures. The victim agrees to this disposition of his or her body, as if there were no other way to deal with the problem. Specific technologies of population management, technologies requiring a class of professionals and managers, achieve epidemic proportions with the spread of disease, and profound changes have been known to occur in the course of history in such a seemingly inadvertent way.[1]

The plague of 1348 provided the occasion for Boccaccio's *Decameron.* He could have chosen a number of other events troubling Florence during the same decade—the dictatorship of the Duke of Athens, the recent insurrection of the *populo minuto,* or the devastating famine of 1346. But the reason for Boccaccio's choice of the plague is clear enough. The plague, as he imagines it, represents the single greatest threat both to the aristocratic community and to the existence of Florence itself. Boccaccio describes the disease in carnivalesque terms—as something that turns the social order upside down. When she goes out into the streets, he tells us, one well-born woman finds that "the scum of our city . . . go prancing and bustling about" and "singing bawdy songs that add insult to our injuries."[2] Monasteries are said to foster lasciviousness under these conditions, and a home in the country offers sanctuary only if there are faithful servants around. People of worth who remain in the city experience, not fear of death, but a pervasive sense that it is no longer their world. About city life under plague conditions, another stranded woman complains that "no one possessing private means and a place to retreat to is left here apart from ourselves" (60).

To solve the problem posed by the disease, *The Decameron* removes seven women and three men, all of whom are either friends or kin, to the countryside. To while away the time, they move en masse between their various country estates, where they eat tastefully prepared meals, drink the best of wines in moderation, walk in well-groomed gardens, sing, dance, and tell clever tales. If in the process of their story telling these characters resemble scattered bits and pieces of a single body, it is because Boccaccio describes them so. By novelistic standards, these are not well-individuated characters; all are equally intelligent, well bred, full of grace, and fair to look upon. But plague, for someone of Boccaccio's epoch, is not a problem that can be solved by individuation. He deals with it by reinstating sumptuary codes, mating rituals, and kinship ties among the gentlefolk. Thus his erotic tale about the telling of erotic tales reunites the fragments of the elite community into a single social order, self-enclosed and pure.

Although Boccaccio does not write as a member of the ruling elite, he represents it as the community in which artful tales of desire are told. One of his accomplishments as a writer—the responsibility he seems to have felt as an intellectual of fourteenth-century Florence—was to portray the nobility as the only true object of desire. Erotic art was certainly no more or less political than it is today. In early modern Europe, however, the aristocratic body was the object par excellence of erotic art. This body was represented as if its existence were somehow linked to that of the nation itself and no one could wish it to be otherwise. In this regard, England was no different from Florence. Long before 1621, when *The Decameron* was first published in English, individual tales were translated and even adapted for the theater. Moreover, all the evidence suggests that plagues posed the same kind of threat for the literate classes of Tudor and Stuart England as they did for Boccaccio's original readership. Indeed, his imagined solution to the problem posed by the plague bears striking resemblance to the procedures that were supposed to control epidemics in England.

When plague raged in England during the sixteenth and seventeenth centuries, people of birth and wealth fled the cities much as they did in Boccaccio's fantasy. Infected houses were shut up by order of the Privy Council, and all the members of the household, whether healthy or sick, were confined there. During periods when the spread of the plague was at its worst, law terms were adjourned early, fairs were canceled, markets were closed, and vagabonds were persecuted.[3] At these times, the English court did its best to insulate itself from infection. Confronting the plague of 1625, in May of that year the Privy Council ordered that no stranger might come to court to present suits or petitions.[4] By October, the plague had worsened, and members of court were prohibited from passing through infected areas.[5] The nobility constituted itself as an enclosed and restricted community, shut off from the city and unavailable to people of the lesser sort.

Thomas Dekker's description of the plague in *Rod for Run-Awais* (1625) focuses on the social elements from which members of the elite community had so detached themselves. Dekker's tract addresses these persons as if they were Boccaccio's storytellers: "To you that are merry in your Country houses, and sit safe (as you thinke) from the Gun-shot of this Contagion, in your Orchards and pleasant Gardens; into your hands do I deliuer this sad Discourse."[6] Quite another fate, one sharply contrasting with pastoral pleasures, is imagined for those left behind in the city. How these people deal with the plague can be understood, Dekker explains, if one will simply

> looke into Tauernes, looke into Ale-houses; they are all merry all iocund; no Plague frights them. In the Fields they are ... walking, talking, laughing, in the Streets, blaspheming, selling, buying, swearing. In Tauernes, and Ale-houses, drinking, roaring, and surfetting: In these, and many other places, Gods Holy-day is their Worke-day; the Kings Fasting-day, their day of riot. (151)

Here we see something resembling what Bakhtin calls the "mass body" in its carnivalesque phase, apparently inverting all the principles of hierarchy and moderation that were supposed to organize the court.[7] This behavior dramatizes the need for flight and segregation. Early modern England never seems to question the fact that the survival of the nation depends on the survival of its aristocracy.

At the same time, the riot and excess of carnival also implicitly called into being the need for an aristocracy who enforced hierarchy and moderation, an aristocracy whose absence had, in Dekker's words, "left your disconsolate Mother (the City) in the midst of her sorrowes" (145).[8] The conditions that threatened to tear down the barrier protecting those belonging to the privileged classes were therefore conditions that established both the autonomy and the authority of the elite body. The plague appeared to observe certain distinctions within the city that made this especially clear. Records show that the disease visited urban areas already marked by poverty, and that it left the better sections of town mysteriously untainted. In the sixteenth and seventeenth centuries, Paul Slack explains, there was a social topography of disease: "Plague was spread by beggars, migrants, and strangers, and most of the casualties were 'in the families of poor people.' By 1631, these assumptions were so prevalent that when the disease entered a noble household in Yorkshire it went unrecognized because 'no man could suspect a lady to die of the plague.' "[9]

Given the apparent ubiquity of this pattern before the interregnum, there is something shocking about the terms of a proposal written after the plague of 1665, one of the most devastating ever to strike England. Whereas in the past, collective festival had reigned in the city during times of plague, the isolation of urban dwellers was now prescribed; whereas there had been two social groups each with its own integrity and mode of desire, now there was concern only for individual bodies;

and whereas there had been quarantine for the sick and flight for those
of wealth and influence, now there was one policy for the entire population. Dated 7 October 1667, William Petty's "Of Lessening of
Plagues" testifies to nothing less than the presence of a new way of
imagining the body politic. A few lines will show how completely the
idea that England was embodied in its aristocracy has given way to the
idea of a nation composed of households that translated into units of
work:

1. London within ye bills hath 696th people in 108th houses.

2. In pestilentiall yeares, (which are one in 20), there dye 1/6th of ye people
of ye plague and 1/6th of all diseases.

3. The remedies against spreading of ye plague are shutting up suspected
houses and pest-houses within 1/2 a mile of ye city.

4. In a circle about ye center of London of 35 miles semi-diameter, or a dayes
journey, there live as many people and are as many houses as in London.

5. Six heads may be caryd a days journey for 20sh.

6. A family may bee lodged 3 months in ye country for 4sh, so as ye charge
of carying out and lodging a family at a medium will be 5sh.

7. In ye greatest plague wee feare, scarce 20th families will bee infected; and
in this new method but 10th, ye charge whereof will bee 50th pounds.

8. The People which ye next plague of London will sweep away will be
probably 120th, which at £70 per head is a losse of 8,400ths, the half whereof
is 4,200ths.

9. So as 50 is ventured to save 4,200, or about one for 84.[10]

According to Petty's figures, his plan to rescue half of the people destined
to die under earlier quarantine procedures would save the nation no less
than £4,200,000. Unlike previous descriptions of the English nation, that
nation had been inscribed within an economy by the time Petty wrote.
The relationship between disease and national identity is an utterly rational one. Preserving England in the face of plague entails, above all
else, preserving its capacity for work.[11] Dead bodies add up to money
lost, and this loss diminishes England.

If the problem posed by the plague is no longer a matter of how to
perpetuate a bloodline but rather how to minimize economic loss, the
procedures for dealing with the problem are bound to be different. Petty's
rewriting of earlier quarantine measures provides a microinstance where
the new displaces the old. The economic problem posed by the plague
requires the sealing off of each family unit as if it were an elite community
in its own right. He seizes on the strategy of isolation that had previously
applied to elites alone. He converts this strategy into quarantine pro-

cedures for dealing with the urban masses.[12] With this one stroke, flight can no longer separate a nobility from the masses. Instead it breaks down the mass body into a finite number of independent economic units. At every turn in his argument, in plain and practical style Petty insists that to keep England alive is to keep it working. Those at the very top and bottom of the social ladder fade from view as the distinction between them ceases to matter. And by some uncanny property of his "human arithmetic" itself, the author seems to be looking out for the welfare of virtually everyone.

Having said this, we must stress that Petty was hardly unique in imagining a world where power no longer began and ended in the old aristocracy. John Graunt, the only tradesman in the Royal Society, wrote *Natural and Political Observations upon the Bills of Mortality* in 1662. His proposal for a census that would divide the population into laboring and nonlaboring groups refines and clarifies the basic presuppositions behind the idea that England was an economic entity whose power originated in labor.[13] Thomas Sprat's *History of the Royal Society* offers yet another version of the same concept of the nation. Sprat prides himself, as Petty obviously does, on rationality, economy, clarity, and usefulness.

In his depiction of London after the great fire of 1666, Sprat orchestrates these qualities into a highly idealized tribute to the English artisan:

> Nor was their courage less, in sustaining the *second calamity*, which destroyed their *houses*, and *estates*. Thus the greatest losers indur'd with such undaunted firmness of mind, that their example may incline us to believe, that not only the best *Natural*, but the best *Moral* Philosophy too, may be learn'd from the shop of *Mechaniks*. It was indeed an admirable thing to behold, with what *constancy*, the meanest Artificers saw all the *labours* of their *lives*, and the *support* of their *families* devour'd in an instant. The affiliation 'tis true, was widely spread over the whole Nation: every place was fill'd with signs of *pity*, and *commiseration*: But those who had suffer'd most, seem'd the least affected with the loss: no *unmanly bewailings* were heard in the few *streets*, that were preserv'd: they beheld the Ashes of their *Houses* and their *Gates*, and *Temples*, without the least expression of Pusilanimity. If *Philosophers* had done this, it had well become their profession of Wisdom: if *Gentlemen*, the nobleness of their *Breeding*, and *blood* would have requir'd it. But that such greatness of heart should be found amongst the poor *Artizans*, and the obscure *multitude* is no doubt one of the most honourable events, that ever happen'd.[14]

Several changes become immediately evident when one compares such devastation with that characterizing the cities of Boccaccio, Dekker, and others writing before 1667. First, one can see that desirable features from the pantheon of aristocratic virtues—"undaunted firmness of mind," "constancy," and "greatness of heart"—have detached themselves from traditional learning and noble blood to become embodied in the homely artisan. All ignoble features are simultaneously canceled out as Sprat declares, "no *unmanly bewailings* were heard in the few *streets* that were preserv'd: they beheld the Ashes of their *Houses* and their *Gates,* and *Temples,* without the least expression of Pusilanimity."

Whereas despairing men and wanton women had filled the plague-riddled streets of Elizabethan and Jacobean cities, a noble and manly figure arises from the ashes of Restoration London and transfigures it. The city no longer languishes in a state of lawlessness, abandoned by the elite cast of people. Sprat's London feels its loss as one of property and labor power. *Paradise Lost* similarly describes a world that begins anew, from the bottom up, on the basis of labor, and thus it can be said to participate in the same political fantasy. Before explaining just how the poem transforms one concept of the nation into another, however, let us ponder for a moment the character of the labor that has suddenly stepped forward on the cultural stage. During the years immediately following the interregnum, the image of an artisan in an urban environment evidently provided the logic for rethinking the world. It is important to remember, however, that such visibility did not empower artisans.[15] They had always had a hand in shaping the political and economic life of Renaissance cities and towns. For at least a century prior to Sprat's acknowledgment of this fact, certain families in the villages and certain networks of people in England's larger urban centers controlled the various trades within their regions. Even larger networks of kinship and clientage allowed the guilds to regulate trade in the cities. They influenced the quality of goods and services, the stability of prices, the number of people who could practice a given craft, and the flow of goods from one place to another. Artisans' households were nothing like our households; they were neither organized around biological reproduction nor confined to the immediate family. A typical household included apprentices (often from other artisan families) and journeymen, as well as the master craftsman, his kin, and servants, all of whom were involved one way or another in the production of goods. Yet members of this powerful social group were seldom portrayed in Renaissance literature as having the nobility that Sprat attributes to them.[16]

A second fact concerning artisans is perhaps still more perplexing. The preponderance of historical evidence suggests that when this figure did make a glorified appearance in texts of various kinds written after the interregnum, the power of the artisanal culture had already begun a slow but inevitable decline.[17] To understand what kind of project was carried out through the cultural remapping of England that occurred during those years, then, we have to factor in the riddle of the artisan. We must not confuse an older class of artisans with the class that displaced the old aristocratic order; artisans were part of that order and its decline coincided with their own. Indeed, we must assume that although Restoration authors turned to the artisan for an alternative to the reigning political hierarchy, they were in a sense spelling his doom. For as the artisan acquired visibility, it appears that visibility ceased to be a source of power. It indeed subjugated one to new forms of domination. As these authors contrasted the artisan's honest and arduous way of life with the extravagance and corruption of the aristocracy, their visions of the state simultaneously pitted another kind of labor against that of the artisan.

Sprat's *History of the Royal Society* illustrates how the artisan offered the model and metaphor for a form of authority that depended on rising above manual labor. Members of the Royal Society linked their own labor with that of the artisan in dedicating themselves to "the promotion of natural and useful knowledge."[18] Sprat's *History* begins as a paean to such knowledge, declaring that the Royal Society would devote itself to writing histories of trade and to performing experiments. Clearly flushed with a sense of the power of knowledge, Sprat predicts that the new history of trade "will be found to bring innumerable benefits to all the practical *Arts.*" Similarly, the knowledge gained from experiment will further "the *Manual Arts* . . . either by the discovery of new *matter,* to imploy mens hands; or by a new *Transplantation* of the same *matter,* or by handling the old subject of *Manufactures* after a new way."[19] Although Sprat attributes great value to artisanal labor, then, he does not simply pit this residual set of values against those of courtly life. His celebration of artisanal labor deflects value away from the artisan and onto himself; it identifies scientific knowledge as the agent of progressive change; and it identifies the "manual arts" as the material that must undergo transformation in order for progress to occur. Though labor exists in the abstract, the statement itself takes possession of manual labor and, by implication, subordinates those who work with their hands to those who think and write.[20]

Writing was obviously crucial to the project, for it was through words that thought did its work. As Sprat recounts it, the Royal Society "exacted from all its members, a close naked and natural way of speaking . . . bringing all things as near to the Mathematic plainness, as they can: and

preferring the language of Artizans, Countrymen, and merchants, before
that, of Wits and Scholars."[21] Such a statement stands in sharp contrast
with the Elizabethan attitude toward the rhetoric of artisans. When
George Puttenham, for example, wrote his treatise on rhetoric in 1589
he specifically warned against "the speach of a craftes man or carter, or
other of the inferiour sort, though he be inhabitant or bred in the best
town and Citie in this Realme."[22] By taking up a position that directly
opposed the rhetoric dominating the Elizabethan, Jacobean, and Caroline
court culture and politics, the Royal Society did not mean to challenge
the monarch's authority as it might have been understood fifty or sixty
years earlier. It is fair to say that where the Elizabethan and Jacobean
courtier served the monarch by producing exalted images of his person
and power, these Restoration intellectuals, nearly all men of privilege,
sought to do much the same thing by purging English of "all the am-
plifications, digressions, and swellings of style" that marked an aristocratic tradition of letters. It was thus in a conservative spirit that Sprat
condemned courtly rhetoric: "When I consider the means of *happy living*, and the causes of their corruption, I can hardly forbear ... con-
cluding that *eloquence* ought to be banish'd out of all *civil Societies* as
a thing fatal to Peace and Good Manners" (112). Opposing eloquence,
another voice nevertheless emerges—moral where corruption was supposed to have prevailed, conciliatory where there had been internal division, reasonable where excess and self-display had held sway. This con-
scientiously ineloquent rhetoric identifies itself as "the only Remedy that
can be found for *extravagance*" (113). It is Sprat's wish that through the
works of the Royal Society, English will eventually "return back to the
primitive purity, and shortness, when men delivr'd so many *things*, almost
in an equal number of *words*" (113).

Petty and Sprat identified the domain of rational truth with the artisan—his city, his nature, his body, his discourse, his labor. So defined,
the domain of the rational observer took shape in writing and flourished
as a celebration of work. Appearing more method than metaphor, the
new style of writing was opposed to writing that was rhetorically inflated
on the one hand or unlettered on the other.[23] Authorized by the claim
to represent a truth that was already there in the world, such writing
extended the power of gathering information, naming, classifying, and
evaluating over cultural territories that educated people had never bothered with before. By "territories" we mean more or less what Foucault,
in his study of the archaeology of the human sciences, describes as domains of knowledge.[24] The power of such knowledge rested on its anti-

rhetorical claims, which presupposed that transparent referentiality was possible. Truth in the modern sense began its rise to authority by making a distinction between truth and rhetoric. This distinction made it possible for John Locke, toward the end of the century, to gender the rhetorical use of language. "Eloquence," he writes, "like the fair sex, has too prevailing beauties in it to suffer itself ever to be spoken against. And it is in vain to find fault with those arts of deceiving, wherein men find pleasure to be deceived."[25]

Before the English Revolution, English culture acknowledged the power of the nobility. As the symbol of symbols, the monarch stood at the center of a culture that understood how thoroughly symbolic power really was.[26] Obviously aware of the authority that culture had vested in her body, and capable of manipulating that power to her own ends, Elizabeth I went to great lengths to control reproductions of her image.[27] Her portraits deliberately identified the condition of the nation with the condition of her body—as, for example, in the famous Ditchley portrait where she is standing on a map of Great Britain. Supported by the direct patronage—or, as was more common, the titular patronage—of the nobility, Renaissance artists, authors, and playwrights in return served the greater and lesser nobility by representing them as the source of title, land, and wealth. Manor house poetry identified the plentiful fields, streams, trees, fruit, robust peasants, and stately halls with the lord of the manor. To look at Appleton House or Penshurst was to recall the family name. In "To Penshurst," Ben Jonson observed this aesthetic; he represented the estate and its architecture, family members and dependents, and grounds, as well as the banquet table loaded with their bounty, as laudable attributes of Sir Robert Sidney himself.

To emphasize the single-mindedness of the principle underlying all the great art of the Renaissance does not in any way diminish the ingenuity with which various monarchs and the artists whom they patronized made their own marks on the tradition. As the center of the culture, the monarch's preferred style of self-presentation necessarily modified a whole system of symbolic practices to make it his or hers. As we hope to demonstrate, the peculiarities of Caroline art were particularly important to the composition of *Paradise Lost* and therefore to our account of how the poem changed the categories that both organized that heritage and were authorized by it. Whereas Elizabeth thought it advantageous to see herself as Astrea or the Virgin Queen, James I preferred to display himself in the midst of his immediate family.[28] This was his way of saying that his crown (in contrast with Elizabeth's) came to him according to the strict law of primogeniture and in turn guaranteed a line of descent. Charles I chose to memorialize his father with a mural on the ceiling of Whitehall portraying him in the godlike posture of passing a sentence on those beneath. No less taken with his self-image than James, Charles often preferred to display himself with his queen, Henrietta Maria. As Roy Strong has noted, however, Caroline painting and literature stressed the supernatural quality of Charles and Henrietta's relationship; it made them the great lovers of art and legend.[29] Honthorst's painting, *Buckingham Presenting the Liberal Arts to Charles and Henrietta,* cast the couple as Apollo and Diana perched upon a cloud. Jonson's 1630 masque *Love's Triumph through Callipolis* identified the royal couple as exemplars of the purest form of love mortals could experience. In *Coelum Brittanicum,* Carew had the gods vow to reform heaven according to the example set by Charles and his queen, and in Davenant's *Temple of Love* the pair themselves became divinities of love. The rules for representing monarchs were no doubt much more elastic than one can indicate in such a brief glance at the received tradition; even so, the point remains that Renaissance art and literature exalted monarchy whenever it attributed certain qualities to a particular monarch.

The deep distrust of eloquence expressed by Petty, Sprat, Locke, and others was, as we have said, an attack on the generation of intellectuals who wrote before the Revolution. They authored much of the literature of that period and, along with the nobility, made up the audience for whom it was produced. It can be argued that no one more fully possessed the learning qualifying someone for this role than John Milton. His humanist education at St. Paul's and then at Cambridge trained him to read Latin and Greek. But perhaps more to the point, his education directed that reading toward mastery in disputation and oratory.[30] Such training was supposed to produce the people who would serve the state—whether by moving from the Inns of Court into government or, as Milton originally intended, by taking orders and serving in the church. Some critics describe his years at Cambridge as his period of extremism; but Milton apparently felt no conflict between his intention to enter the church and his ardent ambition to write the kind of poetry for which his education had prepared him. Indeed, the young Milton wrote poetry that resembled the subject matter and verse forms of his Cavalier contemporaries.[31] Events took an unexpected turn in the years following Cambridge, however, and his religious convictions forced Milton to join the debate on church discipline. Yet even though his polemical writing opposed the position of the king and the bishops as well as the Cavalier poets who supported the Laudian church, it in no way quelled his poetic ambitions.[32] The well-known opening to the second book of *The Reason of Church Government* (1642) expresses Milton's unflagging resolve to do for the English language what Ariosto had done for Italian: "What the greatest wits of Athens, Rome, or modern Italy, and those Hebrews of old did for their country, I, in my proportion, with this over and above of being a Christian, might do for mine."[33] Events saw to it that his dual ambitions did not remain compatible for long.

It might be argued that because Milton's career incorporated so fully the historical discontinuities and contradictions of prerevolutionary British culture, the English Revolution produced a revolution in his writing.[34] When he became Secretary of Foreign Tongues to the Council of State in 1649, the middle-aged Milton abandoned the kind of verse dominating the *Poems of Mr. John Milton* (published in 1645), most of which had been written in the style of the Caroline court. When the return of Charles II in 1660 made it dangerous to write polemics against monarchy, Milton turned back almost exclusively to poetry and produced the biblical epics for which future generations would revere him. Tradition has it that the older man succeeded as a poet because he had failed in politics. But it is just as plausible to say that the later poetry mounted a critique, however inadvertently, of the entire universe of meaning that a humanist education had prepared Milton to reproduce. We will go so far as to suggest that in writing *Paradise Lost* (1667), *Paradise Regained,* and *Samson Agonistes* (both published in 1671), Milton entered directly into a struggle through which the ideals he held as a Protestant reformer and political activist eventually triumphed. This was a struggle for the signs and symbols of political reality itself, a struggle, therefore, to say what that reality was.

If there is any truth in Hill's claim that the English Revolution was a revolution in thought, then *Paradise Lost* has to be seen as a pivotal moment in this process. The fall of man is both the means and the marker whereby poetry ceased to reproduce one idea of England and began to produce another. The new nation that Milton imagines is the same world that Petty reconstructs from the city under plague and that Sprat envisions in the London leveled by fire. Milton's revision of the political world may be distinguished from theirs, however, because it takes place through consciousness rather than through the enclosure of property or the regulation of bodies. One could argue that in this respect Milton lags behind his more practical-minded contemporaries; they, it would seem, are tampering with the material of political history itself.

But that argument assumes that writing enters into history and acts upon the body through legal, scientific, or even philosophical discourse rather than through poetry. And such an assumption fails to explain why Milton's later poetry was taken to heart by the late-seventeenth- and eighteenth-century readership on both sides of the Atlantic, and why it still makes an important contribution to the self-conception of the dominant groups in England and America. The fact that Milton's later poetry grew in popularity whereas the other authors we have mentioned were not nearly so widely received, even though they were laying out much the same vision of the world, indicates that poetry is historically the more important kind of writing; this in turn implies that the most important changes do not necessarily take place where history says they do. *Paradise Lost* represents the sudden visibility of labor and an economic definition of the nation as part of a larger revolution in consciousness.

In his Edenic passages, Milton portrays the unfallen Adam and Eve as the sacred couple celebrated by Caroline art. In this way, what had been a rather worn political convention in the years leading up to the English Revolution emerged in the years after the Restoration as part of a revisionary poetics. It could be said of Milton's Eden that in it the sacred couple steps forward one last time as the center of aristocratic culture. All the world belongs to them by divine entitlement: "Godlike erect, with native honor clad / In naked Majesty," the pair "seem'd Lords of all" (IV, 289–90).[35] Eve epitomizes the beauty of unfallen nature. Resembling the idealized female of manor house poetry in this respect, she sums up the bounty of the estate and testifies to the generosity of the lord of the manor. The well-known account of her creation draws precisely this equation:

> Under his forming hands a creature grew,
> Manlike, but different sex, so lovely fair,
> That what seem'd fair in all the World, seem'd now
> Mean, or in her summ'd up, in her contain'd.
> (VIII, 470–73)

More than any other of his creatures, Eve displays the poet's creative power. The poem can be said to make its most magnificent lyrical ascent with the celebration of her solitary body.

To describe the coupling of the sacred couple, Milton piles up literary allusions so that the moments of their copulation become the climax of an entire tradition of verse as well. Appearing to contain all of the creation within her, Eve is also embedded alongside her mate within a magnificent landscape. The passages beginning "Hail, wedded love" (IV, 750) and

"Now Morn her rosy steps" (V, 1) provide two of the more memorable scenes of such conjugal love. By enclosing the estate in the woman and then enveloping the couple within the landscape, the poem fuses political relations to sexual relations. At that moment, sexual relations cease to provide a natural analogue for the bond uniting father and son and subordinating client to patron. Having just transformed the account of the creation of man into an account of the creation of woman, the poem exalts conjugal love over and above the tie that binds man to God and male to male. Indeed, the poet makes the angelic world imitate the heterosexual couple:

> Whatever pure thou in the body enjoy'st
> (And pure thou wert created) we enjoy
> In eminence, and obstacle find none
> Of membrane, joint, or limb, exclusive bars:
> Easier than Air with Air, if Spirits embrace,
> Total they mix, Union of Pure with Pure
> Desiring; nor restrain'd conveyance need
> As Flesh to mix with Flesh, or Soul with Soul.
> (VIII, 622–29)

With this gesture, Milton sows the seeds of future conflict in the materials of aristocratic culture.

Even to be considering, as we are, how the female came to be the site of an epic struggle between God and Satan is in itself a departure from the tradition of Milton criticism. Such a line of inquiry suggests that Milton was doing something hostile to the material of Renaissance culture.[36] For, unlike any previous epic or romance, *Paradise Lost* makes domestic relations so central to the poem that everything else takes on meaning only in relation to Adam and Eve.[37] It is their bond that is at stake, after all, in the ultimate outcome of the struggle between God and Satan—the conflict between desire and divine interdiction that takes place in and through Eve, and Adam's subsequent rebellion against patriarchal authority, as well as in the possibilities for redemption that Michael spells out near the end of the poem. By the end of book IX, the epic struggle between God and Satan has been replaced by a domestic squabble that only the couple themselves can resolve. This transformation does not at all diminish the political importance of the Fall, however. It simply shifts the theater of political change from the battlefield to the household. Marriage has ceased to offer the means of a political alliance among houses, lines, or businesses. Instead, marriage defines a personal domain where, in theory, the state cannot intrude. It is well worth noting what makes this fundamental difference between an earlier aristocratic age and one that so clearly resembles our own.

Milton uses the Fall to produce the change in sexual practices. He strips the defeated angel of almost all the powers he possessed as part of an elite community, leaving only his eloquence intact. To represent the viewpoint of someone excluded from that community, Milton again draws upon Renaissance poetry—the Petrarchan lyric.[38] In this verse form, the aristocratic woman symbolizes a lack—the blood the courtier does not possess, the community into which he cannot gain entry, the property and power to which he has no title.[39] Gazing at his mistress only intensifies the courtier's awareness of what appears to be a metaphysical distance separating him from her. Burning with the desire for his patron's power and tormented by envy of those who do enjoy that bounty, Satan speaks the language of such a courtier.[40] The splendor of Eve's body and the erotic pleasure that she and Adam experience simply inspire a more grandiose version of the same kind of longing that found its way into Petrarchan verse:

> Sight hateful, sight tormenting! thus these two
> Imparadis't in one another's arms
> The happier *Eden*, shall enjoy thir fill
> Of bliss on bliss, while I to Hell am thrust,
> Where neither joy nor love, but fierce desire,
> Among our other torments not the least,
> Still unfulfill'd with pain of longing pines.
>   (IV, 505–11)

Issuing from Satan's mouth, the clichés of courtier rhetoric take on a refreshingly literal meaning.[41] The choice of such Petrarchisms to express the most profound resentment that could be felt toward divinely ordained patrilineage is an important one, especially since Milton gives this language such an important role in his version of the Fall.

With God's military victory over Satan, their political struggle is hardly over. From Milton's perspective, it has really just begun. The battle within the elite community becomes a battle over the signs and symbols of political power—the Edenic landscape and the human body. The battle ultimately detaches these symbols from their creator, putting meaning itself in question. Although it presupposes a source outside the elite community, the poetry of lack and longing observes the same ideological imperative as poetry written in gratitude for aristocratic generosity. Capable of acknowledging but one source of power, Satanic rhetoric does nothing to overturn God's authority—nothing, that is, until that rhetoric begins to operate in and through a woman. In this regard, Milton's poem seems to share the Royal Society's view of eloquence as the fall of language from an original state of purity where meaning was immanent in words and words mirrored things. He indicates such purity by eliminating the distinction between Eve's body and its reflection in the pool as well as between that image and her self-conception. As God explains, "What there thou seest fair Creature is thyself" (IV, 468).

This conflation of sign, meaning, and referent constitutes precisely the kind of iconicity that Milton destroys by means of the Fall. Its disintegration begins as Satan whispers in Eve's ear "discontented thoughts / Vain hopes, vain aims, inordinate desires" (IV, 807–8). He tells her a story of a tree that would require her "utmost reach" and how all the creatures "with like desire / Longing and envying stood" around the tree (IX, 591–93). He claims he enhanced his own position by "vent'ring higher than [his] Lot" (IX, 690). Such is the power of his language that it induces Satanic longing, and Eve imagines that forbidden knowledge will do as much for her: "render me more equal, and perhaps, / A thing not undesirable, sometime / Superior" (IX, 823–25). As the fruit fills her body with a common, garden variety of desire, she ceases to embody aristocratic value and becomes the unruly woman, leveler of hierarchies. Once she has "Greedily ... ingorg'd without restraint," Eve is "hight'n'd as with Wine, jocund and boon" (IX, 791–93). Eating the fruit detaches Adam from her by the same principle that separates Boccaccio's elite community from the carnival of death occupying the city under plague. She entreats him to consume the fruit so that "equal Lot / May join" them, and lest "different degree / Disjoin" them (IX, 881–84); and Adam's fall repeats hers in all its excess:

> As with new Wine intoxicated both
> They swim in mirth, and fancy that they feel
> Divinity within them breeding wings
> Wherewith to scorn the Earth: but that false Fruit
> Far other operation first display'd,
> Carnal desire inflaming, hee on *Eve*
> Began to cast lascivious eyes.
>
> (IX, 1008–14)

The fall of man drains sexual play of all its former spirituality; eroticism becomes the language of misdirected desire; and the luxuries of an aristocratic tradition serve the poet as signs of the fallen condition.

When Eve separates herself from Adam, she also separates herself from her original self. The poem no longer defines both of them as the objects of Petrarchan love; now only Adam is. Eve is now consumed with a sense of lack and the desire to fill it. To come to the decision that she must share the fatal fruit with Adam, by no coincidence, she resorts to the logic of the Petrarchan lover: "So dear I love him, that with him all deaths / I could endure, without him live no life" (IX, 832–33). In her mouth, however, this language dismantles the fantasy that the elite community is a self-enclosed body of blood, at once originary and perpetual. Instead, individuals are objects to one another and the means for ulterior ends. As such, they are not only replaceable but also reproducible objects of potentially adulterous desire. It is when she thinks that she "shall be no more / And *Adam* wedded to another Eve" (IX, 827–28) that Eve finally decides to offer Adam the fruit. To share her mortality he will have to exist in a world infused with Petrarchan envy where women can, indeed must, be possessed, enclosed, clothed, and, once clothed, rendered invisible. They can, according to the logic of the fallen world, no longer be objects of aesthetic display.

This sudden turn of the poetic tradition against itself raises two questions: Why did men who occupied such politically antagonistic positions as Milton and Petty or Sprat all renounce Renaissance luxury and rethink the world as a world of work? And what role did their writing play in the construction of this new and radically prosaic reality? Each author implies that disputation had divided the ruling elite against itself and torn the nation apart. Each also suggests that the collapse of an elite community irreparably compromised the tradition of letters it had formerly patronized. Petty, Sprat, and others, including John Locke, describe figurative language as merely corrupt and misleading. For Milton, however, the turn against courtier rhetoric obviously meant the fall of the entire tradition in which he was trained, and he declares the end of that tradition with such elegiac lines as these: "Earth felt the wound, and Nature from her seat / Sighing through all her Works gave signs of woe" (IX, 782–83); from Adam's "slack hand the Garland wreath'd for *Eve* / Down-dropp'd, and all the faded roses shed" (IX, 892–93). In such lines, the materials of aristocratic culture depart from the domain of truth at once political and spiritual, to compose a new category of mere rhetoric or adornment. The poet who is attracted to such materials will resemble the unsuccessful courtier who has mistaken fashion for a noble bearing; neither personal gratification nor aesthetic value can reside

> in the bought smile
> Of harlots, loveless, joyless, unindear'd,
> Casual fruition, nor in Court Amours,

> Mixt Dance, or wanton Mask, or Midnight Ball,
> Or Serenade, which the starv'd lover sings,
> To his proud fair, best quitted with disdain.
>   (IV, 765–70)

Milton invokes the carnival of night to describe Restoration society and
the poetry that caters to it. This, then, is what poetry does that cannot
be done in the rational prose style of the Royal Society. It consigns a
whole world of writing to obsolescence.

This is in itself a politically ambitious purpose, but the poem does
more than eliminate the possibility of using the humanistic tradition of
learning in the grand old way. It breaks down this tradition into the
materials of a world—at once domestic and personal—that had not existed before, at least not in Renaissance literature. With Eve's corruption,
the distinction between elite and popular bodies collapses, and a new
opposition begins to organize the materials of the poem.

Milton made Eve out of writing drawn from two potentially contrary
traditions. He gave her a body that celebrates aristocratic power, but he
composed her thoughts and speech out of material drawn from handbooks on domestic economy and from puritan sermons and treatises on
marriage, which were adamantly opposed to the luxury of aristocratic
display.[42] Her frugal talk would certainly have struck a chord familiar to
the readership of 1667, no matter how far that talk was out of tune with
the lush description of her body. To prepare for Raphael's visit, Adam
asks Eve to "pour / Abundance fit to honor and receive" (V, 314–15).
She responds by arguing for the practical value of objects over their value
as signs of God's abundance and of man's supremacy over the rest of
creation. Contradicting the meaning that such things have in an aristocratic tradition of letters, she claims that

> small store will serve, where store,
> All seasons, ripe for use hangs on the stalk;
> Save what by frugal storing firmness gains
> To nourish, and superfluous moist consumes.
>   (V, 322–25)

Having registered her objections, Eve obediently assembles a feast fit to
show "that here on Earth / God hath dispenst his bounties as in Heav'n"
(V, 329–30). The dialogue between man and woman nevertheless makes
it clear that two different economies exist in potential conflict even in
Eden.

On the one hand, Adam speaks from within the economy whose end
is conspicuous consumption. His logic underwrites aristocratic cultures

and opposes the accumulation of capital. From the perspective of a protocapitalist economy the luxury and display of aristocratic culture appears impractical, wasteful, and decadent.[43] Milton's poem has established a perspective within the very heart of aristocratic culture from which to see a patron's immodest displays of generosity as wasteful and, on this basis, aesthetically displeasing. It is against the old notion of pleasure that Eve coaxes Adam to divide the labor between them. Precisely because they take so much pleasure in each other's company, she reasons, "Our day's work brought to little, though begun / Early, and th' hour of Supper comes unearn'd" (IX, 224-25). In agreeing, Adam submits to a practical standard that sees the plenitude of unfallen nature as unruly excess rather than the earthly equivalent of heavenly perfection. Within Eden, then, the materials of Renaissance art run up against the economy of the plain style according to which pleasure is supposed to come with labor and turn to misery when coupled with extravagance. The Fall allows Milton to divide heaven and earth between the two competing styles.

He is far from insensitive to what such a change means for someone who writes poetry. Where he once—as a young man—approached the role of poet with patriotic zeal, he sees himself late in life as someone stranded in the wilderness, singing

> with mortal voice, unchang'd
> To hoarse or mute, though fall'n on evil days,
> On evil days though fall'n, and evil tongues;
> In darkness, and with dangers compast round,
> And solitude.
>   (VII, 24-28).

The political impact of the revolution occurring within *Paradise Lost* becomes clear when one considers what relationship between the author, his readership, and "woman" such a voice establishes. The poem itself offers a particularly telling comparison between this relationship before the Fall and the changed relationship after the Fall. The angel Raphael visits the sacred couple in their unfallen state to tell them (and the reader, of course) just where they stand among the emblems of God's power and how they shall live at their patron's pleasure. It is His knowledge and power they both embody. Satan and his legions demonstrate the consequences of exclusion: their bodies are grotesque after the Fall: "all transform'd / Alike, to Serpents all as accessories / To his bold Riot" (X, 519-21). Loss of God's bounty afflicts this monstrously writhing mass with a "scalding thirst" and "hunger fierce" (X, 556) that resemble the endless hunger of the grotesque body in Bakhtin's account of Rabelaisian culture.[44] Once the sacred couple has taken on the features of the grotesque body, the angel Michael comes to explain the new basis for their identity. The contrast between the domestic scenes before and after the Fall is all-important.

Milton's epic account of the Fall carries aristocratic conventions into new semiotic territory, where order is grounded in domestic relations and the primacy of the individual. Political order ideally depends on the individual's consent, just as morality depends on his conscience. This is the conclusion that Adam and Eve reach in debating their relative culpability: morality falters or prevails within the individual, and it does so to the degree that domestic life either erodes or fortifies him. It is important to note that even before nature and culture undergo the cataclysmic changes that make them modern, turbulence erupts both between the sexes and within each one to endow them with a conflict-ridden individuality more like our own (IX, 1099–1186). On the one hand, as we have already suggested, Adam and Eve are no longer themselves once they have fallen from their original estate; the magical stirrings of internal conflict divide the aristocratic body on the basis of sex to make it fit for labor. On the other hand, the pair have acquired what future generations of readers would regard as authentic selves, the raw material out of which social character is fashioned and moral value acquired. Upon this notion of origins hinge the Enlightenment concepts of mind and state as they were articulated in its philosophy, as well as in the narratives of personal development that prepared the way for the novel.[45] Like the last two books of Milton's poem, both theory and fiction located the beginnings of the nation in a prior state of nature, the beginnings of consciousness in some initial act of perception, and the development of the individual in a series of exchanges between individual and state that conventionally begin and end in the family.

Power in the world so constructed depends upon literacy. The last two books of *Paradise Lost* lay down the conditions for acquiring such power. Even a hasty comparison between Michael's vision of the future and Raphael's earlier account of man's prelapsarian past illustrates how problematic language has suddenly become. The purpose of Raphael's story is to reveal a divine truth, which clearly exists prior to its revelation. Communication in Eden resembles this angelic discourse. It too presumes that a thing, being the handiwork of God, contains its own meaning. But like the language Satan uses to distort Eve's view of things, the language Michael uses with Adam is curiously ambiguous and requires interpretation. Adam's second dialogue with one of God's emissaries redefines truth as something that is produced by and within the individual rather than a message delivered from above.

In this new situation, language is not only of man's making, it is also the making of man. To demonstrate the implications of this new property of language, we have chosen the section of Michael's instructions to Adam where the daughters of Cain entice the sons of God:

> by thir guise
> Just men they seem'd, and all thir study bent
> To worship God aright, and know his works
> Not hid, nor those things last which might preserve
> Freedom and Peace to men: they on the Plain
> Long had not walkt, when from the Tents behold
> A Bevy of fair Women, richly gay
> In Gems and wanton dress; to the Harp they sung
> Soft amorous Ditties, and in dance came on.
>   (XI, 576–84)

Let us follow the "Bevy of fair Women" through the dialogue between man and angel. "Soon inclin'd to admit delight," Adam jumps to the conclusion that with their appearance history has suddenly taken an upward turn (XI, 596–602). Not so, according to the angelic historian, who admonishes him thus: "Judge not what is best / By pleasure, though to Nature seeming meet" (XI, 603–4). These women may resemble "Goddesses, so blithe, so smooth, so gay," but they are "empty of all good wherein consists / Woman's domestic honor and chief praise" (XI, 615–17). This is indeed a striking new development in the poem—a body whose beauty as an object indicates its deficiency as a subject.

As morality opposes eroticism and becomes the standard of beauty in the poem, the female body loses all iconicity. It provides the language for an invisible essence—or "mind"—that requires interpretation. Again beguiled by earthly beauty, Adam assumes that the "Bevy of fair Women" acquires meaning as the simple negation of unfallen beauty: "But still I see the tenor of Man's woe / Holds on the same, from Woman to begin" (XI, 632–33). And again the angel intervenes. Meaning does not inhere in things themselves at all, he now insists. It is not from woman but "From Man's effeminate slackness" that man's woe begins (XI, 634). Michael's moral interpretation of the scene detaches meaning from the object and relocates it within the viewing subject as the sign of his "effeminate slackness." His instruction of Adam thus allows us to witness the transformation of the aristocratic woman into attributes of her new beholder—the rational observer.

Let us return to the scene of instruction itself and see how the disciplinary behavior of language modifies the power relations organizing that scene. The poetry of the fallen world is didactic poetry. It does not celebrate the patron's generosity. It identifies human deficiencies and establishes a standard for perfection. By bearing witness to human history, Adam acquires the knowledge of human progress required to produce such interpretations. Paradoxically, this knowledge—committed to rationality, delayed gratification, frugality, self-enclosure, and the division of labor—distinguished Eve's practical approach to her role as gardener from Adam's extravagance, and it instigated her rebellion. Yet a version of Eve's way of thinking is what ensures man's redemption in the new world. Where practical knowledge was represented as feminine knowledge by an aristocratic tradition of letters, the same knowledge takes on a masculine identity after the Fall. So altered, it is no longer a source of disruption but the guarantee of self-regulation and domestic stability. Milton, in other words, represents the Fall as the emergence into dominance of the kind of thinking found in handbooks on domestic economy and in puritan marriage manuals.

The world in which Milton leaves the reader at the end of *Paradise Lost* is a world of work. It cannot appear other than a place of scarcity in comparison with the copious beauty of Eden. But the fact remains that this new world belongs to an entirely new kind of man, a man empowered by production rather than conspicuous consumption. This is a man for whom patronage is no longer the means of distributing wealth and maintaining hierarchy and social order. Milton represents Adam's disobedience as a refusal of patronage, which caused him to be cast out of the elite community and set to work building a version of that community on a mundane and personal scale. If before the Fall the sexual division of labor produced a fissure in the elite community, after the Fall that division becomes an ordering principle in its own right. Upon this division of labor depends the integrity of political and personal life. That is made clear by Michael's instructions. As the "Bevy of fair women" mixes into the political affairs of men, both men and women are sullied.

Feminist criticism has recently made a second fact at the end of the poem almost as apparent as the first. The male world of politics and history is dominated by intellectual rather than manual labor. Why else did Milton have a powerful impact on the culture that arose from the destruction of monarchy's exalted images, particularly that of the Caroline version of heavenly love?[46] Michael genders political information when he narcotizes Eve during Adam's history lesson. Thus he differentiates male from female on the basis of the knowledge each should possess, before he condemns the one to productive and the other to reproductive labor. The categories of labor that organize the new world are defined by the most fundamental distinction of all: between those who work only with their bodies and those whose labor is invisible because it is intellectual. This distinction is always implicit in the distinction between productive and domestic labor that marks modern industrial cultures.

That *Paradise Lost* provided (indeed, still provides) an instrument for reproducing the distinction between intellectual and manual labor in and among readerships becomes apparent if one examines subsequent editions of *Paradise Lost*. Footnotes were added to explain the scientific knowledge, the theological debates, and the body of philosophical and literary material to which the poem alludes. These editions implied that one had to master an enormous body of knowledge in order to read this one poem, and people who negotiated the web of allusions and references as they read the poem could think they possessed a superior form of literacy. In the fourth printing of the poem, the poet added the "Arguments." In 1674 an engraving of the poet's head was published with the poem.[47] As early as 1695, a body of critical commentary began to accumulate around the poem, attributing to it an exalted imagination and moral insight.[48] These critical remarks considered the poem a testimony to the greatness of the individual in whom the poem was supposed to have originated. Leslie Moore explains why Jonathan Richardson, one of Milton's most influential early commentators, argued that (in Moore's words) "*Paradise Lost* [should] be treated like Scripture, like the revealed Word of God": "The commentator on Milton is a scribe working with a sacred text; while he may tamper with the 'Prophane' writings of antiquity, he may not alter or improve *Paradise Lost*."[49] Given this absolute authority, the text in turn authorizes the work of the educated critic or commentator.

Richardson tells the reader of *Paradise Lost*:

> Whoever Profits, as he May, by This Poem will, as *Adam* in the Garden, Enjoy the Pleasures of Sense to the Utmost, with Temperance, and Purity of Heart, the Truest and Fullest Enjoyment of them; and will Moreover perceive his Happiness is Establish'd upon a Better Foundation than That of his Own

> Impeccability, and Thus possess a Paradise Within Far more Happy than that of *Eden*.[50]

Richardson promises the reader that when he has mastered the poem, he will have acquired a form of cultural capital, or "profit," that provides access to a superior "Eden." The new Eden is at once a morally sanctified world of leisure ("Truest and Fullest Enjoyment") and an elite interpretive community.

In this way, Milton had something to do with the rise to power of the class of people for whom he served as the very model of "the author" and the personification of a form of knowledge-power possible only through literacy.[51] The poem offered a means of identifying those who had the cultural knowledge required to read it as a cut above those who did not. By so revising the effect of literacy, furthermore, the poem changed what it meant to write, who could do it, and what could be said in print; and the consequences of so redefining and redistributing literacy were immediate. Despite all the official measures to turn back the historical clock, where literacy was concerned the change was permanent. The importance of *Paradise Lost* increased as literacy began to allow some people to participate in a whole new world of English information, from which those less educated were excluded. Reading and writing provided the basis for self-definition and testified to the growth and quality of consciousness. The ability to read and write vernacular English identified those who possessed it as the true English people, those fitted by nature and obligated by culture to rule and reproduce themselves. On the terrain of writing, then, England underwent a transformation that meets the marxist criterion for revolution: it brought a new class of people into power. In another and equally important sense, it brought those people into being as a modern ruling class.

CHAPTER FIVE

The Vanishing Intellectual

Everything begins with reproduction.
> Jacques Derrida,
> *Of Grammatology*

During the 1640s, the state lost control of published information. Political opinion escaped from the charmed circle of the elite in which it had circulated, and what for centuries had been the privileged knowledge of this small group became the subject of public debate.[1] Although, as we will argue, this publicizing of what had been private constituted only one component of the cultural revolution we are trying to identify, the results were unquestionably profound. One can regard the rise of the English newspaper as symptomatic of the change in question. Before 1641 there were sporadic publications that reported on foreign events, but the only ways to find out about debates in Parliament and discussions of government policy were through personal participation in the political life of the nation, regular attendance at court, or periodic residence at the Inns of Court. In other words, to be informed about decisions having the most direct and pervasive influence over one's life, one had to have direct access to the handwritten reports, the letters, the conversation, or the gossip of those involved. Political information was confined to the private world of the political elite. Thus one may safely assume that, before 1641, a cultural gulf separated "the public" and "the political," as those spheres are understood today.[2] With the dismantling of the royal censorship procedures and the events that began to unfold in 1642, however, the whole notion of what could be argued about in print was transformed.

In July 1641, Parliament abolished the Star Chamber, which had enforced the censorship regulations; and by "November 1641 the first news-paper dealing with events in England could be bought in the vicinity of Old Bailey."[3] Within two weeks of the first paper's appearance, a second appeared, and two weeks later a third. These were soon followed by many more.[4] A glance at the Thomason Tracts is all one needs to get a sense of how rapidly information proliferated during this period. A book-seller by trade, George Thomason sought to acquire every publication—licensed and unlicensed—published during the 1640s and 50s. Although the collection was far from complete in its day and has not come down to us intact, 23,000 items have survived.[5] The collection includes broad-sides, sermons, prophecies, newsbooks, and a variety of other publica-tions that poured off the presses from the early 1640s on. Even after the revolutionary government succeeded in establishing some control over the flow of information, unlicensed material continued to proliferate. And if certain interest groups wished to publish and distribute printed matter legally, they could, like many a Royalist sympathizer, obtain a license. By resorting to literary forms that included elaborate allegories, Italianate genres, and various modes of pastoralism, apparently they could publish rather controversial ideas.[6]

These few examples should indicate that the censorship measures put into practice by the king, Parliament, the protector, and eventually the Licensing Act of 1662, included within their purview a lot of material we no longer consider especially political, while excluding some that we do. The ready availability of means by which to avoid government cen-sorship suggests that Milton, whether he was putting out tracts in the 1640s, serving as a censor under Cromwell, or writing as a poet and historian during the 1660s, always made a political decision to write as he did. As a result, he was continuously involved in an intense struggle that would determine who controlled the production of truth. If only temporarily, print produced something like a public sphere of debate and gave rise to an entirely new kind of political literacy.

However, one must deal with the fact that censorship returned with new vigor in 1662. This is what killed off the political Milton, leaving us with the poet—or so a tradition of criticism has claimed. Between the moment of renewed censorship and the beginning of what Raymond Williams calls "the long revolution" in 1695, there exists a significant gap. During this time, in Williams's words, "the situation becomes ex-tremely difficult to analyse. The imperfect evidence that we have, in a number of fields, suggests on the one hand a continuation of the general pattern of expansion—slow growth of the serious public, more rapid growth of the occasional public, but also the apparent confinement of the expansion to a growing middle class."[7] Williams posits a thirty-year period of suspended animation between 1663, when the first surveyor of the press was appointed "with a virtual monopoly in printed news," and 1695, when Parliament "declined to renew the 1662 Licensing Act, and the stage for expansion was now fully set" (180). Like Christopher Hill, Williams assumes that the Revolution was ultimately a bourgeois revolution. He finds that between 1662 and 1695 the literacy of an aristocratic culture did indeed give way to that of an expanding middle-class readership. Yet he refuses to consider these signs of middle-class empowerment as evidence that a bourgeois revolution had already occurred, preferring instead to regard the expansion of middle-class literacy as the "confinement" and delay of revolutionary effects.

Did revolution stop dead in its tracks because the Licensing Act was renewed? We cannot believe Hill and Williams actually mean to suggest that change has to be legal before it can be called revolutionary. From the data they provide, it is difficult to understand how any legal attempt to contain the political sphere could have succeeded once the means of producing information had spread beyond the court and Parliament. It strikes us as far more likely that the Licensing Act was renewed several times in centuries to follow precisely because print had gotten so far out of hand. Indeed, indications are that beginning in the 1640s the power struggle in England shifted onto the plane of writing. The question was not entirely—or even primarily—a question of who won the battle of words. What mattered more was that once the political struggle shifted onto the plane of writing, the struggle itself could not fail to empower those who produced and disseminated information. But, adhering to a modern notion of what belongs to the category of the "political," neither Hill nor Williams discusses the political impact that this shift had on England during the years immediately following the Restoration.

The same evidence that fuels their argument that the political effects of the Revolution were not felt immediately—during the period between the publication of *Paradise Lost* and, say, *Robinson Crusoe*—also indicates that a major cultural change had in fact taken place. This evidence shows that a substantial number of people had already put their thoughts into words and had them printed. There is no evidence to suggest that these people stopped thinking of themselves as authors, or of authors as people like themselves, simply because the official censorship had been renewed. If they had indeed stopped thinking of themselves in this way, it seems unlikely there would have been the veritable explosion of print in 1695 which Williams identifies as the beginning of "the long revolution." The Licensing Act of 1662 sought to limit the number of master printers to twenty.[8] This act was designed for preventing "the frequent Abuses in printing seditious, treasonable and unlicensed Books and Pamphlets and for regulating Printing and Printing Presses."[9] Soon after the act was passed, Roger L'Estrange was appointed surveyor of the press. He was, in Marvell's words, one of the "public tooth-drawers of the press."[10] Known to have named Milton as the possible author of a pamphlet that "runs foul, [and] tends to a tumult," L'Estrange apparently thought the popular press presented a threat to royal interests.[11] Indeed, Hill tells us, "when in 1663 L'Estrange issued proposals for licensing the press, his main target was 'the great masters of the popular style' of the interregnum, who 'speak plain and strike home to the capacity and humours of the multitude' because they wrote 'in times of freedom.' "[12]

When L'Estrange referred to "popular style" and "plain speech," he clearly meant something different from what Petty, Sprat, and Locke meant when they advocated a style of writing that displayed the virtues of practicality, clarity, and referential fidelity. From a more modern vantage point, one can see that in taking issue with the florid rhetoric and Latinate polemics of Caroline intellectuals, these men were not speaking on behalf of what L'Estrange called "the multitude." To the contrary, members of the Royal Society were attempting to set a standard for vernacular English. Their definition of the ideal English prose style should be understood as a rather overt attempt to regulate the printed word and confine the spread of political information to the middle-class readership—which, Williams insists, they succeeded in doing. It is misleading to think of the development of what would later be called "the plain style" as an advance of freedom in the wider, more popular sense as Williams represents it to be. It is more accurate to see that development as the emergence of a new language of power, one that could not only expand the political sphere well beyond court and Parliament but also restrict the production of truth to those who possessed a particular brand of literacy.

Each line of inquiry pursued so far in this book leads to the question of what kind of people wrought so central a change—the change, we are arguing, that marks the onset of modernity. In Milton criticism, as we argued in an earlier chapter, one regularly stumbles over the man's banishment from one domain of writing and his confinement to another. And this cultural redefinition of the source where writing was presumed to come from obviously had a lot to do with what Milton wrote. In turning to historical accounts of the English Revolution, we found a similar reluctance to focus on events taking place at the level of information, its production and distribution. Though Stone and Hill as much as admit that the Revolution was a revolution in thought if not in words, they nevertheless seek out other, more primary causes for change, and they extend the process fifty years or more into the future in order to catch up with other, more important effects. Historians of the family find themselves working with quite different bodies of data from the periods before and after the Revolution. Some, like Laslett, project backward in time the presence of emotions that only later are put into writing; others, like Stone, infer an absence of these intimate feelings from the absence of documentary evidence concerning personal life. For both groups, information about the presence or absence of information constitutes "extra" information—even noise—in the system. Such information never operates as a narrative element in their accounts. Yet in failing to address that information directly, they fail to answer these questions: What was revolutionary about the English Revolution? How did the household become the haven for private individuals in a heartless public world? And why is Milton the first modern literary author?

To address these questions, one must first consider how such different people as John Milton, John Locke, William Petty, and Daniel Defoe came to reformulate their world as one based on labor and composed of enclosed private worlds. As we have suggested, no single person could have accomplished this radical reconception of England. To imagine the English Revolution as a revolution in words, it is necessary to imagine how a group of disparate individuals turned as if with a single mind to the task of reorganizing countless varied bits of information into a new political classification system. Our reading of *Paradise Lost* argued that the authors who took part in this unacknowledged revolution were not in fact reproducing something that was already in place. For like Petty's proposed plague precautions, Sprat's account of the noble artisans, and Defoe's story of Crusoe's island kingdom, the history lesson in the last two books of *Paradise Lost* establishes an entirely new set of principles for evaluating human beings. Circumstances did not allow these men to collaborate directly. Yet each obviously felt a certain commitment to the labor of his pen and a belief in its power to improve the world in some finite and practical way. From this conviction—rather than from an innate longing for freedom—developed the concepts of mind, family, and nation that we have been describing.

If there is some truth in these speculations, then any attempt to deal

with the advent of modernity must come to terms with what, for con-
venience, we are calling "intellectuals" and "intellectual labor."[13] The
question of who "intellectuals" are and what relationship exists between
them and other members of industrialized societies has a long and trou-
bled history, which seems to begin, along with the other questions we
have been considering, during the time of Milton's career. The historian
Harold Perkin has referred to intellectuals as "the forgotten middle
class," but as he himself admits, this is a somewhat misleading epithet.[14]
He holds these people—whoever they were—responsible for rearticulat-
ing social relations in terms of the kind of work one did (if any), and
the source of one's income. In so doing, intellectuals saw to it that
educated people would regard "the aristocratic, entrepreneurial, and
working-class ideals as the three major class ideals contending for supremacy in early nineteenth-century England" (252). Thanks largely to
the reclassification that began with the efforts of such men as Milton,
Petty, and Sprat, our cultural past is often described as a procession of
class oppositions, in which a conflict between aristocracy and bourgeoisie
somehow gave way around the end of the eighteenth century to a conflict
between owners and workers. Yet, as Perkin notes,

> there was another class and another ideal, without analysing which it is still
> not possible to understand the struggle between them. An extraordinary pro-
> portion of the spokesmen of the first three ideals were members of none of
> the three classes.... To what class did this collection of lawyers, doctors,
> public officials, journalists, professors and lecturers belong? To the middle
> class, certainly, but not to the capitalist or professional middle class, a class
> curiously neglected in the social theories of the age. (252)

The point is well taken, whether or not one agrees that writers and
intellectuals constitute a fourth class.

Zygmunt Bauman has argued that intellectuals coined the term "intellectual" at the beginning of our own century as part of an effort "to
recapture and reassert that societal centrality and those global concerns
which had been associated with the production and dissemination of
knowledge during the age of Enlightenment."[15] The term both exalted
the power of knowledge and testified to the obsolescence of that power.
Ironically, by the time it was coined people could no longer believe in
the possibility of an enlightened state that operated on behalf of the
entire population—if in fact they ever did. This irony is compounded by
another. Intellectuals formulated a self-description that relegated their
power to the past at precisely the moment when intellectual labor had
come to dominate other social and economic practices in the most bla-

tant and undeniable way. How could it be seen otherwise? What had
seemed a subordinate sector of the middle class made up of managers,
professionals, experts of various kinds—"the philistines" Arnold called
them—was running England by the 1860s. The problem was, according
to Bauman, that the term "intellectuals" lumped together journalists,
poets, artists, and culture critics with scientists, bureaucrats, professional
people, and public figures. "By the time the word was coined," he explains, "the descendants of *les philosophes* or *la république des lettres*
had already been divided into specialized enclaves" (1). In this respect,
the word was no more than a rallying cry to revive the old tradition of
"men of knowledge." In another respect, and one more closely related
to the difficulty at hand, the lament for the passing of the power of
knowledge was a way of denying the present location and the effects of
that very power. The lament for the post-Enlightenment intellectual
served to mystify intellectual labor.

Bauman notes that "while the mythology of Enlightenment mesmer-
ized much of eighteenth-century Europe, England had her own way of
conceptualizing this new notion of the nation. The Puritan personified
the intellectuals' plans for the better, rational society" (193). Bauman's
puritan was not simply an "imaginary" puritan. He was an idealized self-
representation whom intellectuals invoked whenever they wanted to
identify what modern culture was lacking: "Behind every 'carrier of rationality' the intellectuals appointed, the Puritan was lurking, and the
recognition of this disappearance made all further painting of likenesses
gratuitous" (193). The figure of the puritan harked back to a time when
intellectual labor was not in ascendance. Furthermore, the modern intellectual appeared to have none of the political power that had once
adhered to the puritans. Because the puritan seemed in both instances
to occupy the underdog's position, intellectuals could invoke this figure
to legitimize their labor. By lamenting the disappearance of the Enlightenment intellectual, intellectuals represented themselves as what was
needed to restore faith in England's foundational assumption—that men
could progress collectively toward a more reasonable and humane state
through education and moral reform. In this respect, the puritan was
both an obsolete formation and a possibility that had not yet been realized, his regime already over and not yet begun; he identified intellectuals with a salutary force that was somehow always beyond their reach.
Consequently, they could exercise what power they did possess from a
position that appeared to have little political impact or none at all.[16] Yet
all the elements needed for defining the role of intellectuals were already

there by the time Marx and Engels began their study of political economy. Only the fact that the theory of capital subordinated intellectual labor to productive labor made the intellectual's vanishing act possible. And his departure from the arena of politics, as we will try to demonstrate, made his labor all the more powerful. Let us examine a few passages from Marx to illustrate this point.

Marx rejected out of hand the proposition that any statement merely "reflected" the material circumstances of its existence. He regarded it as a defect of all previous "materialism . . . that the thing, reality, [the sensible world] is conceived only in the form of the *object of contemplation,* but not as *sensuous human activity, practice,* not subjectively."[17] This question of whether the mind dominates the body grew still more perplexing whenever Marx and Engels tried to account for the mind-body relationship in terms of class struggle. At one point in *The German Ideology,* for example, they seem to make mental production less important to the rise of capital than material production; yet paradoxically they say that mental production is absolutely necessary in order for capitalism to succeed.

> The class which has the means of material production at its disposal, has control at the same time over the means of mental production, so that thereby, generally speaking, the ideas of those who lack the means of mental production are subject to it. The ruling ideas are nothing more than the ideal expression of the dominant material relationships, the dominant material relationships grasped as ideas; hence of the relationships which make the one class the ruling one, therefore, the ideas of its dominance. (64)

By asserting that possession of the means of "material production" entails possession of the means of "mental production," the first sentence in the quotation acknowledges that ideas do something, if only by virtue of suppressing the ideas of those who do not possess the means of material production. The second sentence asserts that "ruling ideas" are "nothing more" than an "expression of the dominant material relationships." Thus this second sentence relocates power in a cause prior to ideas, detaching that power from ideas. Ideas cannot cause anything to happen because they are "mental" rather than "material." A number of commentators have noted those moments when Marx and Engels open the possibility that the class struggle was a struggle between intellectual and productive labor. On these occasions the question of intellectual labor usually fades back into the opposition between labor and capital referred to in the passage just quoted.[18]

In *Capital,* however, Marx offers a just-so story that translates the struggle between labor and capital into a struggle between productive and intellectual labor, revealing the concealment of the second narrative of struggle within the first. To explain how surplus value comes into being, he imagines the mental process by which the vulgar capitalist decides to reward himself for his own labor. At the end of his chapter entitled "The Sale and Purchase of Labour Power," Marx stages the onset of this process:

> A certain change takes place . . . in the physiognomy of our *dramatis personae*. He who was previously the money-owner now strides out in front as a capitalist; the possessor of labour-power follows as his worker. The one smirks self-importantly and is intent on business; the other is timid and holds back, like someone who has brought his own hide to market and now has nothing else to expect but a tanning.[19]

What causes the change in the money-owner's self-conception that so demoralizes the possessor of "labour-power"? In his next chapter, "The Labour Process and the Valorization Process," Marx explains how capital begins to dominate labor, as if the power of money to do so were directly related to the capitalist's inflated self-definition. But whether capital produces the sense of superiority displayed by those who buy labor, or whether something else makes the capitalist feel superior to the workers and thus prompts him to use money exploitively, is not at all clear. Marx creates the second possibility in his attempt to argue for the first.

The story is therefore double: "The process of consumption of labour power is at the same time the production process of commodities *and* of surplus value" (279, our italics). But this distinction within the object between process and product, or value and what Marx calls valorization, cannot be detected in the commodity itself. To understand the semiotic composition of the object, we must leave the domain of "the market or the sphere of circulation" and penetrate the secret of the commodity fetish. Or so Marx enjoins the reader: "Let us therefore, in company with the owner of money and the owner of labour-power, leave this noisy sphere, where everything takes place on the surface and in full view of everyone, and follow them into the hidden abode of production, on whose threshold there hangs the notice 'No admittance except on business' " (279–80). To understand the valorization process, presumably one must first understand the labor process.

The next chapter of *Capital* takes up the story after a man brings his labor power to market for sale as a commodity. By virtue of the intellectual component, labor in this state has taken a quantum leap beyond "the first instinctive forms of labour which remain on the animal level"

(283). Admittedly, "a bee would put many a human architect to shame by the construction of its honeycomb cells. But what distinguishes the worst architect from the best of bees is that the architect builds the cell in his mind before he constructs it in wax" (284). Originally, then, intellectual labor distinguishes human labor as both human and labor, lending value to the products of that labor that does not inhere in the natural object. Indeed, the comparison of the architect and the bee suggests that commodities cannot exist without intellectual labor. At this point in the story, the capitalist intervenes and purchases both the means of production and labor power.

Although the moment when the owners of money take control of labor is the focal point of Marx's theory, and the very thing his microhistory is meant to explain, the narrative introduces that event as a disruption of the normal course of events. "Let us now return to our would-be capitalist. We left him just after he had purchased, in the open market, all the necessary factors of the labour process" (291). The capitalist's intrusion into the process transforms the material as well as the labor that converts it into a commodity: "Now the raw material merely serves to absorb a definite quantity of labour. By being soaked in labour, the raw material is in fact changed into yarn, because labour-power is expended in the form of spinning and added to it; but the product, the yarn, is now nothing more than a measure of the labour absorbed by the cotton" (296–97). The story about spinning cotton into yarn resembles the fairy tale about spinning straw into gold. Marx says the product undergoes this transformation because of "the labour-process . . . expended in the form of spinning and added to it." Thus he leaves us with the impression that cotton is the "material" and manual labor the "means," or magical ingredient in the recipe. Marx's capitalist initially thinks he will make a profit on his yarn by purchasing the labor as well as the cotton, but this is not to be. Since "the value of the product is equal to the value of the capital advanced, . . . no surplus value has been created and consequently money has not been transformed into capital" (297–98).[20]

To proceed to the next step in the story of capital, Marx turns away from the logic of production in order to dramatize how the capitalist, having turned money into material and labor, turns that material and labor back into money at a profit to himself. The capitalist changes the way he conceptualizes the problem and especially the role he assigns to himself in the production process. "He gets mad," Marx tells us. "He makes threats. He will not be caught napping again" (298). The capitalist learns from his mistake. "Let him therefore console himself with the reflection that virtue is its own reward," Marx cautions. "But no, on the contrary, he becomes insistent. The yarn is of no use to him, he says. He produced it in order to sell it" (299).

Were this a fairy tale, a Rumpelstiltskin would enter at this point and offer to spin the straw into gold on the sly in exchange for the vulgar capitalist's first child. But this chapter of *Capital* is a modern narrative, and the magic must take another form. The tale requires what Vladimir Propp would call a "donor" in order for the hero to emerge and be recognized as such.[21] Marx turns the intervention of the donor into an operation of the capitalist's consciousness. The wonders of imagination, the capacity to grow or develop, a flash of insight—all seem to produce something out of nothing, much as they do in nineteenth-century fiction. In this way, whenever Marx cannot find a material cause for the production process, he locates that cause in the capitalist's mind, and that mind consequently grows less vulgar. Indeed, it can be argued that Marx turns to the devices of fiction, and specifically to the trick of personification, whenever he wants his theory to take a step forward. Nowhere is this clearer than when he explains how production can yield surplus value.

Marx has the capitalist redefine labor so that the trouble it took for him to purchase yarn and labor power can be called work: "Can the worker produce commodities out of nothing, merely by using his arms and legs?" With some indignation the capitalist asks further, "Did I not provide him with the materials through which, and in which alone, his labour could be embodied?" (299). This is not simply the arrogance of capital but that which comes with the prestige belonging to men who work with their minds as opposed to their "arms and legs." A closer examination of what happens to the capitalist's state of mind would show him marshaling the righteousness of puritan rhetoric, combining it with the logic of Enlightenment epistemology, and then adding a dash of the worker's humility. When actually challenged by those who own the labor on which he depends, the owner of money mimics their voice. He takes on "the unassuming demeanor of one of his own workers and exclaims: 'Have I myself not worked? Have I not performed the labour of superintendence, of overseeing the spinner? and does not this labour, too, create value?' " (300).

When he took possession of the means of material production, the capitalist apparently gained possession of the means of mental production. Although Marx does not tell us how it came to be, the capitalist's ideas appear to count more than anyone else's. For what, according to *The German Ideology*, is a "ruling idea" but "the dominant relationship grasped as ideas; hence of the relationships which make the one class the ruling one, therefore, the ideas of its dominance" (64)? Such ideas are determined by economic relationships; they conceal the truth of these relationships. In Marx's account of surplus value, these ideas first collapsed the means of production (labor) into the materials (cotton). Then, through an act of equivocation, the capitalist rationalized his own contribution to the process ("Did I not provide him with the materials through which, and in which alone, his labour could be embodied?"). This rationalization displaced the value of manual labor and substituted the labor of the capitalist, enabling him to conceal the true source of surplus value and claim all the profits as his.

At this point in the story, the struggle between labor and capital has become a struggle between labor and intellectual labor. Indeed, the capitalist appears to have solidified his domination over the worker and to have secured the worker's subservience by translating the conflict between their respective interests—namely, labor and capital—into a conflict between manual and intellectual labor. Where Marx had initially bonded the two functions to one another in comparing human labor with that of bees, he used the figure of the capitalist to break this bond and to set the two forms of labor in opposition. So redefined, the intellectual component that had been indistinguishable from human labor becomes capable of acting on its own behalf; intellectual labor dominates the manual component of the labor process; and valorization displaces labor value. But to place such stress on irrational, mental phenomena, as Marx does whenever he turns his narrative over to personification, is to threaten the logic of economic determinism. His use of personification injects the rhetoric of fiction into the logic of political economy. Surely, Marx cannot allow this rhetoric to remain in place for long. Let us read further.

The story of the production of surplus value is not quite over once the owner of money reclassifies labor and assumes the humility of the worker. The reason why his claim to have labored was accepted as true by his fellow capitalists and workers has yet to be explained; and everything, according to this all-important though apparently epiphenomenal narrative, hinges on that acceptance. Securing the acceptance of capitalism, one discovers, is not something the capitalist can do for himself: "The whole litany he has just recited was simply meant to pull the wool over our eyes" (300). The capitalist is in the business of making a profit, not of rationalizing it, even though securing that profit seems to depend on his conceptual as well as his rhetorical appropriation of surplus value. "He leaves this," Marx reminds us, "and similar subterfuges and conjuring tricks to the professors of political economy, who are paid for it" (300). The intellectual can thus be regarded as the personification of the brainstorm—a rationalizing faculty that originated inside the capitalist's mind: "Have I myself not worked? Have I not performed the labour of superintendence, of overseeing the spinner? and does not this labour, too, create value?" (300). The capitalist in turn ceases to be an intellectual, returns to his former role as owner of money, and, as the personification of capital, dominates both the labor process and the valorization process.

In light of this fable, how is one to regard the uninterrupted flow of logic that concludes the twin histories entitled "The Labour Process and the Valorization Process"? On the one hand, Marx does take us into what he calls "the hidden abode of production" in order to explain how the incorporation of labor value in the product changes the marketing and circulation of goods. Returning from this venture into the labor process ordinarily concealed by the professors of political economy, he offers the reader a mathematical formula that is supposed to reveal precisely how the purchase of labor power on a mass basis reduces the cost of production, creating a surplus value (or valorization) where there had been only exchange value before. With that, he can say: "The trick has at last worked: money has been transformed into capital" (301). Viewed from the perspective of this theoretical statement, Marx's caricatures of capitalist and worker and the narrative of their changing relationship seem merely rhetorical embellishments—an entertaining narrative that presents the intricate dynamic of the class struggle as an interaction between two personifications.

To disregard the rhetoric of fiction in favor of the logic of theory may be how our cultural reflexes tell us to understand the relationship between rhetoric and logic, or fiction and theory. But Marx's account does something to these familiar oppositions that occasionally requires us to put fiction first. As Marx says of the architect, before his labor can acquire any value at all, it must have a purpose, and that purpose comes from the intellectual component of his labor. After capital intervenes in the process of production, the process of valorization seems to require a story of its own. At least Marx gives it one. Contained within a personification which is in turn contained within a fable, the process of valorization comes to the reader as a digression from the master narrative, or process of production. Closure of the two plots is accomplished by the gesture of the mathematical formula as a kind of coda and by the sudden addition of experts—professors of political economy—to the plot. Despite the secondary and derivative position that Marx seems to give the process of valorization by dissociating it rhetorically from the process of production, he cannot preserve the logic of his master plot without the rhetoric of fiction. Where does surplus value come from, if not from the ideas that give the capitalist confidence and that make his money more valuable than the labor it purchases? The transitions in Marx's fable take place as intellectual labor transforms the meaning of labor and changes both the self-conceptions of those who perform it and the distribution of money and goods. Theory cannot steer a straight course through the hidden abode of production by pursuing the fate of labor power or even that of money. It must pass through the domains of language and consciousness as well. Only fiction can make this digression without compromising Marx's attempt to bring Hegel down to earth. Fiction allows Marx's theory to remain logically grounded in the world of real people, money, and the things that they make.

To protect his theory of capital, furthermore, Marx has to conceal his own intellectual labor, much as his own antihero, the vulgar capitalist, conceals his behind the humility of manual labor. Marx turns to fiction— his novelette about the capitalist, the worker, and the professor of political economy—whenever it is necessary to shift from an account of how the world works and consider instead how it is represented. He maintains the crucial distinction between fiction and theory this way, but he also reveals how profoundly his theory depends upon these rhetorical gestures—not only to create the categories required by his logic but also to conceal the fact of his own labor in making them.

One finds further indication that "ruling ideas" can actually cause things to happen whenever Marx and Engels try to imagine the defeat of capitalism. Workers will not triumph until they begin to understand that owning labor is better than owning money and to rethink the state as one of "propertyless producers." For nothing short of such a reconception of their relation to their own labor would shatter both the "self-importance" and the "rationality" of the money owner.[22] Whenever Marx and Engels formulate a narrative for the emergence of socialism, it always takes intellectual labor to undo the subordination of manual labor to capital. It may be inferred that this is because intellectual labor created the difference between one kind of labor and another in the first place.[23] That is, for owners of labor to think of themselves as superior to those who work with their "arms and legs," they must, as Marx and Engels suggest, become their own intellectuals. Such moments demonstrate the degree to which capitalism depends on certain forms of knowledge and the special forms of literacy that allow one to gather, classify, and distribute that knowledge. Yet because the intellectual function is either embodied in the capitalist or disembodied and dispersed among experts who seem detached from the means of production, the distinctive character and role of intellectuals quickly fade into the categories of class conflict. What Perkin calls the fourth class easily disappears into the other three.

The most influential attempt to sharpen the definition of intellectuals within a marxist model of class analysis is Antonio Gramsci's. Gramsci theorized precisely the problem we have just identified in Marx. In so doing, he thought he could eliminate that problem by giving intellectuals separate bodies from workers and capitalists and then assigning all three functions to two preexisting classes. In this way, their contributions could be analyzed without disturbing Marx's model of class conflict. Gramsci granted that intellectuals did something other people did not do. "There are historically formed specialised categories," he stated, "for the exercise of the intellectual function."[24] But this was not, he thought, grounds for calling them an autonomous group: "It can be observed that the 'organic' intellectuals which every new class creates alongside itself and elaborates in the course of its development, are for the most part 'specialisations' of partial aspects of the primitive activity of the new social type which the new class has brought into prominence" (6). Intellectuals are not supposed to achieve autonomy for themselves. They are supposed to lend autonomy to the class whose interests they serve: "every social group, coming into existence on the original terrain of . . . economic production, creates together with itself, organically, one or more strata of intellectuals which give it homogeneity and an awareness of its own function not only in the economic but also in the social and political fields" (5). Rather than define intellectuals as a group in their own right, then, Gramsci identified them as part of "the ensemble of the system of relations in which these activities (and therefore the intellectual groups who personify them) have their place within the general complex of social relations" (8). Given this, what role do intellectuals play in the class struggle?

Gramsci drew out a residual argument in Marx when he contended that "one of the most important characteristics of any group that is developing towards dominance is its struggle to assimilate and to conquer 'ideologically' the traditional intellectuals," a struggle that intensifies as the rising group defines its own brand of intellectual in opposition to the reigning tradition. When an emergent group thus begins to contest the class in power, the struggle will be enacted on a symbolic plane. Gramsci confined that clash of codes to a specialized (cultural) arena of the larger socioeconomic class struggle—a part never quite capable of redefining or displacing the whole. He posited a struggle for the means of intellectual production within a struggle for the means of production. Such a conception of the intellectual makes it possible to place Milton in political history even after he stepped out of political office, but it leaves us with two problems.

The first might be called the problem of fragmentation. Gramsci's intellectual is a function of a class that already exists as such. This definition of the intellectual invariably places his labor in a secondary and derivative relation to productive labor, or labor per se. According to Gramsci, there can be no nonintellectual forms of labor: "*homo faber* cannot be separated from *homo sapiens*" (9). However, because his theory requires two definitions of intellectuals, he contends that all men both are and are not intellectuals: "All men are intellectuals, one could therefore say: but not all men have in society the function of intellectuals" (9). Gramsci defined "the function of intellectuals" as all labor from which the manual component is missing. This attempt to invert the thinking of Marx's vulgar capitalist by giving productive labor two functions rather than one puts an obvious strain on the concept of intellectual labor. The idea that intellectual labor is labor from which the manual component is missing allows intellectual labor to blossom into subcategories that undermine the whole point of defining it in the first place. Technocrats, teachers, bureaucrats, and alienated artists are all intellectuals, and yet all seem to speak for different and often competing interests. At one point, the problem of fragmentation appears in this manner: "Intellectuals articulate the rules of the social order and the theories that give them sanction, but at the same time it is intellectuals who criticize the existing order of things and demand its supercession."[25] Of course, these are contrary functions only if meaning derives from preexisting classes. As we saw in *Paradise Lost*, criticizing the rules can be the same as articulating them. And as we saw in Marx's account of the valorization process, intellectual labor tends to disappear into the labor process at the very moment when it has redefined that process in the interest of the capitalist.

A second problem, that of self-contradiction, arises from the problem of fragmentation. In order to hang on to the classical marxist categories of class, Gramsci must posit a class identity for intellectuals and a class function for intellectual labor, and these sometimes openly contradict one another. According to Gramsci, the intellectuals of an emergent class are " 'specializations' of partial aspects of the primitive activity of the new social type which the new class has brought into prominence" (6). At the same time, he also argues that the special task of these intellectuals is to define the class from which they come, for they are the ones to "give it homogeneity and awareness of its own function" (5). In order to account for intellectuals without destabilizing the categories of class based on productive labor, Gramsci has each class create its own intellectuals. But then what are intellectuals for, if not to return the favor by defining the class of people who have created them? It is instructive to trace the tautology organizing this influential description of intellectuals through a series of contradictions that unfold at other sites in Gramsci's writings where intellectual labor bursts out of its subordinated position and takes over the logic that attempts to confine it.

We turn first to his notes on the fetish. Drafted around 1933, this sketch of an idea can be understood as an attempt to rethink Marx's concept of the commodity fetish.[26] Marx foresaw a situation when men would no longer decide what they produced and consumed; instead, things would tell people what to desire in one another as well as in the world of objects. What he described was not only an object capable of inverting the relationship between people and things, but one that also overturned the relationship between signs and their users. Gramsci, too, attempts to explain the circumstances under which things get the upper hand on their makers and determine social relationships. He looks to the intellectual component of the object—the properties that transform it from an object to a sign that is capable not only of displacing the thing to which it refers but also of redefining those who consume it. Gramsci uses the logic of the fetish to spell out the tautology of the intellectual in a narrative form. Individuals accept a notion of themselves as a collective that they themselves have formulated: "A collective organism is made up of single individuals who form the organism in that they have given themselves a hierarchy and a determinate leadership which they actively accept" (243). It may be that some people accept what others have formulated on the basis of yet a third set of interests and values, so long as one presumes that the end of the story (i.e., the collective) exists in the beginning as that story's reason for being. The differences among sender, receiver, and context do not presuppose different social groups, so long as these functions identify positions within the collective. But what happens when the idea in fact succeeds in objectifying individual needs and wishes as a single idea—the idea of the collective? The collective then resembles the commodity that has incorporated the labor power that went into its manufacture as a property of the object itself: "If each of the single components thinks of the collective organism as an entity extraneous to himself, it is evident that this organism no longer exists in reality, but becomes a phantasm of the intellect, a fetish" (243). The fetish inverts the natural relationship between ideas and both their makers and their consumers. Like the commodity fetish, the collective takes on a sinister life of its own. It situates individuals in relation to one another according to a will that cannot be reduced to the sum total of individuals that have either produced or actively accepted the collective will as their own. In this respect, the collective is no longer the collective, Gramsci argues, but an ossified structure—resembling the church hierarchy—that survives on past the time when individuals actively made it universal and accepted it as such. The church objectifies the labor power that went into establishing the idea as a compelling feature of the belief system itself. These two different phases of the collective correspond to the two different kinds of intellectuals that enter into the class struggle at the level of ruling ideas.

Gramsci's sketch does not explain how the struggle to define the collective figures in the larger class struggle. He uses the marxist notion of the fetish analogically. By using the logic of commodity production to think about the production of ruling ideas, however, Gramsci suggests that mental and material production can indeed be thought about in similar terms. In both cases, it is the intellectual component—the object's capacity to signify—that goes haywire. If the commodity fetish represents the moment when people cease to be defined as producers and come to be understood in terms of what they consume, then the objectification of such bases for identity in writing effects a similar inversion. People cease to write and start to be written instead. At this point, the argument becomes curiously metaphorical and agentless. Gramsci's note on the fetish concludes: "An orchestra in rehearsal, each instrument playing for itself, gives the impression of the most dreadful cacophony. And yet these rehearsals are necessary for the orchestra to live as a single 'instrument' " (245). Does this mean that some fiction of unity, some score, is necessary in order for the collective to exist in the first place? If so, then the true collective would remain true only until its purely intellectual nature became evident as such. Then it would become the ossified structure that replaces the collective.

The essential continuity between ossified and spontaneous forms of social unity becomes apparent when one turns back to an essay Gramsci wrote fifteen years before the notebook entry on fetishism. In an article published in 1918, Gramsci refutes the accusation that Lenin's utopianism was arousing emotions and raising workers' economic expectations that could not be met in postrevolutionary Russia.[27] Gramsci confronts the argument for economic determinism on its own ground by disputing the principle that "political constitutions are necessarily dependent on economic structure, on forms of production and exchange" (45). An increase in earnings does not necessarily translate into a new quality of life, he insists. The worth of men should be seen not only "in terms of their weight, their size, and the mechanical energy they derive from muscles and nerves" but also "in the fact that they have a mind, that they suffer, understand, rejoice, desire and reject" (45–46). In a revolution, he claims, the "mind" is the "unknown variable." Who knows why it suddenly coalesces from the collective "*élan vital*" of a nation, especially when the minds of men coalesce to form a collective. On the assumption that "no act remains without consequences," he begins to consider what act could possibly cause men to assume that "mysterious form" called "humanity" (46).

"Theory," he reasons, "has its own particular impact on action" (46). While it is true that he stops well short of regarding "theory" as a political action in its own right, Gramsci does, on the other hand, situate what might be called intellectual events prior to changes in the conditions under which people work, making intellectual labor the necessary supplement to manual labor. He does this by shifting from "theory" to "interpretation": "It is not the economic structure which directly determines political activity, but rather the way in which that structure and the so-called laws which govern its development are interpreted. These laws," he continues, "have nothing in common with natural laws—even granting that natural laws too have no objective, factual existence, but are the constructs of our intelligence designed to facilitate study and teaching" (46). As in Marx, then, the professors are held responsible for transforming the interplay of modes of power into natural law. Only certain interpretations acquire the status of "laws," or "ruling ideas," and these ideas, rather than the economic structure itself, determine the political success or failure of that structure.

Gramsci's defense of vanguardism thus grants a temporary priority to intellectual labor over productive labor. Fully aware of the pitfalls of idealism to which this position is subject, he tries to give back with one hand what he has taken away with the other. He splits the intellectual in two. He distinguishes one from the other on grounds that one tells the truth (namely, Lenin) and the other speaks fiction (in the form of the ossified notion of the state that Gramsci would later sketch out in his account of the fetish). To make this distinction, he breaks apart the conventional coupling of economic necessity with fact. He then recombines these elements with another conventional pair—nonreferential language and fiction—and links nonreferential language with fact and economic necessity with fiction. Once he has shown that Lenin needed the element of intellectual labor to materialize the fantasy of a new political order, Gramsci puts causality back on the shoulders of productive labor. He returns to the idea that the distinction between intellectual and economic production is a distinction between fiction and fact. Gramsci concludes this discussion of utopianism by explaining how the imagined community will become real.

To meet the conditions of his argument in defense of Lenin, Gramsci describes revolutionary change as the growth of the public sphere:

> An uncultivated individual gets a chance to improve himself in the discussion over the election of his representative to the Soviet—he himself could be the representative. He controls these organs because he has them constantly under review and near to hand in the community. He acquires a sense of social responsibility, and becomes a citizen who is active in deciding the destiny of his country. Power and awareness are passed on, through the agency of this hierarchy. From one person to many: society is such as has never before appeared in history. (51–52)

Gramsci solves the problem of defending Lenin without subordinating productive to intellectual labor. He casts the worker, represented by the pronoun "he," in the role of narrative agent: he controls, he has the soviets constantly under review, he acquires, he becomes active. The worker is the grammatical subject of these sentences, but he is not the subject of the discourse. To have any agency at all, the hero of this narrative has to have a source of magic. In this tale, the donor gives the worker a chance to improve himself. The donor also sees to it that power and awareness are passed from one person to many ("through the agency of this hierarchy"). If the worker "controls these organs" of power-knowledge, it is only because power-knowledge allows him to do so; the worker controls the intellectual function of his class only as intellectuals make it possible for him to do so. He becomes one of them, not the other way around. They are his agency.

In this respect, Gramsci's story of the emergence of Soviet socialism reproduces Marx's account of surplus value. Both insist on the theoretical distinction between the production of words and of things. Both temporarily invert the materialist priority of things and ideas in order to attribute to people a power of knowledge over a world of things that includes their own labor. This move arguably situates a theoretical description of revolution within the framework of a magical narrative, or fiction. If their effort to exalt productive labor ultimately requires Marx and Gramsci to smuggle intellectual labor back into the argument through the subterfuges of fiction, then something equally curious results from efforts to isolate the intellectual function and grant it historical agency in its own right.

The idea that intellectual labor could provide the basis for an autonomous set of class interests was popular among social critics who sought to explain the dilemma of eastern Europe from the 1950s through the 80s. Under the Soviet style of socialism, bureaucrats did not appear to serve the interests of capitalists, and yet they had certainly broken their bond with the working class.[28] To launch a critique of this caste of intellectuals, George Konrad and Ivan Szelenyi declare: "We believe that the Eastern intellectual vanguard abused our epistemological innocence and, while pretending to carry out the 'historical mission of the proletariat,' in fact gradually established its own class domination over the working class" (3). Following Gramsci, Konrad and Szelenyi make productive labor the basis of political power. It gives them a moral basis for opposing the intellectuals in power. In contrast with Gramsci, however, they lived to see the Soviet-style bureaucracy become an objectification (of the state) rather than a living idea, much as the church was for Gramsci. They accordingly represent the new power of knowledge much as Gramsci did the fetish—as an idea that takes on a life of its own independent of the people who originally brought it into being. This is how they deal with the fact that "in planned economies especially under the bureaucratization of the state and the socialist labour movement, intellectuals gained a certain autonomy" (10).

Forty years of Soviet-style bureaucracy in eastern Europe made it increasingly difficult to explain who intellectuals were in terms of the class from which they came. Dissidents such as Konrad and Szelenyi saw party intellectuals and bureaucrats as people who had betrayed their class mission. They viewed these intellectuals as an aberration rather than an extension of the logic of class relations, as a class whose very identity derived from their violating the logic of class. The argument that eastern European intellectuals constituted a fourth class thus left the classical marxist model of class relations undisturbed. Like the theory of the fetish, fourth-class theory attached intellectual labor to classes that were economically determined and saw the intellectuals' quest for autonomy as a hallucination of the material conditions.

Barbara and John Ehrenreich's concept of a "professional-managerial class" is perhaps the most influential American attempt to create a new category for intellectual labor, no doubt because their observations tend to ring especially true for contemporary Americans.[29] The Ehrenreichs postulate a new class for those possessing the power of knowledge. The apparent autonomy of intellectuals is not an aberration of the class system, as the Ehrenreichs construe that system, but an extension of its logic. Around the end of the nineteenth century, conditions in the United States created a class within a class. The emergence of monopoly capitalism was marked by the emergence of a class specializing in the social and cultural reproduction of the modern ruling class. Although this new class is a "derivative" one, its appearance, according to the Ehrenreichs, "drastically altered the terms and conditions of class struggle at the workplace: diminishing the workers' collective mastery over the work process and undercutting the collective experience of socialized production" (15). Unlike the old "middle class," this new class was not made of self-employed artisans, shopkeepers, investors, professionals, or farmers. It was formed of those employed by capital to consolidate capital's "cultural hegemony over the working class, as the army of counselors, psychologists, teachers, etc., swelled from the twenties on" (25).

A generation or two down the line, the class interests and consciousness of such people necessarily diverged from those of the "ruling class," a divergence that shifted the basis of their power from economics to culture. "The son of the chairman of the board may expect to become a successful businessman (or at least a wealthy one) more or less by growing up; the son of a research scientist knows he can only hope to achieve a similar position through continuous effort" (19). Crucial to membership in the professional class is the kind of beginning a child receives in the home and the kind of education he receives at the university. As a result of professionals' insecurity about their own class reproduction, their anxiety settles around two cultural focal points:

All of the ordinary experience of life—growing up, giving birth, child rearing—are freighted with an external significance unknown in other classes. Private life thus becomes too arduous to be lived in private; the inner life of the PMC [professional-managerial class] must be continuously shaped, updated and re-

vised by—of course—ever mounting numbers of experts: experts in child raising, family living, sexual fulfillment, self-realization, etc., etc. The very insecurity of the class, then, provides new ground for class expansion. (30)

The rise of the professional class was therefore marked by a proliferation
of experts in the techniques of daily living and by the expansion of
university systems.

In that it posits an additional class whose interests oppose those of
both capitalist and worker, the argument for a new professional-managerial class resembles the argument for a fourth class put forward by
social theorists who were trying to account for the Cold War conditions
in eastern Europe. Both sets of arguments attempt to deal with the question of what happens when intellectuals get out of hand. Because the
American model relocates the basis of class interests in what might be
called cultural capital, it defines "intellectuals" as a category capable of
encompassing professors and artists, as well as doctors, lawyers, scientists,
and bureaucrats.[30] Remaining essentially true to Marx's categories of
class, the Ehrenreichs argue that a change in the demographic character
of the bourgeoisie had to occur before the bourgeoisie could secure its
hegemony. For this purpose, a new caste of experts assumed a position
of increasing importance within the newly established bourgeoisie. In so
doing, the experts eventually changed the means of class domination.[31]
They shifted the locus of power from the arena of production to that
of reproduction, from economic to cultural capital.

The idea of a new class emerging within a preexisting class would
appear to be the perfect compromise between a classical marxist model
of class and more recent accounts that are aware of the often independent
and central role that intellectuals, information, and the media play in
twentieth-century politics. The Ehrenreichs position intellectuals within
political economy, alongside the owners of money. Together, these two
classes consolidate the mental and material forms of domination. Although the two achieve social prominence by quite different means, in
the Ehrenreich's essay the professional-managerial class (PMC) exhibits
a fundamental spirit of cooperation with the capitalists. Both are defined
in relation to the family—the capitalist class produces and sustains it
biologically, the PMC reproduces it culturally. The capitalist is thus situated in the primary role, as the one who produces the bodies, while
the expert is placed in the secondary role of giving those bodies the
qualities associated with a ruling class—straight teeth, athletic proficiency,
social graces, and music lessons. The capitalist's role fades quietly from

this picture as the child grows and experts begin to hatch their own little experts. The capital of the capitalist has been translated into something else. Social reproduction has outstripped production. Thus the family provides the Ehrenreichs with the logic of an evolving class formation: kids grow up, and for them to do so in one way rather than another requires experts. Experts have children. These children require more experts.

In his analysis of intellectual labor, Rudolf Bahro elaborates the conflict between the operations of economic and cultural capital that are spliced together by the Ehrenreichs' narrative.[32] Bahro puts collective flesh on a relationship that takes the personified form of "the son of the chairman of the board" and "the son of a research scientist" in the Ehrenreichs' example. The moment reproduction outstrips production, in Bahro's view, the contradiction posed by the second function of Marx's capitalist begins to blossom into a cultural division of labor with far-reaching economic consequences.

During the 1970s, Bahro was first imprisoned and then exiled from what was then East Germany. Well aware of the risks of doing so, he asserted that Soviet socialism had created a situation where intellectual labor seemed to be undervalued. It would not entitle one to higher wages than productive labor. When both are calculated in terms of "units of labor," he argues, the ordinary reward for work done ceases to hold (209). From his perspective as a Communist Party member, it became obvious that those who were highly skilled had stopped competing to produce more or better products. In the absence of economic rewards, they were competing on some other basis. When money ceases to motivate labor, he reasoned, the quest for the "positions in the multi-dimensional system of the social division of labour, becomes the specific driving force of economic life characteristic of actual existing socialism" (212). His term for this driving force is "bureaucratic rivalry." Bureaucratic rivalry changes the whole system of economic relations into a struggle for administrative power, which is identified with maximum access to those above and minimum accountability to those below—both of which depend on the ability to gather, hoard, and dispense information. Bahro understands the formation of a professional-managerial class much as the Ehrenreichs do, as a shift from economic to cultural capital; but he rejects the idea that such a class arises from and ultimately serves the interests either of capital or of labor. His model gives intellectual labor the power to subordinate and eventually displace productive labor. Because it does so, however, Bahro's argument returns us to something like the position of Konrad and Szelenyi, which grants intellectuals the power to constitute themselves an autonomous class.[33]

At the risk of oversimplifying what is in actuality a complex series of responses to very different historical circumstances, let us conclude by summarizing the two ways in which theory has sought to resolve the contradiction posed by intellectual labor. One way overvalues productive labor by making intellectuals a subcategory of economically determined classes; but the effects of intellectual labor tend to disappear into the effects of productive labor, only to reappear in magical explanations for the emergence of capitalism (Marx) and socialism (Gramsci). We would be content to rest with this first way, if making intellectual labor a function of some economically predetermined class could explain the changes that occurred during the English Revolution. The second alternative we considered seems, in contrast, to overvalue intellectual labor; it assigns to intellectuals a position independent or even hostile to productive labor. This overvaluation may explain what went wrong in eastern Europe from the late 1940s until the late 1980s. But granting such autonomy to intellectuals cannot account for the intellectual component of capitalism that we have seen in the self-representation of Marx's owners of money, the self-serving services provided by the Ehrenreichs' professionals and managers, and the self-legitimating strategies that characterize modern authors. Where the first solution suppresses the conflict between intellectual and productive labor, the second allows a conflict within the modern middle class to overshadow the conflict between that class and those whom it succeeded in subordinating.

In fact, one can argue that both approaches undervalue intellectual labor, for neither uses the idea of intellectual labor to modify the economistic explanation of class. The example of the English Revolution invites us to remember that in so-called modern cultures the people in charge are always literate people who determine what literacy is, how one acquires it, and therefore who has access to the specific knowledge and privileges accompanying it. One finds, further, that modernity itself coincides with the rise of such people to a new position of authority. All this is commonplace. What is less readily acknowledged is the role that writing—simultaneously the means and the product of intellectual labor—played in the process, or how it acquired the power to displace permanently the aristocracy. The rest of this book considers the possibility that the class emerging in the wake of the English Revolution was at first made up of the owners of knowledge and only later and secondarily the owners of money. We think of the capitalist as a later sub-species of the intellectual. Such a hypothesis is the only way to get around the logical conundrum we have been elaborating. Theories that leave intellectuals out of the picture at the beginning of the modern period seem unable to account for intellectual labor later on. In the next chapter we try to show how many of the problems that haunt accounts of the transition from early modern to modern England can be resolved. We argue that the English Revolution was revolutionary because it allowed intellectual labor to get out of hand.

CHAPTER SIX

Signs of Personal Life

If the politics of sex makes little use of the law of the taboo
but brings into play an entire technical machinery, if what is
involved is the production of sexuality rather than the repression of sex, then ... we must shift our analysis away from
the problem of "labor capacity" and doubtless abandon the
diffuse energetics that underlies the theme of a sexuality repressed for economic reasons.

Michel Foucault,
The History of Sexuality: An Introduction

Let us return to Marx's capitalist at the point where, full of himself, he
dreams up the idea of surplus value. At this moment, Marx laminates
intellectual labor onto labor power much as fairy tales endow their heroes
with the special properties of a donor. Here and at all the little narrative
turns along the way that make the moment of the vulgar capitalist's
transformation possible, theory steps quietly aside and fiction becomes
the operative mode of narration. Political economy does not feel the
least bit threatened by the temporary suspension of logic; it is confident
that theory will be given credit for the whole affair. Ours is a culture
that will not grant historical agency to writing—a culture, moreover
where fiction is written transparently; it has no materiality in its own
right but confers reality on the type of people it is "about." If, on the
other hand, one wants to pursue the possibility that in a literal and quite
material sense writing is more than the thing it describes, then it stands
to reason we should seek out those places in our cultural past that
announce themselves as being nothing other than writing. We should
focus on writing that situates one where no one can really be situated,
that offers a view of the world through someone else's eyes, someone
in the process of authoring the kind of self we generally believe ourselves
to be. It is this anterior view of a self like ourselves that Milton offers
his readers, and this is why subsequent generations of readers alternately
admired and disapproved of him. Eighteenth-century fiction also offered

such a perspective on our own beginnings, but that fiction declared that its view was a fiction rather than truth.

If Marx succeeded in removing intellectuals from history, or at least in placing them to the side as spectators of and commentators on it, then our task is clear. It is necessary to question narratives that oppose intellectual to productive labor, dividing the world into the subjects and objects of discourse, respectively. By privileging productive labor, Marx and Gramsci were simply trying to bring theory—their way of classifying individuals and representing the destinies of nations—down to earth and make it socially responsible. Under the conditions that Marx describes in his chapter on fetishism, however, it is precisely this distinction between intellectual and productive labor that no longer obtains; its absence characterizes our time. Any concept of materialism that restricts causality to productive labor and to money simply takes up the other side of the idealism Marx was intent on refuting well over a century ago. We live in an age when the material effects of writing can no longer be denied.

The term "intellectual labor" sums up the disjunction between the terms "intellectual" and "labor" and indicates the logic we will pursue in showing the two concepts to be in fact one. Since most historians and social theorists deliberately choose not to reconsider the relationship between the two concepts, and especially the primacy of "labor," we have gone elsewhere for a narrative model that would allow us to look at the "intellectual" as an undervalued term in most accounts of late seventeenth-century English culture. Benedict Anderson has come up with the concept of "print capitalism" to describe the formation of a new kind of nation made of individuals who were affiliated with one another by the kind of literacy they shared.[1] Anderson does not provide a chronological account of this formation. He is not especially concerned with the process that transformed seventeenth-century England into the enormous bureaucracy of a modern imperial nation-state. Rather, he focuses on the difference between seventeenth-century Europe and an eighteenth-century American culture—a difference he represents by shifting geographical rather than historical frames of reference. There are certain things we can do with this model precisely because it does translate time into space. First, it is elegantly simple. It allows us to factor intellectual labor into the picture without either adding a new class or splitting an existing one into opposing factions. As Anderson shifts from one side of the Atlantic to the other, he also shifts the class struggle onto the plane of intellectual labor. His concept of "print capital" invites us to reconceptualize the struggle among economically determined classes as a struggle between intellectual and productive labor; this struggle brought economic domination to those who held a monopoly on information, knowledge, or truth. Second, Anderson illustrates the principle of print capitalism by focusing on what happened during the seventeenth century when the traditional ideals of Europe were carried abroad.

According to Anderson's account, an entirely new kind of nation was formulated in the New World as information was produced and distributed in vernacular English, French, Spanish, Dutch, or Portugese. Scattered throughout the New World to do the business of Europe were functionaries and bureaucrats who carried on an economic relationship, largely in print, with those who wrote and presumably spoke in their respective colonial environments the same European language as they spoke with their families, business partners, and government officials back home in Europe. Without print, Anderson surmises,

> the diversity of spoken languages, those languages that for their speakers were (and are) the warp and woof of their lives, was immense; so immense, indeed, that had print-capitalism sought to exploit each potential oral vernacular market, it would have remained a capitalism of petty proportions. But these varied idiolects were capable of being assembled, within definite limits, into print-languages far fewer in number. (46–47)

As European print languages circulated among those who no longer lived in their countries of origin, a new kind of individual came into being. This individual understood himself or herself as part of a community that shared a body of information acquired from newspapers and novels. The community so imagined connected the New-World European to Europe through the information that traveled back and forth across the Atlantic.[2] Literacy thus distinguished individuals who understood themselves in this way from the creole population with whom they lived and worked.

At the same time, their literacy made those of European parentage understand what they shared with those who were not of European birth. The two groups were bound together by their exclusion from the homeland. The New-World Europeans were a minority, both in relation to those with whom they did business back home and in relation to the creole population with whom they worked in America; nevertheless, they "constituted simultaneously a colonial community and an upper class" (59). Anderson proposes

> that neither economic interest, Liberalism, nor Enlightenment could, or did, create *in themselves* the *kind*, or shape, of imagined community to be defended from these regimes' depredations; to put it another way, none provided the

framework of a new consciousness—the scarcely-seen periphery of its vision—
as opposed to centre-field objects of its admiration or disgust. In accomplishing
this specific task, pilgrim creole functionaries and provincial creole printmen
played the decisive historic role. (65)

This concept of modern nationalism as an "imagined community" allows
Anderson to construct a narrative potentially compatible with Foucault's
concept of "discourse." Anderson's claim that the emergence of a new
form of literacy produced at once a new nation and a new ruling class
also recalls what Raymond Williams calls "the long revolution" in
England.[3]

By translating time into spatial terms and investigating the historical
effects of the information revolution in the New World, however, Anderson can show us certain things that Foucault and Williams cannot.
Foucault posits an absolute rupture between early modern monarchies
and the uses of representation that characterize institutional cultures;
Anderson explains how a whole new set of class interests formed around
the technologies of discourse as print became the basis on which a new
ruling class would rule.[4] Anderson's model has all the advantages of
Robinson Crusoe. It extends the logic of centralized European monarchy
beyond the reach of the European metropolis, allowing us to see how
the same logic might have begun to serve a contrary ideological purpose
in a setting with an entirely different past, a territory the European could
imagine as having no past at all.

The very term "print capitalism" also identifies the link between intellectual labor and the rise of a new middle class, and this is perhaps
what is most surprising. Sociologists, political theorists, and historians
have defined the modern "middle" class in a number of ways, but few
have accounted for the fact that literacy was what members of this class
obviously had in common at the dawn of modernity. The people whose
emergence and rise to power is chronicled by modern history were first
and foremost literate people. The increase in their ranks was commen-
surate with the spread of their brand of literacy, and from the beginning
they felt that their power depended on reproducing in print the information, news, and literature that spoke to their interests.[5] However various their means of making a living might seem, the livelihood of these
people was thus linked in some instrumental way to intellectual labor,
specifically that of authors.

According to Anderson's account, intellectual labor made the crucial
difference between the nations of the Old World and those of the New.
Precisely because he represents change in purely spatial terms, however,

Anderson gives us no way of explaining how a new class came into power back in Europe, or what this change had to do with the development of print capitalism in North America. We understand Anderson's disinclination to regard American history as a later chapter of western European history. However, it does not make sense to say that the New and the Old World parted company with the formation of American nations and thenceforth pursued independent historical trajectories. If the American colonies must be understood as a development and transformation of European history, it seems only reasonable to see modern Europe through the lens of New World nationalism—as cultures in which the print vernacular gained sudden and unprecedented authority, just as it had overseas. To do so, we need to make some relatively minor adjustments to Anderson's model.

Anderson abandons a rather traditional account of European history just when the European nations were about to enter the modern period. By shifting to the New World at exactly that moment, he does not have to consider what the circulation of new forms of information had to do with the onset of modernity in Europe—how did the monarchies of the seventeenth century turn into the great imperial bureaucracies of the nineteenth and early twentieth centuries? Anderson notes that print vernaculars were available in England well before print began to proliferate in British America. Still, he argues, "nothing suggests that any deep-seated ideological, let alone proto-national, impulses underlay this vernacularization where it occurred" (44). In his estimation, print vernaculars simply provided "well positioned would-be absolutist monarchs" with an instrument of centralization: "There was no idea of systematically imposing the language on . . . various subject populations" (44). In this way, Anderson helps to clarify the gap characterizing the literary and historical scholarship discussed in the first three chapters of this book. Social theory has also failed to consider adequately the effects of the writing that began to circulate in print during the late seventeenth and early eighteenth centuries. In order to account for this wide-reaching cultural change, then, one simply has to translate Anderson's concept of "print capitalism" back into European terms and approach the so-called revolution in words accordingly.

In *Discipline and Punish,* Foucault juxtaposes what he calls "the spectacle on the scaffold" with the architecture of the modern penal institution, the point being that a profound transformation of political power occurred at some time during the second half of the seventeenth century. Similarly, Williams describes the popular press as starting up suddenly at the end of that century; he thus represents this event as a radical break from monarchy rather than as an extension of older technologies of domination. With the monarchy's failure to renew its legal hold on the press, he contends, many previously suppressed interests were able to assert themselves in print, and English culture eventually got out from under the thumb of the old government. Although Foucault rejects narrative histories that emphasize the continuity between one age and the next, his account is actually quite compatible with the one proposed by Williams. Foucault cannot explain how the modern exercise of power emerged from what came before it, without subverting his effort to show that modern power operates through entirely different means and on an entirely new subject.

Most of us are disposed, along with Foucault and Anderson, to assume that during the seventeenth and eighteenth centuries social, political, and cultural events occurring in Europe should be given historical priority over those occurring in British America. Scholars and critics tend to assume that culture flowed westward from Europe to America. Especially when it comes to the English language, how can one doubt that it came from there to here in space as well as time? Yet recent research suggests otherwise. Having reviewed this material, Michael Warner calls attention to the often overlooked fact that during the last half of the seventeenth century, there were actually more presses in the colonies than in England.[6] Equally important, those who immigrated to the New World during the seventeenth century possessed a much higher rate of literacy than the population back in Europe. "By 1765," Warner tells us,

> print had come to be seen as indispensable to political life, and could appear to men such as Adams to be the primary agent of world emancipation. What makes this transformation of the press particularly remarkable is that, unlike the press explosion of the nineteenth century, it involved virtually no technological improvements in the trade. . . . The material constraints on the press—such as the scarcity of paper or the lack of skill to cast type domestically—remained in force until the end of the eighteenth century. Nevertheless, printing changed both in character and in volume, after 1720 growing much faster even than the population. (32)

Such a gap between literacy and its technological manifestations gives substance to Foucault's hypothesis that epistemology precedes technology. From the explosion of print, one can infer that the colonies were populated by individuals who had been so educated as to feel compelled, once they were overseas, to represent themselves in print precisely because they were deprived of the highly developed English-speaking culture to which they had belonged back in England. If the geographical dislocation of these people gives Anderson an agent and motive for the emergence of a new print culture, why not adopt his model to think about the impact of the spread of print back in Europe? In certain respects, late-seventeenth- and eighteenth-century England can be understood as an emergent nation too.

It is not necessary to identify what was revolutionary about a revolution whose political effects were felt much later on, if one is willing to take quite literally Hill's and Stone's point of agreement—that the English Revolution was a revolution in words.[7] It seems more reasonable to understand the empowering of words (or what Anderson calls "print capital") as the immediate and irreversible effect of the upheavals England experienced during the 1640s. Even when in 1660 a Stuart monarch was returned to the throne, the power of the monarchy was never to be the same again. One could argue that this was because the power of words had changed so profoundly. From what we know about the writing that appeared in the years immediately following the Restoration, it is fairly obvious that no renewal of censorship could succeed in reversing this change. The urgency with which Roger L'Estrange tried to restore the aristocratic monopoly on printed information only seems to testify to the fact that an older style of monarchy was impossible in the new semiotic environment.[8] In effect, one could say, the iconicity of Renaissance culture disintegrated with the severing of the monarch's head, and the most cherished signs and symbols of English culture took up a life independent of the monarch's body. No longer under the control of church and state, meaning was decided elsewhere and served other interests. As Williams's account of "the long revolution" suggests, meaning was decided by a community of educated people. And Foucault's theory of "discourse" implies that, as the locus of that meaning changed, the power of determining what and how things could mean increased exponentially.[9] If one follows Foucault's line of argument to its conclusion, one can understand how the practices that began to cluster around writing might have acquired a power that produced not only new class affiliations but a new form of nation-state as well.[10]

By thinking of Foucault's story of the rise of discourse as a European version of Anderson's account of the relationship between print and emergent nationalism in North America, we do not have to add a new class or to turn up new evidence of social change. To imagine English history in terms of the change that Anderson uses in describing the difference between the Old and the New World, one simply has to reverse

the priorities implied by the Ehrenreichs' chronology.[11] Foucault's ge-
nealogies of power indicate that what the Ehrenreichs call "the old middle class" was never really a class of money owners as that class is
generally assumed to be, at least not in the North American colonies.
Anderson suggests another reason why writing should suddenly become
the kind of authority we are suggesting. Where the nobility could be
illiterate and still be powerful, he contends, the bourgeoisie could only
come "into being as a class in so many replications" (74). Intellectual
labor did not play the secondary role in Anderson's narrative of New
World nationalism that it did in most histories of Europe. Writing could
not have empowered those who had already established themselves by
economic means. Indeed, if there is any lesson to be learned from Anderson's account, it is simply that print capitalism had to be in place
before the colonies secured economic independence from England.[12] To
suggest how the power of literacy might also have remodeled the mother
country in the image of its former colony in this one respect, however,
we have to correct a second omission in Anderson.

Anderson not only abandons England at the moment when the print
vernacular was about to serve interests hostile to monarchy, he also
neglects to say what role fiction played in making the New World nations.
Novels, even more than newspapers, seem to offer Anderson the best
example of an "imagined community" that characterizes New World
nationalism.[13] Anderson assumes that the appearance of newspapers and
novels is the unmistakable symptom of a nation's modernity, without
explaining what part they themselves play in its modernization. What
else if not newspapers and novels refashioned the whole idea of class
and nation by calling a modern readership into being? Yet Anderson
denies the logical implications of his own argument, refusing to let it
challenge European historiography. "What brought together, on the same
page, *this* marriage with *that* ship, *this* price with *that* bishop," he insists,
was not fictions but "the very structure of the colonial administration
and the market system itself" (62). In this way, he reasserts the idea that
"real" capitalism controlled "print" capitalism and gave it meaning: what
brought information together on the same page was "the very structure
of the colonial administration and the market system itself." How does
this square with his assertion that the nation in question was one made
by print? In order for print to form the basis of an "imagined community,"
"*this* marriage" had to be placed in a specific relationship with "*that*
ship." If newspapers presented an already existing relationship between
these kinds of information, then in what sense did print revise the idea

of the nation? Alternatively, if newspapers produced what Anderson calls an "imagined community," then who could have produced the "imagined community" characterizing an emergent nation if not people who already thought they belonged to that community? If such a profound and irreversible change in the basis for national affiliation did occur, what made it happen? The question of agency rears its head; and neither page, nor print, nor the ability and desire to read print qualify for this role.

The dualism that makes things appear more real than the words that define them is apparent not only in the phrase "print capitalism" but in "imagined community" as well. Embedded in Anderson's terminology is the assumption that where there is an "imagined" community there must be a "real" one that is outside and prior to its imaginary counterpart. Print, in other words, transformed the way of life in which people had exchanged objects and information with the same people they met in church, with whose families they might intermarry. In order to feel the affiliation that molded them into a new ruling class, people did not have to meet, trade, marry, or even contemplate a relationship beyond that of reading the same information in the same language. Anderson postulates a real community based on economic relations as the cause of the "imagined community" which comes into being with print capitalism. Foucault, on the other hand, can prevent our argument from collapsing back into the epistemology of realism that haunts most accounts of intellectual labor.

Foucault prevents this collapse by including words and things within a single field of cultural practices, over which print suddenly began to exercise unprecedented power sometime during the late seventeenth century. He circumvents the kind of rationalism (once celebrated by the Royal Society) that makes one look through words to people and things. He reconstructs a moment in history when power shifted from a human agent and the practices of the body, to writing and the mind of the subject. The people whose emergence into power marks the advent of modern history did not so much write, in Foucault's account, as they *were written.* New techniques of gathering, organizing, and disseminating information not only empowered certain people but also made them who they were—each a world of consciousness bounded by the body.

Foucault is among a handful who locate agency in print itself, on the grounds that it changes those who use it. He is practically alone in identifying the most personal recesses of the subject as precisely the territory that writing opened to social exploration and conquest. In contrast with both Williams and Anderson, he refuses to posit an economic cause for a textual effect. Instead, he asks us to reconsider the relationship between our most personal feelings, the world of work and government external to our selves, and the textualizing practices that appear to mediate between them. He also calls for a history that explains how these fundamental and enduring differences between subject, object, and writing came into being in the first place. By the time he wrote *The History of Sexuality,* Foucault had already provided a sequence of off-center, many-stranded histories to suggest that historical change could not be represented in any other form. His work that preceded *The History of Sexuality* suggested, further, that such change was accomplished largely through small revisions, new connections, filaments of explanation broken off and rearticulated to new objects that would therefore serve very different ends.

One strand of a Foucaultian account of historical change might begin with the proliferation of grammar books and a whole battery of new genres that emerged during the late seventeenth century in England. Then it might trace the effects of such writing on speech and emotion until, some time late in the eighteenth century, these texts began to determine how people thought of themselves as human beings. It has been deftly argued that during the eighteenth century, "ideas about language firmly distinguished those who were within the civilized world from those who were completely outside it."[14] Those who used a refined version of English were supposedly "rational, moral, civilized, and capable of abstract thinking," while the use of what were regarded as "baser" forms revealed the speaker as someone limited by "the concerns of the present, an interest in material objects, and the dominance of the passions" (3). Speech produced a fundamental division between classes by distinguishing one person from another, and it was through a form of speech based on writing that one class gained prestige and power over the other. To make this point, Olivia Smith writes:

> Bishop Lowth, author of the first comprehensive grammar (1762), Samuel Johnson, author of the *Dictionary of the English Language* (1765), and James Harris, author of *Hermes* (1751), the major theorist of universal grammar in England, form something of a linguistic trinity. These three seminal works, appearing almost within a decade of each other, indicate the acceleration of the study of language, making its initiation into a more prominent social role and simultaneously perpetuating the even greater role that it would have later. (4)

When books by Bishop Lowth and John Wesley made grammar the sign of a person's innermost character, they were more explicit but not es-

sentially different in either kind or effect from other books that attempted
to regulate the use of the English language. All reflect a situation where
print played a more substantial role in English culture than formerly.

As Smith points out, the "following sentence which Lowth asks his
students to parse combines an exercise in grammar with a lesson in
morality: 'The power of speech is a faculty peculiar to man, and bestowed
upon him by his beneficent Creator for the greatest and most excellent
uses; but alas! how often do we pervert it to the worst of purposes' "
(8–9). To compile such statements and put them into print is to put into
operation a twofold assumption about the status of print. The statement
proceeds on the assumption that a person's writing represents the way
he or she speaks, which in turn represents the way he or she thinks and
feels, and thus his or her capacity for action.[15] But the same statement
also proceeds on the assumption that writing produces specific forms of
speech, thought, and emotion. To regulate the English language in print,
then, was to produce a whole new set of motivations and behaviors that
became meaningful in relation to the written word. By the mid-eighteenth
century, writing had acquired the power to classify other forms of labor
and to define those who performed them on the basis of whether they
possessed or lacked literacy.

But it is not enough, for our purposes, to call attention to the increasing power of written communication in England. If that strand of
historical information is to say something about the emergence of a new
class of people, one must not assume that that class existed as such
before its members used language in one form rather than another. On
this one point, we would take issue with Smith, who sees grammar as
something that imposes the standards of class on people who have already
formulated an identity outside the language community. Cultural historians critical of the middle-class hegemony tend to think of culture as
something that represses human nature; however, Foucault asks us not
to think of culture in such negative terms. He argues that writing in fact
produces precisely what it seems to be repressing, denying, constraining,
or otherwise regulating. To suggest what made the difference between
the old and new societies within England itself, then, we have to examine
another strand in the snarl of microevents that so changed the status and
effects of writing.

A group of cultural historians primarily associated with the *annaliste*
tradition of French historiography have recently begun to investigate the
development of a private sphere around sexual reproduction and child
rearing.[16] It must be stressed, however, that public and private are not

necessarily separate; this was pointed out by Philippe Ariès in his introduction to the third volume of *A History of Private Life*. In the late
Middle Ages, Ariès argues, an individual and his or her family "moved
within the limits of a world that was neither public nor private as those
terms are understood today or were understood at other times in the
modern era," for "private was confounded with public, 'chamber' with
exchequer."[17] In order for the modern individual to emerge, privacy as
it was understood by early modern individuals had to undergo a radical
change. Privacy traditionally referred to activities that took place within
the inner sanctum of elite culture—namely, the political policy-making
activity located within royal and aristocratic households, from which the
vast majority of people were excluded. What would it have meant for
political policy to constitute a private domain secured from the eyes of
the populace? To this question Ariès responds, "First, and crucially, it
meant that . . . many acts of daily life were, and for a long time would
continue to be, performed in public" (1). Privacy had nothing to do with
sexual reproduction except in those rare cases where marriage or childbirth was a state secret. Drawing on the work of Norbert Elias, Roger
Chartier concludes that "in England by the end of the seventeenth century
and in France during the eighteenth, a private space began to develop
outside of government."[18] Yves Castan characterizes the early modern
period as one of equipoise between the two concepts of privacy; one
referred to the government's power over the people—its right "to govern
their work, their leisure, and the use they made of their property, positions, and even, in the case of the family, their bodies."[19] The other had
to do with "the authorized defense of the civil liberty of each individual
insofar as that individual's behavior was not governed by law or the
duties of office" (43). Together, this particular group of historians argues
that the emergence of the second meaning of "privacy" marks the onset
of modernity in Europe.

Such a reversal of cultural meaning and valences goes right to the
heart of our argument. For one thing, it links the history of the family
to a set of values and a rhetorical position that are hostile to those of
centralized monarchy. For another, the shift of "privacy" from elite political circles to the sanctuary of the ordinary household implies a relationship between writing and the practices around sexual reproduction.
As one examines what might seem an insignificant change in daily practices having to do with reading, writing, the care of the body, and the
creation of a private living space, pieces of a narrative begin to fall into
place. The narrative describes a relatively abrupt and irreversible change

that took place in the most basic categories of western European culture.

From what we can gather from the French historians of the family, the struggle that transformed the meaning of "privacy" was the same struggle that brought the modern family into being. Jacques Gélis describes the early modern family as one among whom "the blood tie was so powerful that . . . [the] body was not totally individual, totally independent of the family."[20] Under these circumstances, the child was "a public child" who belonged to the family (311). At about the same time, in the urban centers the child was beginning to occupy a space of its own: "Increasingly it was seen as the property of the individual, not the family" (316). In effect, such an argument suggests that the privatization of the family changed the whole idea of what a family was. What had previously been a single body of individuals, any one of whom could be replaced, became a cluster of spatially fixed, individuated bodies, each of which had a unique identity. In the introduction to the second section of A History of Private Life, volume 3, Roger Chartier supports Gélis's contention that the family underwent a profound change during the seventeenth century, by showing how during this same period people were beginning to regard the body as something that was supposed to be owned and controlled by the person inhabiting it. Jacques Revel offers evidence that it became unfashionable to display openly the emotions that had once testified to the sensibility that distinguished members of the aristocracy. Crying became something one should do only in private—and this helped to produce the modern notion that anything leaking out from inside the body should be regarded as strictly one's own.[21] Jean-Louis Flandrin substantiates the same line of thinking as Revel when he shows how certain changes in the rules of hygiene shifted the focal point of cleanliness from the visible surface of the body—linen, hands, and face—to the covered, sexual parts and bodily orifices.[22] This change in the definition of dirt was another way of remaking the symbolic distinction between private interior and social exterior. Together, these bits of information add up to a rather clear equation between the privatization of the family and the production of the modern individual.

The French historians of the family also reveal a curious correlation between, on the one hand, the privatization of practices having to do with sexual reproduction and child rearing, and on the other, the redefinition of certain intellectual practices. Probably as many essays in the second and third volumes of A History of Private Life consider the practice of writing as deal with changes in the concept of the individual. The essays on writing examine the practice of memoir and journal writing, the collection of souvenirs, and the customs of silent reading and of private writing, for signs that a modern individual was present in these events. Indeed, historians seeking out the origins of private life have to deal with the fact that the practice of writing memoirs and journals was already flourishing among the elites during the seventeenth century. And with this fact inevitably come certain questions: If certain areas in early modern culture were already reserved for what we now consider private experiences, then what change occurred in the character and capabilities of those areas during the course of the century?[23] What brought this change about, and how did it empower a new class of people? Why, as Jean Marie Goulement asks, was all literature "influenced by a similar affirmation of private life" (385)? "It is tempting," Goulement argues, "to assume that this evolution was relatively simple and clear-cut: that a private space did emerge, that its emergence aroused resistance, and that it became a site of transference and investment of new values" (385). But evidently that is not the way it was. The kind of privacy that developed around the ordinary care of the body, emotional life, and sexual reproduction did not constitute a space outside of the social, but one both within society and outside of the state. In so reclassifying these activities, writing can be said to observe the logic of supplementarity, whereby inclusion of an extra element substantially changes the system of relationships as a whole. But although they lead readers toward this conclusion, the French historians of the family cannot make them rethink history accordingly.

Content to draw suggestive parallels between the practice of writing and the privatization of whole sectors of daily experience, these historians repeat the mistake of their English counterparts in taking the relationship between writing and personal life for granted. They assume that any change in the way life was written somehow proceeds from changes in the way life was lived. At the very moment when they should reconsider the relationship between verbal and sexual experience, they reinstate the traditional categories of history. They assume that words more or less accurately interpret people and events that already exist. They do not look beyond diaries, journals, accounts of manners, conduct literature, and other writings about the family for evidence of the changing status and meaning of privacy. By confining their research on privacy to information that we now consider relevant to the family, they inadvertently betray their own first principle and take the modern concept of "the private" for granted, as well as its distinction from the category of "the political."

Not all historians have taken the category of "the private" for granted, however. Jacques Donzelot, for one, identifies the moment of its self-enclosure as the moment when the family became politically powerful in an entirely new way. His *Policing of Families* elaborates a web of subtle but mutually authorizing connections between maternal authority and the medical profession.[24] This web provided the nearly invisible means of cutting the family free from the state and also, as Donzelot's title suggests, of "policing" the family. The web sealed the family hygienically around the child to keep out social contaminants, and it also charged the mother with the all-important work of maximizing the physical and mental potential of that child. Claiming to exist solely for the well-being of the child, the mother-doctor nexus established once and for all the unquestionable value of each human body in the abstract. At the same time, however, the mother-doctor nexus subordinated what had been powerful forms of lay knowledge—often female forms of knowledge—to the expertise of professionals. Extrapolating from Donzelot's example, one could argue that the privatization of the family not only necessitated the redefinition of the nation as a population but also brought that nation under the care of professionals. When he made certain changes in the family central to the history of the family, then, Donzelot also made those changes in the family central to the history of the state. Thus one can say that the formation of the private sphere was not a minor event but a reconception of cultural categories that transformed the political sphere as well.[25]

Donzelot describes a specific site at which the division of public and private occurred. He allows us to imagine how the political authority that was once part of the elite conception of privacy was split off from the private and then subordinated to the heads of respectable households, and from there given over to the professional people who grew in numbers and power as they took over the care of these households. In this respect, he gives us reason to locate the formation of what the Ehrenreichs call the professional-managerial class at a much earlier point in modern history, where these specialized caretakers have a central role to play in the middle-class hegemony. But one thread of vital importance to our narrative remains disconnected from the historical bundle whose interdependence we are trying to establish. Donzelot does not really help make the connection between, on the one hand, the privatization of the family and the empowerment of a new class of people, and on the other, the proliferation of print. It is to Foucault that we must return in order to figure writing into the process.

Foucault's multivolume study of the history of sexuality begins by invoking the conventional view that the advent of modernity was marked by a puritanical form of censorship leveled against individual sexuality: "The seventeenth century, then, was the beginning of an age of repression emblematic of what we call the bourgeois societies, an age which perhaps we still have not completely left behind. Calling sex by its name thereafter became more difficult and more costly."[26] But this gesture at giving convention its due is the beginning of a process by which Foucault turns the whole concept of censorship upside down. If, as we have argued, people did not renounce literacy or stop thinking in writing during the periods when censorship was officially imposed, then it is equally possible that censorship was not actually lifted simply because Parliament failed to renew the Licensing Act of 1662. The Licensing Act was replaced by a different form of censorship—different in its effect as well as in its object and means. "Areas were thus established," Foucault reminds us, "if not of utter silence, at least of tact and discretion: between parents and children, for instance, or teachers and pupils, or masters and domestic servants. This almost certainly constituted a whole restrictive economy, one that was incorporated into that politics of language and speech" (18). But whereas silences seem to have been "imposed" where previously statements had been made and desires enacted, practically the opposite phenomenon occurred at the level of what Foucault calls "discourse." When we shift our focus away from *what* people were supposed to be saying and doing, and onto *how* they were saying and doing it, the repressive hypothesis no longer holds: "There was a steady proliferation of discourses concerned with sex—specific discourses, different from one another both by their form and by their object: a discursive ferment that gathered momentum from the eighteenth century onward" (18).

By the "discourse of sexuality," Foucault does not simply mean either material that made mockery of the new code of decency or information directly concerned with sexual reproduction—although attempts to suppress sexually explicit subject matter were indeed involved in the "ferment."[27] During the eighteenth century, man's sexuality, and during the nineteenth, woman's sexuality, were infiltrating all manner of writing at the very time when Williams, Anderson, Smith, Chartier, and others tell us that the amount of print was increasing exponentially and its power escalating as well. Sexuality had to be taken into account not only in medicine but also in the law and in political theory. During the nineteenth century, as Anita Levy has persuasively argued, the human sciences developed around the problem of working-class sexuality (i.e., sociology), the sexuality of colonial populations (i.e., anthropology), and the sexuality of white, middle-class women (i.e., psychology).[28] Thus, as she demonstrates, the restrictions on sexuality cannot be understood as restrictions on desirous individuals who already existed as such. At some point during the late seventeenth century, the older form of censorship became obsolete even before its repeal. The form of censorship that mattered was the one that worked hand in glove with the discourse of sexuality. For it produced the very thing it was intended to repress—a desire present in each individual's body at birth, an identity prior to that given him by the state, an energy hostile to the social order and requiring new strategies of management. It was true that "one had to speak of sex . . . publicly and in a manner that was not determined by the division between licit and illicit," as Foucault explains:

> One had to speak of it as of a thing to be not simply condemned or tolerated but managed, inserted into systems of utility, regulated for the greater good of all, made to function according to an optimum. Sex was not something one simply judged; it was a thing one administered. It was in the nature of a public potential; it called for management procedures; it had to be taken charge of by analytical discourses. (24)

Volume 1 of *The History of Sexuality* argues, in effect, that sexuality was essential to all aspects of Enlightenment rationalism. It lurks in the transparent language of the Royal Society and in the grammars that aimed at suppressing English dialects—for what, if not the sexual elements of human nature, are the materials that must be screened out as hostile to linguistic transparency? What are the seductive qualities of rhetoric, if not signs of irrational thoughts in the mind of the author and an invitation to readers to share them?

It is difficult to imagine how rationalism could have acquired much authority if it had not come into being alongside a notion of sexuality that defined human desire as something requiring mental control. But the discourse of sexuality had arguably its most lasting impact through literature. Theater tended steadily toward melodramas that turned on the repression or absence of sexual gratification and that consequently produced countless ways of representing the feelings that accompany the lack of gratification and sexual fulfillment. Poetry tended with equal determination toward dramatic monologues that accomplished much the same thing during the Victorian period. As our final chapter shows, the fiction which came into fashion during the eighteenth century rearticulated social relationships in terms of the urge—however misunderstood, thwarted, displaced, or twisted—to form a modern family unit. On the discovery, containment, and redeployment of what was understood as a single reproductive drive was made to depend not only the wholeness of the individual as an individual but also the survival of the state as a free and all-encompassing nation.[29]

Foucault's brief history of sexuality during the modern period shows that "sexuality" began in prose; it passed from there into speech, where it was used to interpret behavior; and eventually it came to produce thoughts, feelings, wishes, and dreams. So the very sexuality that we seek to liberate when we try to undo repression, is likely to be the sexuality first formulated in writing and disseminated in print about three centuries ago. Foucault does not stress the tendency on the part of modern social critics to equate this sexuality with freedom; but we see this tendency in a sexual utopianism that recurs periodically throughout the modern period as the alternative and antidote to middle-class culture. Engels succumbed to this cultural impulse in his treatise on marriage and the family.[30] In *Culture and Anarchy*, Matthew Arnold apparently had much the same set of alternatives in mind when he argued for high "culture" as the means of countering the ordinary Englishman's belief in "doing as one likes."[31] One has to credit Arnold with an understanding of the power of culture, in the modern sense of the term. In proposing culture as a means of government, he returns us to the twin issues of literature and censorship with which this chapter began. He argues that neither the courts of law, nor speeches made in Parliament, nor the religious debates rocking England during his time, nor even the most probing and extensive scientific reports, decided who people thought they were, what they wanted, and what they were entitled to do as Englishmen. The official discourses of any culture have authority only to the degree that they appropriate meanings and messages formulated at a more basic level that might be called everyday life. Art alone, in Arnold's opinion, was able to intervene at this level and infuse some attitudes and practices with beauty and morality, while identifying others with the darkness.

Even if we reject Arnold's conviction that the world would be a better place were high culture to manage low culture through education, one has to concede his point that middle-class authority works far more effectively through consent than coercion. Neither official nor analytical discourse has anything like the power of fiction to regulate and to persuade. It is arguably not so important what people think about the state when they know they are under its power. They may, as Marx and others have argued, be aware of the precise nature of their exploitation and nevertheless go to work with perfect regularity. Much more important is what it means *not* to be under the thumb of owners, supervisors, police, institutions, or parents. That mass cultures induce people to do certain things under these circumstances is what really keeps a modern population in line. People are, Foucault suggests, governed by the concept of freedom—as defined by literature, and especially fiction, but also by sketches and line drawings, newspapers, photo albums, and more recently, radio, sound and video recordings, television, and film. The formation of leisure as a space to be progressively occupied, managed, and commodified cannot be distinguished from the proliferation of the very genres that Arnold wants to subordinate to the themes and procedures of elite culture. As a leisure-time activity, we are suggesting, information in the print vernacular began to organize a cultural space for people to occupy when they were not at work or under the supervision of the state in any way. And while they were enjoying this form of freedom, it infiltrated their fantasies and dreams and whispered in their heart of hearts just who they could and could not be in order to be truly themselves.

Having thus brought Anderson's narrative of New World nationalism back to Europe and infused it with Foucault, one must come face to face with a surprisingly simple conclusion. Simple, because we have described the modern middle class not as a class of owners and merchants so much as a class of people whose power derives from a monopoly on information, knowledge, or truth. Surprising, because such a conclusion goes a long way toward reconciling Foucault's claim that the power of discourse governs modern history with Marx's claim that the power of capital governs modern history. Our conclusion allows us to leave marxist historiography intact and still account for intellectual labor without either subdividing each class or adding another. One simply has to enlarge and specify historically the category of intellectual labor. All our sources point in this direction.

In a letter to Marx written in 1858, Engels voiced his frustration that "this most bourgeois of all nations is apparently aiming ultimately at the possession of a bourgeois aristocracy and a bourgeois proletariat *as well as* a bourgeoisie."[32] He was referring to the power of English culture to reproduce itself—a power no other national culture seemed to have exercised with quite the same efficiency. In this letter, Engels identifies the power of the "bourgeoisie" with the aggressive appropriation and remodeling of an earlier, aristocratic culture. This distinguishes the English bourgeoisie from that of other nations. Lawrence and Jeanne C. Fawtier Stone refer to this letter only to disagree sharply with it (410–11). Where Engels saw the whole nation becoming middle class, the Stones think of modernity as the spread of genteel culture. They imagine culture as something that originated in an aristocratic England and descended upon the aspiring classes from above. In their view, the landed elites "psychologically" co-opted "those below them into the status hierarchy of gentility" (410). For the Stones, then, the emergent class was made up of people who sought gentility by emulating everything they associated with the elite way of life.

There is no question that, as the Stones suggest, the emergent class did appropriate many of the features of the culture it was replacing. However, the Stones ignore the fact that this appropriation might well have been part of a struggle between the two groups for control of the most cherished signs and symbols of English culture. The Stones do not see culture in terms of a conflict by means of which the new class consolidated itself and acquired power. Like Engels, they do not acknowledge the radical nature of such aggression. Moreover, they ignore the most important implication of their own theory of cultural change— namely, that the acts of cultural appropriation that brought modern culture into being were propelled, not by the English love of freedom, but by the inherently conservative desire of every man of independent means to be the monarch of his own little castle. When taken up by a new group of people, however, the fantasy that property could constitute an autonomous political sphere transformed an aristocratic England. Rather than a society organized around the court and manor houses, this fantasy legitimated a society composed of individuated and privatized family units. The same fantasy authorized a cast of intellectuals and bureaucrats to manage that society.

The Reproductive Hypothesis

It is through abolishment of dietary taboos, partaking of
food with pagans, verbal and gestural contact with lepers, as
well as through its power over impure spirits that the message of Christ is characterized and, as is well known, compels
recognition in a most spectacular manner—superficial perhaps
but striking. Those indications should not be construed as
simply anecdotal or empirical, nor as drastic staging of a po-
lemic with Judaism. What is happening is that a new arrangement of difference is being set up, an arrangement whose
economy will regulate a wholly different system of meaning,
hence a wholly different speaking subject. An essential trait
of those evangelical attitudes or narratives is that abjection is
no longer exterior. It is permanent and comes from within.
Threatening, it is not cut off but is reabsorbed into speech.

Julia Kristeva, The Power of Horror

The forbidden fruit of *Paradise Lost* indicates that in placing prohibitions
on human nature, culture calls a whole new form of nature into existence,
a nature that requires precisely such regulations. This is Foucault's revision of what he calls "the repressive hypothesis." Foucault lived in a
culture that prides itself on its scientific and materialist models for explaining the mysteries of nature and the vicissitudes of history. Where
Milton could simply credit God with making and enforcing the rules,
Foucault has to locate such cultural agency elsewhere. It is significant,
then, that in arguing for the productive effects of certain prohibitions,
Foucault steadfastly refuses to locate agency either in individuals or in
the class from which they come. He turns the picture around and tries
to see how writing and the institutional practices giving it the character
of "discourse" in turn wrote both the subjects *(The History of Sexuality)*
and human objects *(Discipline and Punish)* of knowledge. In this way,

he represents writing as being like any other kind of work that transforms the material universe into a world of meaningful objects, one that determines not only what relationships bind those who do such work to one another but also how they feel about themselves and others.

We have already explained how Foucault stresses the individuating capacity of the writing that proliferated during the late seventeenth and the eighteenth century. This writing identified those who possessed a certain kind of literacy as people who lived a certain kind of life as well. By reproducing the constellation of symbolic practices that belonged to personal life, however, this writing was not representing something that existed elsewhere or in some other way. As Foucault explains, the language in question was most literary precisely where it appeared to be most faithful to nature. An individual's sexual desires no longer played the role of the devil in man's continuing struggle to overcome temptation and achieve redemption. After a certain point in history, talking about desire was not talking about temptations or the vicissitudes of the soul, it was talking about the natural claims of the body and one's ability to manage them. In purporting to discover the facts of human nature (that is, the facts of body and mind and their relationship) beneath the veneer of religion, writing, as Foucault describes it in the first volume of *The History of Sexuality,* produced the kind of individuals who could be known, evaluated, and governed strictly through writing. Foucault attends to the production of the self-enclosed individual, but he takes the framework in which this occurs—that is, the nation—largely for granted.

Benedict Anderson's concept of "imagined community" might be said to err in the other direction. In focusing on the formation of a new kind of nation, Anderson takes the existence of such self-enclosed individuals for granted. He assumes that the connections of *"this* marriage with *that* ship, *this* price with *that* bishop" have to be made in order for such individuals to form a collectivity.[1] It probably was, as he says, "the very structure of the colonial administration and the market system itself" that caused these connections to be made on the pages of colonial newspapers. But by virtue of coexisting on the page, it can be argued, the bits of printed matter in turn helped produce a social organization that ultimately challenged the European bureaucracy. The economic and political information that bound individuals to an early modern administration and maintained the commercial relationship between two continents became the basis for a new system of differences in the colonies. These bonds became the "exterior" facts of a remote and disconnected "interior" existence. What linked New-World Englishmen to one another in a coherent community was not so much their connection with the monarch and his surrogates back in Europe as the fact that they could share their personal isolation in the colonies. Cut off from one another as much as from the people back home, their self-enclosure in families and villages was made known to them through letters, sermons, and a variety of published accounts of others who existed in a similar situation, individuals whom they were likely never to know in any other way.[2] Fact had no special advantage over fiction in this respect. If anything, fiction had the edge.

Yet neither Foucault nor Anderson takes fiction all that seriously. As a culture developed the kind of "imagined community" associated with New World nationalism, Anderson reminds us, it tended to produce great novels—works of fiction written in the creole language that simultaneously declare what is specific to that culture and place the emerging nation among the other novel-producing nations. Anderson cites the example of such novels to illustrate the intricate network of linguistic relationships in which a mass readership both imagines itself to be living and, through the activity of reading, actually exists as a nation. He describes such fiction as "a device for the presentation of simultaneity in 'homogeneous empty time,' or a complex gloss upon the world of 'meanwhile' " (31). In this respect, only the novel resembles the community that Anderson has in mind. Of the writing available in print, only the novel is composed of various acts that may all be "performed at the same clocked, calendrical time, but by actors who may be largely unaware of one another" (31). These characters are nevertheless "embedded in societies" that have a "firm and stable reality." The print vernacular makes these otherwise disconnected bits of information into a unity that can be contained "in the minds of omniscient readers. Only they see the links" (31). Anderson may imply that people are what they read under these circumstances, but his account preserves the distinction between fiction and social fact. Somehow the imagined community that exists upon the printed page provides Anderson with both the prototype and a reflection of the affiliation that bound actual people into a community. Even though these people could hardly get to know one another any other way, Anderson locates the two communities—imagined and imaginary—on separate ontological planes; "the idea of a sociological organism moving calendrically through homogeneous, empty time," he writes, "is a precise analogue of the idea of the nation" (31).

Foucault, in contrast, concentrates on the fictional dimension of other kinds of discourse—memoirs, medical treatises, social scientific writing, educational pamphlets, as well as personal confessions—to support his allegation that such intellectual activity produced the recesses of the self and the regions of private experience that authors were claiming to discover. He identifies the properties and the powers we associate with modern fiction in a wide array of cultural materials; but he does not consider, in turn, the historical properties of fiction. In this respect, he maintains his affiliations with the disciplines of philosophy and history.

More than any other medium available at that time, fiction proved able to represent the inner world of the solitary individual. It was very much like modern love in this respect—namely, a relationship among people who did not work with one another but who did share their personal lives. Newspapers may, as Anderson claims, have prompted readers to imagine all the other people perusing their morning newspapers and, at that moment, to feel part of a community of newspaper readers. Fiction interpellated "a readership" in much the same way. At the same time, however, fiction resembled a diary. It provided special access to information that was not, by definition, publicly shared. It was so personal that short of living it oneself or violating someone else's privacy, one could not get such information. Fiction, one might say, was the public form of information that was becoming privatized.

Such information must have been necessary to the kind of national culture Anderson describes. Why else would fiction have emerged predictably to dominate the scene whenever cultures began to privilege the distinction between fact and fiction? Such cultures abandoned epic poetry. Subsequent poets had a right to complain that *Paradise Lost* was the last successful epic poem to be written in England; but they were wrong to blame Milton for that. He obviously saw the end arriving, and he was at least as sorry about the advent of the culture of the novel as subsequent poets could ever be. When he put Eve to sleep and gave Adam a history lesson, Milton was anticipating the framework in which he would be read and achieve notoriety—that of a culture that linked fact with business, and fiction with personal matters, as if it were all a dream dreamed by the slumbering Eve. Yet he also knew there was nothing like a sexual desire to send history reeling in one direction rather than another, and nothing like the reading and interpretation of a story about the fatal consequences of seduction when it came to understanding and managing sexual impulses in oneself. It may be true, then, that Milton was the last English poet to write a poem that summed up a long and exalted tradition of learning—which was received by an entirely new readership, unfamiliar with the culture that had trained Milton's mind and forged his ambitions to be a poet. But those ambitions and the project they inadvertently initiated hardly ended with Milton. If it can be argued that the endeavor to return to a world of origins—a world from which one has been permanently exiled—organized and empowered *Paradise Lost,* then the ambitions driving the poem can be said in turn to find their most perfect realization in subsequent fiction. By ambition, then, we do not mean Milton's professed ambition to do for English poetry what Ariosto had done for Italian. Rather, we are interested in how, under new historical circumstances, the same ambition to produce a national literature might have accomplished something through the poetry that was unanticipated by the man.

In using *Paradise Lost* to formulate a model of what modern culture would do with an aristocratic tradition of letters, one is naturally tempted to rely on the poem's closing lines—to assume they offer an elegiac farewell to the old epoch and, however apprehensively, venture forth into the new. However, the culture that developed in the wake of the English civil war was infused with nostalgia from the start. The fiction whose development cannot be distinguished from that of middle-class culture as a whole, produced an inherently conservative narrative that looked back with longing. That fiction, and the writing which preceded and accompanied it into cultural prominence, was trying not so much to formulate a new world as to reproduce one that had been lost. To do so, such writing had to break up and redefine the materials of the old landowning England. It remade that world in miniature, in the process reconceptualizing the nation as a cluster of individuated worlds. One can understand how such an attempt to return to a largely imaginary earlier state of peace and plenitude might have displaced the culture we described in chapter 4—the culture where (as in Milton's Eden) an aristocracy stood at the center of all meaning and value. We present the materials of this chapter in just this way. The impulse on the part of late seventeenth-century authors to restore continuity with the past is the demiurge of modernity in the story we are telling. The gesture to restore the past in writing is a gesture that displaces, a gesture through which writing becomes the supplement. This chapter attempts to trace the development of a new self and nation that was at first a fiction, as we have suggested, but nonetheless real for being so.

Paradise Lost suggests that the fiction of "personal life" began in marriage treatises and handbooks of domestic economy. This is the material out of which Milton composes Eve's proprietorial notion of how nature should be regarded, and the same notion of nature as private property organizes the cultural fantasy of a new social world that begins to develop as the modern heterosexual couple departs from Eden. Milton anticipates the privatization of the English household by having his poem conclude: "They hand in hand with wand'ring steps and slow, / Through *Eden* took thir solitary way" (XII, 648–49). Having read the poem as an account of cultural change, one faces the possibility that Eve's minority viewpoint injecting individual autonomy in the midst of Edenic wholeness and harmony changed forever the aristocratic culture it had infiltrated. If, however, we consider how little influence the puritan family household and its concern with economy appears to have had on early seventeenth-century culture, a contrary picture emerges. Before the English Revolution, the conflict between aristocratic and puritan representations of the household did not amount to a conflict between old and new. To begin with, the puritan family was not infused with the qualities of personal life but was a miniature version of the aristocratic state. Puritan treatises on marriage and household management simply argued that the state should renounce certain sumptuary habits; that it should continue the process, begun under Henry VIII, of reforming the church; and that in certain cases—such as matters of household management— the monarch's power ought to stop when it encroached on the authority of the man who rules the "little commonwealth."

The title of Robert Cleaver's popular work *A Godly Form of Household Government* (London, 1598) makes clear the analogy between the government of the household and that of the state: "A household is as it were, a litle commonwealth, by the good gouernment whereof, God's gloree may bee aduanced" (1). This comparison is commonplace in books on marriage and the family published during the first half of the seventeenth century. As if the church and the government of England also hung in the balance, the author of one such book declares: "Now a family must be gouerned as wel as maintained (yea verily it cannot be maintained without gouernment). . . . The man must be taken for Gods immediate officer in the house, and as it were the King in the family . . . the woman an officer substituted to him."[3] The author was a well-known puritan preacher; but the family hierarchy he proposed was not hostile to the idea of monarchy. James I was fond of representing himself as *parens patriae,* and he reminded Parliament that in the scriptures "Kings were also compared to Fathers of Families."[4] This figure of speech continued to serve the interests of monarchy as late as 1642, when *His Majesties Answers to the Nineteen Propositions* was published. Until this historical moment, it was possible to contend that noblemen stood in relation to their households as the king to his people, as may be gathered from Edward Topsell's dedication of a marriage treatise to Richard Sackville, Earl of Dorset: "The first thing wherein your Hon: must now shew your selves to the worlde, is your household gouernment. *Household Gouernment*, I say, the Parent and first beginner of common-wealthes."[5] William Gouge, author of one of the most popular puritan treatises on marriage, echoes these very sentiments when he writes, "The family is a little Church and a little Commonwealth."[6]

It is perhaps not surprising that men, from king to puritan preacher, could describe their different relations to the state in much the same terms; a patriarchal hierarchy both empowered and constrained virtually everyone capable of expressing his political opinions in print. Until the late 1630s, puritan sermons and descriptions of family government never contested the concept of monarchy. They seem consistently dutiful in displaying respect toward the king.[7] However, during the pamphlet wars of the 1640s that preoccupied Milton and his contemporaries, the situation changed decisively. No doubt because the family offered such a well-established analogy for the state, raising questions about the nature of the family became a way to make controversial statements about the nature and distribution of political power.

To define the family was also to seize hold of one of the instruments of power. Indeed, the family was perhaps second only to the covenant between God and Adam in the frequency with which it provided an analogy for state power. Each side argued that marriage provided a mirror of the contract between king and subject and, in doing so, maintained the system of relationships God originally had in mind. Royalists insisted that the bond between husband and wife required the same absolute obedience from the wife as the bond with the king required from his subjects. Parliamentarians argued that there were unstated limitations on a husband's prerogative, just as there were on a monarch's. In the course of one such debate, Henry Parker drew this comparison in support of parliamentary rule: "If men, for whose sake women were created, shall not lay hold upon the divine right of wedlock, to the disadvantage of women; much less [shall] princes who were created for the peoples sake, challenge any thing from the sanctity of their offices, that may derogate from the people."[8]

The theory of rights raised the possibility that the contract between monarch and subjects could be nullified if the king were to act irresponsibly. In his *Doctrine and Discipline of Divorce* (1643) Milton used the marriage analogy to argue that the marriage contract was subject to the exercise of individual conscience. It did not take an irresponsible husband to dissolve the contract that binds husband to wife or, by analogy, the contract that binds monarch to subject.

> He who marries, intends as little to conspire his own ruine, as he that swears Allegiance: and as a whole people is in proportion to an ill Government, so is one man to an ill mariage. If they against any authority, Covnant, or Statute, may by the soveraign edict of charity, save not only their lives, but honest liberties from unworthy bondage as well may he against any private Covnant, which hee never enter'd to his mischief, redeem himself from unsupportable disturbances to honest peace, and just contentment.[9]

In this statement, the offending spouse and the monarch remain in separate domains and are related to one another only by analogy. But the injured spouse and the oppressed subject have become one and the same. The individual who consents to both marriage and government has not agreed to endure either a bad marriage or unjust government.

By 1645, however, when Milton came to write *Tetrachordon*, marriage and government no longer merely provide analogies for one another but are causally related. The argument of *Tetrachordon* moves the issue of divorce yet another notch away from the Royalist position. The marriage metaphor has so infused political discourse that Milton could not criticize existing marriage practices without challenging the king's claim to absolute rule. Indeed, it might even be argued that one could not help but challenge the monarchy itself. For in talking about marriage, one had to consider whether the monarch gave individuals the right to consent (and could therefore withdraw that right) or whether it was their consent that entitled him to rule.[10] The dispute over how the king's power related to that of husbands and fathers grew so intense that the meaning of marriage itself was up for grabs. Charles I could not control its meaning; one of the favorite Stuart images had slipped out of the monarch's grasp.

In *Tetrachordon*, Milton declares that the outward and public form of marriage "is not sufficient to distinguish matrimony from other conjunctions of male and female, which are not to be counted marriage. *Joyning man and women in a love, &c.* This brings in the parties consent; until which be, the mariage hath no true beeing."[11] According to this argument, "consent" cannot be ordained by God, for it is a matter of choice. But neither can consent bind one in "error." In the world before the Fall, Milton explains, "Nature made us all equall, made us equall coheirs by common right and dominion over all creatures" (661). In such a world, there was no possibility of marrying someone less worthy than oneself. As it is, however, some people are less capable of love than others. As even God acknowledges, divorce is sometimes necessary: "hee suffer'd divorce as well as mariage, our imperfet and degenerat condition of necessity requiring this law among the rest, as a remedy against intolerable wrong and servitude above the patience of man to beare" (661). Consent is not consent unless it operates for the good of the individual. True consent, according to Milton, "is a love fitly dispos'd to mutual help and comfort of life."[12] This is the "true beeing" as opposed to the mere form of marriage. To argue that marriage has to be organized from outside (by the state) and inside (by the individuals involved) rather than simply arranged by God has serious political implications. It means that a comparison with husband and wife does not necessarily authorize the hierarchal relations between the monarch and his subjects. If it does not, then the argument for divorce implicitly challenges the argument for absolute monarchy. Moreover, if the argument for divorce is also an argument on behalf of individual rights, then marriage, rather than rank and station, is by implication the bond that holds individuals who have acquired those rights together in a well-governed nation. At this point, the marriage metaphor seems not only to challenge monarchy but also to put marriage in the place of government, much as Milton does in the last books of *Paradise Lost.*

It is not difficult to imagine why the story of man's first disobedience was regularly invoked in the face of such challenges to patriarchal authority. The story links man's disobedience directly with that of his wife. It shows that her obligation to obey him cannot be separated from his obligation to obey God, and tampering with either hierarchy violates the laws both of God and of nature. When in 1643 Phillip Hunton anonymously published *A Treatise of Monarchy,* questioning this analogy on the grounds that it did not apply after the Fall, the response was swift. Henry Ferne wrote *A Reply unto Severall Treatises,* which he published later that same year; and four years later Robert Filmer's *The Anarchy of a Limited or Mixed Monarchy* (1648) was published. The patriarchalists used the story of Genesis to reestablish the link between marriage and monarchy at their point of mutual origin, in order to invert the parliamentarian contention that government should, like marriage, be based on consent. They all claimed that divorce violates the original principle of government. Perhaps the most ardent of the patriarchalists, Filmer begins by attacking Hunton's misuse of Genesis:

> Our author first confesseth, 'It is God's express ordinance there should be government', and he proves it by Genesis iii,16, where God ordained Adam to rule over his wife, and her desires were to be subject to his; and as hers,

so all theirs that should come of her. Here we have the original grant of government, and the fountain of all power placed in the Father of mankind. . . . This paternal power continued monarchical to the Flood, and after the Flood to the confusion of Babel.[13]

Filmer repeats the argument against consensualism in his *Observations concerning the Originall of Government* (1652). Claiming that the patriarchal order of the family was divinely ordained, he singles out for attack Milton's *Defensio pro Populo Anglicani,* which had appeared on 31 December 1650. In this treatise, Milton distinguishes between the father to whom we are born by nature and the king by whom we consent to be governed. Filmer objects to such use of the family to challenge the legitimacy of patriarchal rule:

Father and King are not so diverse, it is confessed that at first they were all one, for there is confessed *paternum imperium et haerieditarium,* . . . and this fatherly empire, as it was of itself hereditary, so it was *alienable* by the parent, and *seizable,* by a usurper as other goods are: and thus every King that now is hath a paternal empire, either by inheritance, or by translation or usurpation, so a Father and a King be all one. (236)

As the first subject and father, Adam was supposed to extend into the household the vertical chain of command headed by the king, as Milton had him do in the Edenic sections of *Paradise Lost.*

During the interregnum, however, something evidently happened to the symbolic properties of marriage, so that one could not mention it without admitting the possibility that the individual subject had natural rights. Although Adam occupies the center of this controversy from one end of the seventeenth century to the other, by the 1660s he was playing a role that directly contradicted the one he had been assigned during the period leading up to the interregnum. First printed in 1689–90, John Locke's summary of the argument of the first treatise of his *Two Treatises of Government* clarifies the political implications of such tinkering with aristocratic culture at the level of the household. By attacking Filmer's interpretation of Genesis, Locke attacked the basis of the argument for absolute monarchy. At times resembling the angel Michael in *Paradise Lost,* Locke renders aristocratic codes obsolete on the grounds that they violate the laws of nature and God that were established in the beginning. Locke offers this summary of the first and therefore true authority of the father:

1. That *Adam* had not either by natural Right of Fatherhood, or by positive Donation from God, any such Authority over his Children, or Dominion over the World as is pretended.

2. That if he had, his Heirs, yet, had no Right to it.

3. That if his Heirs had, there being no Law of Nature nor positive Law of God that determines, which is the Right Heir in all Cases that may arise, the Right of Succession, and consequently of bearing Rule, could not have been certainly determined.

4. That if even that had been determined, yet the knowledge of which is the Eldest Line of *Adam's* Posterity, being so long since utterly lost, that in the Races of Mankind and Families of the World, there remains not to one above another, the least pretence to be the Eldest House, and to have the Right of Inheritance.[14]

Even though Cromwell's government collapsed and a Stuart returned to the throne, the cultural effects of the dispute over the family could not be reversed, as the patriarchalists discovered. The argument separated the household forever from the political sphere and made it potentially autonomous. Indeed, to oppose such autonomy would only underscore the fact of the household's detachment from an earlier political sphere.

In the *Two Treatises of Government*, Locke assumes, like William Petty and Thomas Sprat, that labor provides the basis for his nation's power. On this assumption, he generates a theory of property designed to supplement the aristocratic distribution of power with a new form of power that could also descend genealogically from father to son.[15] However, labor power does not originate wholly within the father and, by implication, the collective body of the elite community as a whole. Labor power is potentially both self-generated and self-generating. "Thus," Locke proclaims, "*Labour*, in the Beginning gave a *Right of Property*, where-ever any one was pleased to imploy it, upon what was common . . . and is yet more than Mankind makes use of" (II.45.1–4). In mixing his labor with the objects of the world, man gives those objects value.[16] They become useful. They also become part of the person who uses them. The political fantasy that both demands and sustains these assumptions is a familiar one, taking the form of a space wholly usable but never wholly used. Such a space allows for the limitless expansion of laboring man's domination over a nature that is either wasted or waiting to be used and is therefore ripe for appropriation—in theory, at least, a nation created from the bottom up.

For precisely the reason that it posed a contradiction to traditional patriarchy, however, the logic of property could not unfold very well within seventeenth-century England. To imagine a world that developed according to this logic, Locke has to imagine an empty space, a *terra nullius*.[17] To do so, he draws upon the figure of the fallen world and redefines that world as a space that is not so much full of sin as simply lacking value. Having emptied this space, he can represent the difference between nature that has been mixed with human labor and nature that has not been so mixed as the difference between something and nothing.

> There cannot be a clearer demonstration of any thing, than several Nations of the *Americans* are of this, who are rich in Land, and poor in all the Comforts of Life; whom Nature having furnished as liberally as any other people, with the materials of Plenty . . . yet for want of improving it by labour, have not one hundreth part of the Conveniencies we enjoy: And a King of a large and fruitful Territory there feeds, lodges, and is clad worse than a day Labourer in *England*. (II.41)

A world where a king lives "worse than a day Labourer in England" can only be a fallen world. Yet the idea of a *terra nullius* obviously held forth certain utopian possibilities.

A territory uninscribed by history offers exactly the right space in which to unfurl a theory of property. "Thus in the beginning," Locke proclaims, "all the World was America, and more so than that is now" (II.49.1).[18] In taking his examples from Genesis, on the one hand, and from America on the other, Locke imagines a nation based on labor developing in another time and place. Although it substitutes the laboring body for the body that houses noble blood, his theory of power stops well short of openly opposing absolute monarchy. It envisions no practical means of replacing the power of inherited wealth and entitlement with power that inheres in the individual body. One might say that he resembles Petty and Sprat in this respect, for their remodeling of political categories takes place within conceptual spaces that have been wiped clean of aristocratic culture by plague and fire, respectively. Locke not only refutes one form of patriarchy by positing another, he also ignores the practical implications of the political contradiction that he creates by doing so. The contradiction between private property and monarchy exists for Locke only on the plane of ideas and for purposes of philosophical debate. In a chapter of the *Second Treatise* entitled "Of Paternal Power," however, Locke does take the concepts of Petty and Sprat a step further historically. He represents the family as the alternative form of patriarchy, thus destroying the analogical relationship between the household and the state.

It is significant that Locke has to redefine the basis of power yet again in order to accomplish this effect. The *Treatises* argue that labor is the source of political power; this particular chapter makes a similar—indeed, analogous—argument on behalf of intellectual labor. "Of Paternal Power" introduces the idea that "reason" provides the basis both of individual rights and of political domination. In contrast with their father, Locke argues, Adam's children were not born under the law of reason. Indeed, "he that is not come to the Use of his *Reason*, cannot be said to be *under this Law;* and *Adam's* Children being not presently as soon as born, *under this Law of Reason* were not presently *free*" (II.57.8–10). To make this principle into a law of nature, Locke simply extends "*Adam's* Children" to include all children: "The *Power,* then, *that Parents have* over their Children, arises from that Duty which is incumbent on them, to take care of their Off-spring, during the imperfect state of Childhood. To inform the Mind, and govern the Actions of their yet ignorant Nonage, till Reason shall take its place" (II.58.1–5). Like unused territory, the child's mind represents a lack of knowledge that translates directly into a lack of political rights. When the child has acquired the kind of knowledge that will allow his self-government, however, he will no longer be under his parents' thumb. He will have the same power under the law that his father possesses. After the son's "Understanding be fit to take the Government of his Will," father and son "are equally Subjects of the same Law together, without any Dominion left in the Father over the Life, Liberty, or Estate of his Son" (II.59.26–30). To insist upon the rights of the individual householder over and against the monarch described by Filmer, Locke sets up a benevolent dictatorship within the household. He gives reason absolute power over both prerational and irrational states of mind, as well as over the bodies inhabited by them. Thus the child acquires the right of self-government only when he acquires the rationality that distinguishes the father from both the child and the mother.

Particularly noteworthy is the mother's place in this argument. Locke gives her authority over her son "in the imperfect state of childhood." Resembling the father in this respect alone, her authority over the child overrides even the prerogatives the king claims over each of his subjects. Thus she establishes the absolute nature of parental authority and, with it, the perfect autonomy of the household. But her authority cannot be based on reason, for then she would be entitled to certain rights under the law. Such independence on the part of the mother would, in theory, threaten the autonomy of the household by breaking the little chain of dependency that presupposes a male parent at its head. By the pronouns that he uses in describing the child's developing rationality, Locke clearly restricts the growth of reason to men, thereby restricting political rights to fathers and sons.[19] Once her son matures and she has fulfilled her role as parent, Locke's theory leaves the mother in some netherworld of self and politics and proceeds to argue for the enfranchisement of her male children.

By shifting the basis of hierarchy from the symbolic surface of the body onto the mind, Locke produced a self-contained system of relationships that England had never seen before, at least not in so many words. At the head of Locke's model household was not necessarily a member of the nobility; rather there was an educated man, one whose economic power was based not on labor so much as on his ability to think rationally, or what might be called intellectual labor. In thus shifting the emphasis, Locke did not do away with the old system of primogeniture completely. One generation had power over the next, and the men of either generation had prerogatives that their female counterparts lacked; rationality came only to men, and to them only through education. Nevertheless, by grafting internal, mental qualities onto the physical categories of gender and generation, Locke equipped the old system to behave in new ways. He defined a new basis for political entitlement as he described the qualities of mind that went by the name of "reason." However restrictive in terms of gender this concept might have been, it was in theory available to any man who could acquire the right kind of education.

Perhaps more important than the apparent democracy of Locke's family model is the potential of the model's paired dissymmetries of gender and generation to ensure its own replication from within. Individuals who work hard and think rationally are, according to the logic of paternal power, not only qualified to exercise sovereign power over affairs within their households but also obligated to rule those who do not yet (or perhaps will never) possess the capacity to rule themselves. It can indeed be argued that in the logic of paternal power resides the nascent logic of social reproduction, where lies in turn the secret of the modern family's hegemonic power. However, because Locke still viewed the household as a model of the state and a way of limiting state power, we must still regard the politics of his chapter "On Paternal Power" as the view of the loyal opposition. His argument on behalf of paternal power sought to enfranchise those men who possessed the qualities of mind found in someone like Locke, and in the Earl of Shaftesbury, whom Locke served.[20] In pursuing this objective, Locke's model did mount a powerful argument against absolute monarchy. But it also kept the patriarchal family at the center of the political arena.[21] The concept of paternal power went one step beyond the rest of *The Second Treatise of Government*, historically speaking; but it stopped one crucial step short of the argument Locke would develop a few years later in his *Essay Concerning Human Understanding*. There he works out the logic of property in pragmatic terms, but does so on a purely personal terrain. Some time between these two publications, Locke ceased to imagine a household modeled on the state and began to imagine a state made of individual householders. And this made all the difference. To demonstrate why it proved to be far more effective to modify political relations at the micro level of the individual rather than at the macro level of the nation, we must shift momentarily away from Locke and look at a kind of diary writing that flourished along with puritan treatises on marriage and handbooks on household management.

We shall begin our brief history of the modern individual during the years immediately following the English Revolution when this individual had clearly emerged in writing and there was as yet no evidence of such a self fully enclosed within the body or of a personal existence enclosed within the home.[22] During the past twenty-five years, as we indicated in chapter 3, a small but impassioned school of English social historians has focused on the history of the family, the events and practices attending biological reproduction, and the emotions that people experienced during various periods in social history. In the ensuing debate as to whether parental affection was natural and normal for all times or whether it must be regarded as a very recent development, the diary of Ralph Josselin—one of a handful of such accounts surviving from this period—turns up with notable regularity on both sides of the question. Between 1641 and 1683, this prosperous and apparently good-natured vicar filled nearly 185 pages in minuscule handwriting with his observations on daily life in England. Certain passages from this manuscript have been used to support arguments to the effect that (1) the family was a repository of affection, which dissipated with the rise of the factory system and (2) the family was a cold, unfeeling hierarchy which gave way to affectionate relationships with the rise of the modern middle classes and the formation of the nuclear family.[23]

To isolate the beginnings of personal life, then, let us see for ourselves how Josselin classified what his modern counterparts take to be the most personal of domestic experiences. And let us begin with an entry that has fueled debate among historians of the family as to how Josselin felt about the deaths of his children. Historians who have been sympathetic to the views of either Laslett or Stone tend to ignore the economic and political information woven into Josselin's accounts of what most of us consider the most heart-wrenching experience a parent can feel. For

Josselin, however, the death of his son is mingled with anxieties about the weather, his inheritance, his cattle, and clearly most important of all, his standing in the eyes of the Almighty—all curiously equivalent components of a world in a state of perpetual dissolution.

> June 15 [1673] about one a clocke in the morning my eldest sonne Thomas and my most deare child ascended early hence to keepe his everlasting Sabbath with his heavenly father, and Saviour with the church above[.] his end was comfortable and his death calme, not much of pain til the Satturday afore. in my course this morning I read Josh;I: which had words of comfort, god making his word my counsellour and comfort[.] He was my hope. but some yeares I have feared his life, god hath taken all my first brood but Jane. lett all live in thy sight sanctified[.] a wett morning, the heavens for some time have mourned over us.
>
> 17. Son buried. June.23. rid to Braintry. by coach to London and returnd safe with An very ill home July. 3. a wett flouding yeare like that in 48. god in mercy looke down upon us.
>
> July 20: God afflicts mee, my An ill and deafe and therby unchearfull, and so I scarce can comfort her soule: Lord marre not my inheritance, a black cow died suddenly of the blacke gargett. my heart pants after god as my hope, and my trust is in him for good, lord leave mee not[.] some good days in answer of prayer the lord will adde more.[24]

Alongside accounts of death and marriage, Josselin sometimes recorded dreams. They reveal an element of intellectual ambition not necessarily unbefitting a man of God but occasionally resituating that very man at the center of political power. It was as if there were no difference between public and private in Josselin's world, at least no difference that Josselin felt he had to reproduce in making sense of himself in writing. His relation to God appears to have been much more important than his relation to his family in determining his written identity.

On the basis of passages such as the following, one might conclude that this seventeenth-century mind was performing its most important dreamwork, not through the symbols of familial relations and infantile sexual desires, but through figures drawn from theology and contemporary politics.[25]

> No. 13 [1650]. at night, my thoughts having beene much on the kingdome of christ that shal bee sett up in the world, and desirous of god my eyes might see his salvacon, I dreamd that wee of our nation were instrumentally imployed about that worke in France, and that the court thereof was pure, I was making joyned worke to use there and that I should receive a letter from the grandees of the army in Scotland the latter part thus as for that academicall opinion what wee shall doe in that wee knowe not. Erit aliquando [quo] nunc est viz

> a kingdome of christ in the world—implying that work is begun already in
> England. . . . our actings in France in my apprehension were not above 2 or
> 3 years hence in a short time.

Though such grandiose political ambitions were strictly confined to his
dreams, Josselin never wavered in his conviction that England would
soon be transformed. Nor did he abandon his wish to participate in this
event. Yet, from what we can tell, he neither acted upon that wish nor
meant it for eyes other than God's and his alone. It is as if the diary,
like the dreams it sometimes recorded, constituted a medium of communication between Josselin and his God.

When coupled with another dream, reported in the diary five years
later almost to the day, the figures shaping what would today be private
fantasies may alter how one assesses the significance of any single child
in Josselin's culture:

> No. 19 [1655]. the litle boy at the priory, died this morning, Mr R.H. senior.
> very ill, the lord in mercy watch over him for good: 21: spent at Chappel,
> where I was sole arbitrator in the Nevils busines with hope to end it; 22.
> married Tibball and his wife, towards morning 23. I dreamed I was intimate
> and secretary to the Protector, who appeared to mee young, I advised him to
> heed the interest, and the kingdom of Christ. solus inter nos, at the first
> entrance to this advice he interrupted mee, told mee I must first mention not
> a word of any such thing for it was an unpardonable fault with the Council;
> it seemed as if not so to him, it would countenance the Anabaptists and other
> sects, but I might advise to make good lawes against dronkeness and other
> vices.

Though written a mere two or three decades before Locke used the body
to mark the line where the power of the monarch ended and that of the
householder began, neither the spatial boundaries of the household nor
the language of family relations appears to have served that purpose for
Josselin.

His wishes are not so much those of a son or father, as those of a
would-be adviser-functionary of the revolutionary regime. Whenever he
dreams of breaking the restrictions that came along with his position in
life, his wish takes the form of a political revolution that occurs primarily
through language. He might imagine himself helping to establish the
kingdom of Christ, as the first dream suggests, or authoring laws for
secular reform, as the second dream seems to imply. In both, however,
one can observe the power of the word moving out of the domain of
theology to become a full-fledged secular power capable of displacing
the authority of both church and aristocracy. By positioning the indi-

vidual who possesses this new literacy close to the center of power, the dream imagines a government founded on law rather than on divine right or entitlement. The dream also suggests that this historical change was one that took place on the terrain of consciousness—and even of unconscious wishes—before it could reshape the institutions of government.

However, having noted the culture-specific form of Josselin's dreams, we must put the family back into the picture and historicize that most recalcitrant of cultural material. To understand the role the family played in Josselin's fantasy life, we turn to a lesser-known work by one of the English Republicans, Henry Neville's *Isle of Pines*. This extremely popular work, first published in 1668, was written from a peculiarly destabilized position within English society; this made it likely that any fantasy of a new world would be aimed directly against the English status quo.[26] Neville's fabulous travel account tells of the discovery of an island off what is now Australia inhabited by "10 or 12,000 persons," all of whom speak "good English."[27] What follows is the history of an imaginary nation, named the Isle of Pines after its founder, George Pine, and (by inverting the vowels of the plural form of his surname) the means by which it was populated. Shipwrecked on the beach of a deserted island with three white women and a black maid as his only companions, this ship's bookkeeper sets to work to ensure the necessities of life for his little community. Nature frustrates his efforts at manual labor from the beginning, however. Indeed, Pine confesses, the island proves so free of hardship, so comfortably abundant, that "this place, had it the culture that skilful people might bestow on it, would prove a Paradise" (11). Having placed his hero in a setting that resembles Eden, Neville then supplies several women with whom he could engage in something resembling prelapsarian sex.[28]

Pine proceeds to create a nation of people by means of sexual union with his former master's daughter, her maids, and a slave whose country of origin is never specified. The result is a single family of man that pledges allegiance to a paternal government embodied in Pines (the name of the people as well as the territory) and his official wife, Sarah English. This family is a nation homogenized by gender and generation but one carrying within it the basis for future divisions of race and class. Pine's offspring are divided not only into male and female but also into black and white and into descendants from the slave, from the servants, and from the master's daughter. These differences become visible as the body is stripped of Old World status distinctions, presumably stripped down to nature itself.[29] In this nation as extended nudist colony, reproduction of the body is what counts; and count them the bookkeeper-patriarch does, thereby allowing readers to understand a kingdom as a population.

Though Neville's irreverent story was as public as Josselin's diary was private, it can be argued that they observe a single cultural logic, one that turns reproduction into a basis of political power. In both instances, a new conception of the body as a self-replicating mechanism replaces the aristocratic notion of the body as the means of perpetuating noble blood. This body allows both authors to represent the biological family as a basis of social organization and a source of political power. To link Josselin to Neville in this way, of course, one has to understand the fantasy of a new nation as the utopian underside of the good vicar's extraordinarily perishable household. Whenever Josselin tallied up his offspring, resigning himself to every loss and cautiously celebrating every gain, he was thinking along lines that bear significant resemblance to Neville's bookkeeper. Josselin was watching a kingdom increase or deteriorate. We would argue that all the elements of a new political fantasy seem to be there: the desire for self-replication, the use of sexual reproduction to express this desire, and the idea of rebuilding a kingdom from the inside out or from the bottom up. It is particularly evident in Neville's narrative that sexual reproduction allows him to reimagine the origins of an island nation.[30] But the distinction between political and personal experience organizes neither one of the fantasies in question; consequently, they belong to an earlier moment in British cultural history. If *The Isle of Pines* represents the "political" as a family of commoners, then Josselin's diary observes the early modern (i.e., political) notion of privacy. Political secrets are confined to the sanctuary of dreams; family matters constitute the politics of daily life. Modern cultures, on the other hand, locate power in householders by inverting this pattern. Modern cultures privatize the sexual, and they open state policy to public scrutiny and discussion.

More than Neville's sexual utopia, curiously enough, it is Josselin's diary that sets us on the trail of the modern subject. Coupled with the compulsive character of the diary itself, Josselin's dream of serving in Cromwell's bureaucracy suggests that the desire to reproduce himself biologically is not nearly so compelling as the desire to produce himself in words. For here one sees Josselin, a relatively unimportant figure in the new ecclesiastical establishment of revolutionary England, imagining that the role of "Intimate and secretary to the Protector" can place him close to the very heart of the new government. His privileged relationship to the language of the church and thus to God earns him entry to the innermost sanctuary of political life. As he gains entry to this closed circle of power, however, it is significant that the power of words undergoes transformation. When Josselin dreams that Cromwell has detached the language of theology from that of politics, he dramatizes the passing into obsolescence of an earlier language of power. The dream begins with the proposition that the word of God (as represented by the phrase *solus inter nos*) will direct the course of history, but it confronts the apparent reality of politics—namely, that although many different sects can presently speak with the voice of God, only one can speak with the voice of law, and that sect shall dominate England. Thus we may watch the dream placing a form of censorship on an earlier language of power— the Latin of *solus inter nos*—in order to banish it from political life in favor of a fully secular morality which talks in terms of "dronkeness and other vices."

Although Josselin never deviated from the older notion of privacy even in his dreams, one cannot overlook the fact that he saw fit to reproduce himself in writing day by day in careful detail over a period of forty years. He was apparently carrying on a relationship with God by accounting for himself so exhaustively and receiving what he obviously felt were signs of self-affirmation through his dreams.[31] Although the record of this relationship fails to conform to modern accounts of personal experience, be they religious or therapeutic, the diary must also strike the modern reader as remarkably self-enclosed.[32] In much the same self-centered manner as *Robinson Crusoe,* Josselin's diary records all information in relation to its author. Not only does this author transcribe the details of his life and mind for forty years with no one else in mind besides himself and God, he also dreams of transforming the power of God into that of language.[33] This change portends the end of Josselin's intimacy with God and the complete self-enclosure of the material of the diary—which indeed tends to be received today by the British historians of the family as the self-reflection of a single human consciousness very much like their own.

After 1690 the narrative of the individual mind parted company from that of the state, and God dropped out of the picture.[34] This had to happen, we might speculate, before the relationship between public and private could undergo the inversion that marks the onset of modernity. In his *Essay Concerning Human Understanding,* Locke gave to each entity—the subject and the object worlds respectively—its own originary fable and made each knowable in different terms. Thus to tell either story was to reproduce a certain division of cultural knowledge. But when he enclosed the subject within an individuated body separated by its skin from an external world of objects, he also bound the subject to this world through an exchange that was essential to the character of each. It is significant, we feel, that he imagined these relations in terms of writing: a body that inscribed itself through labor on the things of nature, and a subject on whom objects inscribed themselves through sensation. This exchange itself produced an indelible difference between self and nonself that locates Locke's representation of the subject on the other side of a historical fault line from that of Josselin.[35]

By showing how the rational mind develops, Locke's critique of absolute monarchy turns into something else. What had served to illustrate the limitations of monarchy in the second of his *Two Treatises of Government* begins to assume the dimensions of a new theoretical model. This model posits a world confined within the individual body and bearing certain structural similarities to the world of objects on the other side of its skin. Given the emptiness of this world, Locke can construct and legitimate a social order by means of a power that arises strictly from within the self—a world, that necessarily positions the self at its center. By positing an interior space, furthermore, Locke can write as if such a world were being constructed in the here and now of late seventeenth-century England. Rather than situating individual man within empty space, *An Essay Concerning Human Understanding* situates an empty space within individual man. By means of this space, Locke situates a second source of power within the given social world—a source of power within the individual body but, unlike productive labor, an extension of that body into the domain of knowledge.

Indeed, his use of the "white Paper, void of all Characters, without any *ideas*" to describe this world in its original state reveals how closely he identified the production of human understanding with his own act of writing—the degree to which he not only relied on writing to conceptualize "mind" but also used the concept of labor to authorize writing.[36] He encourages the reader to consider the world that develops inside the mind as sensation becomes subject to reason. This world is simply the complement to the world of property. Consciousness begins as an empty space "void of all Characters" and acquires knowledge according to the same principle of appropriation by which the body acquires property. Sensations originate in the world of objects and provide the very substance of ideas without which, he insists, the mind cannot become sensible even to itself. On this basis, Locke grants the world of objects a kind of primacy in his theory. But he also posits a second "Source of

ideas [that] every Man has wholly in himself . . . call'd internal Sense"
(II.i.4). In this way, the mind establishes a relationship among sensations,
and from these it extrapolates the laws organizing objects in the world.
The process of internal division described in the chapter on paternal
power and again in the opening to the second book of the *Essay Concerning Human Understanding* repeats itself without requiring any reorganization of the framework within which the territory in question has
been embedded. Thus, in his theory of mind, Locke grants power over
the world of objects to the knowledge that comes from within the mind
itself, much as he previously granted power to the father over his son.
Indeed, as in the chapter from *Two Treatises* entitled "Of Paternal
Power," he again draws an analogy between the child's physical growth
and the growth of his mental faculties, this time positioning sensation
as prior to reason but inferior to it along a natural continuum.[37]

When he uses the example of sleep to demonstrate the superiority of
reason over sensation, however, Locke introduces a contrary logic into
his model of consciousness. This logic rattles the classification system
that contains it. The body asleep is a body that is not working, one can
almost hear him say. Thought in such a person is similarly idle. Yet who
would be so foolish, he asks, as to suppose the soul had departed from
the body during sleep and gone somewhere else to think? Thus to detach
soul from body in this way is, in his estimation, much the same thing as
supposing the soul capable of inhabiting another body (II.i.12). To demonstrate that it is absurd to think the soul is not contained within a single
body, he imagines what it would be like within two:

> Let us . . . suppose the Soul of *Castor* separated during his Sleep, from his
> Body to think apart. Let us suppose too, that it chuses for its Scene of Think-
> ing, the Body of another Man, *v.g. Pollux*, who is sleeping without a Soul:
> . . . I ask then, Whether *Castor* and *Pollux*, thus, with only one Soul between
> them, which thinks and perceives in one, what the other is never conscious
> of, nor is concerned for, are not two as distinct Persons? (II.i.12)

At this point in his argument, the body can no longer serve as a metaphor
for the soul. The body literally surrounds and contains the soul, and
together they constitute a single individual for whose condition the mind
is, ideally, responsible.

By so embodying soul, Locke incorporates it within a model of understanding that makes rationality the basis of political power. In so
embodying soul, however, he transfigures the body. As a result, neither
body nor soul can provide the basis for human identity, as they did in
early modern culture. Each link in this chain of somatic allusions brings

us historically closer to a familiar figure—that of a mind enclosed within a body, a body fully individuated because it has been emptied of noble blood and Christian soul and reconceptualized as the metaphysical space of consciousness. Once the soul has been relocated in the body, describing that body becomes a way of describing—quite literally, it appears— the condition of the soul. "Thus, methinks," says he, that "every drowsy Nod shakes their Doctrine, who teach That the soul is always thinking" (II.i.13). Having refuted the idea of a soul independent of the body, Locke ought to have no trouble identifying "soul" with the "white Paper" on which, he claims, all the ideas an individual possesses are written. This would allow him fully and finally to subordinate the Christian notion of soul to the Enlightenment notion of reason.

However, once he has enclosed the soul within the body and linked it with consciousness, the magical qualities of the old Christian concept reappear within the enclosed world of consciousness in the form of dreams. Apparently not all those who sleep must dispute the "doctrine ... That the soul is always thinking." For Locke quickly qualifies his equation between consciousness and thought: "Those, at least, who do at any time *sleep without dreaming,* can never be convinced, That their Thoughts are sometimes for four hours busy without their knowing of it" (II.i.13). Dreams indicate that the soul is busy even though reason sleeps when the body sleeps. Dreams therefore threaten not only the regime of reason but also the autonomy of the subject world. If only briefly, they shake the metaphorical foundations of Enlightenment thought. For dreams threaten to make soul, and not reason, equivalent to thought and thus to personal identity.

To avoid this conclusion, Locke again turns to the body. He recounts a story suggesting that, like the healthy body, the mind is normally inactive during sleep: "I once knew a Man, that was bred a Scholar, and had no bad Memory, who told me, he had never dream'd in his Life, till he had that Fever, he was then newly recovered of, which was about the Five or Six and Twentieth Year of his Age" (II.i.14). However, this attempt to pathologize dreaming apparently failed to solve the problem that has entered his theory with the mention of dreams. For Locke goes on to suggest that even when a healthy person dreams, those dreams proceed from an idle body. In this way, he makes dreams resemble the wasteland of America before human labor transformed it. If the soul "has no memory of its own Thoughts; if it cannot lay them up for its own use, and be able to recall them upon occasion; if it cannot reflect upon what is past, and make use of its former Experiences, Reasonings, and Con-

templations, to what purpose does it think?" (II.i.15). If this is not enough
to dismiss dreams, Locke covers the exceptional instance of individuals
who have retained some impression from their dreams. He finds even
these impressions useless: "How *extravagant* and incoherent for the most
part they are; how little conformable to the Perfection and Order of a
rational Being" (II.i.16).

Any discussion of the metaphors shaping Locke's theory must finally
come to terms with the attention he devotes to dreams. That attention
extends well beyond the logical requirements of his argument. As we
have implied, he is clearly intent on working his way out of the opposition
between spiritual and secular definitions of "soul," the argument organizing cultural production during the early modern period in social history—what is usually called Christian Humanism. He wants to situate
himself within a purely secular definition of consciousness and argue on
behalf of reason. Dreams supply the negative term that, once and for
all, allow him to incorporate the "soul" of an earlier culture within the
material body of man. But in using them, Locke has done more than
solve the problem with which his reference to sleep began. He has opened
up an entirely new argument. That he spends too many sentences putting
dreams in their place tells us not only that his attack on the Christian
notion of soul placed him in a minority position within his culture but
also that his notion of rationality depended in some profound way upon
the presence of the irrational.

We are not saying that the repetitious nature of his attack upon dreams
indicates that Locke really needed to beat irrationality into the ground
so as to assert the superiority of reason. To the contrary, we are suggesting
that he needed the old culture in order to describe a new one. His concept
of rationality required the presence of man's innate irrationality (a transparent secularization of the Christian notion of soul) as the thing that
must be overcome. To be sure, in Locke's argument the "irrational" and
"frivolous" domain of dreams is in logical terms no more than it lin-
guistically declares itself to be: the negation of everything rational. In
figurative terms, however, and thus in terms of the history that we are
tracing, the intrusion of dreams into Locke's theory of consciousness
operates as yet another empty space that offers itself for cultural inscription. Along with the orderly operations of reason, this space is part and
parcel of modern consciousness. Indeed, in the century elapsing between
Locke and Malthus, authors developed the cultural space inhabited by
dreams in order to determine a new basis for human identity. Essentially
opposed to reason, this space was implicitly female; but within its bound-

aries, a virtually infinite number of distinctions could be made—distinctions of race, class, and ethnicity, as well as distinctions of gender.

Finally, it is important to our purpose to consider the displacement of the "soul" by "irrationality" in terms of the narrative of self-inscription that it made possible. We have insisted all along that fiction was instrumental in producing a new imagined community that was the basis for both a nation and a new ruling class. Daniel Defoe's *Robinson Crusoe* provides a partial fable for the emergence of the modern middle class, a fable that subsequent generations of intellectuals have felt compelled to complete in one way or another. In this respect, the novel might be called an instrument as well as a model of the process we want to articulate. This particular novel begins within the same epistemological framework as Locke's *Two Treatises of Government*. An irrational drive compels Defoe's hero to reject his designated place in the world of his father and strike out for new territory. Once he has been shipwrecked on the island, however, reason seems able to overcome all obstacles in the way of his desire to convert the entire space into personal property. At this point, we argue, Defoe has reclassified the source of power in the same way that Locke did in the chapter "On Paternal Power," thereby creating the basis for his later theory of knowledge.

The story of *Robinson Crusoe* moves decisively beyond Locke's moment, in that it concentrates more on the irrational than on the rational mind in formulating a new basis of political power.[38] Defoe identifies Crusoe as someone from "the middle estate." From the beginning, however, Crusoe possesses irrational qualities not expected in someone who should be, as his father says, "in easy Circumstances sliding gently thro' the World."[39] The irrational alone positions Crusoe as a subject in opposition to the world of objects, enabling him to conquer that world simply by conquering himself.[40] As if he were living out Locke's political fantasy, the shipwrecked Crusoe sets immediately to work mixing his labor with the things of the world around him. Apparently, though, Defoe felt that such industry required some prior motive. He goes to elaborate lengths to redefine the cause and effect of Crusoe's fear, once he is stranded on the island.

In the old world, fear existed purely as the effect of natural disasters inflicted on man by a punitive God. Thus, for example, Crusoe initially understands his misadventures at sea as God's way of punishing his filial disobedience. On the island, however, fear wells up from within Crusoe's body unbidden by the rational mind. Rather than the wrath of God, demons of the mind ensure the survival of the individual. Such fear can and must eventually be conquered by reason, redefining the real struggle as a struggle and triumph of the mind. It can be argued that Crusoe initially fears a nature that bears certain similarities to Hobbes's nature. However, he discovers nature upon the island to be otherwise, and that Hobbesian view of nature quickly recedes into the past along with human ignorance. The novel characteristically identifies the predatory world with an earlier society. It transforms nature into demons of the mind that can be conquered by rationality when the mind is English, and by external manipulation of those demons when the mind is incapable of exercising rationality on its own behalf.

Crusoe writes in his journal, "I walk'd about the Shore almost all Day to find out a place to fix my Habitation, greatly concern'd to secure my self from an Attack in the Night, either from wild Beasts or Men. Towards Night I fix'd a proper Place under a Rock" (57). He writes this from a fortified enclosure erected on that spot. Fear inspired by a world in which his father and the Christian God hold sway has compelled Crusoe to create walls within walls, separating himself from everything else in the world. This fear places supreme importance on his body as the object in relation to which all other objects suddenly acquire practical value. In doing so, moreover, this fear produces a self-enclosed consciousness. Defoe describes Crusoe's emotions as if they led a life of their own. The island is not there simply to be inscribed with value by his labor. It is also there, in marked contrast with the old world, to provide a space devoid of referents for most of Crusoe's fears. For the time being at least, beasts and savages belong strictly to the world he has lost. In having his hero fear them now, Defoe makes the figures of the savage world serve as phantoms of the human mind, making visible the irrational faculties that respond to various forms of stimulation and control.[41]

Let us use one well-known episode to illustrate the point. Eager to vary his diet, Crusoe cooks up a sea turtle and immediately develops a fever. Illness transforms his helpless body into the theater of a struggle between rationality and feverish states of mind, internalizing the argument about political authority in much the same way that illness did in Locke's account of his scholarly "friend." During a rare moment of lucidity, Crusoe consumes all the water remaining in his hut and prays to God for help. These actions bring relief from the fever and a period of restful sleep, but sleep brings a still graver threat. "In this second sleep," he recalls, "I had this terrible dream. . . . I saw a Man descend from a great black Cloud, in a bright Flame of Fire, and light upon the Ground: he was all over as bright as a Flame, so that I could but just bear to look towards him; his Countenance was most inexpressibly dreadful, impossible for Words to describe" (70). Having dished out pure convention, Defoe adds a modernizing twist to his classical and biblical materials: "He was no sooner landed upon the Earth, but he moved forward towards me, with a long Spear or Weapon in his Hand, to kill me; . . . he spoke to me, or I heard a Voice so terrible, that it is impossible to express the Terror of it" (70). Once again defeating expectation, Crusoe quickly and clearly recounts the words that inspired so much fear: "*Seeing all these Things have not brought thee to Repentance, now thou shalt die.*" Savage man is the more horrific for speaking with the familiar voice of the Christian god and not the inarticulate mumbling of an aborigine. Savage man, so represented, no longer represents either God or savage man, however, but combines them both into a representation of Crusoe's irrationality—Crusoe the Other, as he might appear to a normal European.

Defoe offers us this interesting bit of protoanthropological reasoning. He represents God as the personification of natural forces hostile to man, forces that can be conquered by reason. The vision equates God's intervention in human affairs with savagery, and Crusoe's terrors during the bout of fever with those of the savage mind. In this way, the novel transforms the old nature animated by God into what might be called a discourse of personal life, the world as felt and reflected upon by the individuated subject, a world thereby enclosed within his body. Images testifying to the presence of dangerously irrational territories within the self place a premium on self-control, which becomes the answer to every problem Crusoe subsequently encounters. God remains in Crusoe's world to the degree that He helps to supply this answer; but God is radically transformed, we find, as Crusoe's reason achieves a decisive advantage over the fever. To produce a cure, Crusoe draws upon knowledge, acquired during his travels in South America, concerning the medicinal effects of tobacco. This recollection initiates something like a magical undoing, whereby through his own agency Crusoe can master all the outside forces that once threatened him, including God himself. He experiments with some leaves until he settles upon a method of inhaling smoke from tobacco soaked in rum. While thus filling his head with "vapour," he recounts, he "took up the Bible and began to read." Drugged at his own initiative, Crusoe's body recovers. Once he has acquired God's word through the labor of reading, furthermore, Crusoe's mind regains unprecedented tranquility. Like information concerning the therapeutic properties of tobacco, the word of God can operate on behalf of the individual when it has been appropriated as useful knowledge.[42]

Thus integrated into one's personal life, God becomes therapeutic—disciplinary rather than punitive.[43]

But what about the "Print of a Man's Naked foot" that Crusoe discovers one day in the sand? Does this not send him catapulting back into the demon-haunted world he has tried to master by means of reason? Upon the appearance of the footprint, Crusoe describes his state of mind as one "thunderstruck" by "an apparition" that once again fills his "Head full of Vapours" (125). The reappearance of the language Crusoe used to describe his state of mind altered by fever seems to return the hero to his earlier relationship with objects in the world. But the novel does not take us back to earlier confrontations between self and other. Having been banished from the story upon Crusoe's arrival on the deserted island, savage man returns in the brand-new form of a body that embodies irrationality. As such, he may now be conquered by rationality rather than violence. His reappearance constitutes a fundamental change in Crusoe's conception of what people are; this change is dramatized by a radical about-face in Crusoe's relation to other men.

Upon first spying the footprint, Crusoe plans an ambush. He is so full of the impulse to kill them all "that I often dream'd of it; and sometimes [it seemed] I was just going to let fly at them in my Sleep" (132). Domination through a monopoly on violence—according to Foucault, the early modern conception of government—was the method Crusoe used to deal with wild beasts and savage men before he was washed ashore on the island (22). No sooner does he take up the old fantasy of power, however, than he rejects such violence outright in favor of what proves to be a more effective means of physical domination. It is as if, having dislodged sensation completely from referents in the world, Defoe can shift the theater of domination from nature and the world of property to human nature and the world of consciousness. On the one hand, Crusoe's relationship with Friday suggests that the nation of orderly individuals develops according to the same principle on which Locke bases a theory of education. The man who arrives at a desired state of rationality is obligated to reproduce that state of mind in others. This obligation not only entitles him to political power; it is in itself a form of political power. But Locke's argument never pauses to ask the practical question that Defoe's narrative has gone to so much trouble to raise: If rationality manifests itself as self control—control, that is, of one's own irrationality—then by what means does one reproduce that state of mind in others?[44]

Upon reconsidering the footprint, Crusoe abandons his attempt to impose rationality on the world of nature. He directs the same strategies of division, enclosure, and observation at the savage mind. But it becomes clear that the patient methods of instruction by which he enlightens Friday's mind are impractical on a mass scale. Crusoe may be able to domesticate Friday, but once a mutinous crew of men from old Europe washes up on his beach, the metaphor of paternal authority—defining the relationship between state and subject as one between father and son—no longer translates into an effective method of socialization. There are simply too many other people for Crusoe to deal with, and they are of very different nationalities, religions, and social positions. Subtle forms of fear seem to provide him with a far more effective means of managing such a population than reason does.

Having emptied the island of baseless fears, Defoe promptly fills it with a mutinous population. Understanding himself to be decisively out-numbered, Crusoe decides to subdue these men by the methods he de-veloped for purposes of mastering his own worst nightmares and imag-inary fears. To achieve rationality, he has had to fix each sensation to an object in the world, discovering by this process the real order of things and purging the island of all sources of superstitious fear. Being reason-able, however, he comes to depend on the assumption that sensations—grasped as signs—have their source in things that exist outside the self. Is it not curious, then, that Crusoe decides to exploit the potential gap between signs and things which characterizes irrationality in general and dreamwork in particular? For this is indeed what he does when he creates a governor—a completely rational individual, apparently omniscient and omnipotent—who has neither voice nor body and thus no power outside of fiction. By means of this fiction, Crusoe reproduces in his subjects much the same state of fear and awe that the apparition of a savage god inspired in him. In noting this parallel between dreams and political power, however, we must note as well precisely where the two diverge. Fiction ultimately proves far more powerful than dreams in Defoe's story about the founding of the modern nation; it is invisible and cannot be tested against the world of objects. Fiction, in this sense, is superior to things; it cannot be refuted but fills the space of the island and determines what people experience there.[45]

Although Locke's theory of property insists that political power de-rives from property, which in turn derives from productive labor, Defoe's novel abandons such labor. Instead it represents intellectual labor as the source of political power. Rather than set intellectual labor to work on the blank space of the savage mind in the way he set productive labor to work on the blank space of the island, Defoe splits off the power of knowledge as it is personified in Crusoe from productive labor as it is embodied in Friday. It is important to note that the worker seems to find this division of labor entirely beneficial. Indeed, Crusoe reports that Friday is concerned because "there is much more Labour upon me [Crusoe] on his Account" (166), even though "in a little Time *Friday* was able to do all the Work for me, as well as I could do it my self" (166). How can this be? The contradiction quickly resolves itself when one remembers that Marx's vulgar capitalist claimed that he did as much work as his employee because the capitalist had to supervise the laborer.[46] In having the capitalist give voice to this line of reasoning, Marx is simply giving back to the capitalist the rationale that Defoe put in the mouth of Crusoe's surrogate son and grateful servant Friday. As he takes up the role of paternal authority in its most benevolent form, Crusoe explains: "He [Friday] . . . let me know, that he thought I had much more Labour upon me on his Account, than I had for my self; and that he would work the harder for me, if I would tell him what to do" (166). A similar division of labor occurs when it comes to administering violence. Crusoe takes up a musket once more after Friday's appearance, in order to hand over the business of bloodshed to the servant. Crusoe is the better tactician, but Friday proves the more effective marksman during his very first attempt: "*Friday* took his Aim so much better than I, that on the Side that he shot, he kill'd two of them, and wounded three more; and on My side, I kill'd one, and wounded two" (182). Within four paragraphs, the two have parted ways. Crusoe claims to have "kept my Piece in my Hand still, without firing, being willing to keep my Charge ready," while Friday "pursu'd the flying Wretches with no Weapon in his Hand, but his Hatchet; and with that he dispatch'd those three" (184).

As a result, the hero of the story is no longer so much self-made man as self-reflective man—the man who can manage other men because he has learned to regulate himself. The project of this man—and presumably of those whose interests he will come to represent—is not so much to produce a habitable world outside the self as to reproduce the world of self within others. Why, then, does he achieve this political effect by producing irrational fears in his subjects? If such irrationality defines him as uniquely qualified to oversee such a population, then his rationality provides the technology with which he reproduces precisely those fears.

This answer provides us with a way around the trap awaiting readers of *Robinson Crusoe*. The novel asks to be read as a story about the property question, whether it ultimately comes down on the side of an older and more limited concept of ownership or lends support to possessive individualism. As a fable of the origins of private property, it also asks to be read as the fable of a developing self. These two positions can be identified with two of Defoe's most famous readers, Rousseau and Marx. In *Émile,* Rousseau states that *Robinson Crusoe* is the first book his hero needs. Reading this book will encourage the boy "to examine the behaviour of his hero, to see if he has not forgotten something, or if he could have done better."[47] Thus Rousseau uses Defoe's fable about the making of the modern state as a model of personal development. On the other hand, Marx used the story of Robinson Crusoe to kick off his account of capitalism. The novel provided him with a model of nation formation.[48] Each adopts one-half of the novel as the basis of his theory; but neither theory connects the narrative of personal development with that of national history, even though *Crusoe* demonstrates, as perhaps no other narrative does, that they are mutually dependent fables. The nation that comes into being on the imaginary island is composed of self-governed subjects. Thus the modern Crusoe preexists the modern state. At the same time, it is the business of that state, as represented by his island kingdom, to produce the kinds of individuals who want to submit to it. Subsequent interpretations underscore the discontinuity and yet interdependence of the "inside" (the mind) and the "outside" (the state), which Defoe's narrative joins in the manner of a Moebius strip.[49] No matter what developmental model it favors—personal or political—in interpreting this novel, the critical tradition focuses squarely on the "rational" structures of the text, namely, on the production of property and the triumph of knowledge over both nature and imaginary fear. Yet the connection between the world of objects and that of subjects does not meet the test of rationality. Our brief genealogy of dreams has sought, in contrast, to stress the production of irrationality—uninscribed territories which appear to be already there outside of language but are in fact produced by the work of fiction itself.

Foucault's notion of discipline has pointed our reading in this direction. It helped us to shift attention away from the terrain of property as the first location of cause, and onto that of mind. Events on this terrain were, to our way of thinking, no less political than events that supposedly occur outside and prior to words. Moving into Defoe's fiction from Locke's *Essay Concerning Human Understanding,* one is struck by the fact that reason is never quite able to contain in a stable classification system the simple impressions made by things in the world upon the blank slate of the European mind. To the contrary, reason does its best work on materials that made sense in pre-Enlightenment England. It stripped these materials of any empirical basis. Formerly the innate stuff of a Christian soul and aristocratic body, under the dictates of reason they became the stuff of unfounded fears, fancies, and dreams.

For our purposes, the transformation of early modern culture into irrational territories of mind—not a white sheet of paper devoid of characters, but regions hopping with demons and fraught with violence—must be regarded as the most important work Defoe did. The existence of these territories intruded into Lockean theory and shifted the locus of cultural controversy inside the individual body and onto a psychological plane. In *Robinson Crusoe,* however, the irrational affords the semiotic terrain on which an entirely new political project can unfold—that which Foucault calls discipline. This project empowered a class of writers, editors, bureaucrats, bookkeepers, and printers—the kind of people whom Benedict Anderson calls the petit bourgeoisie of print capitalism, as well as the kind of people who engineered what Raymond Williams describes as "the long revolution" in print. In this revolution, such people reproduced themselves in words and managed to define their image as that of England itself. But these people neglected to explain what their intellectual labor had contributed to the success of the image. They made it seem as if England itself had improved, grown wiser and more just. Through fiction in particular, they wrote themselves out of the picture; in doing so, they made it convenient for subsequent generations of reformers, bureaucrats, writers, and intellectuals to locate agency outside themselves—in money and heads of state. Foucault alone grants their intellectual labor the place it probably deserves in modern history.

Foucault allows us to read *Robinson Crusoe* as the agent of the change that gave writing unprecedented authority because this work of fiction helped to determine how individuals would eventually be classified; but there is something that only such authors as Locke, Defoe, and ultimately Richardson can in turn tell us about Foucault. If we position Foucault at the other end of the historical trajectory we have been investigating, and grant Locke and Defoe a certain degree of explanatory power on the basis that writing actually does something to the things to which it refers, we can return to the observation with which we began this chapter: Foucault, like Locke, has divided his account of modern culture into the history of the state *(Discipline and Punish)* on the one hand, and the history of personal life *(The History of Sexuality)* on the other. In this respect Foucault has reproduced the interior difference produced by

Locke, naturalized by Defoe, and gendered by Richardson. By writing a separate history of personal life, after all, Foucault does suggest that the story of modern institutions can be understood apart from what he calls "the discourse of sexuality" and what we mean by "personal life." On the other hand, he has been the most forceful proponent of the idea that in discovering new interiorities of the human mind, the writing that proliferated around sexuality during the eighteenth century produced something that literate people eventually took to heart as their very nature. Locke acknowledged the category of consciousness that would later house sexuality, simply in order to represent everything that rationality was not. Indeed, he considered it impossible for there to be a second self within the self that reason had excluded from the domain of knowledge. In Foucault's account, the irrational self—which invariably made its presence known in sexual terms—did not step forward and submit itself to classification and analysis until the early nineteenth century, when hysterics, homosexuals, children, paupers, and criminals were seen as manifestations of its existence.

Defoe tells a somewhat different story. His fiction demonstrates that, at the beginning of the modern period, the categories characterizing rational discourse were mapped onto haunted ground. The interior landscape of the modern subject was, in a very real way, the dumping ground of materials from an earlier culture; as Crusoe's dream suggests, these materials were both natural and holy. This territory provided the optimal site for cultural activity that divided the social world into the cellular structure realized perhaps most perfectly in Jeremy Bentham's Panopticon. Bentham thought up the Panopticon prison as a practical means of disciplining prisoners by supervision. The prisoners were to be housed within an architectural setting that made both their every move and their moments of idleness visible to an invisible observer at the prison's center. It was assumed that the prisoners would internalize that supervisor by thinking and behaving as if they were being constantly watched and evaluated. It is important to recall that the Panopticon was inspired by a workshop that Bentham's brother Samuel designed for Prince Potemkin in 1786. Jeremy not only seized upon his brother's design and adapted it for a prison but also reformed the prison according to the general principle of social discipline in an institutional setting. The Panopticon provided Bentham with the model of the welfare state that would replace the existing Poor Law.[50] Locke, Defoe, and countless others first set this logic in motion when they divided a certain form of individual off from everything and everyone else in the world.

But between their moment and that of Foucault—our moment—something equally profound occurred, for which we have merely set the stage with our reading of *Robinson Crusoe:* the gendering of the writing subject. Richardson obviously knew what he was doing when he described the writing subject as someone subjected to rather than empowered by the laws of property. He was guided by the Lockean metaphor of the self as self-inscription just as surely as by the logic of a state based on private property. Even in granting women a certain "parental authority" over their children, Locke never suggested they were capable of the development that entitled one to self-government. If some of the best-known heroines of eighteenth-century fiction appear to have some of the power once reserved for men, it is because Richardson gave them the compensatory power of writing. Writing does not allow Pamela and Clarissa to enter into a contract with the state; but it does allow them to refuse and (in Pamela's case at least) renegotiate a relationship with a man of superior station to themselves. It allows them to challenge the absolute power of such men. In this respect, Richardson—and writers like him—pried writing loose from the powers and privileges that earlier writers had embodied in the male. Richardson represents writing as a power in its own right. Writing could not override the twin powers of law and property, but it could overwrite them. And so writing could determine whether those powers were considered necessary, desirable, or right.

At first glance, Crusoe might appear to be the prototypical writer in this respect. In his hands, writing recapitulates in miniature the fate it suffers in the works of Josselin and Locke. Crusoe's journal starts out as an attempt to account for himself in the eyes of God, but words drift away from this project and begin to stick to things—reckonings of the hoarding of goods, the acquisition of new property, and the production of the food to supply a kingdom. Indeed, in calculating the weather, words cease to operate on behalf of the soul and its salvation and begin to exercise control over nature. Anything and everything (including even God himself) that can be converted into words can be appropriated according to the logic of property, and can be subjected to the faculties that organize information within the mind. It is with a stroke of the pen and not the sweat of Crusoe's brow that divine authority gives way to a secular culture organized around the individual. But theocentricity capitulates to logocentricity only so long as the person who authors himself authors all—a population fathered by the dissemination of information much as Pine's kingdom was created by the distribution of his seed alone.

Once Crusoe returns to England, his language lacks the power of patriarchal authority, authorial presence vanishes, and the organization of his miniature kingdom in the Caribbean reverts to a state resembling Hobbes's nature. Crusoe's island is not quite an imagined community in the modern sense of the term. Writing does not permanently displace the speech community.

By giving the implements of writing to abducted women, Richardson hit upon a situation in which writing could do what ordinary labor could never accomplish, at least not in England. It could appropriate vast territories of culture and attach them to the name of the author, creating a world in words that neither vanished in the face of inherited authority nor openly contested that political order. It occupied another territory, a space at least as empty as America, because it was unknown until he wrote about it. This territory might be compared with that defined by the map in the Borges story, from which Baudrillard borrows his well-known figure of the simulacrum: the map is so exact in size and detail that people soon forget that it completely covers what was once the territory.[51] The genius of the mapmaker vanishes along with the artificiality of the map; objectification turns into object; and the world becomes one vast empire of visible signs, one must suppose, belonging exclusively to those people who know how to read it. To call Richardson an author and compare him with Borges's mapmaker is to relocate the moment when words gained power over things in the first half of the eighteenth century. It is to say that we are not undergoing the inversion of sign and referent at the present moment, as Baudrillard wants us to believe. The present crisis of meaning simply marks the moment when it is becoming obvious that no such inversion in fact occurred.[52] If history seems to be vanishing, as Baudrillard and a number of other theorists of culture complain, it is because the map is fraying and there appears to be nothing of substance underneath. The appearance of a reality "beneath" or "outside" of discourse, not the world made out of words, is the hallucination. Only the fact of writing supports the Enlightenment world of fact.

For a model of the rise of writing, we turned from Anderson and Foucault to Defoe and Richardson. But to call Richardson an author and use him to personify the capacity of words to produce a writing subject who would not otherwise be available to public view, does not identify the hero of the story. The question with which we began this book therefore resurfaces. We must consider just how Richardson authored an author who, though only fictional, would strike a chord of truth for an expanding readership. Anderson has argued that only writing could produce a basis for collective identity in America; but we have not yet developed an explanation of how something similar might have happened back in Europe. Neither Defoe nor Anderson can tell us that; whereas Foucault, like Richardson, takes up the story as if writing were already empowered. The success of *Pamela* and *Clarissa* demonstrates that indeed it was. It remains for us now to consider what happened between Defoe's time and Richardson's that made it possible for a print vernacular to behave in England much as Anderson claims it did in North America.

CHAPTER EIGHT

Why Categories Thrive

No doubt I made a strange sight in a dark coat, borrowed
from the captain, over sailor's pantaloons and apeskin san-
dals. Did they think of me as Cruso's wife, or had tales already reached them—sailor's haunts are full of gossip—of the
Englishwoman from Bahia marooned in the Atlantic by Portuguese mutineers? Do you think of me, Mr Foe, as Mrs
Cruso or as a bold adventuress? Think what you may, it was
I who shared Cruso's bed and closed Cruso's eyes, as it is I
who have disposal of all that Cruso leaves behind, which is
the story of his island.

J. M. Coetzee, *Foe*

Each chapter of this book has converged on the question raised by the
tautology that it takes an author to create an author. How, then, did the
author first come into being? Literary historians generally agree that the
rise of the English novel has everything to do with the rise of the modern
middle class and thus with the onset of modernity. Our final chapter will
reconsider the rise both of that class and of its favorite genre. We will
try to imagine the conditions for the emergence of the kind of writing
subject that Richardson created when he made a novel by stringing together personal letters supposedly written by an abducted servant girl.
By questioning the origins of the English novel, we want to challenge
the tendency among scholars and critics to assume that modern fiction
has to originate in some earlier European genre. To think about the
origins of the English novel, we will try out a narrative more like one
that might be used to describe the emergence of new cultures on *this*
side of the Atlantic. We want to think of England as part of a larger
nation whose boundaries extended overseas to North America. In order
for this nation to exist on both sides of the Atlantic, as a number of
scholars have recently noted, the English developed print technologies
which in turn played a crucial role in the formation of a culture peculiar
to the colonies.[1] In time, Benedict Anderson has suggested, writing and

ultimately print replaced other agents of government.[2] In time, he has speculated further, writing and especially print displaced the kinds of speech communities that could be overseen by the monarchs of early modern Europe. In this way, the technologies of power that had developed in order to extend England into the New World began to exercise a kind of power in their own right.

To this point in our argument, we could perhaps be charged with swapping a Eurocentric narrative of lineal descent for what might loosely be termed American exceptionalism. Indeed, we are suggesting that the English novel constituted itself as an exception to the European tradition of letters, much as American culture did. If exceptionalism is used to rethink the traditional accounts of English modernity, however, and if this same fantasy of self-origination took hold in Europe and propelled the sort of changes now identified with modern cultures, then exceptionalism can no longer be considered the exception.[3] One has to regard it as some new and highly infectious rule. Nor, from the perspective we are taking, was the novel first and foremost a European genre, but rather one that simultaneously recorded and recoded the colonial experience. With this in mind, we want to imagine what happened to the print culture that bound early modern English people on one side of the Atlantic to those who had ventured to the other. As it underwent the strange mutation that created a new basis for English identity in the colonies, this culture had to have a profound effect upon European Englishmen as well. But while any number of scholars have shown how English culture changed in the colonial setting, few if any have bothered to consider what happened when colonial writing flowed back across the Atlantic to England.

We like to think this way of reconceptualizing the problem of cultural origins has a midwestern origin. One September night in 1988, our first in Minneapolis to be exact, we happened to tune in a public television show that documented how one Minnesotan decided to spend the last years of a life sadly foreshortened by leukemia. Knowing his days were limited, this man marshaled most of his family's resources—not only its savings but time and devotion as well—to build a replica of a Viking ship capable of sailing from Duluth, through the Great Lakes, up the St. Lawrence, and across the Atlantic to a small town on the western coast of Norway. Bent on demonstrating that Minnesota had been visited if not in fact settled by Norsemen four to five hundred years before Columbus's first voyage, the ailing patriarch passed away before the boat could make its maiden voyage. As the dream of return was taken up by his children, however, it became the basis for a more complex and ambitious theory of origins.

They imported a crew from Norway to rebuild the vessel and to navigate it through the treacherous waters of Lake Superior. Somewhere in the process, someone, perhaps only in jest, raised the possibility that certain towns on the western coast of modern Norway might have been founded by an expedition of North American settlers intent on returning home. Even the Norwegians involved in the project were captivated by this possibility. They assured the makers of the documentary that Lake Superior was by far the roughest part of the entire journey and agreed with their American counterparts that "anyone who could make it through Superior could make it all the way to Norway." Two months later, when the boat bearing its binational crew made land on the Norwegian coast, communities on both sides of the Atlantic regarded the success of the venture as proof positive that each could well have been the forebear of the other. Our purpose for drawing this parallel between the origin of the English novel and that of Norwegian Americans is not only to cast the whole project of discovering cultural origins in a slightly ridiculous light but also to consider the historical consequences of understanding ourselves and our novels in that way.

The eighteenth-century English novel might be called the perfect creole. Novels characteristically claim to have begun as another kind of writing, as a diary, a journalistic account, a handbook for letter writing, a travel narrative, a criminal confession, a romance, or just plain history. Yet each English novel also insists it was the product of England alone, the record of a true-born speaker of the mother tongue. And critical tradition has respected this claim. In the past few years, among the most influential studies of the eighteenth-century English novel, one finds several new attempts to locate the origins of that genre in texts written and published in England before there was anything like the novels that would eventually be canonized.[4] Yet in order to disagree over which genre provided the prototype of the English novel, all the authors of these studies assumed that it sprang from a strictly English past. Because they understood that past in modern terms, as an England confined to the British Isles, these scholars failed to consider the events that produced the modern nation. None of their historical accounts factored the rise of the novel into the process that identified the English nation with the print vernacular. We will use Samuel Richardson's first novel, *Pamela,* to argue that no such product of modern English culture can be explained by events occurring strictly within English culture if we restrict our definition of England to modern England alone.[5] To discover precisely where the printed word first began not only to refer back to a source in an epistolary heroine but also to derive extraordinary authority from qualities that supposedly inhered in that individual alone, one has to go to British America. One has to go to America, in other words, to understand where novels come from.

Published in 1740 and generally considered the first domestic novel, *Pamela* recounts a scandal which takes us right to the heart of our argument. The heroine, a poor but honest serving girl, is held captive on a country estate. In order to have his way with her, the master of the estate dresses up as a drunken maid and pretends to doze off in Pamela's bedchamber. After a housekeeper, who takes part in the conspiracy, has wedged herself in bed next to the naked heroine, Mr. B. slips out of his disguise and joins them, pinning Pamela's free arm beneath him. Except for her mouth, she is completely immobilized. She screams, she pleads, and then she faints. The sequence of events promises almost certain rape. Merely by shifting from excessive speech to silence, however, Pamela keeps her virtue magically intact; and, by thus refusing to give her consent, she continues to occupy the role of heroine. In a letter written to her parents upon regaining consciousness, she reports the effectiveness of so withholding herself from a libertine master: "This, O my dear parents! was a most dreadful trial. . . . I hope, as [Mr. B.] assures me, he was not guilty of indecency; . . . God, . . . by disabling me in my faculties, empowered me to preserve my innocence" (214).

What does it mean that Mr. B. cannot possess her simply because she refuses to give her consent? A case might be made that by withholding consent she has succeeded in redefining her body and her labor as hers alone to exchange or to withhold. But to make this case would be to suggest that Richardson was claiming for women much the same rights to labor and property that Locke had claimed for certain men. We prefer to argue that Richardson has Mr. B. plot so many assaults on Pamela's body in order to prove that she does not have a body—at least, not a body that can serve as the object of libertine desire. During the course of the novel, as in the scene above, the repeated assaults upon Pamela's chastity cause her body to disappear along with her status as servant. She stops working and does nothing but write personal letters. As she does so, she ceases to exist as a sexually desirable woman and becomes a unique source of written speech. The transformation proves curiously self-empowering. It is arguably the first time in English literature that readers were asked to care about the personal happiness of a servant and to believe that her chances for happiness depended upon her maintaining her virginity.[6] And care they did, so much so that in 1740 Richardson's *Pamela* launched the tradition of the novel. In subsequent novels by both male and female authors, the future of the ruling class—their suitability for rule—would continue to hinge on their adherence to courtship procedures that demonstrated extraordinary concern for the feelings of otherwise quite ordinary women. Fiction established a new standard for membership in the ruling class.

A great deal thus hinges on the question of the origin of the English novel: Where did the power to define a class of people come from? What could possibly make the body of an ordinary woman matter so much to a readership? Even granted that she was rather well educated for someone in her position and that her parents were once substantially better off, why should educated readers care about the feelings of this housemaid, a ditch digger's daughter? There was nothing in previous fiction to suggest that a woman's ability to write letters was alone sufficient compensation for what she lacked in wealth and position. Nor was there any precedent to suggest that Richardson's readers would have been shocked either at the idea of several people sharing the same bed or at the idea of a wealthy landowner having his way with a servant.[7] They might have found it strange that such a man could fail despite the artfulness of his attempts at seduction. And they would probably have been scandalized to learn that the same man was willing to marry that woman. Richardson anticipated such responses. When her tormentor hesitates to force himself upon Pamela out of respect for her sentiments, his collaborator, Mrs. Jewkes, regards such hesitation with a mixture of contempt and incredulity: "And will you, sir, . . . for a fit or two, give up such an opportunity as this?" (213). Knowing full well that common sense was against him, Richardson was nevertheless intent on overthrowing the housekeeper's sense of propriety and her master's sexual prerogative. Richardson wrote two extremely popular novels that set the hymen of a nonaristocratic woman above the wishes of a gentleman.[8]

Many literary historians regard Daniel Defoe as the father of the English novel. *Robinson Crusoe* appeared around 1719, some twenty years before *Pamela,* and there are important similarities between the two works of fiction. Richardson, one could argue, simply replaces Crusoe's island in the New World with the interior spaces of the household, the female body, and the private world of the emotions as revealed in Pamela's letters to her parents. But it is one thing for a community to reclaim an individual who has undergone a personal transformation in captivity; it is another thing to reabsorb an individual who has elsewhere grown politically powerful and self-aware. Unlike Pamela, Crusoe comes back as the exception rather than the rule of European culture, and he remains on its periphery at the conclusion of the novel.

The difference between Defoe's narratives and the domestic fiction that flourished later in the century boils down to a difference in their use of gender. When Defoe used female narrators, they were always entrepreneurs, excellent businesswomen who actually made a go of it in the colonies.[9] These women did not win readers' admiration by warding off seducers. Defoe obviously entertained his readership by showing just how far his women got by giving in. As a result, the story of *Moll Flanders* was excluded from the canon long after *Robinson Crusoe* was taken in, even though Defoe withdrew this heroine from the marketplace at the end of the story and gave her all the respectability of marriage. *Crusoe* was Defoe's only novel to be listed among the books appropriate for nineteenth-century women and children to read, no doubt because Crusoe was the only one of Defoe's protagonists to conduct himself in the manner of a Richardsonian heroine. Crusoe single-mindedly preserves intact the magical boundary defined by his skin from any and all invaders. He rings himself round with ditches, fences, fields, and walls, creating a domain as internally compartmentalized and temporally ordered as the household Pamela describes in the tediously protracted conclusion to her narrative. Faced with threats to his body, however imagined or real, he takes the girl's option where Moll Flanders throws in her lot with the boys.[10] Where he goes domestic, she goes native and becomes a whore among whores, a thief among thieves. Would Defoe have switched the sexes of his two most memorable protagonists had he known that eighteenth-century readers were going to identify their interests with the perpetuation of a household that in turn depended on a woman's sexual purity? Hard to say. We can only speculate that he did not know how the gender game would be played out in fiction and that by the time Richardson was writing *Pamela*, the rules were absolutely clear.

The notable success of Defoe's domestic hero invites us to consider what gender had to do with the political change taking place in eighteenth-century England. Recent controversy over the origins of the novel (which is also a controversy over the origins of middle-class culture) has not come up with a theory that is significantly better than those of Ian Watt and the preceding generation of critics as to why an assault on the body of a common Englishwoman should carry such a political and emotional charge.[11] In an effort to identify the source of fiction's ob-

sessive concern with the potentially deleterious effects of low-life figures
and their criminal behavior, Lennard Davis offers criminal confessions as
a possible prototype for the novel. But while such writing may account
for the non-elite features of the novel, it cannot explain why narratives
of courtship should acquire such enormous appeal. Michael McKeon's
admirably exhaustive account of the origins of the English novel encourages us to understand *Pamela* as "a progressive specification of romance to the conditions of eighteenth-century domestic service" (370).
Although he identifies this aspect of *Pamela* with the counterfeiting of
letters of reference and the crisis in domestic service that marked the
period, his theory does not shed much light on the question of why
sexual assault proved so meaningful to an eighteenth-century readership.
In suggesting a panoply of other sources, J. Paul Hunter forces one to
consider how Anglocentric the search for the origins of the English novel
has always been.[12] Although Armstrong's book on the political history
of the English novel focuses on gender, she too confines herself to English
materials when she locates the prototype for domestic fiction in female
conduct books of the seventeenth and eighteenth centuries. *Desire and
Domestic Fiction* does explain why the hero of eighteenth-century fiction
is usually and most powerfully a heroine. It is certainly important to see
how novels used a female narrator to open a discursive space for the
writing subject. It is equally important to see that the bourgeois subject
began not only as a female subject but also as a writing subject. But it
is perhaps even more important to understand why gender's power as a
historical category cannot be understood within the tradition of English
letters, as that tradition is currently defined.

Created in part by the extraordinary popularity of domestic fiction, a
revolution in reading habits during the eighteenth century changed the
notion of what it meant to be English, at least among the literate classes.
Novel readers were not asked to locate England's strength and their own
security exclusively within the health and well-being of the English aristocracy. Instead, the survival of respectable people and the perpetuation
of their domestic way of life began to matter.[13] To understand where
Pamela's hermetically sealed body might have acquired its unprecedented
ideological charge, one must determine where two discursive phenomena
converge. Where, if anywhere prior to *Pamela*, did Englishness come to
be embodied in a nonaristocratic female? And where, if anywhere prior
to *Pamela*, was the female in question a virtually inexhaustible source
of English prose? Certainly not in England. But such a woman does appear

in captivity narratives written in the North American colonies during the late seventeenth and eighteenth centuries.

Among the earliest accounts of encounters with the indigenous peoples of the Americas are those of Cabeza de Vaca (1542) and Juan Ortiz (1557), Johann von Staden's *Warhaftige Historia* (1557), and Job Hortop's *The Travailes of an Englishman* (1591).[14] These accounts are curiosities. They never became an important genre in and of themselves, although they were certainly familiar enough to the reading public and could appear as interpolated tales, as "The Captive's Tale" does in *Don Quixote*. Reading through collections of captivity narratives into the late seventeenth century, one can observe the genre proliferating and subdividing, though not exactly along national lines. Among the Indian captivity narratives, one kind in particular begins to reshape and dominate the genre. Of primary importance is the fact that this kind of captivity narrative was not produced b·· emissaries of church or state. It differs in this respect both from Johr ith's account of his three weeks in captivity in Virginia and from the grisly accounts of the physical torture experienced by the Jesuit Fathers Jogues, Bressani, Garnier, Chaumont, and Hennepin.[15] In the captivity narrative that we will identify with the English novel, the captives tend to be European settlers from rather ordinary backgrounds who wanted to establish a home in North America.

One version of this type of narrative combines a modern authorial consciousness with early modern Protestant hagiography to produce a distinctively English experience and testimony. Always present in these accounts is the possibility of going native. We will not discuss such accounts as those of John Marrant or Mary Jemison, in which the captive becomes assimilated to another culture. But we do want to note that during the seventeenth and early eighteenth centuries, these stories existed as a kind of anti-tale within the hagiographical narrative. The reader of captivity narratives was always aware of the story that would have to be told were the captive to lose her English character, just as later readers were aware of the pornographic narrative that would at once develop were Pamela to let her guard down and fall prey to Mr. B.'s seduction.[16]

Throughout the eighteenth century, one of the most popular captivity narratives on both sides of the Atlantic was Mary Rowlandson's account. Within the year of its publication, 1682, it went through three editions and several printings in British America.[17] That same year a fourth edition was published in England, and by 1720 a fifth edition appeared there in print.[18] Encapsulated versions of the same story appeared in published sermons, in publishers' reports, and as advertisements included on the back pages of other books.[19] A late-seventeenth- or early-eighteenth-century reader could see Rowlandson's name and fill in the substance of her testimony without actually having to read the words in which she told it. Once created, furthermore, the appetite for narratives of this kind never diminished with the rising popularity of fiction on both sides of the Atlantic.[20] By the end of the eighteenth century, almost thirty editions of Rowlandson's account had appeared, most in the last thirty years of the century, which certainly suggests that her story continued to be well received even after English readers had developed their prodigious appetite for novels. Along with Rowlandson's account, a number of other captivity narratives went through several printings on both sides of the Atlantic. If first editions of many of these accounts are extremely rare or even nonexistent today (as in the case of Mary Rowlandson's), it is no doubt because they passed through so many hands; one can assume that the readership was even larger than the publication history indicates.

Mary Rowlandson anticipated Crusoe in representing the English in the New World as an abducted body. When captivity narratives began to be published on both sides of the Atlantic, however, the bodies so endangered were usually—though not always—female bodies.[21] Even when the storytellers were men, these men wrote of their experience as Englishmen enslaved by Indians.[22] Captive men owned neither their labor nor their bodies, according to legal theory of the period, and under such conditions there is reason to think that an eighteenth-century readership would not have considered them men. It can be argued that Englishmen in captivity wrote from a position akin to that of women and children. Scholars have pored over these late-seventeenth-century accounts for information about colonial life and the cultures of the indigenous peoples. But the most obvious fact that leaps off the page is that these narratives required readers to change the way they imagined being English, because they had to imagine being English in America.[23] The exemplary captive existed for the early eighteenth-century reader as a kind of epistolary heroine, whose ability to read and write, more than anything else, distinguished her from her Indian captors.[24] Moreover, in later captivity narratives, literacy also distinguished the English individual from men and women of European birth. The French—and during the revolutionary period, the English—posed a threat to the English character. The temptations of religious conversion, in the first case, and of treason, in the second, could sever the individual's connection to home and community just as permanently as going native.[25]

To describe *Pamela* as a captivity narrative is, by implication, to construct a theoretical link between Benedict Anderson's account of New World nationalism and Foucault's account of European modernity. As we explained in chapter 6, Anderson believes the journey to the New World set in motion a process which transformed the basis on which certain Englishmen understood their relationship both to England and to one another. As the print vernacular circulated among them, they began to imagine themselves as a nation made up of people who read and wrote in vernacular English. But Anderson's narrative never takes one back to Europe, even though the formation of New World nationalism took place at the very time when the modern English state was emerging out of an earlier form of monarchy, and despite the fact that the print vernacular gained unprecedented importance during the same period. Foucault, on the other hand, does not consider how information from the colonies might have triggered the massive project of reclassification that he identifies with the emergence of a modern institutional culture. Indeed, he deliberately avoids the whole question of causality. He describes the so-called rise of the middle classes as a process whereby writing gained supremacy over a field of discursive practices in which it had formerly played a minor role. His account of the transformation of early modern into modern Europe is Eurocentric; the process is entirely self-enclosed. Mary Rowlandson's narrative allows us to connect the historical narratives of Anderson and Foucault, both of whom neglect the impact of gender and of fiction.

A closer look at Rowlandson's account of her captivity will indicate what advantages might have accrued to writing that appeared to have a female source. In contrast with Robinson Crusoe, Mary Rowlandson could be incorporated within an English (albeit colonial) community after enduring captivity and exile among the Indians. The female Crusoe could return without overturning the status quo. Yet, in doing so, she brought a new and distinctively modern basis for political identity into the mainstream of European thinking. It is true that she made a difference between Englishmen in England and in the colonies, when she made writing the means of maintaining an English identity overseas. But, as *Pamela* leads us to believe, literacy established a new basis for identity back in England as well.

The captivity narrative described an experience that people of "the middling sort" in England could not have imagined were it not for the colonial venture; it asked its readers to imagine being English in America. Although it is an ordinary voice—and most often a female voice at that—

the voice of someone captured by Indians speaks with authority because it speaks out in isolation and testifies to the individual's single-minded desire to return home. Such a voice predisposes us *not* to think of the English as intruders who were decimating the native population and driving them from their homeland.[26] Indeed, Rowlandson frequently describes the indigenous population as if it were the invader of an English land. On one occasion, she recalls how "the Indians quickly spread themselves over the deserted English fields, gleaning what they could find."[27] A landscape from which the signs of English life have vanished is a setting where the solitary body of the Englishwoman exists in imminent peril—more so in Rowlandson's America than on Defoe's uninhabited island. Rowlandson recounts, for example, "the hideous insulting and triumphing that there was [among the Indians] over some Englishman's scalps they had taken (as their manner is)" (330). In later captivity narratives, even other Europeans can resemble savages in their barbarous treatment of English women. Hannah Swarton is but one example of a captive who suffered much the same kind of anxiety at the hands of the French as other English women did when held captive by North American Indians. "Yea, sometimes the papists, because I would not turn to them, threatened to send me to France," she explains, "and there I should be burned because I would not turn to them."[28]

But despite repeated allusion to such atrocities (which could include even cannibalism), the captivity narrative does not make us care so much about the body of an English woman as about what Rowlandson calls the English "heart," which introduces some of the language of later Gothic romance into the puritan narrative:

> Now away we must go with those barbarous creatures, with our bodies wounded and bleeding, and our hearts no less than our bodies. About a mile we went that night, up upon a hill within sight of the town, where they intended to lodge. There was hard by a vacant house (deserted by the English . . .). I asked them whether I might not lodge in the house that night, to which they answered, "What will you love English men still?" (325)

Surrounded by "nothing but wilderness, and woods, and a company of barbarous heathens," the English subject becomes poignantly aware that survival depends on her ties to a community that cannot be experienced directly (342–43). It requires her captivity in a strange and hostile place to equate the enduring love for signs of Englishness with what is most essential about the protagonist herself.

For lack of English inscriptions, the American landscape exists for Rowlandson—as it did for Locke in his *Second Treatise of Government*—

as a blank space lacking cultural inscriptions of any kind.[29] Out of lack comes longing, and out of longing, words. Having emptied the landscape, Rowlandson's words proceed to inscribe it with signs of the absent homeland. "As we went along," she writes, "I saw a place where English cattle had been. That was comfort to me, such as it was: quickly after that we came to an English path which so took with me, that I thought I could have freely lain down and died" (335). What is a landscape where "English cattle had been"? Certainly it is something more on the order of a rotten nature than nature either raw or cooked.[30]

Rowlandson describes her solitary state as a significantly fallen one in contrast with direct participation in the community of believers. But that same state of isolation gives her—though she is in no other way distinguished among English women—decisive superiority over native Americans. She is self-reflective and thus a whole world unto herself; Indians exist in her account as mass man, devoid of individuated interiority and thus lacking the capacity for self-examination. Whenever Rowlandson finds herself spiritually lacking in the eyes of God, she testifies to the presence of a peculiarly English consciousness.

> When I came to the brow of the hill that looked toward the swamp, I thought we had been come to a great Indian town (though there were none but our own company). The Indians were as thick as the trees: it seemed as if there had been a thousand hatchets going at once: if one looked before one, there was nothing but Indians, and behind one, nothing but Indians, and so on either hand, I myself in the midst, and no Christian soul near me, and yet how hath the Lord preserved me in safety! (334)

It is one of the great ironies of Western history that, in standing in for the original speech community in this way, Rowlandson's written English distinguished its author from members of that original community as well as from those people who neither spoke nor wrote English at all.

Rowlandson's account presupposes a single community that is united on the basis of literacy. This community is more English than Christian, though it is certainly Christian, and indeed puritan.[31] Rowlandson frequently refers to the Bible in her effort to sustain herself in solitude. These references suggest that her body is infinitely valuable, not because it contains a Christian soul—presumably that could survive without a body—but rather because it houses a unique sensibility, the source of the language composing the narrative and thus of the meaning that clings to those words across the ocean and down through the ages.[32] Her writing separates Rowlandson from England, then, and from all other forms of cultural exchange—not only speech but also the exchange of labor, goods, and all the symbolic gestures that are now considered part of daily life. But in doing so, the narrative simultaneously converts a form of literacy based on the print vernacular into a new basis for English identity.[33] It is not difficult to imagine how such narratives produced the kind of nationalism that was especially strong in those areas of New England where print was abundant and literacy high.[34] But what of the fact that these accounts circulated back to England and were avidly consumed there? On this matter scholars may have had little to say, but fiction has a great deal to tell us.

The kind of captivity narratives we have been discussing simultaneously record and create a new source of value that contemporary scholars neglect to factor into their accounts of earlier periods. Rowlandson's narrative demonstrates how an individual could acquire value quite apart from wealth and station simply because she was the source of writing. She emphasized her separation from her culture by organizing her account as a series of "removes" or marches. Richardson capitalized on the popular appetite for such narratives when he separated Pamela from her parents and then filled her with a single-minded desire to return. Throughout her account of captivity, Pamela reaffirms this solitary wish: "And now, my dearest father and mother, expect to see soon your poor daughter, with an humble and dutiful mind, returned to you" (31). Instead, of course, her master removes Pamela still further from the sanctuary of the family to whom she writes. Rather than send her home to them, he takes her to a more remote estate where he contrives to weaken her resistance. To be sure, these removes expose her to the seduction of a wealthy landowner rather than the violence of heathens. Yet each remove takes her farther into a world bent on destroying her cultural identity, which she tries to maintain by writing letters.

Were it not for the fact that Pamela is locked away in the heart of an older, agrarian England, the terms of her captivity would certainly have reminded scholars before now of Mary Rowlandson and all the other English women captured by Indians. "I find I am watched and suspected still very close; and I wish I was with you," Pamela confides in a letter to her parents. "But that must not be, it seems, this fortnight. . . . It will be a tedious and a dangerous one to me" (217). A second generation of captivity narratives that appeared around the time of *Pamela*'s publication attempted to close the gap between the theological discourse found in captivity narratives and the language of sentimental fiction. One captive describes her experience in terms that might have come straight from the heroine of a Gothic novel. "I dreaded the tragical design of my master," Elizabeth Hanson confesses, "looking for his coming to execute his bloody will upon us."[35] Though rape, as Mr. B.'s housekeeper puts it, may not seem "so bad as cutting her throat," most readers appear to have accepted Pamela's view that it was better to die than have sex with anyone but one's husband. Could it be that they heard in her protests the sentiments of colonial heroines responding to the Indian menace? What else would have made the loss of her virtue equivalent to losing one's English identity? "I trust," writes Pamela in a voice that might be mistaken for Mary Rowlandson's, "that God who has delivered me from the paw of the lion and the bear . . . will soon deliver me from this Philistine, that I may not *defy the commands of the living God!*" (218).[36] Rowlandson's account of her captivity may seem worlds apart from Richardson's protracted tale of attempted rape—until one considers what each accomplishes by gendering the writing subject.

Something of great importance to the respective readerships hinges on the fates of these women. Rowlandson is taken from her husband and turned into an Indian's slave. Pamela is taken from her parents and turned into the object of a libertine's desire. In both cases, the trials of the body matter less than the mental cruelties the women suffer. The captive's ability to return to the fold depends entirely upon qualities of mind that resist illegitimate forms of domination. That both New England Indians and old English aristocrats are inferior to the ordinary ("true") English person is indicated by their women. Rowlandson describes one of her master's squaws as "a severe and proud dame . . . bestowing every day in dressing herself neat as much time as any of the gentry of the land: powdering her hair, and painting her face, going with necklaces, with jewels in her ears, and bracelets upon her hands" (351). The description could easily be transported into Richardson's fiction to describe a woman of the upper gentry. Indeed, Mr. B.'s sister fits this stereotype. In either case, this kind of woman is contrasted with the ordinary English woman, whose virtues are identified with the virtues of the English in general. This is the point of the strange and seemingly extravagant ritual by which the newly reformed Mr. B. plans to introduce Pamela—now his fiancée—into polite society dressed in her rustic homespun. "I have told them the story of your present dress, and how you came by it," he informs her:

> One of the young ladies begs it as a favour, that they may see you just as you are: and I am the rather pleased it should be so, because they will perceive

you owe nothing to dress, but make a much better figure with your own native stock of loveliness, than the greatest ladies arrayed in the most splendid attire and adorned with the most glittering jewels. (286)

We might even regard Pamela's appearance in this emblematic form as Richardson's way of acknowledging the relationship between his epistolary heroine and the authors of captivity narratives.

If, as we are claiming, *Pamela* is a captivity narrative, then how might this interpretation redefine that novel and the whole tradition of sentimental and Gothic fiction that it inaugurated? Richardson located his captivity narrative in an aristocratic manor house, the symbolic center of early modern England. There he made readers care about the chastity of an otherwise insignificant serving girl in the same way they had already come to care about English women who had been abducted by Indians in British America. An advertisement for Rowlandson's narrative appearing in the first American edition of *The Pilgrim's Progress* (1681) suggests how such concern was generated: "Before long there will be published . . . the particular circumstances of the Captivity, & Redemption of Mrs. Mary Rowlandson; and of her children. Being pathetically written, with her own hand."[37] The emphasis shifted from the pathetic to the sensational when advertisers wanted to appeal to the readership back home in England. Here, for example, is an announcement that appeared in the *Term Catalogues*: "The history of the Captivity of Mrs. *Mary Rowlandson*, a Minister's Wife in *New England;* with her cruel and inhumane Usage amongst the Heathens for Eleven Weeks, and her Deliverance from them. Written by her own Hand, and now made Publick."[38] Her English publisher emphasized Rowlandson's position as an abducted wife rather than as a mother sent into captivity with her children.

Rowlandson changed English identity by maintaining her own identity among the heathens. Richardson made the ruling classes appear unfit to rule because its members seemed incapable of ruling themselves. He made their sexual practices testify to that inability. One must agree with Henry Fielding that the real scandal of *Pamela* is not her abduction but the fact that Richardson gave her the authorial prerogative not only to represent her own behavior but also to evaluate that of her master.[39] That prerogative could not have been imagined, much less taken seriously, without the power behind it that print had apparently acquired in North America. The captivity narrative requires the captive to ward off the threat of another culture by preserving the tie to her mother culture through writing alone. But there is another requirement for Pamela's prototype, which is directly related to the gender of the individual from whom writing comes. The captivity narrative requires that the detached—and thereby individuated—individual be reincorporated into the culture from which she has been separated.[40] Robinson Crusoe cannot quite manage such a return. Even though he finds his way back across the Atlantic, he feels compelled to leave again; he fails to fit into early modern British society after becoming rich and powerful overseas. Let us consider, then, how Pamela does what female captives such as Rowlandson could and Crusoe could not accomplish.

On the level of plot, Rowlandson ends up pretty much where she begins, in the bosom of her family and friends. Indeed, she seems to return to the same community that was in place before the Indian uprising, and her return appears to restore that community's original state of wholeness. Her narrative no doubt acquired some of its enormous popularity on both sides of the Atlantic from its insistence that English people could not be at home except with other English people and that English women could feel secure only with a specific English male and the offspring they produced together. But even this appeal to family feelings is not sufficient to explain the cultural-historical importance of captivity narratives. Their peculiar form of narrative closure does not simply close the gap between the narrating subject and her object of desire, the community from which she has been separated. Nor do those narratives merely elevate the English way over all other ways of being human; they also distinguish the New World community to which the captive returns from the Old World community she left behind. At least, this is what one gathers from comparing the female captivity narratives with *Pamela*.

The opening of Rowlandson's account represents the original community in this fashion: "Some in our house were fighting for their lives, others wallowing in their blood, the house on fire over our heads, and the bloody heathen ready to knock us on the head, if we stirred out" (323–24). When the Indians invade Rowlandson's New England household, that household is made up of Christians, largely women and children. The reader cannot tell individual families apart, much less individual bodies. It takes the solitude of her captivity to turn the narrator into a separate individual. When she is absorbed back into the community at the end of her captivity, however, her narration does not lose its self-enclosed character.[41] Her separation from that community paradoxically defines what and who she is even after her return to friends and family, and the community necessarily changes once it has opened its doors and admitted such an individual.[42] The captive's return transforms that community into one in which the individual counts. Though her description of the initial onslaught of Indians reveals little grief on her part for those family members who were lost, the search for a lost plenitude and wholeness continues to motivate her account as Rowlandson awaits the recovery of each and every child remaining in captivity. A continuing lack thus characterizes the reunion with her husband: "We were now in the midst of love, yet not without much and frequent heaviness of heart for our poor children and other relations who were still in affliction" (362). And when all the pieces of the family so incinerated, dismembered, and dispersed are finally reassembled, it is a markedly different social unit from what it was before; it is now a family organized around the heterosexually monogamous couple and their immediate offspring. Nested in a household that is nested in a community of such households, the family becomes the ideological cement between the isolated authorial consciousness of Rowlandson and a community of readers.

As we noted in chapter 7, the early-seventeenth-century puritan authors thought of the household as a little commonwealth, an autonomous domain within early modern England at whose doorstep the power of the monarch ideally stopped. But something happened to this century-old model for Protestant dissent when it was restaged in a colonial setting. By rebuilding the original household, Rowlandson's account fills the imaginary space onto which *Paradise Lost* opens in the last few lines of book XII. This space was cleared by the fire that swept through Thomas Sprat's London as well as by the plague that William Petty sought to combat by proposing that all families—not only those of the elites—be moved to houses within a day's carriage ride of London. The household that assembles around Rowlandson upon her return is one made up of individuals whose place is determined by their demonstration of endurance, compliance, sensitivity, and devotion. These faculties may take various symbolic forms, or so the heroine's trials suggest. But by far the most powerful demonstration of her personal worth is the published word—the captivity narrative itself. Along with printed sermons, almanacs, and local newsletters, it indeed provided a means of consolidating all those who participated in the English diaspora.[43] Apparently believing the print vernacular was capable of reuniting what the colonial experience had torn asunder, these people, one could argue, reinvented English for themselves. As print began to serve this purpose, it produced a whole new concept of the nation as a people detached from the European country of origin to which they were reconnected by a literature. It is in this way that the formation of New World nationalism allows us to imagine how eighteenth-century readers back in England began to reconceive that nation as a readership.

Is this reconception of England—as a nation made up of families that are in turn made up of literate individuals—not precisely what Richardson's fiction tries and manages to do? Is this not the purpose of detaching Pamela from a family who sent their offspring into service with the local landowners, thereby relinquishing whatever authority they might have had as parents? From the very beginning Pamela seeks to return to her family. But her return from her Gothic remove into the heart of old England is not a return to her original state so much as the production of new origins for herself and for English society as a whole. Indeed, this is more obviously so in *Pamela* than in New World captivity narratives.[44] In making a place for the letter-writing subject within it, the community becomes one of equally self-enclosed individuals whose sentiments appear to matter as much as their birth. By showing that Richardson's narrator goes through the same process of exile and return as Rowlandson did, we are suggesting that the insertion of such private spaces within an earlier landowning culture could just as well have transformed England too.

The abduction and return of these women perform a transformation that could not be accomplished in overtly political terms. They begin as wordless objects in an exchange among men, but both evolve into bodiless subjects of writing. In doing so, they distinguish an earlier, apparently more primitive aristocratic culture from one in which every literate individual matters. The community to which they belong changes accordingly, from one governed by a monopoly on violence to one where mastery is exercised strictly through words. In returning to their mother cultures, then, they quietly and almost imperceptibly change that culture forever. In both cases, a speech community gives way to one for which writing not only establishes the model but also poses as speech, as thought, and by way of speech and thought, as human nature itself. Of this discursive formation, something remains to be said concerning the secret of its longevity.

We have focused on the captivity narrative as the means of individuating English consciousness and of placing it in a position of mastery over all that it surveys—including an alien landscape, the indigenous peoples of the Americas, other English people, and even one's own body. The capacity of her writing to perpetuate the individual under circumstances so hostile to individuality remained unequalled, perhaps, until the publication of *Pamela*. By connecting Rowlandson to Richardson, we have used the captivity narrative as the basis of a theoretical model that supplements both Anderson's and Foucault's accounts of modernity by articulating each to the other. We used Anderson's account of how the traditional bases of English identity were transported to North America to explain the sudden emergence of what Foucault calls discourse. In using Anderson to supplement Foucault's Eurocentric account of modernity, we have also reversed Anderson's tendency to see culture as moving from Europe to America. The extension of English into the colonies, together with a radical redefinition of what an author was and who could be one, necessarily changed the culture of origin. Its most cherished signs and symbols no longer had to be embodied, circulated among a restricted group of people, or carried across the ocean on a ship. If one can imagine how culture, so called, came to be embodied in print, it does not take much of a leap to consider how vernacular English began to carry on a life apart from speech and thus from the place where it originated and especially from the things to which it once referred. As print joined the European metropolis to points scattered throughout the colonies, and all these points to readers back in England, in time readers came to think of themselves as occupying positions within the vast and intricate network of such relationships that identifies a modern culture.

Let us retrace the logic that brought us to this conclusion, a logic which, we have argued, can be extrapolated from *Paradise Lost*. As Milton's attempt to reproduce a culture from which he had irrevocably separated, the poem offers a paradigm for the operations of a peculiarly Anglo-American brand of imperialist nostalgia.[45] His sense of separation from an originary speech community compelled the translation of English culture into the writing that subsequently became the basis for a new kind of community. To represent the new world that came into being through the American adventure, authors of captivity narratives were, like Milton, looking backward, and their accounts are infused with a poignant longing to return. In the case of an originary speech community, however fantastic to begin with, this desire on the part of North American Englishmen to return compelled the reproduction both of that community in writing and of the primal lack of a speech community that written words can never fill. In this instance, one might say, language lost its innocence—its Adamic character—and began to behave as signs, writing, or the supplement, which relocated the preindustrial speech community still further in the past with each and every replication. Noting how Richardson actively displaced an older landowning England as he reproduced it in Pamela's letters, our argument moved from the present time back to the late seventeenth century in search of a work that might have empowered the author so that no other form of cultural authority was necessary save that of writing. For such would have to be the prototype of the sentimental fiction identified with Richardson.

If literary or cultural scholarship remains within the boundaries of the English nation as writing would later define it, virtually all the materials that went into making the English novel can indeed be found in England. However, nowhere did such an earlier England pull these materials together in any way that anticipated the magic Richardson obviously had to have in order to found the genre. Thus we shifted our attention to Mary Rowlandson's account of her captivity. We found in it a perfect demonstration of what happened when the print vernacular came to be the only tie between an Englishwoman in exile—stripped of all the other powers and properties of being English—and the culture of her origin. If one regards her account as the first appearance of the author who is an entire world of consciousness and an authentic source of language, then her narrative can be used to imagine how a new basis for nationality came into being. What distinguished her and others like her from previous authors was her desire to return to a preindividuated speech community. What made her narrative important to English readers was the promise that she would put an end to writing, dissolve the world she represented, close the gap that written words produced between herself and other people, and communicate in speech. That, of course, is something that writing can never do. Such an attempt to return to a lost speech community though writing did not make authors vanish but put them on the sociopolitical map. After the New England colonies made a return to an earlier England fundamental to their own identity, Richardson appropriated the same equation between the writing subject and the English subject for an Old World setting. At that point, *Robinson Crusoe* could be incorporated in a national literary tradition that went back to *The Pilgrim's Progress* and *Paradise Lost*.[46] Rather than identify any such origin for the novel, however, our purpose has been to question the whole venture of doing so.

Programs in English and American literature generally ignore the thoroughgoing transformation that English culture underwent in the New World. With flawless consistency most scholars and critics still assume that American literature originated in England.[47] Even on this side of the Atlantic, high culture remains steadfastly Eurocentric. By the time they enter our classrooms, students have already been taught, much as we ourselves were, to regard *Pamela* and *Clarissa* as prototypes both for English domestic fiction and for the American novel, from Rowson and Cooper to Hawthorne and James. And Mary Rowlandson's narrative exists for most educated Americans as an anomaly of America's pre-literary past that has little or nothing to do with the English literary tradition.[48] This fact requires us to consider, in closing, the effects of any analysis that relies on origins to explain what a cultural object is. Because it is joined to the present by a narrative that seems to be carried along by history itself, the point of origin—once so designated—tends to remain impervious to questions, and all things American still seem to have begun in Europe. More specifically, the captivity narrative reveals how deeply ingrained is the habit that causes any quest for origins to posit a source for language in an authorial consciousness. An author in turn implies a nation (in whose language she or he is writing) and a family (that is presumed to generate the author's deepest and most natural emotions along with the body containing them).

To the cultural formation that one inevitably reproduces in the name of returning to origins, we have given the name Imaginary Puritan. We believe that the attempt to return to origins operates on a transnational scale to obscure what might be called the logic of supplementarity, by which the colonial world revised the so-called culture of origin. In con-cluding our study of the relationship between the emergence of the author and the transformation of England into a modern nation state, we feel compelled to stress the problematic nature of the term "origins" contained in the subtitle of this book. If this chapter has claimed to return in time and place to the beginnings of English fiction, let it now dispel that illusion.

By implying that English fiction comes from captivity narratives, we have tried to illustrate how those narratives succeeded in producing their own origins, in turn producing a world of things and people that seemed to be outside and prior to writing, however long ago those people and those things vanished into the past. By regarding *Pamela* as a continental version of the American captivity narrative, we called attention to the power the novel attributes to the printed word; it is nothing less than the power to create the authorial consciousness from which print hence-forth appeared to come and the readership among whom it would cir-culate. In telling the story of the English novel in this way, then, we have not really recaptured the origins of the novel. We have used the novel to imagine a moment when words on the page acquired the subtle and enduring power to produce the human source from which they came.

Notes

INTRODUCTION

1. For an insightful elaboration of this point, see H. D. Harootunian, "Prologue: Historians' Discourse and the Problems of Nativism," in *Things Seen and Unseen: Discourse and Ideology in Tokugawa Nativism* (Chicago: University of Chicago Press, 1988), pp. 1–22.

2. Gayatri Spivak briefly summarizes the disagreement between Derrida and Foucault in her preface to Jacques Derrida, *Of Grammatology*, trans. Gayatri Chakravorty Spivak (Baltimore: Johns Hopkins University Press, 1976), pp. lix–lxii. At the time, she notes that Derrida's 1963 critique was aimed at "a dated Foucault, the Foucault of the sixties" (lx). In his "Cogito and the History of Madness," in *Writing and Difference*, trans. Alan Bass (Chicago: University of Chicago Press, 1978), pp. 31–63, Derrida specifically critiques the Foucault of *Madness and Civilization* for pretending to know a consciousness not his own that exists on the other side of language. Foucault responded to this critique in "Mon Corps, ce papier, ce feu," published in the second edition of *Histoire de la folie à l'âge classique* (Paris: Gallimard, 1972), pp. 583–603; but his *Discipline and Punish*, trans. Alan Sheridan (New York: Vintage, 1979; first published in French, 1975), and *The History of Sexuality*, trans. Robert Hurley (New York: Pantheon, 1978; first published in French in 1976), address the heart of the problem that beset his earlier project. The later works do not, as far as we can see, take consciousness as the object of knowledge but trace the production of that object in and through writing. See also Ann Wordsworth, "Derrida and Foucault: Writing the History of Historicity," in *Post-Structuralism and the Question of History*, ed. Derek Attridge, Geoff Bennington, and Robert Young (Cambridge: Cambridge University Press, 1987), pp. 116–25.

3. This is not to say that writing is the same thing as discourse. Indeed, as Geoff Bennington argues in "Demanding History," in *Post-Structuralism and the*

Question of History, pp. 15–29, collapsing the terms is no way to save deconstruction for marxism. We would argue that deconstruction's attack on the sign as the sign of what is not and never was there, is, indeed, as Bennington contends, "the most historical of discourses imaginable" (17).

4. In *Desire and Domestic Fiction* (New York: Oxford University Press, 1987), for example, Nancy Armstrong shows that the woman-centered household of middle-class culture existed in writing fifty to seventy-five years before it organized everyday life for the range of people from gentry to small independent farmers and shopkeepers we now call middle-class or even for select groups within this class.

5. Hayden White, *Metahistory: The Historical Imagination in Nineteenth-Century Europe* (Baltimore: Johns Hopkins University Press, 1973), p. xi.

6. Fredric Jameson, *The Political Unconscious: Narrative as a Socially Symbolic Act* (Ithaca: Cornell University Press, 1981).

7. For an interesting critique of the current tendency to set the hegemonic against the counterhegemonic possibilities of narrative, see Jochen Schulte-Sasse, "Introduction" and "Can the Disempowered Read Mass-Produced Narratives in Their Own Voice?" *Cultural Critique* 10 (1988): 5–18, 171–99.

8. In this book, we will use such terms as "ruling ideas," "discourse," "literacy," and "cultural capital" analogically and, on occasion, interchangeably, depending on the materials under discussion.

9. Michel Foucault, "The Subject and Power," afterword to Hubert Dreyfus and Paul Rabinow, *Michel Foucault: Beyond Structuralism and Hermeneutics* (Chicago: University of Chicago Press, 1982), pp. 208–26. The quote is on p. 211. ("Conscience" may be a misleading translation of the French *conscience,* by which Foucault probably meant something more like "consciousness.")

10. Rather than observe the marxist division of history based on modes of production—feudalism or capitalism—we have adopted the terms "early modern" and "modern" commonly used by social historians. Because it designates the early seventeenth century as a period that was neither medieval nor modern, the term "early modern" allows us to grant importance to the fact that English culture underwent some kind of transformation which marked the onset of modernity.

11. In tracing the use of the term in the sixteenth and seventeenth centuries, Paul Christianson has argued that it should be reserved to describe a very small number of people; it is misleading to apply the term "puritan" to most of the reformist movements within the English church. See his "Reformers and the Church of England Under Elizabeth I and the Early Stuarts," *Journal of Ecclesiastical History* 31 (1980): 462–82.

12. Our notion of the Imaginary Puritan was helped along by two provocative adaptations of the Lacanian "imaginary." Our earliest speculations along these lines were prompted by Anthony Wilden's *The Imaginary Canadian: An Examination for Discovery* (Vancouver: Pulp Press, 1980), where he replaced Barthes's concept of "mythology" with "imaginary" to suggest the same thing at a macro level. Wilden explains that although he first came to know about the "imaginary" from his translation of Jacques Lacan's *Language of the Self* (Baltimore: Johns Hopkins University Press, 1968), his own use of the "concept of

Imaginary relations is not derived from the same source as Lacan's. . . . The *relationships* it refers to are primarily social and economic relations, rather than 'psychoanalytic' ones. Indeed, if we now look back at the social and economic analysis of capitalism in the work of Marx, for example, we find that much of his discussion of the effects of alienation under the power of modern capital is, in retrospect, a discussion of Imaginary relations (notably his analysis of what he called 'the fetishism of commodities')" (63). A study to which we are particularly indebted recuperates an element of Barthes's mythologies that gets lost in Wilden's Anglo-materialism. In *Scenarios of the Imaginary: Theorizing the French Enlightenment* (Ithaca: Cornell University Press, 1987), Josué V. Harari argues that while the imaginary speaks through images, the conventional notion of the relationship between the image and the real is seriously mistaken. An image, as he explains, "depicts not the real *in itself,* but rather the real *in its absence,* that is stripped of reality. . . . [Such an] image (representation) does not refer back to the real that it allegedly reproduces, but rather points to the real by means of the network of signification it lends to the real." Thus, he concludes, "we must reverse the relationship between thing and image, implying by this reversal that *there is no experience of the real without an image.* In order for the real to signify, it must borrow its meaning from the image-inary" (58).

13. Thomas Babington Macaulay, "Milton," in *Literary Essays: Contributed to the Edinburgh Review* (London: Oxford University Press, 1937), p. 45.

14. For accounts of Milton's reputation and influence in the eighteenth and nineteenth centuries see John W. Good, "Studies in the Milton Tradition," *University of Illinois Studies in Language and Literature* 1, nos. 3–4 (1915); R. D. Havens, *The Influence of Milton on English Poetry* (Cambridge: Harvard University Press, 1922); Ants Oras, *Milton's Editors and Commentators from Patrick Hume to Henry John Todd: A Study in Critical Views* (New York: Haskell House, 1964); W. R. Parker, *Milton's Contemporary Reputation* (New York: Haskell House, 1971); George Sensabaugh, *Milton in Early America* (Princeton: Princeton University Press, 1964); John T. Shawcross, ed., *Milton: The Critical Heritage* (New York: Barnes and Noble, 1970), and *Milton, 1732–1801* (London and Boston: Routledge and Kegan Paul, 1972); Joseph Wittreich, ed., *The Romantics on Milton: Formal Essays and Critical Asides* (Cleveland: Press of Case Western Reserve, 1970); Dustin Griffin, *Regaining Paradise: Milton and the Eighteenth Century* (Cambridge: Cambridge University Press, 1986), especially pp. 11–42.

15. Macaulay, "Milton," p. 3; T. S. Eliot, "Milton II," in *On Poetry and Poets* (New York: Farrar, Straus and Cudahy, 1957), p. 168.

16. For two quite different critical perspectives that make this same assertion, see Sandra M. Gilbert and Susan Gubar, *The Madwoman in the Attic: The Woman Writer and the Nineteenth Century Literary Imagination* (New Haven: Yale University Press, 1979), pp. 200–1, and Fredric Jameson, "Religion and Ideology," in *1642: Literature and Power in the Seventeenth Century,* ed. Francis Barker, Jay Bernstein, John Coombes, Peter Hulme, Jennifer Stone, and Jon Stratton (Colchester: University of Essex, 1981), p. 335.

17. Roland Barthes, "Myth Today," in *Mythologies,* trans. Annette Lavers (New York: Farrar, Straus and Giroux, 1972), p. 130.

18. In part III, section iv, of *A Philosophical Inquiry into the Origin of Our Ideas of the Sublime and Beautiful,* Edmund Burke declares Milton's portrait of Satan to be one of the most perfect examples of a sublime description.

19. Joseph H. Summers, *The Muse's Method: An Introduction to Paradise Lost* (Cambridge: Harvard University Press, 1962), pp. 30–32; Harold Bloom, *A Map of Misreading* (Oxford: Oxford University Press, 1975), pp. 125–26.

20. Sensabaugh, *Milton in Early America,* pp. 3–4.

21. F. O. Matthiessen, *American Renaissance: Art and Expression in the Age of Emerson and Whitman* (Oxford: Oxford University Press, 1941), p. 103.

22. Robert Weisbuch notes that by the nineteenth century such writers as Shakespeare and Milton were viewed as part of the common English heritage, "common because it was pre-colonial." To this end he quotes Cooper: "The authors, previously to the revolution, are common property, and it is quite idle to say that the American has not just as good a right to claim Milton, and Shakespeare, and all the old masters of the language, for his countrymen, as an Englishman." *Atlantic Double-Cross: American Literature and British Literature in the Age of Emerson* (Chicago: University of Chicago Press, 1986), pp. 16–17.

23. Quoted in Matthiessen, *American Renaissance,* p. 103.

24. Toward the end of the nineteenth century, for example, there was a revival of the movement to discover—more accurately, to insist upon—the Englishness of the American past by invoking the Anglo-Saxon origins supposedly common to both. This racial movement extended from folklore studies and literary scholarship to the writing of revisionist accounts of American history. Peter Novick has argued that among historians this movement expressed both a reaction to the waves of immigration from southern and eastern Europe and a desire to justify American imperialism. It became accepted practice to discover the racial influence of an originary Anglo-Saxon culture in "pure" American politics and institutions. Thus, for example, Edward Channing in his popular six-volume history of the United States claimed that the "English race" was responsible for our political system, while other historians described the American Revolution as a regrettable quarrel among "race brothers" and sought to make amends for the "race feud" that had torn "two kindred peoples" apart. During and immediately following the First World War, a similar racism apparently prompted a number of historians to establish a common heritage for England and America in the Anglo-Saxon love of liberty. The quoted material as well as the examples from American history come from Peter Novick, *That Noble Dream: The "Objectivity Question" and the American Historical Profession* (Cambridge: Cambridge University Press, 1988), pp. 81–82. The same ideology can be found in the history of English literary studies. Among his examples of efforts, during this period of superpatriotism, to blur the distinctions between English and American literature, Gerald Graff includes a college textbook edited by two Renaissance scholars, Edwin Greenlaw and James Holly Hanford. Published in 1919, this anthology was jingoistically titled *The Great Tradition: Selections from English and American Prose and Poetry, Illustrating the National Ideals of Freedom, Faith, and Conduct.* Of the introduction, Graff writes: "The editors described the selections as 'landmarks in the march of the Anglo-Saxon mind from the beginning of the

modern period.' " *Professing Literature: An Institutional History* (Chicago: University of Chicago Press, 1987), p. 130.

25. In *Shakespeare's Perjured Eye* (Berkeley: University of California Press, 1987), Joel Fineman describes Shakespeare as having the kind of mind that, we are claiming, Milton embodies for modern readers. Fineman's ingenuity paints Shakespeare as an anomaly in his age though not in ours. Perhaps it is because *Paradise Lost* formulates a self-enclosed, internally coherent individual only in the last two books that generations of critics have felt compelled to translate the discontinuities of the poem into contradictions within the personality of its author.

26. It should be acknowledged that Hayden White's *Metahistory* informs chapters 2 and 3. It is difficult to imagine our performing those "readings" of history without his ground-breaking work.

27. Our readers will find a variable use of the third-person singular pronoun. We saw no way around it and resolved at the first moment of awkwardness to offer the following explanation. To refer to the generic "individual" of early modern culture or the individual represented in writings of the period, we use the generic male pronoun. In the interests of historical accuracy, "he" in these instances does not refer to males in general but to those males who were members of the elite class of people that comprised Milton's audience for the poetry he wrote prior to 1645, and whose codes of conduct that poetry authorized. It would be impossible to say just whom Milton imagined he was addressing in his late poetry, but it is certainly neither the laboring man he portrays in books XI and XII of *Paradise Lost* nor the rational man of Lockean political theory and epistemology. In the early eighteenth century, the latter had certainly become the referent for the masculine pronoun, but we do not substitute the modern "he or she." Unless the pronoun refers to female, pronoun references to the "individual" or "reader" would be understood to designate male individuals and readers, and we have chosen to remain faithful to that meaning of "he." Only in cases where those who refer to "readers" are referring to both male and female do we use the form "he or she."

28. On this point, see Leonore Davidoff and Catherine Hall, *Family Fortunes: Men and Women of the English Middle Class, 1780–1850* (Chicago: University of Chicago Press, 1987).

29. For a sophisticated reconsideration of the relationship between literature and other aspects of historical change, see John Frow, *Marxism and Literary History* (Oxford: Basil Blackwell, 1986), pp. 103–24.

30. Joan Wallach Scott, "On Language, Gender, and Working-Class History," *Gender and the Politics of History* (New York: Columbia University Press, 1988), pp. 53–67.

CHAPTER 1

1. Roland Barthes, "Myth Today," in *Mythologies,* trans. Annette Lavers (New York: Farrar, Straus and Giroux, 1972), p. 135.

2. Douglas Bush, *English Literature in the Earlier Seventeenth Century, 1600–1660* (Oxford: Clarendon, 1945), pp. 359–60.

3. In his 1948 presidential address to the Modern Language Association, Bush defined his own practice in contrast with that of the critic—by whom he meant the New Critic—as one in which the scholar tries to view a text "through the minds of its author and his contemporaries." Douglas Bush, "The New Criticism: Some Old-Fashioned Queries," *PMLA* 64, supplement (1949): 18–21. For a discussion of the circumstances of this speech, see Gerald Graff, *Professing Literature: An Institutional History* (Chicago: University of Chicago Press, 1987), pp. 183–90.

4. By the same token, Bush, like many historical critics of his generation, seems never to have questioned the modernity of his own aesthetic. Instead, he proclaimed a belief in the unchanging "conception of poetry which reigned for some 2,500 years, through the greatest periods of literature." Quoted in Graff, *Professing Literature,* p. 186.

5. Balachandra Rajan, *Paradise Lost and the Seventeenth Century Reader* (Ann Arbor: University of Michigan Press, 1967; first published 1947), p. 21.

6. Joseph H. Summers, *The Muse's Method: An Introduction to Paradise Lost* (Cambridge: Harvard University Press, 1962), p. 30.

7. Summers specifically draws the comparison between Milton and Henry James: "Milton anticipated, I believe, one of Henry James's favourite and most successful devices for involving the reader directly in the moral action of his stories, the technique of the 'guilty reader.' In *The Aspern Papers, The Wings of the Dove,* and in a number of the stories, James managed to seduce all but the most attentive readers into identifying initially with a point of view which seems sensible and, if not absolutely good, at least human and sympathetic" (30–31).

8. Stanley E. Fish, *Surprised by Sin: The Reader in Paradise Lost* (Berkeley: University of California Press, 1971), p. xiii.

9. For an insightful reading of Fish's place within an American tradition of pluralist criticism, see Ellen Rooney, *Seductive Reasoning: Pluralism as the Problematic of Contemporary Literary Theory* (Ithaca: Cornell University Press, 1989). Rooney points out that a flight from history characterizes a variety of pluralist critics (235).

10. Louis L. Martz, *Poet of Exile: A Study of Milton's Poetry* (New Haven: Yale University Press, 1980), p. 79.

11. Harold Bloom, *A Map of Misreading* (Oxford: Oxford University Press, 1975), p. 125.

12. In a trenchant article on American poetry, "Poetry in America: The Question of Gender," *Genre* 22 (1987): 153–70, Maria Irene Ramalho de Sousa Santos argues that Bloom's theory that every poem desires to redefine its own origins reproduces an essentially American trope. She writes, "The specificity of American poetry in Bloom's theory is, therefore, that it deliberately ignores its own belatedness, and offers its repetitions as immaculate beginnings, knowing that they are repetitions. Between actual posteriority and the willful ignorance thereof, between experiences of life with death as term and the myth of boundless innocence (or first origin) as illusion of immortality, American poetry goes on reinventing the language" (155–56).

13. It is because we are interested in the discursive Milton that our argument does not directly engage the rich and complex debate over Milton's treatment of women that has commanded the attention of some of our best Milton scholars for at least fifteen years. Among the articles and books we consulted are Marcia Landy, "Kinship and the Role of Women in *Paradise Lost*," *Milton Studies* 4 (1972): 3–18; Barbara K. Lewalski, "Milton on Women—Yet Once More," *Milton Studies* 6 (1974): 4–20; Sandra M. Gilbert, "Patriarchal Poetry and Women Readers: Reflections on Milton's Bogey," *PMLA* 93 (1978): 368–82; David Aers and Bob Hodge, " 'Rational Burning': Milton on Sex and Marriage," *Milton Studies* 13 (1979): 3–33; Joan Webber, "The Politics of Poetry: Feminism and *Paradise Lost*," *Milton Studies* 14 (1980): 3–24; Christine Froula, "When Eve Reads Milton: Undoing the Canonical Economy," *Critical Inquiry* 10 (1983): 321–47, and her response, "Pechter's Spector: Milton's Bogey Writ Small; or, Why Is He Afraid of Virginia Woolf?" *Critical Inquiry* 11 (1984): 171–78; Diane Kelsey McColley, *Milton's Eve* (Urbana: University of Illinois Press, 1983); Mary Nyquist, "Gynesis, Genesis, Exegesis, and the Formation of Milton's Eve," in *Cannibals, Witches, and Divorce: Estranging the Renaissance*, ed. Marjorie Garber (Baltimore: Johns Hopkins University Press, 1987), pp. 146–208, and "The Genesis of Gendered Subjectivity in the Divorce Tracts and in *Paradise Lost*," in *Re-Membering Milton: Essays on the Texts and Traditions*, ed. Mary Nyquist and Margaret W. Ferguson (New York: Methuen, 1987), pp. 99–127. For a noble effort at recasting the debate in a historical perspective, see Joseph Wittreich's survey of women readers' responses to Milton between 1700 and 1830 in *Feminist Milton* (Ithaca: Cornell University Press, 1987).

14. Sandra Gilbert and Susan Gubar, *The Madwoman in the Attic* (New Haven: Yale University Press, 1979), p. 191.

15. On the more general problem of the belief system that supports liberal feminism, see Nancy Armstrong, "The Gender Bind," *Genders* 3 (1988): 1–23.

16. Herman Rapaport, *Milton and the Postmodern* (Lincoln: University of Nebraska Press, 1983), p. 12.

17. *Re-Membering Milton*, ed. Nyquist and Ferguson, p. xii.

18. Terry Eagleton, "The God That Failed," in *Re-Membering Milton*, ed. Nyquist and Ferguson, p. 346.

19. It seems to us that anything represented in aesthetic terms is especially prone to losing historical specificity. The aesthetic object is one that appears to have ceased participating in political conflict and to be meaningful primarily through what it says about the individuated consciousness that moderns attribute to "authors" and "readers." As we argued above, for example, Stanley Fish reads *Paradise Lost* as the encounter between the two. He personifies historically inaccessible material as the superior consciousness of Milton, the genius, poet, and educator; personifies modern literacy as "the reader"; and then identifies the difference between the two as the degree to which ordinary literacy falls short of the kind of learning it takes to be a humanist scholar.

20. Fredric Jameson, "Religion and Ideology," in *1642: Literature and Power in the Seventeenth Century*, ed. Francis Barker, Jay Bernstein, John Coombes, Peter Hulme, Jennifer Stone, and Jon Stratton (Colchester: University of Essex, 1981), pp. 315–36.

21. David Norbrook, *Poetry and Politics in the English Renaissance* (London: Routledge and Kegan Paul, 1984), p. 239.

22. One can clearly see this language in the notion of the social contract later elaborated by Rousseau. But, as we will show in chapter 6, perhaps nowhere is this language more deliberately employed than in the twin discourses of property and understanding theorized by Locke.

23. Harold Perkin notes: "There is no English word for *bourgeoisie* because, until the nineteenth century at least, the thing itself did not exist, in the sense of a permanent, self-conscious urban class in opposition to the landed aristocracy. In every generation the richer citizens and townsmen who, if socially frustrated, might have galvanized their neighbours into a powerful class were themselves transmuted into country gentlemen, thus making room for other townsmen at the top, and setting in train a general upward movement." *The Origins of Modern English Society, 1780–1880* (London: Routledge and Kegan Paul, 1969), p. 61.

24. Quoted in Michael Zuckerman, "Identity in British America," in *Colonial Identity in the Atlantic World, 1500–1800,* ed. Nicholas Canny and Anthony Pagden (Princeton: Princeton University Press, 1987), p. 116.

25. Renato Rosaldo, "Imperialist Nostalgia," in *Culture and Truth: The Remaking of Social Analysis* (Boston: Beacon Press, 1989), pp. 68–87.

26. For a discussion of the process by which this group came to dominance, see Leonore Davidoff and Catherine Hall, *Family Fortunes: Men and Women of the English Middle Class, 1780–1850* (Chicago: University of Chicago Press, 1987).

27. On the role the idea of the skin plays in imagining the body, see Julia Kristeva, *The Power of Horror,* trans. Leon S. Roudiez (New York: Columbia University Press, 1984).

CHAPTER 2

1. For an extended discussion of the eighteenth- and nineteenth-century use of the word "revolution" in historical writing, see R. C. Richardson, *The Debate on the English Revolution Revisited* (London: Routledge, 1988), pp. 65–86, and Michael G. Finlayson, *Historians, Puritanism, and the English Revolution: The Religious Factor in English Politics before and after the Interregnum* (Toronto: University of Toronto Press, 1983), pp. 1–76.

2. Finlayson cites the example of the Tory critic J. W. Croker, who was angered at what he considered Guizot's confusion between the events of the civil war and the Commonwealth period, on the one hand, and those of the Glorious Revolution, on the other. Croker wrote, "I admit that the first helped to produce the other as a dungheap helps to produce asparagus, as filth produces food, but they are not the same thing" (24).

3. François Guizot, "Introductory Discourse on the History of the Revolution of England," *History of the English Revolution of 1640: From the Accession of Charles I to His Death,* trans. William Hazlitt (London: George Bell and Sons, 1878), p. 1.

4. "A Review of Guizot's Book, 'Why Has the English Revolution Been Suc-

cessful?' " in Karl Marx and Frederick Engels, *Articles on Britain* (Moscow: Progress Publishers, 1971), p. 95.

5. Finlayson, *Historians*, pp. 21–22.

6. Hume, as J. G. A. Pocock has argued, cannot be considered a "vulgar" Whig historian, for he believed that at least three constitutions could be identified in England's past. *The Ancient Constitution and the Feudal Law: A Study of English Historical Thought in the Seventeenth Century, A Reissue with a Retrospect* (Cambridge: Cambridge University Press, 1987), p. 376.

7. R. C. Richardson notes of Gardiner, "his religious affiliations had kept him out of Oxford in earlier life and for years he had to submit to the drudgery of schoolteaching to eke out a living. . . . He had an Oxford research fellowship by 1884, was offered (and declined) the Regius Chair ten years later." (82).

8. On narrative strategies employed in nineteenth-century historiography, see Hayden White, *Metahistory: The Historical Imagination in Nineteenth-Century Europe* (Baltimore: Johns Hopkins University Press, 1973).

9. Samuel Rawson Gardiner, ed., *The Constitutional Documents of the Puritan Revolution, 1625–1660* (Oxford: Oxford University Press, 1906), p. x.

10. In his summary view of Charles at the end of *The History of the Great Civil War, 1642–1649* (London: Longmans, Green, and Co., 1894), Gardiner elaborates this view: "Even on the scaffold he reminded his subjects that a share in government was nothing appertaining to the people. It was the tragedy of Charles's life that he was entirely unable to satisfy the cravings of those who inarticulately hoped for the establishment of a monarchy which while it kept up the old traditions of the country . . . would yet allow the people of the country to be to some extent masters of their own destiny" (4:327).

11. Matthew Arnold identifies a similar feature as essentially English. Unlike Gardiner, however, Arnold thinks that such desire leads straight to anarchy: "[According to Jacob Bright, the MP from Manchester] the central idea of English life and politics is *the assertion of personal liberty*. Evidently this is so; but evidently, also, as feudalism . . . dies out, and we are left with nothing but our system of checks, and our notion of its being the great right and happiness of an Englishman to do as far as possible what he likes, we are in danger of drifting towards anarchy. We have not the notion, so familiar on the Continent and to antiquity, of *the State*—the nation in its collective and corporate character, entrusted with stringent powers for the general advantage, and controlling individual wills in the name of an interest wider than that of individuals." *Culture and Anarchy*, ed. J. Dover Wilson (Cambridge: Cambridge University Press, 1986), pp. 74–75.

12. Gardiner, *Constitutional Documents*, p. x.

13. There are a small number of contemporary historians who still refuse to use the word "revolution" to describe the events of the mid–seventeenth century. They understand their views to be iconoclastic. See, for example, Ivan Root, "The Late Troubles in England" (Inaugural lecture delivered at the University of Essex, 1969), pp. 8–10. The most famous example of this practice is Peter Laslett's *The World We Have Lost: England before the Industrial Revolution* (New York: Scribners, 1970).

14. Lawrence Stone. "The Results of the English Revolutions of the Seven-

teenth Century," in *Three British Revolutions: 1641, 1688, 1776,* ed. J. G. A. Pocock (Princeton: Princeton University Press, 1980), p. 62.

15. Perez Zagorin, *Rebels and Rulers, 1500–1600,* vol. 2, *Provincial Rebellion: Revolutionary Civil Wars, 1560–1660* (Cambridge: Cambridge University Press, 1982), p. 185.

16. Lawrence Stone holds a similar position: "For a short time, and perhaps for the first time, there came onto the stage of history a group of men proclaiming ideas of liberty not liberties, equality not privilege, fraternity not deference. These ideas were to live on, and to revive again in other societies in other ages." *The Causes of the English Revolution, 1529–1642* (New York: Harper and Row, 1972), p. 146. This view is echoed by Christopher Hill's claim, "So although the Puritan revolution was defeated, the revolution in thought could not be unmade." *The Century of Revolution: 1603–1714* (New York: Norton, 1980), p. 163. See also Hill's *The World Turned Upside Down: Radical Ideas during the English Revolution* (London: Penguin, 1975), p. 381. Hill's *Some Intellectual Consequences of the English Revolution* (Madison: University of Wisconsin Press, 1980) is devoted entirely to this issue.

17. J. H. Hexter, "Power Struggle, Parliament, and Liberty in Early Stuart England," *Journal of Modern History* 50 (1978): 29.

18. The transhistorical nature of this desire can be seen in J. H. Hexter's declaration that "in the seventeenth century for the first time men tried effectively to limit the power of the state over its subjects in many of the same ways and for precisely the same reasons as we do today." "The Early Stuarts and Parliament: Old Hat and the *Nouvelle Vague,*" *Parliamentary History* 1 (1982): 208.

19. For the classic formulation of this belief, see Christopher Hill, "The Norman Yoke," in *Puritanism and Revolution: Studies in Interpretation of the English Revolution* (London: Secker and Warburg, 1965), pp. 50–122.

20. *The English Revolution: An Essay* (London: Lawrence and Wishart, 1955; originally published 1940). In this early version of his argument, Hill explicitly describes this class as a middle class (135). For an account of Hill's consistent historiographic assumptions, see Harvey J. Kaye, *The British Marxist Historians* (Cambridge: Polity Press, 1984), pp. 99–130.

21. Christopher Hill, "A Bourgeois Revolution?" in *Three British Revolutions,* ed. Pocock, p. 111. This has been perhaps the most persistent proposition in Hill's theory of the English Revolution for over fifty years. In one of his earliest pieces, Hill quotes Engels's *Anti-Dühring* on this point: "This mighty revolution in the economic conditions of society was not followed by any immediate corresponding change in its political structure. The state order remained feudal, while society became more and more bourgeois." Hill, *English Revolution,* p. 140. The concept of a bourgeois revolution has been challenged by various scholars. See, for example, Lawrence Stone, "The Bourgeois Revolution of Seventeenth-Century England Revisited," *Past and Present* 109 (1985): 44–54.

22. Conrad Russell, "Parliamentary History in Perspective, 1604–1629," *History* 61 (1976): 3. For a more complete account of Russell's position, see his *Parliaments and English Politics, 1621–1629* (Oxford: Oxford University Press,

1979). When Russell challenged the notion that there was such a thing as an opposition to the Crown in Parliament, he touched a nerve among historians. Since Gardiner's magisterial account, most renderings of the seventeenth century had represented the origins of the English Revolution in terms of one or another simple opposition: Puritans versus Anglicans, Parliament (by which was usually meant the Commons) versus the Crown, city versus country, and so on. Such an opposition is particularly useful if one is going to produce a progressive or evolutionary emplotment to the historical narrative. Apparently the need for this sort of opposition is so compelling that Theodore K. Rabb, for example, has argued that even if Russell were correct in disputing the existence of any clear political opposition, there were nonetheless disputes, conflicts, and thus "opposition beliefs." "The Role of Commons," *Past and Present* 92 (1981): 55-78. See also Derek Hirst, "Parliament, Law, and War in the 1620s," *Historical Journal* 23 (1980): 455-62 as well as his *Authority and Conflict: England, 1603-1658* (Cambridge: Harvard University Press, 1986), pp. 126-59, especially pp. 135 and 149-50.

23. The year following the publication of Russell's provocative essay in *History*, the *Journal of Modern History* 49 (1977) devoted an issue to largely revisionist views of the English Revolution. This issue included essays by Paul Christianson, "The Peers, the People, and Parliamentary Management in the First Six Months of the Long Parliament"; James E. Farnell, "The Social and Intellectual Basis of London's Role in the English Civil Wars"; and Mark Kishlansky, "The Emergence of Adversary Politics in the Long Parliament." Another example of this kind of work that appeared at the same time is Kevin Sharpe, "Introduction: Parliamentary History, 1603-1629," in *Faction and Parliament: Essays in Early Stuart History*, ed. Kevin Sharpe (Oxford: Oxford University Press, 1977), pp. 1-42.

24. Russell begins his essay by comparing the traditional historian to a man who reads the last chapter of a detective story first. The historian is thus always at risk "of letting hindsight lead him to see the evidence out of perspective," and doing so is "particularly tempting for historians who describe the years before the revolution." "Parliamentary History in Perspective," p. 1.

25. Christianson, "The Peers, the People, and Parliamentary Management."

26. John Morrill, *The Revolt of the Provinces: Conservatives and Radicals in the English Civil War, 1630-1650* (London: Longman, 1976); Anthony Fletcher, *The Outbreak of the English Civil War* (London: Arnold, 1981). See also John Morrill and J. D. Walter, "Order and Disorder in the English Revolution," in *Order and Disorder in Early Modern England*, ed. Anthony Fletcher and John Stevenson (Cambridge: Cambridge University Press, 1985), pp. 136-65.

27. Mark Kishlansky, *The Rise of the New Model Army* (Cambridge: Cambridge University Press, 1979).

28. Mark Kishlansky, *Parliamentary Selection: Social and Political Choice in Early Modern England* (Cambridge: Cambridge University Press, 1986). Kishlansky challenges positions such as that of Derek Hirst. In *The Representatives of the People: Voters and Voting in England Under the Stuarts* (Cambridge: Cambridge University Press, 1975), Hirst claimed that Parliament had come to rep-

resent the political and ideological interests of the electorate; Kishlansky insists that "before 1640 ideology was absent from the process of parliamentary selection," and members were elected for local reasons (16).

29. Paul Christianson, "Reformers and the Church of England under Elizabeth I and the Early Stuarts," *Journal of Ecclesiastical History* 31 (1980): 463–82. Unhappy with the way historians since Gardiner had used the term to indicate a political/religious opposition to Anglican practice, Christianson limits "puritan" "to exclude all but those reformers who worked within the Established Church for ministerial parity and a severely attenuated liturgy" (481).

30. Lawrence Stone, "The Century of Revolution," *New York Review of Books* 34 (February 26, 1987): 43. For equally strong attacks that seek to protect the traditional Whig/liberal accounts of Parliament and the emergence of representative democracy against the charge of an ideological bias, see Hexter, "Power Struggle," and especially his "Early Stuarts and Parliament." See also "Revisionism Revised: Two Perspectives on Early Stuart Parliamentary History," 1: Rabb, "Role of Commons," and 2: Derek Hirst, "The Place of Principle," *Past and Present* 92 (1981): 79–97; Christopher Hill, "Parliament and People in Seventeenth-Century England," *Past and Present* 92 (1981): 100–124. Mary Fulbrook has tried to reinscribe the revisionist critique within those very approaches that revisionism critiques, "The English Revolution and the Revisionist Revolt," *Social History* 7 (1982): 249–65.

31. Christopher Hill, "Under the Tudor Bed," *New York Review of Books* 34 (March 13, 1987): 36.

32. J. C. D. Clark, *Revolution and Rebellion: State and Society in England in the Seventeenth and Eighteenth Centuries* (Cambridge: Cambridge University Press, 1986).

33. For an exchange on Clark's historiographical assumptions, see Joanna Innes, "Jonathan Clark, Social History and England's 'Ancien Regime,'" *Past and Present* 115 (1987): 165–200 and Jonathan Clark, "On Hitting the Buffers: The Historiography of England's Ancien Regime," *Past and Present* 117 (1987): 195–207.

34. The effect of the revisionist assault has been such, Barry Coward has written, that "there is ... a danger of suggesting that the consequences of what happened between 1640 and 1660 were either totally negative or irrelevant in explaining many later developments in England." When Coward turns then to justify his own use of the phrase "the English Revolution," he is noticeably defensive: "My case for keeping the phrase 'the English Revolution' is not so much that the period did see some undeniably revolutionary events, especially in the winter of 1648–49, but that it is the one that is now most widely used by historians writing on the 1640's and 1650's. Those who use it are not necessarily waving an ideological banner." "Was There an English Revolution in the Middle of the Seventeenth Century?" in *Politics and People in Revolutionary England*, ed. Colin Jones, Malyn Newitt, and Stephen Roberts (Oxford: Basil Blackwell, 1986), p. 10.

35. Roland Barthes, "Myth Today," in *Mythologies*, trans. Annette Lavers (New York: Farrar, Straus and Giroux, 1972), p. 138.

36. We are taking Benedict Anderson's suggestion in *Imagined Communities:*

Reflections on the Origin and Spread of Nationalism (London: Verso, 1983) and assuming that the form a nation is generally believed to have is only imagined as such by particular groups of its citizens. By the same token, those who write a nation's history extrapolate a certain collective or corporate body from the information preserved or handed down by those groups, even when such authors consider that the nation is a complex entity made up of different regions, status groups, and dialects. Histories of seventeenth-century England invariably begin with the assumption that the events of that period produced a nation defined by neither its aristocracy nor its rural poor but by the "middling sort."

37. This is also known as "history from below." Such histories focus on oppositional political practices at the local level and upon forms of religious radicalism that challenged those of the ruling elites. Typical is the thrust of Clive Holmes's essay, that "it was 'the middling sort' of the fenland villages—minor gentry, yeomen, richer husbandmen, some tradesmen—who played the crucial role in organising the local resistance, including riots, to the drainers' activities" (186). "Drainers and Fenmen: The Problem of Popular Political Consciousness in the Seventeenth Century," in *Order and Disorder*, ed. Fletcher and Stevenson, pp. 166–95. Other examples of such history include David Underdown, *Revel, Riot, and Rebellion: Popular Politics and Culture in England, 1603–1660* (Oxford: Oxford University Press, 1987); *Radical Religion in the English Revolution*, ed. J. F. McGregor and B. Reay (Oxford: Oxford University Press, 1987); *Popular Culture in Seventeenth-Century England*, ed. Barry Reay (London: Croom Helm, 1985); and Hill, *World Turned Upside Down*. For a brief survey, see Richardson, *Debate on the English Revolution Revisited*, 173–86.

38. The closing paragraph of Wolfe's study captures this concept of Milton as radical humanist:

> The identification of personal sin with man's political failures in *Paradise Lost* throws into sharp relief Milton's rich contributions to the progressive thought of the Puritan Revolution. In contrast to the political implications of his great epic, these contributions were secular in the main and humanistic. The timeless arguments for intellectual liberty found in *Areopagitica* transcend all theological creeds; they breathe, indeed, a revolutionary fervor that would open all creeds to pitiless criticism, leaving no institution unchallenged, no social assumption static or secure.... This humanism, together with his extreme Protestant individualism, drove him away from the royalists and the Presbyterians, justified the toleration and republicanism of the Independents, and sustained the democratic arguments of *The Tenure* and *The Defense*. To go further than this Milton's environment and training and his theological convictions forbade. Here was his place in the Puritan Revolution.

Don M. Wolfe, *Milton in the Puritan Revolution* (New York: Humanities Press, 1963; first published 1941), p. 351.

39. Christopher Hill, *Milton and the English Revolution* (Harmondsworth: Penguin, 1979). The dedication reads: "This book is dedicated in gratitude to the memory of Don M. Wolfe, who devoted a lifetime to the study of Milton, but never forgot Richard Overton and Gerrard Winstanley" (v).

40. Hill, *Century of Revolution*, p. 163.

41. Hill, "A Bourgeois Revolution?" p. 111.

42. Hill, *Century of Revolution*, p. 163.

43. Hill, *Milton and the English Revolution*, p. 63.

44. Hill assumes that this so-called third culture was inherently oppositional and progressive except when debased by "the intellectuals of lower-class origin" who wanted to get on in the world. As E. P. Thompson pointed out in "The Moral Economy of the English Crowd in the Eighteenth Century," *Past and Present* 50 (1971): 76–136, and in "Eighteenth-Century English Society: Class Struggle without Class," *Social History* 3 (1978): 133–65, there was nothing inherently progressive about protests initiated by the lower social orders. In the seventeenth century as in the eighteenth, their activity, their interests, and their ideas could often be in alliance with those of court and king against the political elites of village, town, and city. The Declaration of Sports by James I and later by Charles I, Dover's Cotswold Games, royal encouragement of church ales, morris dances, and maypole festivities, and the implicit support for traditional forms of recreation and pastimes were aimed at curtailing the effectiveness of the reformers. It produced an alliance of sorts between those at the top and those at the lower end of the social hierarchy. On this point, see Underdown, *Revel, Riot, and Rebellion*, pp. 44–72, and Leah S. Marcus, *The Politics of Mirth: Jonson, Herrick, Milton, Marvell and the Defense of Old Holiday Pastimes* (Chicago: University of Chicago Press, 1986).

45. Hill has always used the language of class to characterize seventeenth-century society. In "Parliament and People," he responded to those of his critics who faulted him for using a nineteenth-century classification system to describe social relations in the seventeenth century. As he explains, some argue that "it is inappropriate to talk in terms of class in the seventeenth century, because contemporaries had no such word in their vocabulary. There are those who argue that we not speak of revolution in seventeenth-century England because the language had no word for it. But people can experience things before they invent a name for them" (117).

46. Hill, *Milton and the English Revolution*, p. 462.

47. Barthes, "Myth Today," p. 130.

48. Even Herbert Marcuse uses Milton to characterize the first individualist: "The principle of individualism, the pursuit of self-interest, was conditioned upon the proposition that self-interest was rational, that is to say, that it resulted from and was constantly guided and controlled by autonomous thinking.... In the context of radical Puritanism, the principle of individualism thus set the individual against his society.... The theme has nowhere been more fittingly expressed than in Milton's image of a 'wicked race of deceivers, who ... took the virgin Truth, hewd her lovely form into a thousand peeces, and scatter'd them to the four winds. From that time ever since, the sad friends of Truth, such as durst appear, imitating the careful search that Isis made for the mangl'd body of Osiris, went up and down gathering up limb by limb still as they could find them.'" "Some Social Implications of Modern Technology," in *The Essential Frankfurt School Reader*, ed. Andrew Arato and Eike Gebhardt (New York: Continuum, 1987), p. 140.

49. Hill writes in a passage that is intended to sum up the accomplishments of the English Revolution: "A great revolution. Absolute monarchy on the French model was never again possible. The instruments of despotism, Star Chamber and High Commission, were abolished for ever. Strafford has been described as

a frustrated Richelieu; the frustration of all that Strafford stood for was complete and final." *Century of Revolution*, p. 161.

50. Hill, *Milton and the English Revolution*, p. 65.

51. As David Masson noted over a century ago, however, there was a great deal published during these years which simply ignored the Licensing Order. Milton's own antiprelatical tracts are a case in point. David Masson, *The Life of John Milton* (Gloucester: Peter Smith, 1965), 3:266–69.

52. These constraints are discussed in Ernest Sirlock's introduction to the *Complete Prose Works of John Milton* (New Haven: Yale University Press, 1959), 2:158–64.

53. Lawrence Stone has written: "The revolutionary nature of the English Revolution is perhaps even more convincingly demonstrated by its words than by its deeds. The mere fact that it was such an extraordinarily wordy revolution— well over 22,000 sermons, speeches, pamphlets and newspapers were published between 1640 and 1661—would by itself strongly suggest that this is something very different from the familiar protest against an unpopular government." *Causes of the English Revolution*, pp. 49–50.

54. Williams writes: "As 1688 is a significant political date, so 1695 is significant in the history of the press. For in that year Parliament declined to renew the 1662 Licensing Act, and the stage for expansion was now fully set. . . . The expansion was not slow in coming for in the years between 1695 and 1730 a public press of three kinds became firmly established: daily newspapers, provincial weekly newspapers, and periodicals. Between them, these new organs covered the whole range of the cultural expansion." Raymond Williams, *The Long Revolution* (New York: Columbia University Press, 1961), pp. 180–81. For an account of the history of the Licensing Act from 1662 to 1695, see James Sutherland, *The Restoration Newspaper and Its Development* (Cambridge: Cambridge University Press, 1986), pp. 2–25.

55. We should also note E. P. Thompson's critique of Perry Anderson and Tom Nairn on the grounds that they attempt to see the English Revolution and its aftermath in a monolithic fashion. Thompson is particularly emphatic about the role of literacy in the formation and maintenance of an agrarian capitalism throughout the eighteenth century. "The Peculiarities of the English," in *The Poverty of Theory* (London: Merlin, 1978), pp. 245–301.

56. Stephen Greenblatt, *Renaissance Self-Fashioning* (Chicago: University of Chicago Press, 1980), p. 97.

CHAPTER 3

1. In what has become one of the standard surveys of the field, Michael Anderson's *Approaches to the History of the Western Family* (London: Macmillan, 1980) divides historical research on the family into three approaches: the demographic, the affective, and the domestic economic. We discuss examples of the first two schools in this chapter while reserving discussion of the third for chapter 6. We will not observe distinctions quite so precise as Anderson's, however, since in recent years historians in each group have drawn on the research conducted in the other areas. In addition to surveys of the debate on the history

of the family discussed in this chapter, other discussions can be found in Tamara K. Hareven, "Modernization and Family History: Perspectives on Social Change," *Signs* 2 (1976): 190–206; Mary Lyndon Shanley, "The History of the Family in Modern England," *Signs* 4 (1979): 740–50; Mark Poster, *Critical Theory of the Family* (New York: Seabury Press, 1979); Stephanie Coontz, *The Social Origins of Private Life: A History of the American Family* (London: Verso, 1988), pp. 7–40.

2. Keith Wrightson, *English Society, 1580–1680* (New Brunswick: Rutgers University Press, 1982), p. 73.

3. Ralph A. Houlbrooke, *The English Family, 1450–1700* (London and New York: Longman, 1984), p. 156.

4. Michael MacDonald, *Mystical Bedlam, Madness, Anxiety, and Healing in Seventeenth-Century England* (Cambridge: Cambridge University Press, 1983), p. 82.

5. Angus McLaren, *Reproductive Rituals: The Perception of Fertility in England from the Sixteenth to the Nineteenth Century* (London: Methuen, 1984), p. 28.

6. See, for example, Linda A. Pollock, *Forgotten Children: Parent-Child Relations from 1500–1900* (Cambridge: Cambridge University Press, 1983). In a similar vein is Alan Macfarlane, *Marriage and Love in England: Modes of Reproduction, 1300–1840* (Oxford: Basil Blackwell, 1986). This study of expressions of parental joy upon the announcement of pregnancy or birth may be added to the work of Houlbrooke, MacDonald, and McLaren. Indeed Macfarlane's earlier work on the unchanging nature of the individual and the English family system from 1250 to the present day is often cited by historians in support of attempts to place certain aspects of family life outside of history. See his *Origins of English Individualism: The Family, Property and Social Transition* (New York: Cambridge University Press, 1979) and *The Family Life of Ralph Josselin, a Seventeenth-Century Clergyman: An Essay in Historical Anthropology* (Cambridge: Cambridge University Press, 1970). For an important critique of Macfarlane's selection and interpretation of data that extend the middle-class family backward in time, see Stephen D. White and Richard T. Vann, "The Invention of English Individualism: Alan Macfarlane and the Modernization of Premodern England," *Social History* 8 (1983): 345–63. Seeking to defend her view of children, Linda Pollock finds different grounds for the modern middle-class family's universality, *Forgotten Children*, pp. 1–32. See also Houlbrooke, *English Family*, 14–15, and MacDonald, *Mystical Bedlam*, p. 89 n. 77.

7. Peter Laslett, *The World We Have Lost*, 2d ed. (New York: Charles Scribner's Sons, 1971). Our citations are to this edition, which has a revised text and updated bibliography and footnotes. The first (1965) and second editions have been the most influential in promoting the sentimental view of the history of the family. Although its argument is consistent with that of the first two editions, the third edition was so substantially rewritten as to require a modification in the title: *The World We Have Lost—Further Explored* (London: Methuen, 1983).

8. This account of the genesis of Laslett's book is based on the preface to *The World We Have Gained: Histories of Population and Social Structure: Essays*

Presented to Peter Laslett on His Seventieth Birthday, ed. Lloyd Bonfield, Richard M. Smith, and Keith Wrightson (Oxford: Basil Blackwell, 1986), pp. viii–x.

9. In a general note to the second edition, Laslett explains: "The specific source in unpublished documents for the first edition of *The World We Have Lost* was the embryo of the collection of listings of inhabitants of English communities before 1801, which has now become one of the files (File 3 in the succeeding notes) of the Cambridge Group for the History of Population and Social Structure. This file remains the most important for the development of the studies described in an introductory way in the present work, but all the other files of the Group are relevant to them, and have been used in this second edition" (254). Although his book was not written in the format associated with the demographic approach, in it Laslett relies on the same data on which he relies in his later work in historical demographics.

10. Peter Laslett, introduction to *Household and Family in Past Time,* ed. Peter Laslett and Richard Wall (Cambridge: Cambridge University Press, 1972), p. 46.

11. Peter Laslett, "Mean Household Size in England since the Sixteenth Century," in *Household and Family in Past Time,* ed. Laslett and Wall, p. 127.

12. In the third edition of *The World We Have Lost,* this statement was dropped; however, all the other passages we quote are retained. Thus the same model of the family continues to inform the third edition.

13. This has proved to be one of the most hotly contested notions Laslett put forward in the book. For a review of the various attacks and counterattacks, see R. S. Neale, *Class in English History, 1680–1850* (Oxford: Basil Blackwell, 1981), pp. 68–99. For an analysis of the paternalistic myth that underlies the Laslett model, see E. P. Thompson, "Eighteenth-century English Society: Class-Struggle without Class?" *Social History* 3 (1978): 133–65.

14. Laslett writes: "When all allowance has been made for the very different assumptions about the very different kinship relations too, it remains the case that there ordinarily slept together under each roof in 1600 only the nuclear family with the addition of servants when necessary" (249). Laslett finds support for this conclusion in the fact that "the evidence we now have suggests that household size was remarkably constant in England at 4.75 persons per household from the late sixteenth until the early twentieth century" (93). He further elaborates: "No two married couples or more went to make up a family group. . . . When a son got married he left the family of his parents and started a family of his own" (94). See his "Mean Household Size" for an account of how he arrived at this conclusion. Neither Laslett's conclusions nor his method have been universally endorsed. For a brief survey of the criticism, see Anderson, *Approaches,* pp. 27–38. A useful cautionary can be found in Lutz Berkner, "The Stem Family and the Developmental Cycle of the Peasant Household: An Eighteenth-Century Austrian Example," *American Historical Review* 77 (1972): 398–418. Berkner argues that while statistics may lead one to believe the overwhelming majority of households were organized around a nuclear family, in many societies the nuclear family was in fact a phase through which the extended family passed, or else another model organized the household even when it is not visible as a

statistical mean. Also critical of Laslett's normative assumptions is Tamara K. Hareven, "Cycles, Courses, and Cohorts: Reflections of Theoretical and Methodological Approaches to the Historical Study of Family Development," *Journal of Social History* 12 (1978): 97–109. Another challenge to Laslett's ideological assumptions comes from Miranda Chaytor, "Household and Kinship: Ryton in the Late 16th and Early 17th Centuries," *History Workshop Journal* 10 (1980): 25–60. Keith Wrightson responds in "Household and Kinship in Sixteenth-Century England," *History Workshop Journal* 12 (1981): 151–58. A response to Wrightson and Laslett's response on the ideological implications of their demographic categories is offered by Olivia Harris, "Households and Their Boundaries," *History Workshop Journal* 13 (1982): 143–52.

15. This argument seems to arise on all fronts. For example, in a study of the history of divorce, *Putting Asunder: A History of Divorce in Western Society* (Cambridge: Cambridge University Press, 1988), p. 362, Roderick Phillips argues that men and women put up with one another—indeed required each other—for economic survival. Thus "expectations were low and flexible, and there was a correspondingly high tolerance of what we might think of as negative behavior." It was the growth of the factory system that made it possible for individuals to survive economically. Phillips does point out that the conjugal relationship had other functions besides the economic one. The entire thesis is doubly suspect, however. Phillips not only assumes that the increase in divorce, "consensual unions," homosexuality, and nontraditional relationships within the last one hundred and fifty years means that industrialization destroyed the family as Laslett imagines it. He also assumes that in earlier cultures men needed women and women needed men to survive economically. Why, one might ask, should heterosexual monogamy be the only basis for ensuring collective survival?

16. *The World We Have Lost,* p. 167. In a review essay, Christopher Hill declared that every serious historian since the seventeenth century has either agreed with Oliver Cromwell that there was a revolution or with Clarendon that there was a great rebellion. "A One-Class Society," in *Change and Continuity in Seventeenth-Century England* (Cambridge: Harvard University Press, 1975), pp. 205–18.

17. Stone declares that what he calls the restricted patriarchal nuclear family "began in about 1530." *The Family, Sex and Marriage in England, 1500–1800* (New York: Harper and Row, 1977), p. 7. It is surely more than a coincidence that, without specifying why, Stone dates the origin of the change in family structure close to 1528. His earlier book on the causes of the English Revolution had identified that as the year in which originated the first of the causes of the English civil war.

18. Stone admits that his data favor "a small minority group, namely the literate and articulate classes, and has relatively little to say about the great majority of Englishmen," but he justifies this bias as favoring "the pacemakers of cultural change" (12).

19. In *A Little Commonwealth: Family Life in Plymouth Colony* (Oxford: Oxford University Press, 1970), John Demos contends that "from the very beginning of settlement at Plymouth the family was nuclear in its basic composition and it has not changed in this respect ever since" (181). He also assumes that

Laslett is essentially correct in his views on the distant history of the nuclear family (62). Thus he does not consider the fact that the founding of Plymouth Colony was a social experiment and that life there was meant to differ in certain important respects from life as it was lived back in England. Even so, his chapter on household membership has to deal with the fact that servants were part of the structure of the family. The mere presence of the "servant" category along with those of "husband," "wife," and "children" in the family should alert us to the fact that this is not exactly the modern nuclear family.

20. Susan Stewart, *On Longing: Narratives of the Miniature, the Gigantic, the Souvenir, the Collection* (Baltimore: Johns Hopkins University Press, 1984), pp. 37–69.

21. *Beyond the Pleasure Principle* in vol. 18 of *The Standard Edition of the Complete Psychological Works of Sigmund Freud,* trans. and ed. James Strachey, Anna Freud, Alix Strachey, and Alan Tyson (London: Hogarth Press, 1955), 14–16. Freud named this game after observing his grandson's habit of throwing a wooden reel over the edge of the bed to make it disappear *(fort)* and then pulling it back with the attached string to make it appear *(da)*. Freud reads the game in this manner: "The interpretation of the game then became obvious. It was related to the child's great cultural achievement—the instinctual renunciation (that is, the renunciation of instinctual satisfaction) which he had made in allowing his mother to go away without protesting. He compensated himself for this, as it were, by himself staging the disappearance and return of the objects within reach" (15).

22. Melanie Klein, *Envy and Gratitude* (New York: Basic Books, 1957) and *Love, Hate, and Reparation* (London: Hogarth Press, 1937).

23. Martin Ingram's *Church Courts, Sex and Marriage in England, 1570–1640* (Cambridge: Cambridge University Press, 1987), for example, concludes from the records of church court cases that romantic love motivated individuals during the early modern period (103–26). For an important critique of the assumptions that lie behind E. A. Wrigley and R. S. Schofield's *The Population History of England, 1541–1871* (London: Edward Arnold, 1981), see Henry Abelove, "Some Speculations on the History of 'Sexual Intercourse' During the 'Long Eighteenth Century' in England," *Genders* 6 (1989): 125–30. Typical of the modern assumptions used to make the categories for reading earlier material is Ralph Houlbrooke's *English Family Life, 1576–1716: An Anthology from Diaries* (Oxford: Basil Blackwell, 1988). Houlbrooke's selections are arranged according to categories that emerged only in the eighteenth and nineteenth centuries in narratives of personal development: "Courtship and Marriage," "Married Life and Widowhood," "Pregnancy, Childbirth and Infancy," "Childhood," "Adolescence and Departure from Home," "Parents' Old Age and Deaths," and "Other Kinsfolk."

24. Roland Barthes describes a popular proverb as "a rural statement of fact, such as 'the weather is fine.' " "Myth Today," in *Mythologies,* trans. Annette Lavers (New York: Farrar, Straus and Giroux, 1972), p. 154.

25. Laslett defines the family for the purposes of a "history of the domestic group" in the introduction to *Household and Family in Past Time:* "A preliminary definition of the family in this sense in contrast to the other senses which are

possible is to be found in everyday experience. The domestic group is the family which the suburban worker leaves when he catches his bus in the morning, and returns to in the evening; it was the family which the English husbandman or petty farmer of our pre-industrial past sat with at table and organised for work in the fields. It consists and consisted of those who share the same physical space for the purposes of eating, sleeping, taking rest and leisure, growing up, child-rearing and procreating (those of them belonging to the class of person who society permits to procreate)" (24–25). Stone defines the family on pp. 21–23. In a particularly harsh review of the book, E. P. Thompson shows how "the modern family" is the hero of Stone's study: "The prospective purchaser [of Stone's book] is supposed to squeal excitedly: 'Darling, look, the history of *us!*' " "Happy Families," *Radical History Review* 20 (1979): 42–50 (reprinted from *New Society,* 8 September 1977, 499–501). The quoted material is found on pp. 43–44.

26. The fact that this model of the family is white as well as elite is demonstrated by its absence from the emergent human sciences; there, other races and ethnicities are seen to lack this particular family structure. See, for example, Anita Levy, "Blood, Kinship, and Gender," *Genders* 5 (1989): 70–85.

27. Nowhere is this clearer than in Engels's idea of emancipated humanity. He cites with obvious approval Lewis Henry Morgan's answer to the question as to whether this form of the family "can be permanent in the future. The only answer that can be given is that it must advance as society advances, and change as society changes, even as it has done in the past. It is the creation of the social system, and will reflect its culture. As the monogamian family has improved greatly since the commencement of civilization, and very sensibly in modern times, it is at least supposable that it is capable of still further improvement until the equality of the sexes is attained. Should the monogamian family in the distant future fail to answer the requirements of society it is impossible to predict the nature of its successor." Frederick Engels, *The Origin of the Family, Private Property, and the State,* ed. Evelyn Reed (New York: Pathfinder Press, 1972), p. 89.

28. Barthes, "The Great Family of Man," in *Mythologies,* p. 100.

29. Claude Lévi-Strauss, *The Elementary Structures of Kinship,* trans. James Harle Bell and John Richard von Sturmer, ed. Rodney Needham (Boston: Beacon Press, 1969), p. 31.

CHAPTER 4

1. The plague of 1348 is credited with increasing the availability of land by killing off approximately 25 percent of the landlords, and with destroying between one-third and one-half of the labor force. The Ordinance of Labourers (1349) was intended to deal with the labor crisis that ensued. It declared that men and women under the age of sixty had to work when required and accept wages paid at the rates of 1346. Rather than holding down wages as intended, the ordinance simply encouraged laborers to relocate. This led to a collapse of traditional patterns of landholding that, for many scholars, marks the beginning of the early modern period. On this point, see Emmanuel Le Roy Ladurie, "A Reply to Robert Brenner," in *The Brenner Debate: Agrarian Class Structure and Economic Development in Pre-Industrial Europe,* ed. T. H. Aston and C. H. H. Philpin (Cam-

bridge: Cambridge University Press, 1985), p. 103; Robert Brenner, "The Agrarian Roots of European Capitalism," ibid., p. 270; Robert S. Gottfried, *The Black Death: Natural and Human Disaster in Medieval Europe* (New York: Free Press, 1983), pp. 94–98; Pauline Gregg, *Black Death to Industrial Revolution: A Social and Economic History of England* (London: Harrap, 1976), pp. 81–88; Bertha Haven Putnam, *The Enforcement of the Statutes of Labourers during the First Decade after the Black Death* (New York: Columbia University, 1908). Even among historians who argue that declines in the population and the work force had begun earlier in the fourteenth century than the onset of the plague, most seem to hold the view of M. M. Postan, who writes, "The part the Black Death played was greatly to aggravate the mortality in the late 1340's, and to delay the recovery from the demographic decline in a subsequent century or century-and-a-half." *The Medieval Economy and Society: An Economic History of Britain in the Middle Ages* (London: Weidenfeld and Nicholson, 1972), p. 38. See also Ian Kershaw, "The Great Famine and Agrarian Crisis in England, 1315–1322," in *Peasants, Knights and Heretics: Studies in Medieval English Social History,* ed. R. H. Hilton (Cambridge: Cambridge University Press, 1976), pp. 85–132.

2. *The Decameron,* trans. G. H. McWilliam (Harmondsworth: Penguin, 1972), p. 60.

3. Although the plague orders drawn up by the Privy Council were largely unchanged from 1578 to 1625, it was not until the act of 1604 that violations of quarantine were made felonies punishable by hanging. Our summary account of the plague orders relies heavily on Paul Slack, *The Impact of Plague in Tudor and Stuart England* (London: Routledge and Kegan Paul, 1985), pp. 207–16.

4. *Stuart Royal Proclamations,* vol. 2, *Royal Proclamations of King Charles I, 1625–1646,* ed. James F. Larkin (Oxford: Clarendon Press, 1983), p. 35; see also Proclamation 29. For an example during the reign of James I see the proclamation issued 1 November 1606, "forbidding all Londoners and other inhabitants of places infected, to resort to the Court," vol. 1, *Royal Proclamations of James I, 1603–1625,* ed. James F. Larkin and Paul L. Hughes (Oxford: Clarendon Press, 1973), 151–52.

5. Such prohibitions were rare and nearly unenforceable. Charles F. Mullett, *The Bubonic Plague and England: An Essay in the History of Medicine* (Lexington: University of Kentucky Press, 1956), pp. 142–52.

6. *The Plague Pamphlets of Thomas Dekker,* ed. F. P. Wilson (Oxford: Clarendon Press, 1925), p. 145.

7. Mikhail Bakhtin, *Rabelais and His World,* trans. Helene Iswolosky (Cambridge: MIT Press, 1968).

8. The same language can be found in other kinds of writing recording the effects of the plague. On 10 September 1625, for example, Joseph Mead transcribed a doctor's account of the effects of the plague on London in a letter for a friend. Particularly noteworthy is the image of the city abandoned by its most prominent inhabitants: "The want and misery is the greatest here ever any man living knew: no trading at all; the rich all gone; housekeepers and apprentices of manual trades begging in the streets, and that in a lamentable manner as will make the strongest heart to yearn." *The Court and Times of Charles I,* ed. Robert F. Williams (London, 1848), 1:48.

9. Paul Slack, *The Impact of the Plague in Tudor and Stuart Times*, p. 195.

10. *The Economic Writings of Sir William Petty*, ed. Charles Henry Hull (Cambridge: Cambridge University Press, 1899), 1:109.

11. That Petty understood the power of the state as being based on the population's capacity to work is perhaps best demonstrated by his *Verbum Sapienti*, written in 1665 and published in 1691. A chapter entitled "The Value of People" begins with the following calculation: "Now if the Annual proceed of the Stock or wealth of the Nation, yields but 15 millions, and the expence be 40. The labour of the People must furnish the other 25; which may be done, if but half of them, *viz.* 3 millions earned but 8£.6s.8d. *per annum*, which is done at 7d. *per diem*, abating the 52 Sundays, and half as many other days for accidents as Holy days, sickness, recreations, &c." *Economic Writings*, 1:108.

12. Of considerable importance to Petty's calculations is the fact that the poor are likely to die in greater numbers than any other potential victims of plague. This was clear from the bills of mortality. Three plague pamphlets appearing in 1665 argued for the first time against the practice of quarantine, on the grounds that forced enclosure seemed to breed disease among the poor. See *The Shutting up of Infected Houses as it is Practiced in England* (1665); *Golgotha; or, a Looking-Glass for London and the Suburbs thereof. With an humble Witness against the Cruel Advice and Practice of Shutting up unto Oppression* (1665); *Directions for the Prevention and Cure of the Plague fitted for the Poorer Sort* (1665).

13. Both Graunt and Petty argued that an "exact computation" (Petty's phrase) would make the census more accurate, and hence tax collection more efficient. David Quint has noted that this argument "rests upon the idea of economic rationality that governs king and subject alike." Although Petty was very much a conservative, then, his mathematical conception of the population contradicted the idea that state power originated in the monarch's blood. "David's Census: Milton's Politics and *Paradise Regained*," in *Re-Membering Milton: Essays on the Texts and Traditions*, ed. Mary Nyquist and Margaret W. Ferguson (New York: Methuen, 1987), p. 140.

14. Thomas Sprat, *History of the Royal Society*, ed. Jackson I. Cope and Harold Whitmore Jones (St. Louis: Washington University Press, 1958), p. 121.

15. We are not suggesting that artisans were a monolithic group. There are data to suggest that they did not in fact constitute a class in any modern sense but were often divided into groups with conflicting economic and political interests. For a study of this phenomenon with regard to French labor history, see Jacques Rancière, "The Myth of the Artisan: Critical Reflections on a Category of Social History," *International Labor and Working Class History* no. 24 (1983), 1–16, and the responses by William H. Sewell, Jr., Christopher H. Johnson, Edgar Leon Newman, and Nicholas Papayanis, as well as Rancière's reply to his critics, 17–46. See also E. P. Thompson, "Eighteenth-century English Society: Class Struggle without Class?" *Social History* 3 (1978):133–65.

16. Laura Stevenson has surveyed the materials and finds few descriptions of artisan life after the early years of James's reign. We have drawn upon her findings set forth in *Praise and Paradox: Merchants and Craftsmen in Elizabethan Popular Literature* (Cambridge: Cambridge University Press, 1984). The literature

dealing with domestic economy, animal husbandry, and various kinds of practical labor is not discussed in this chapter; we assume that we are dealing with a culture where "work" has not yet become a meaningful category or a way of organizing social relations. Indeed, by lumping them together as "work," middle-class culture would eventually erase the important distinction between the tasks described in practical advice books and the privileged knowledge passed down from artisans to their apprentices.

17. E. P. Thompson has discussed at length the last stages of this process in *The Making of the English Working Class* (New York: Vintage, 1966).

18. Charles Richard Weld, *A History of the Royal Society with Memoirs of the Presidents* (London, 1848), 1:138.

19. Sprat, *History*, pp. 310, 381.

20. Julia Wrigley has shown how the attempt to prevent the division of labor by teaching the new scientific knowledge to artisans actually divided mental from material production, giving greater economic rewards to the intellectual, professional, and managerial classes. Mechanics' institutes were founded in the early nineteenth century for the purpose of training artisans in the sciences that informed the various trades. As the century wore on, however, these institutes focused more narrowly on training artisans only in technical skills. Once the institutes "abandoned the aim of teaching manual workers science," Wrigley writes, educational policy makers "urged that Britain concentrate on teaching managers and foremen scientific principles," "The Division between Mental and Manual Labor: Artisan Education in Nineteenth-Century Britain," in *Marxist Inquiries: Studies of Labor, Class, and States,* ed. Michael Burawoy and Theda Skocpol, supplement to the *American Journal of Sociology* 88 (1982):32

21. Sprat, *History*, p. 113. Writing in 1671 on the virtues of what he calls "Political Arithmetic," William Petty declares his wish to express himself "in terms of number, weight or measure; to use only arguments of sense; and to consider only as causes as have visible foundations in nature, leaving those that depend on the mutable minds, opinion, appetites and passions of particular men to the consideration of others." *The Economic Writings of Sir William Petty,* 1:244. The theological counterpart to Petty and Sprat was another member of the Royal Society, Sir Joseph Glanville, who attacked the rhetorical excesses of divines in his influential *An Essay concerning Preaching: Written for the Direction of A Young Divine* (1678). Glanville called for a new style of preaching that "ought to be *plain, practical, methodical, affectionate*" (11). On the rise of the plain style in the later seventeenth century, see Wilbur Samuel Howell, *Logic and Rhetoric in England, 1500–1700* (Princeton: Princeton University Press, 1956), pp. 364–97.

22. George Puttenham, *The Arte of English Poesie* (Menston: Scholar Press, 1968), pp. 156–57. Howell, commenting on the problem of comparing the poetic and scientific attitudes toward rhetoric, notes that "even if we confined ourselves to a strict comparison between poet and poet or scientist and scientist of the two eras," the contrast would be "striking, and it would still be noticeable" (*Logic and Rhetoric,* p. 390). As Howell notes, this historical shift in both domains of writing coincides with a similar change in the attitude toward the rhetorical style of sermons (390–94).

23. In *English Literature in History, 1730–80: An Equal, Wide Survey* (New York: St. Martins, 1983), pp. 110–76, John Barrell discusses the irony of creating a new standard of English that subjugated "varieties of provincial English, and the modes of expression of different classes, to the norms of the elite." The modern tendency to remove linguistic and cultural matters from the jurisdiction of the state has obscured the equation deliberately drawn by various Enlightenment intellectuals between "the laws of England and the rules of good English, with the aim of revealing that the language community could be structured as a political community" (112).

24. Michel Foucault, *The Order of Things: An Archaeology of the Human Sciences* (New York: Vintage, 1973). In *Man and the Natural World: A History of the Modern Sensibility* (New York: Vintage, 1983), Keith Thomas has shown that in order to reclassify the natural world, Enlightenment theory produced an individual who was both passionate and capable of rationality.

25. John Locke, *An Essay Concerning Human Understanding*, ed. Peter H. Nidditch (Oxford: Oxford University Press, 1975), III.x.34.

26. As Roy Strong has argued, considerable care was taken with making Elizabeth's birthday, saint's day, and accession day the occasions for carefully orchestrating a ceremonial image of the queen. See his three essays on Elizabeth's pageants in *The Cult of Elizabeth: Elizabethan Portraiture and Pageantry* (Berkeley: University of California Press, 1986), pp. 114–91.

27. In 1563 a proclamation was drafted calling for one painter, and one painter only, "to take the natural representation of her majesty," and "to prohibit all manner of other persons to draw, paint, grave, or portray her majesty's personage or visage," *Tudor Royal Proclamations: The Later Tudors, 1553–1587*, ed. Paul L. Hughes and James F. Larkin (New Haven: Yale University Press, 1969), 2:240. Though we have no evidence how the statute was enforced, we do know it was typical of measures taken to regulate her image. On this point see Roy Strong, *Portraits of Queen Elizabeth I* (Oxford: Clarendon Press, 1963), p. 5.

28. Jonathan Goldberg has discussed the politics of the Jacobean and the Caroline representations of the royal family in *James I and the Politics of Literature: Jonson, Shakespeare, Donne, and Their Contemporaries* (Baltimore: Johns Hopkins University Press, 1983), pp. 85–107. See also Graham Parry, *The Golden Age Restor'd: The Culture of the Stuart Court, 1603–42* (New York: St. Martins, 1981), and R. Malcolm Smuts, *Court Culture and the Origins of a Royalist Tradition in Early Stuart England* (Philadelphia: University of Pennsylvania Press, 1987).

29. Roy Strong, *Van Dyck: Charles I on Horseback* (New York: Viking, 1972), p. 70.

30. On Milton's education, see William Riley Parker, *Milton: A Biography* (Oxford: Clarendon Press, 1968), 1:13–115; Donald Lemen Clark, *John Milton at St. Paul's School: A Study of Ancient Rhetoric in English Renaissance Education* (New York, 1948); Harris Francis Fletcher, *The Intellectual Development of John Milton*, 2 vols. (Urbana: University of Illinois Press, 1956–61).

31. Richard Helgerson has argued that despite modern preconceptions about Milton's hostility to Cavalier culture, in fact he wrote a poetic language that he

shared with the collections of poetry published by his royalist contemporaries. *Self-Crowned Laureates: Spenser, Jonson, Milton, and the Literary System* (Berkeley: University of California Press, 1983), pp. 185–282. In *Poetry and Politics in the English Renaissance* (London: Routledge and Kegan Paul, 1984), David Norbrook argues, contrariwise, that the resemblance between the poetry Milton published in 1645 and that of the Cavaliers is at best "superficial" (238).

32. Leah S. Marcus has discussed the manner in which Cavalier poetry participated in the Laudian program so hated by puritans who sought to continue the reformation of the English church. *The Politics of Mirth: Jonson, Herrick, Milton, Marvell and the Defense of Old Holiday Pastimes* (Chicago: University of Chicago Press, 1986).

33. John Milton, *The Reason of Church Government*, ed. Ralph A. Haug, in vol. 1 of *Complete Prose Works of John Milton*, ed. Don M. Wolfe (New Haven: Yale University Press, 1953), p. 237.

34. Typical of such contradictions is the fact that in the antiprelatical pamphlets Milton argued that support for the bishops undermined loyalty to the king. This was first pointed out by Don M. Wolfe, *Milton in the Puritan Revolution* (New York: Humanities Press, 1963), pp. 46–47.

35. John Milton, *Complete Poems and Major Prose*, ed. Merritt Y. Hughes (New York: Odyssey Press, 1957).

36. As has often been noted, as early as 1638 Milton announced his intention to write an epic. First in *Mansus* (lines 78–84) and then two years later in *Epitaphium Damonis* (lines 160–68), he made clear his desire to write an epic based on Arthurian materials. By 1642, with the publication of *The Reason of Church Government*, he had reconsidered the form: "what king or knight before the conquest might be chosen in whom to lay the pattern of a Christian hero." Hughes, ed., pp. 668–69. The Trinity manuscript (?1639–42) makes clear that he was also speculating on various biblical and British subjects for tragedies. These sources provide a rather good sense of what kind of poem Milton may have had in mind before the civil war, as well as what he might have drawn from various biblical, classical, and Renaissance models. For the transcript of the jottings on tragedy, see appendix A, "Milton's Outlines for Tragedies," ed. John M. Steadman, in vol. 8 of *Complete Prose Works of John Milton*, ed. Maurice Kelley (New Haven: Yale University Press, 1982), pp. 539–82.

37. Allan H. Gilbert considers Milton's focus to be such a deviation from that of his predecessors. *On the Composition of Paradise Lost: A Study of the Ordering and Insertion of Material* (New York: Octagon Books, 1972). Although a number of Milton scholars have rightly noted Milton's unusual emphasis on domestic relations, none that we know of has suggested the degree to which this focus was itself revolutionary, except perhaps Harold E. Toliver, "Milton's Household Epic," *Milton Studies* 9 (1976): 105–20.

38. William Kerrigan and Gordon Braden, in *The Idea of the Renaissance* (Baltimore: Johns Hopkins University Press, 1989), pp. 191–218, offer an account of Milton's use of Petrarch in the early poetry and in *Paradise Lost.*

39. For a discussion of the ideology of this form, see Leonard Tennenhouse, "Sir Walter Ralegh and the Literature of Clientage," in *Patronage in the Re-*

naissance, ed. Guy Fitch Lytle and Stephen Orgel (Princeton: Princeton University Press, 1981), pp. 235–58, and *Power on Display: The Politics of Shakespeare's Genres* (New York: Methuen, 1986), pp. 30–36.

40. Arthur F. Marotti, " 'Love is Not Love': Elizabethan Sonnet Sequences and the Social Order," *ELH* 49 (1982): 396–428, discusses how envy and desire provided the language for place and advancement in such poetry.

41. It is particularly appropriate that this language follows what Barbara Keifer Lewalski has described as Milton's parodies of "a major topos of the romance mode—the hero's adventure in a Garden of Love." *Paradise Lost and the Rhetoric of Literary Forms* (Princeton: Princeton University Press, 1985), pp. 70–71.

42. For a discussion of the kind of writing that went into the making of the aristocratic female body, see Ruth Kelso's treatment of the female courtesy book from the late Middle Ages to the Renaissance, *Doctrine for the Lady of the Renaissance* (Urbana: University of Illinois Press, 1956), and Suzanne Hull's descriptive bibliography, *Chaste, Silent and Obedient: English Books for Women, 1475–1640* (San Marino: Huntington Library, 1982). For an account of the domestic-economy and conduct books that opposed aristocratic display, see Nancy Armstrong, *Desire and Domestic Fiction: A Political History of the Novel* (New York: Oxford University Press, 1987), pp. 59–75.

43. Jacques Donzelot says of the two different economic views, "In [the aristocratic model] wealth was produced to provide for the munificence of states. It was their sumptuary activity, the multiplication and refinement of the needs of the central authority, that was conducive to production. Hence wealth was in the manifest power that permitted levies by the state for the benefit of a minority. With [a protocapitalist economic model] the state was no longer the end of production, but its means: it was the responsibility of the state to govern social relations, in such a manner as to intensify this production to a maximum by restricting consumption." *The Policing of Families,* trans. Robert Hurley (New York: Pantheon, 1979), p. 13.

44. Bakhtin, *Rabelais,* pp. 253–55.

45. Published in 1667, the same year that Petty drew up his proposals for the plague and that *Paradise Lost* first appeared, Thomas Willis's *Essay on the Brain and Nervous Stock* located a physical source within each individual's body for something he calls *sensus communis,* by which he meant the perception of experience that affected fantasy, imagination, and memory. Among other things, Willis argued, it is this *sensus communis* that arouses desire by a process of the nervous system for which he coined the word "psychology." What Willis described might be called the essence of the modern individual, an essence that was both verbally articulated and gendered. Klaus Doerner observes that although Willis revolutionized ideas of the nervous system, "the only disorders Willis took over into his nerve theory almost in toto were hysteria and related complaints, removing them from their venerable site in the uterus, and turning them into 'nervous' diseases." *Madmen and the Bourgeoisie: A Social History of Insanity and Psychiatry,* trans. Joachim Neugroschel and Jean Steinberg (Oxford: Oxford University Press, 1981), p. 25.

46. Although she does not address this mid-seventeenth-century revision in the representation of a Platonized heavenly love, Annabel Patterson has discussed

how the romance form was revived for Charles I and Henrietta Maria, and was itself revised during the interregnum to work against the royal image. *Censorship and Interpretation: The Conditions of Writing and Reading in Early Modern England* (Madison: University of Wisconsin Press, 1984), pp. 159–202.

47. The engraving was by William Dolle after the Henry Faithorne portrait. John T. Shawcross, *Milton: A Bibliography for the Years 1624–1700* (Binghamton: Medieval and Renaissance Texts, 1984), entry 318.

48. For an account of the commentary, see Ants Oras, *Milton's Editors and Commentators from Patrick Hume to Henry John Todd, 1695–1801* (New York: Haskell House, 1964; first published 1929). In the course of the eighteenth century, this commentary grew so extensive that an early-nineteenth-century edition (London, 1804) announced on the title page that it offered "an abridgment of the copia and learned notes," along with a life by the Reverend John Evans.

49. Leslie E. Moore, *Beautiful Sublime: The Making of Paradise Lost, 1701–1734* (Stanford: Stanford University Press, 1990), p. 158.

50. Quoted in Moore, *Beautiful Sublime,* p. 159.

51. From this perspective, Stanley Fish's reading of *Paradise Lost* in *Surprised by Sin: The Reader in Paradise Lost* (Berkeley: University of California Press, 1971) becomes especially useful. Fish focuses on the struggle between one kind of literacy and another (marked as a lack) that is conducted through the literary text. One can think of the neophyte reader, badgered by a text that was designed to humble him, as reproducing the false leaps to meaning that Adam makes when he is learning to interpret the world.

CHAPTER 5

1. We realize that "public" is itself a problematic term. The term does not simply designate everything that is not private. Rather, as Nancy Fraser reminds us, modern cultures are marked by a formation that Habermas calls "the public sphere": "This arena is conceptually distinct from the state; it is a site for the production and circulation of discourse that can in principle be critical of the state. The public sphere in Habermas's sense is also conceptually distinct from the official-economy; it is not an arena of market relations but rather one of discursive relations, a theater for debating and deliberating rather than for buying and selling." "Rethinking the Public Sphere: A Contribution to the Critique of Actually Existing Democracy," *Social Text* 25/26 (1990): 57.

2. In "Censorship and English Literature," in vol. 1 of *The Collected Essays of Christopher Hill* (Amherst: University of Massachusetts Press, 1985), p. 41, Hill writes: "It was criminal folly to extend political discussion beyond the charmed circle of the ruling class. Parliament for its part ordered the Lord Mayor of London not to allow the King's answer to the Nineteen Propositions of 1 June 1642 to be printed."

3. Joseph Frank, *The Beginnings of the English Newspaper, 1620–1660* (Cambridge: Harvard University Press, 1961), p. 21.

4. There were of course certain restrictions on the free production and flow of information in print. The early newspapers seldom had long runs, and Parliament made repeated efforts to control them, first in 1643 and again in 1647. Until

1649, however, attempts to censor or otherwise control what could be published had only limited success. For an account of the various attempts at imposing parliamentary censorship in the 1640s, see John Feather, *A History of British Publishing* (London: Routledge, 1988), pp. 43–49, and Frank, *Beginnings,* pp. 41–43, 115–17, 174–75, 197–98.

5. See G. K. Fortescue, *Catalogue of the Pamphlets, Books, Newspapers and Manuscripts Collected by G. Thomason, 1640–1661,* 2 vols. (London: British Museum, 1908).

6. In addition to Hill's "Censorship and English Literature," see also Annabel Patterson, *Censorship and Interpretation: The Conditions of Writing and Reading in Early Modern England* (Madison: University of Wisconsin Press, 1984), and Lois Potter, *Secret Rites and Secret Writing: Royalist Literature, 1641–1660* (Cambridge: Cambridge University Press, 1990).

7. Raymond Williams, *The Long Revolution* (New York: Columbia University Press, 1961), p. 161.

8. According to Feather, *History of British Publishing,* p. 52, at the time of the act at least 59 printers claimed to be entitled to the license to print; by 1666 there were at least 150 individuals who had served apprenticeships as printers.

9. Quoted in James Sutherland, *The Restoration Newspaper and Its Development* (Cambridge: Cambridge University Press, 1986), p. 2. This act, unlike earlier practices, justified censorship on secular grounds. See J. Walker, "The Censorship of the Press during the Reign of Charles II," *History* 25 (1950): 219–38.

10. Quoted in Christopher Hill, "Sir John Berkenhead (1617–79)," in vol. 1 of *Collected Essays,* p. 102. For an account of Roger L'Estrange's activities as surveyor of the press, see George Kitchin, *Sir Roger L'Estrange: A Contribution to the History of the Press in the Seventeenth Century* (New York: Augustus M. Kelley, 1971; first published 1913).

11. Quoted in Christopher Hill, "John Milton and Andrew Marvell," in vol. 1 of *Collected Essays,* p. 166.

12. Hill, "Censorship," p. 51. Sutherland tells of one printer L'Estrange had arrested in 1663, John Twyn, who was found with "some sheets still wet from the press." For attempting to print "a heretical or seditious" publication, Twyn was sentenced to be hanged, drawn and quartered. Sutherland points out: "It is hard for us today to realise that under the Stuarts any criticism of the government could be, and often was in a court of law, interpreted as an attack on the sovereign: on such occasions no real distinction was made between the king's servants and the king himself" (1–3).

13. In defining the modern middle class as one that consolidated itself and rose to hegemony through intellectual labor, we realize we are not only revising the traditional equation between the modern English ruling class and a European bourgeoisie; we are also going against the prevailing notion of "intellectuals" as a group or even a class opposed to the bourgeoisie or at least to its methods of domination. It is certainly not our purpose to question current meanings of the term as it is used, and interrogated, in the definitive collection of essays entitled *Intellectuals: Aesthetics, Politics, Academics,* ed. Bruce Robbins (Minneapolis: University of Minnesota Press, 1990). We are working at the other end of a

continuum that stretches from the late-seventeenth-century members of the Royal Society, John Locke, and others, to the problematic articulated by the essays in Robbins's anthology—namely, the paradox that in order to have the power to criticize the state one must be empowered by state institutions. As Robbins poignantly puts it in his introduction, "these essays are largely animated . . . by a desire to interrogate the received opinion that the 'success' of the left in grounding itself within American educational and cultural institutions since the 1960s must be seen as the 'failure,' betrayal, decline, or demise of the intellectual" (xii).

14. Harold Perkin, *The Origins of Modern English Society* (London: Routledge Kegan Paul, 1969), pp. 252–70.

15. Zygmunt Bauman, *Legislators and Interpreters: On Modernity, Post-Modernity and Intellectuals* (Cambridge: Polity Press, 1988), p. 1. Pierre Bourdieu has a similar view of the ambiguous position of intellectuals in "The Corporatism of the Universal: The Role of Intellectuals in the Modern World," *Telos* no. 81 (1989): 99–110. Raymond Williams dates the use of the term "the intellectual" from the early nineteenth century. "Intellectuals," in *Keyword: A Vocabulary of Culture and Society* (New York: Oxford University Press, 1976), pp. 140–42. In *Culture and Society, 1780–1950* (Garden City: Doubleday, 1959), p. 38, Williams states that the term had come into common usage by the 1820s. Lewis Coser, *Men of Ideas: A Sociologist's View* (New York: Free Press, 1965), identifies the middle of the eighteenth century as the moment of emergence, although nowhere does he document the coining of the term. Finally, Edward Shils finds the notion in use in the Middle Ages. "The Intellectuals and the Powers: Some Perspectives for Comparative Analysis," in *On Intellectuals: Theoretical Studies Case Studies,* ed. Philip Rieff (Garden City: Doubleday and Co., 1969), pp. 25–48. See also Alvin Gouldner, *The Future of Intellectuals and the Rise of the New Class* (New York: Seabury Press, 1979).

16. The rest of this chapter discusses this paradox from Gramsci to Eastern European theorists and the Ehrenreichs. Each reproduces the idea of an originary and pure, or true, intellectual whose interests were the same as those identifying the group for which he wrote. Each sees the modern intellectual as a deviation from that original. We note, however, that this duality persists even in attempts at determining who belongs in the category of "intellectuals" and who must be excluded. Precisely the issue of which of the two opposing concepts of the intellectual defines university teachers and scholars, simultaneously unites and divides the essays in Robbins's *Intellectuals*. On the one hand, Stanley Aronowitz argues in "On Intellectuals" (3–56) that scientists should be included among intellectuals, on the grounds that the work they do is primarily intellectual rather than productive in nature. On the other hand, Barbara Ehrenreich's "The Professional-Managerial Class Revisited" (173–85) insists that intellectuals should not be confused with the professional-managerial class. In her analysis, what kind of work one does is less significant than one's motive for doing it. But although she dissociates the work of intellectuals from that of any other class, she also distrusts the idea that intellectuals belong to a specialized class of their own. She solves the problem semantically, by calling intellectuals a "group" rather than a "class"— a group whose interests cannot be identified with those of any class. In "Defenders of the Faith and the New Class" (101–32), Andrew Ross (correctly, to our minds)

accepts the conflict between the class from which one comes and the interests for which one speaks as the very condition of being an intellectual. He sees the intellectual as the object both of the disrespect that popular culture displays toward official (high) culture and of the respect that is the basis of his or her intellectual authority (106).

17. Karl Marx, "The Thesis on Feuerbach," in Karl Marx and Frederick Engels, *The German Ideology: Part One and Supplementary Texts*, ed. C. J. Arthur (New York: International Publishers, 1985), p. 121.

18. That this observation was central to Gramsci's reading of Marx and Engels and to the thinking that led up to his conceptualization of hegemony has been convincingly demonstrated by Joseph V. Femia in *Gramsci's Political Thought: Hegemony, Consciousness, and the Revolutionary Process* (Oxford: Clarendon, 1987), pp. 61–164, and John Hoffman, *The Gramscian Challenge: Coercion and Consent in Marxist Political Theory* (Oxford: Basil Blackwell, 1984), pp. 19–98. See also Ernesto Laclau and Chantal Mouffe, *Hegemony and Socialist Strategy: Towards a Radical Democratic Politics*, trans. Winston Moore and Paul Cammack (London: Verso, 1985), pp. 47–92.

19. Karl Marx, *Capital*, trans. Ben Fowkes (New York: Vintage Books, 1977), 1:280.

20. In an illuminating essay entitled "Speculations on Reading Marx: After Reading Derrida," in *Post-Structuralism and the Question of History*, ed. Derek Attridge, Geoff Bennington, and Robert Young (Cambridge: Cambridge University Press, 1987), pp. 30–62, Gayatri Chakravorty Spivak shows how "money" operates in Marx's writing both as a theoretical term to suppress an "irreducible heterogeneity" (35) and in the rhetorical position of "the sign of a sign, the possibility of the exchange of signs, not merely language but a *foreign* language" (32). And once money is seen as an unrecognized supplement in Marx," she continues, "it shows all the marks of writing" (33). It is by a parallel logic that we represent the changing behavior of capital in *Capital* as a story about intellectual labor.

21. For our notion of magical narratives in general, we are indebted to Fredric Jameson's "Magical Narratives: On the Dialectical Use of Genre Criticism," in *The Political Unconscious: Narrative as a Socially Symbolic Act* (Ithaca: Cornell University Press, 1981), pp. 103–50. For Jameson's discussion of Propp, see especially pp. 119–29.

22. Nancy Hartsock sums up the view of Marx and Engels: "By generalizing its own condition, by making all of society a propertyless producer, the proletariat has the possibility of creating a classless society," *Money, Sex and Power: Toward a Feminist Historical Materialism* (Boston: Northeastern University Press, 1985), p. 135.

23. We find that whenever modern intellectuals theorize historical change, an element of intellectual labor is always crucial. In *Anti-Dühring* (Moscow: Foreign Languages Publishing House, 1962), Engels, for example, wrote that before the state can "wither away" it must take "possession of the means of production *in the name of society*" (385, our italics).

24. Antonio Gramsci, "The Formation of the Intellectuals," in *Selections from the Prison Notebooks of Antonio Gramsci*, trans. Quintin Hoare and Geoffrey

Nowell Smith (New York: International Publishers, 1971), pp. 5–23. The quote is from p. 10.

25. George Konrad and Ivan Szelenyi, *The Intellectuals on the Road to Class Power*, trans. Andrew Arato and Richard E. Allen (Brighton: Harvester Press, 1979), p. 22.

26. "Fetishism," in *An Antonio Gramsci Reader: Selected Writings, 1916–1935*, ed. David Forgacs (New York: Schocken, 1988), pp. 243–45.

27. "Utopia," *Gramsci Reader*, pp. 45–52.

28. Near the beginning of this century, Kautsky and Lenin compared the intellectual to the proletarian on the grounds that both lived by selling their labor and were therefore likely to be exploited under capitalism. Unlike the worker, however, the intellectual does mental work that often places him in a managerial relation to other workers. So he may live in a manner comparable to that of the bourgeoisie. In thus joining the dominant class, they believed, the intellectual turned his labor (which should, under capitalism, resist the state on behalf of working people) to support the interests of that class. At the same time, Kautsky and Lenin also believed that the intellectual's identity was not completely determined by the dominant class. Indeed, rather than serve the interests of the bourgeoisie, the intellectual had other options. He could criticize the operations of capitalism, or he could support the working-class struggle directly. As George Konrad and Ivan Szelenyi have more recently insisted, however, "both solutions have in common the assumption that the intellectual is capable of rising above his historical determinedness"; if intellectuals tend to behave like the dominant class, it is not out of choice, it is simply in the nature of what they do. This summary is based on Konrad and Szelenyi, *Intellectuals on the Road to Class Power* (the quotation is from p. 13), and Alvin W. Gouldner, *Against Fragmentation: The Origins of Marxism and Sociology* (New York: Oxford University Press, 1985), 14–22.

29. Barbara and John Ehrenreich, "The Professional-Managerial Class," in *Between Labor and Capital*, ed. Pat Walker (Boston: South End Press, 1979), pp. 5–45.

30. It is important to mention Barbara Ehrenreich's more recent qualification of this thesis in "The Professional-Managerial Class Revisited," in *Intellectuals*, ed. Robbins: "The PMC contains many people who are not intellectuals in any sense of the word, and conversely people who ought to be regarded as 'intellectuals' are scattered throughout all social classes" (174). Once having defined intellectuals in terms of the service they perform, first as an outcropping and then as a self-perpetuating displacement of the traditional bourgeoisie, she then retrieves the more traditional definition of intellectual in a way that totally confounds the precision of her first model. She does so, we believe, in response to criticism that rules out the possibility that critical intellectual resistance to the dominant culture is one of the specialized functions of that class.

31. At this point, we must stress the sometimes neglected point that hegemony is not just domination but a relationship. A group acquires hegemony when its viewpoint and its ideas become the viewpoint and the ideas with which all others have to negotiate in order to present their own views, so that any opposition in

fact attests to the dominance of the elite group's views. For this reason, change often comes from conservative quarters. When, more recently, Laclau and Mouffe try to imagine a similar transformation, they, too, understand that it is not enough to identify the appearance of such transformations full-blown in speech and writing. One has to understand the process of cultural negotiations, minor changes, and displacements through which a new group acquired both authority and its distinctive form. "In order to speak of hegemony, the articulatory moment is not sufficient. It is also necessary that the articulation should take place through a confrontation with antagonistic articulatory practices." Laclau and Mouffe, *Hegemony*, p. 135. A specific articulation, in other words, is the end product of a complicated political and historical struggle that excludes and represses some information in order to make statements that have the authority to seem meaningful and right.

32. Rudolf Bahro, *The Alternative in Eastern Europe*, trans. David Fernbach (Manchester: NLB, 1978). We are indebted to Christopher Hitchens for calling this book to our attention.

33. This problem does not arise only within the official bureaucracies of factories and the statehouse. Bahro's principle of bureaucratic rivalry can be expanded to include those intellectuals who represent themselves to the public (and to one another) as occupying a position outside and in opposition to the economic and political spheres. A special issue of *Cultural Critique* (vol. 12, Spring 1989) devoted to "Discursive Strategies and the Economy of Prestige" demonstrates how Bahro's thesis can be extended into the humanities. The editors, Richard Leppert and Bruce Lincoln, argue that the notion of an "economy" based on the exchange, accumulation, and investment of "labor, material goods, and currency" can be used to describe "comparable (but hardly identical) processes . . . in what we would term an economy of prestige, inspired in a loose way by Pierre Bourdieu's call 'to extend economic calculation to all the goods, material and symbolic, without distinction, that present themselves as rare and worthy of being sought after in a particular formation' " (7). Although they draw on Bourdieu's concept of a larger economy in which virtually any symbolic object may participate, Leppert and Lincoln distinguish "the components of an economy of prestige" from an economy per se, on the basis that prestige results from a process "through which members of society formulate, share, and reformulate their opinions" (7). The prestige system can be said to resemble bureaucratic rivalry because not only is it an extension of the economy (in the restricted sense of the term), it also detaches itself from the economy by certain "acts of discourse" (resembling the bureaucratic hierarchy created by the gathering, hoarding, and selective distribution of information). Leppert and Lincoln stress that the prestige system is not identical with the economy but analogous to it, and therefore potentially in conflict with economic value. Three other essays in this collection focus on the operations of prestige in modern European culture: Susan McClary, "Terminal Prestige: The Case of Avant-Garde Music Composition," pp. 57–81; Jochen Schulte-Sasse, "The Prestige of the Artist under Conditions of Modernity," pp. 83–100; and John Barrell, " 'The Dangerous Goddess': Masculinity, Prestige, and the Aesthetic in Early Eighteenth-Century Britain," pp. 101–31. All three describe a process that began in the eighteenth century and,

with increasing consistency, reinflected the value of high-culture objects back onto the personality of their makers, so that the artist rather than the artifact he produced became the source of that object's value.

CHAPTER 6

1. Benedict Anderson, *Imagined Communities: Reflections on the Origin and Spread of Nationalism* (London: Verso, 1983).

2. David Cressy, *Coming Over: Migration and Communication between England and New England in the Seventeenth Century* (Cambridge: Cambridge University Press, 1987); Ian K. Steele, *The English Atlantic, 1675–1740* (New York: Oxford University Press, 1986); Jacob M. Price, "The Transatlantic Economy," in *Colonial British America: Essays in the New History of the Early Modern Era*, ed. Jack P. Greene and J. R. Pole (Baltimore: Johns Hopkins University Press, 1984), pp. 18–42; David D. Hall, "Religion and Society: Problems and Reconsiderations," in *Colonial British America*, pp. 317–44; Norman Fiering, "The Transatlantic Republic of Letters: A Note on the Circulation of Learned Periodicals to Early Eighteenth-Century America," *William and Mary Quarterly* 33 (1976): 642–60.

3. In *The Long Revolution* (New York: Columbia University Press, 1961), Raymond Williams explains how in England a new group of people acquired the means of producing ruling ideas, but he does not seriously entertain the possibility that such a cultural revolution first defined that class of people as such or provided the means for its domination.

4. Foucault begins *Discipline and Punish*, trans. Alan Sheridan (New York: Vintage, 1979), with the dismemberment of Damien, only to shift his focus abruptly to the kind of state power that operates on the mind rather than the body—through a monopoly on truth rather than violence—to produce an internally regulated subject.

5. Since the business of education expresses "the wider organization of a culture and a society," "what is thought of as 'an education' " will always be, according to Williams, "a particular selection, a particular set of emphases and omissions" (125). He demonstrates this principle in describing the growth of a particular kind of literacy and the development of various educational institutions that were tailored to produce a population for an industrializing England (125–213). E. P. Thompson shows in great detail how it took a whole century or more before local forms of labor would be rendered obsolete and a working class produced that could man the factories of nineteenth-century England. *The Making of the English Working Class* (New York: Vintage, 1966). Both Thompson and Williams emphasize the degree to which intellectuals not only classified people but made them fit the intellectuals' categories.

6. Warner's argument effectively challenges Whig interpretations of the spread of print (that technology precedes epistemology) by illustrating how well Anderson's model of print capitalism works in eighteenth-century America. *The Letters of the Republic: Publication and the Public Sphere in Eighteenth-Century America* (Cambridge: Harvard University Press, 1990).

7. See the discussion of Hill and Stone in chapter 5.

8. L'Estrange seems to have desired constraints on printing more rigid and onerous than had ever been in place before. His proposals would have severely restricted the size of the Stationers' Company and empowered his own office well beyond overseeing the printing of newsbooks and newspapers; the proposals would have granted him an indirect hand in the licensing of coffeehouse keepers. By these proposals he sought to create a patronage system—today we might call it a system of bribery and extortion—that would probably have equaled the worst excesses of the patronage system under James I. See Kitchin, *Sir Roger L'Estrange,* pp. 95–189.

9. Foucault has discussed this at length in *The Archaeology of Knowledge,* trans. A. M. Sheriden Smith (New York: Pantheon, 1972).

10. Benedict Anderson provides a good example of this process when he describes how North American nationalism began to define its own historical trajectory in relation to England. The Protestant, English-speaking creoles of New England were more tightly bunched in New England and more "tightly linked by print as well as commerce" than were, for example, the Spanish creoles in Central America (64).

11. Cornelis Disco points out that "revisionist" Marxist critiques of socialism elaborate earlier attacks and predictions that "in spite of the common attack on the orthodox Marxist scenario of the triumph of socialism and the transition to communism, [they have] ... lifted the lid from a certain Marxist nightmare: namely, that the idea of a future "classless society" might turn out to be as mythical as the present idea of "workers' parties." "Intellectuals in Advanced Capitalism: Capital, Closure, and the New Class Thesis," in *Intellectuals, Universities and the State in Western Modern Societies,* ed. Ron Eyerman, Lennart Svensson, and Thomas Söderquist (Berkeley: University of California Press, 1987), pp. 74–75. With regard to the Ehrenreichs' thesis, Disco writes: "The PMC thesis attempts to have the Marxist cake and eat it too by providing a class account of the new professional and managerial strata which leaves the original Marxist class scenario intact. The PMC is regarded as a new class specific to the monopoly stage of capitalism, whose specific place in the division of labor (read: specific *function*) is the reproduction of capitalist culture and capitalist class relations. The PMC is thus the most recent incarnation of the mysterious and interstitial 'petty bourgeoisie,' destined to disappear from the historical stage whenever the essential class contradiction between global capital and global labor reasserts itself" (75–76).

12. There are a number of indications that certain forms of social reproduction precede what are believed to be the corresponding means of social production. In "The Moral Economy of the English Crowd," *Past and Present 50* (1971): 76–136, E. P. Thompson shows how late in the eighteenth century it was before anything resembling a modern middle class could be discerned; social contention took place between landlords and crowds, not between those who owned labor and those who owned money. In *The Machinery Question and the Making of Political Economy, 1815–1848* (Cambridge: Cambridge University Press, 1980), Maxine Berg contends that entrepreneurs associated with mechanization were a despised minority until the great landowners lost their ability to compensate for food shortages and settle local disputes. Fear of the mob, ap-

parently inspired by the French Revolution, created a brief and uncomfortable alliance between the old aristocracy and the owners of machinery. E. P. Thompson's account of the radical press in *Making of the English Working Class*, pp. 713–36 and passim, argues that it was necessary to suppress the radical press because it played a major role in resisting the conversion of older forms of skilled or artisan labor into a "working class." In *The Industrial Muse: A Study of Nineteenth-Century Working-Class Novels* (New York: Barnes and Noble, 1974), Martha Vicinus has shown how broadsides and other products of the popular press expressed hostility to the mechanization of labor as well as to bourgeois sexuality. These publications gave way to what might be called a working-class literature, which emulated the high cultural modes of poetry and fiction. Vicinus suggests that the working class acquired access to the legitimate press in a way that ultimately helped to subordinate their culture to that of the new middle class.

13. It is curious that Anderson does not give novels an instrumental role in the formation of New World nationalism, even though they produce "a precise analogue of the idea of the nation" (31). Doris Sommer has gone a long way toward making this connection. Her ground-breaking study, *Foundational Fictions: When History Was Romance in Latin America* (Berkeley: University of California Press, 1991), shows how nineteenth-century Latin American novels helped to form the nation-states of Central and South America. We would like to thank her for allowing us to read portions of this book in manuscript.

14. Olivia Smith, *The Politics of Language, 1791–1819* (Oxford: Clarendon, 1986), p. 3.

15. Until the early eighteenth century, literacy was assumed by most readers to be male. From about the middle of the eighteenth century on, literacy was assumed to include women, but women readers were thought to have different thoughts and feelings from men. This difference can be seen in the appearance of gendered consciousness in fiction and other popular writing, and in the use of gendered pronouns in reference to readers. For a discussion of this point, see Nancy Armstrong, *Desire and Domestic Fiction: A Political History of the Novel* (New York: Oxford University Press, 1987), pp. 96–160.

16. Lynn Hunt has described this group as "fourth generation Annales historians." Introduction to *The New Cultural History*, ed. Lynn Hunt (Berkeley: University of California Press, 1989), pp. 6–7.

17. Philippe Ariès, introduction to *A History of Private Life*, vol. 3, *Passions of the Renaissance*, ed. Roger Chartier, trans. Arthur Goldhammer (Cambridge: Harvard University Press, 1989), p. 1.

18. Norbert Elias, *The History of Manners*, trans. Edmund Jephcott (New York: Pantheon, 1978), *Power and Civility*, trans. Edmund Jephcott (New York: Pantheon, 1982), *The Court Society*, trans. Edmund Jephcott (New York: Pantheon, 1983); Roger Chartier, "Figures of Modernity," in *History of Private Life*, 3:17.

19. Yves Castan, "Politics and Private Life," in *History of Private Life*, 3:43.

20. Jacques Gélis, "The Child: From Anonymity to Individuality," in *History of Private Life*, 3:309–25. The quote is found on p. 310.

21. Jacques Revel, "The Uses of Civility," in *History of Private Life*, 3:167–205. See especially pp. 188–89.

22. Jean-Louis Flandrin, "Distinction through Taste," in *History of Private Life*, 3:265–307. See also George Vigarello, *Concepts of Cleanliness: Changing Attitudes in France since the Middle Ages*, trans. Jean Birrell (Cambridge: Cambridge University Press, 1988); Norbert Elias, *History of Manners*, pp. 129–68; Peter Stallybrass and Allon White, *The Politics and Poetics of Transgression* (London: Methuen, 1986), pp. 125–48.

23. Roger Chartier argues that the growth of silent reading and private writing helped to create "a new private sphere into which the individual could retreat." "The Practical Impact of Writing," in *History of Private Life*, 3:125. Orest Ranum in "The Refuges of Intimacy," pp. 207–63, argues that certain spaces within early modern culture appear to have been reserved for privacy in the modern, or individualistic, sense. The souvenir space and the souvenir book, for example, "were quite private, having been possessed by an individual unique in space and time. Nevertheless," claims Ranum, "the significance of such spaces and objects was encoded and perfectly comprehensible to others. *The source of the meaning was social*" (210, our italics). In "The Literature of Intimacy," pp. 327–61, Madeleine Foisil makes the same distinction. She says of memoir writers that "to our way of thinking, these seventeenth-century authors lacked awareness of the inner self" (329), and of journal writers that, although "children were loved . . . there was no sentiment about childhood" (346). About the same body of writing, Jean Marie Goulement in "Literary Practices: Publicizing the Private," 363–95, insists: "The genre is an aristocratic one; the individual is reduced in it to his public acts" (381). Given this analysis of genres that are usually regarded either as anticipating the self-enclosed consciousness of modern authors or else as indicating the presence of such consciousness in the past, Goulement is at a loss to say why "by the late 17th and early 18th centuries, all literature was influenced by a similar affirmation of private life" (385).

24. Jacques Donzelot, *The Policing of Families*, trans. Robert Hurley (New York: Pantheon, 1979).

25. Donzelot writes, "To understand the strategic significance of this movement of normalization of the adult-child relationship, we have to recognize that the object of these measures was hygienic and political in nature, the two facets being indissoluble. Doubtless they were aimed at remedying the state of abandonment in which the children of the laboring classes were apt to find themselves, but just as important if not more so, they also sought to reduce the socio-political capacity of these strata by breaking the initiatory ties that existed between children and parents . . . that resulted from the loosening of ancient communal constraints" (78–79).

26. Michel Foucault, *The History of Sexuality: An Introduction*, trans. Robert Hurley (New York: Pantheon, 1978), p. 17.

27. Except with respect to the elite, whose breeding had always been highly codified, the focus on sexual reproduction was a new phenomenon. Peter Wagner discusses the enormous outpouring of erotic literature during this period in *Eros Revived: Erotica of the Enlightenment in England and America* (London: Secker and Warburg, 1988). Frank Mort describes a corresponding growth in the medical practices attending to sexual reproduction, in *Dangerous Sexualities: Medico-Moral Politics in England since 1830* (London: Routledge and Kegan Paul, 1987).

For an account of the moment when childbirth became medicalized, see Robert A. Erickson, " 'The Books of Generation': Some Observations on the Style of the British Midwife Books, 1671–1764," in *Sexuality in Eighteenth-Century Britain,* ed. Paul-Gabriel Boucé (Manchester: Manchester University Press, 1982), pp. 74–94, and his *Mother Midnight: Birth, Sex, and Fate in Eighteenth-Century Fiction (Defoe, Richardson, and Sterne)* (New York: AMS Press, 1986). Finally, Henry Abelove's "Some Speculations on the History of Sexual Intercourse during the Long Eighteenth Century in England," *Genders* 6 (1989): 125–30, shows how permissible sexual pleasure came to be equated with the reproductive act.

28. Anita Levy, *Other Women: The Writing of Race, Class, and Gender* (Princeton: Princeton University Press, 1990).

29. See Armstrong, *Desire and Domestic Fiction,* pp. 59–95.

30. Frederick Engels, *The Origin of the Family, Private Property and the State* (New York: International Publishers, 1942). For Engels, polygamy and free love offer ways of imagining an alternative political order.

31. Matthew Arnold, *Culture and Anarchy: An Essay in Political and Social Criticism,* ed. J. Dover Wilson (Cambridge: Cambridge University Press, 1960). See the chapter entitled "Doing as One Likes," pp. 72–97.

32. Quoted in Lawrence Stone and Jeanne C. Fawtier Stone, *An Open Elite? England, 1540–1880* (Oxford: Clarendon, 1984), pp. 410–11.

CHAPTER 7

1. Benedict Anderson, *Imagined Communities: Reflections on the Origin and Spread of Nationalism* (London: Verso, 1983), p. 62.

2. For a brief overview of the various ways in which written information circulated in British America from the last half of the seventeenth century through the first half of the eighteenth, see Richard D. Brown, *Knowledge Is Power: The Diffusion of Information in Early America, 1700–1865* (New York: Oxford University Press, 1989), pp. 16–64. However, Brown has very little to say in this book about the circulation of fictional materials.

3. William Whately, *A Bridebush or a Direction for Married Persons* (London, 1619), p. 89.

4. *The Political Works of James I,* ed. Charles H. McIlwain (Cambridge: Harvard University Press, 1918), p. 305. For a discussion of this version of the Jacobean and Caroline theory of patriarchalism, see Gordon H. Schochet, *Patriarchalism in Political Thought: The Authoritarian Family and Political Speculation and Attitudes Especially in Seventeenth Century England* (Oxford: Basil Blackwell, 1975).

5. Edward Topsell, *The Householder: or Perfect Man* (London, 1610), ˙5v.

6. William Gouge, *Of Domesticall Duties,* 3d ed. (London, 1634), p. 17.

7. William Gouge, for example, is particularly careful to praise the monarch. One of his marriage treatises explains, "God gaue vs such a King as we now haue, of the stronger sexe . . . furnished with such knowledge and zeale, as neuer King since Christ had." *An Exposition of Part of the Fift and Sixt Chapters of S. Paules Epistle to the Ephesians, wherein is handled all of the duties as belong to Household Gouernment* (London, 1630), p. 3.

8. Quoted in Mary Shanley, "Marriage Contract and Social Contract in Seventeenth-Century English Political Thought," in *The Family in Political Thought,* ed. Jean Bethke Elshtain (Amherst: University of Massachusetts Press, 1982), pp. 80–95. The quoted material is from p. 86.

9. *The Doctrine and Discipline of Divorce,* ed. Lowell W. Coolidge, in vol. 2 of *Complete Prose Works of John Milton,* ed. Ernest Sirluck (New Haven: Yale University Press, 1959), p. 229. The year before (1642), in a very popular tract, Henry Parker had used much the same language when he wrote, "They which contract to obey to their own ruin, or having so contracted, they which esteem such a contract before their own preservation are felonious to themselves." "Observations Upon Some of his Majesties Late Answers and Expresses," in *Revolutionary Prose of the English Civil War,* ed. Howard Erskine-Hill and Graham Storey (Cambridge: Cambridge University Press, 1983), p. 41.

10. By that time, Ernest Sirluck has noted, Milton had "completely integrated the case for divorce with that for Parliament's supremacy." *Complete Prose Works,* 2:157.

11. *Tetrachordon,* ed. Arnold Williams, in vol. 2 of *Complete Prose Works of John Milton,* pp. 571–718. The quote is found on p. 612.

12. Milton identifies the sign of a true marriage with the formation of a "whole man" and a domestic unit. See, for example, *Tetrachordon,* in *Complete Prose Works,* 2:601–13.

13. *Patriarcha and Other Political Works of Sir Robert Filmer,* ed. Peter Laslett (Oxford: Basil Blackwell, 1949), p. 283.

14. John Locke, *Two Treatises of Government,* ed. Peter Laslett (Cambridge: Cambridge University Press, 1988), II.1.1–14.

15. There is a long-running debate among political philosophers concerning Locke's response to Filmer's arguments: Did he come down on the side of the elites who possessed property or on the side of labor and the natural rights of ordinary man? See, for example, C. B. Macpherson, *The Political Theory of Possessive Individualism* (Oxford: Oxford University Press, 1962). For a critique of Macpherson, see Peter Laslett, "Market Society and Political Theory," *Historical Journal* 6 (1964), 150–54; James Tully, *A Discourse on Property: John Locke and His Adversaries* (Cambridge: Cambridge University Press, 1980); Alan Ryan, *Property and Political Theory* (Oxford: Basil Blackwell, 1984), 14–48. For a brief review of Macpherson's historical claims, see Richard Ashcraft, *Revolutionary Politics and Locke's Two Treatises of Government* (Princeton: Princeton University Press, 1986), pp. 150–60; Andrej Rapaczynski, *Nature and Politics: Liberalism in the Philosophies of Hobbes, Locke, and Rousseau* (Ithaca: Cornell University Press, 1987), pp. 177–90. We do not claim to be determining anything about Locke's theory of property beyond the rhetorical strategies that enable its arguments to appear logical. In opposing Filmer's representation of the English social body as the monarch's body, Locke imagines the social body as a genetic, or self-replicating, cellular structure.

16. On this point, see Robert Nozick, *Anarchy, State, and Utopia* (Oxford: Basil Blackwell, 1974), p. 174, and James Tully, *Discourse on Property,* pp. 116–18.

17. We wish to thank Kathryn Milun for sharing her research on the *terra*

nullius trope, as set forth in her manuscript "Pathologies of Modern Space."

18. Neal Wood writes that Locke refers to a so-called "waste land" to make the distinction between land that has a public status as opposed to land owned by parish and country or "commons." *John Locke and Agrarian Capitalism* (Berkeley: University of California Press, 1984), pp. 61–62.

19. Typical of Locke's use of masculine pronouns is this example: "If such a state of Reason, such an Age of Discretion made him free, the same shall make his Son free too" (II.59.11–12).

20. Locke, of course, enjoyed some of the fruits of traditional clientage. But none of the offices he was given through the influence of Lord Ashley—later the Earl of Shaftesbury—were particularly lucrative or politically powerful. The older model of clientage and patronage had quite simply passed away. In the introduction to his edition of the *Two Treatises*, Peter Laslett states in a note: "Locke was so conscious of status, his own in particular, that he actually cancelled the title-page of one of his books because it described him as Esq., and substituted another calling him Gent" (42). Laslett goes on to ask, "Can [Locke] be called, as so often he is, the spokesman of a rising class, the middle class, the capitalists, the bourgeoisie?" and offers this response: "He is perhaps best described as an independent, free-moving intellectual, aware as others were not of the direction of social change" (43–44).

21. However, Locke's model household was still imagined only for a privileged minority in England. It was unlikely, for example, that either the poor family or the working family could provide the kind of household Locke considered suitable for his political model. According to Peter Laslett, Locke thought that the poor existed because of "a relaxation of discipline and the corruption of manners" and that a working family "had no right to expect its children to be at leisure after the age of three" (43).

22. As we noted in chapter 1, both Fredric Jameson and Terry Eagleton respond to a discrepancy between the individuated perspective produced by *Paradise Lost* and the lack of such individuals in the culture for which the poem was written. They consider the discrepancy itself as the historical marker of the poem. See Fredric Jameson, "Religion and Ideology," *1642: Literature and Power in the Seventeenth Century*, ed. Francis Barker, Jay Bernstein, John Coombes, Peter Hulme, Jennifer Stone, and Jon Stratton (Colchester: University of Essex, 1981), pp. 315–36, and Terry Eagleton, "The God That Failed," in *Re-Membering Milton: Essays on the Texts and Traditions*, ed. Mary Nyquist and Margaret W. Ferguson (New York: Methuen, 1987), pp. 342–47.

23. For example, Alan Macfarlane, *The Family Life of Ralph Josselin, A Seventeenth-Century Clergyman: An Essay in Historical Anthropology* (Cambridge: Cambridge University Press, 1970), pp. 105–25, sees Josselin's diary as showing that parental feeling and affective bonds have remained unchanged since at least the early modern period. A similar view of Josselin's diary is maintained by Linda A. Pollock, *Forgotten Children: Parent-Child Relations from 1500–1900* (Cambridge: Cambridge University Press, 1983), pp. 136–37; Ralph A. Houlbrooke, *The English Family, 1450–1700* (London: Longman, 1984), pp. 136–37; and Michael MacDonald, *Mystical Bedlam: Madness, Anxiety, and Healing in Seventeenth-Century England* (Cambridge: Cambridge University Press, 1981), p.

84. But the diary is also seen as supporting quite a contrary view of the family: Lawrence Stone, *The Family, Sex and Marriage in England, 1500–1800* (New York: Harper and Row, 1977), p. 214; Randolph Trumbach, *The Rise of the Egalitarian Family: Aristocratic Kinship and Domestic Relations in Eighteenth-Century England* (New York: Academic Press, 1978), pp. 288–89; Edward Shorter, *The Making of the Modern Family* (New York: Basic Books, 1984), p. 64. See also Stephanie Coontz, *The Social Origins of Private Life* (London: Verso, 1988), p. 29.

24. *The Diary of Ralph Josselin, 1616–1683*, ed. Alan Macfarlane (London: published for the British Academy by Oxford University Press, 1976).

25. In "L'Histoire sociale des rêves," *Annales* 28 (1973): 329–42, Peter Burke identifies some of the material in the dreams recorded by Archbishop Laud, Elias Ashmole, Ralph Josselin, and Samuel Sewell that makes them all unmistakably seventeenth-century dreams.

26. Henry Neville, *The Isle of Pines Or a Late discovery of a fourth Island in Terra Australis Incognita* (London, 1668). Neville is better known for another kind of political tract. Like Harrington's *Oceana*, Neville's *Plato Redivivus* sought to explain what had gone wrong with the old relationship between property and monarchy, leading to the collapse of the latter. In these tracts, the transmission of property ideally followed exact inheritance rules, alleviating the conflict between hereditary rights (represented by the Lords) and property rights (represented by the Commons) that had destabilized monarchy. According to J. G. A. Pocock's introduction to *The Political Works of James Harrington* (Cambridge: Cambridge University Press, 1977), pp. 60–64, Neville's use of the family to argue for strict inheritance rules was precisely what Edmund Burke would later find interesting in republican writing. We, however, see an implicit contradiction between the geneticism organizing the irreverent *Isle of Pines* and the genealogy organizing aristocratic historiography—the difference between replicating the individual and extending the aristocratic body.

27. Neville, *Isle of Pines*, title page. For an account of the enormous popularity of this text in England, France, Germany, Italy, and America, see the introductory essay by Worthington Chauncey Ford, ed., *The Isle of Pines, 1668: An Essay in Bibliography* (Boston: Merrymount Press, 1920).

28. A. Owen Aldridge has discussed the importance of this element in "Polygamy in Early Fiction: Henry Neville and Denis Veiras," *PMLA* 65 (1950): 464–72.

29. From the fourteenth through the end of the sixteenth century, statutes were periodically enacted and royal proclamations issued that were designed to regulate dress. These laws were supposed to make rank visible. Cloth of gold, for example, could only be worn by members of the royal family, velvet by the aristocracy; silk was permitted to the gentry but not to people of low birth; and so forth. The regulations covered cuts, the use of special fabrics and furs, dyes of a particular hue, and thread and trim. The regulation of these features of dress distinguished between members of the royal family, dukes, marquesses, earls, viscounts, barons, and knights, between servingmen, yeomen, and husbandmen, and even between wage earners having incomes of 200, 100, 40, 20, 5, and 2 pounds per annum. Despite the obvious difficulties in enforcing these laws, nineteen such proclamations were issued during the latter half of the sixteenth century.

The proclamations were posted throughout the land to ensure that everyone ranked himself or herself in these terms and interpreted the rank and income of other people accordingly. And even though this legislation was vacated in 1604, there were at least a half a dozen attempts in the first two decades of the seventeenth century to introduce new sumptuary regulations. For an account of this legislation and its impact, see N. B. Harte, "State Control of Dress and Social Change in Pre-Industrial England," in *Trade, Government and Economy in Pre-Industrial England: Essays Presented to F. J. Fisher*, ed. D. C. Coleman and A. H. John (London: Weidenfeld and Nicolson, 1976), pp. 132–65.

30. Michael McKeon contends that the genealogy originating in the otherwise unnoteworthy bookkeeper is not grounded in the aristocratic kinship practices it may seem at first to parody. *The Origins of the English Novel, 1600–1740* (Baltimore: Johns Hopkins University Press, 1987), pp. 251–52.

31. In carrying on a direct conversation between himself and God, Josselin's diary is characteristic of the diaries kept by many devout men and women. For an account of the practice and kinds of diary keeping in England during this period, see Élisabeth Bourcier, *Les Journaux privés en Angleterre de 1600 à 1660* (Paris: Publications de Sorbonne, 1976). For an overview of diaries kept by women, see Sara Heller Mendleson, "Stuart Women's Diaries and Occasional Memoirs," *Women in English Society, 1500–1800*, ed. Mary Prior (London: Methuen, 1985), pp. 181–210.

32. William Haller has explained how diaries kept by puritan saints provided at times biographical information that was appended to the sermons read at their funerals; some kind of personal testimony to one's spiritual struggles was expected to be part of such services. "Always and everywhere in Puritan circles oral tradition extensively supplemented the written hagiography. If the saint had kept no diary, he had at any rate unbosomed himself to his friends." *The Rise of Puritanism; or, The Way to the New Jerusalem as Set Forth in Pulpit and Press from Thomas Cartwright to John Lilburne and John Milton, 1570–1643* (New York: Columbia University Press, 1938), pp. 101–2. Though a diary might supply this kind of information, there is no indication that Josselin's diary was written with such a public ceremony in mind.

33. Diary keeping was regularly thought of as a means of tallying up one's gifts from God. *Rise of Puritanism*, pp. 38–39, 96–99. Owen C. Watkins has discussed this feature with regard to other puritan diarists in *The Puritan Experience: Studies in Spiritual Autobiography* (New York: Schocken, 1972), pp. 18–25. See also George A. Starr, *Defoe and Spiritual Autobiography* (New York: Gordian Press, 1965), pp. 6–7, 28–31; J. Paul Hunter, *The Reluctant Pilgrim: Defoe's Emblematic Method and Quest for Form in* Robinson Crusoe (Baltimore: Johns Hopkins University Press, 1966), pp. 72–73, 82–86.

34. On this point, see Felicity A. Nussbaum, *The Autobiographical Subject: Gender and Ideology in Eighteenth-Century England* (Baltimore: Johns Hopkins University Press, 1989).

35. The framework of a single chapter will not allow us to explain why Hobbes has been excluded from our account of the discursive take-off that allowed words to produce a whole new set of origins both for themselves and for the English "people." But we can suggest (both here and in our later discussion

of Defoe) how we would deal with this question. We would begin with the question that perplexed C. B. Macpherson: How can one "reconcile Hobbes's acceptance of bourgeois morality, and his prescription of a state designed to protect and facilitate a life of competition, with the contemporary bourgeois dislike or neglect of Hobbes's doctrine?" Introduction to Thomas Hobbes, *Leviathan*, ed. C. B. Macpherson (Harmondsworth: Penguin, 1985), p. 53. We would not attempt to answer the question—as Macpherson does, unsuccessfully—by identifying features in Hobbes's political theory that might have set that theory at odds with the ideology of democracy. Such an argument would not explain a thing if, as we argue, the logic that propelled the writing that emerged in the wake of the English Revolution was inherently conservative. In part 1 of *Leviathan*, Hobbes puts forward a creationist definition of human nature; in doing so, he reveals his affiliation with the cultural moment that was passing away rather than with one that was emerging. According to Hobbes's epistemology, the mind neither constitutes a territory unto itself nor acquires knowledge in the same way that men acquire property. He lacks a semiotic, then, that would account for the production of interior (personal) and exterior (political) discursive worlds.

36. John Locke, *An Essay Concerning Human Understanding*, ed. Peter H. Nidditch (Oxford: Oxford University Press, 1975), II.i.2.

37. "Children, when they first come into it, are surrounded with a world of new things, which, by a constant solicitation of their senses, draw the mind constantly to them, forward to take notice of new, and apt to be delighted with the variety of changing Objects ... and so growing up in a constant attention to outward Sensations, seldom make any considerable Reflection on what passes within them, till they come to be of riper Years; and some scarce ever at all" (II.i.8).

38. Daniel Defoe, *Robinson Crusoe*, ed. Michael Shinagel (New York: W. W. Norton, 1975), p. 6.

39. In *Prodigals and Pilgrims: The American Revolution against Patriarchal Authority, 1750-1800* (Cambridge: Cambridge University Press, 1982), p. 69, Jay Fliegelman writes: "The same 'inclination' that in 1697 Locke had identified with passion and insisted must be suppressed is identified with providence in Defoe's novel." See also Starr, *Defoe and Spiritual Autobiography*, pp. 74-81.

40. Literary critics tend either to see *Robinson Crusoe* as a working out of some model of spiritual autobiography or to focus on Crusoe's acquisition of private property. Starr, *Defoe and Spiritual Autobiography*, and Hunter, *Reluctant Pilgrim*, have been particularly useful in directing our attention to the puritan writing upon which Defoe drew. The classic description of Crusoe's economic individualism is in Ian Watt's *The Rise of the Novel: Studies in Defoe, Richardson and Fielding* (London: Chatto and Windus, 1957), pp. 60-92. For readings that seek to reconcile the two opposing trends in *Crusoe* criticism, see, for example, McKeon, *Origins of the English Novel*, pp. 315-37; John Richetti, *Defoe's Narratives: Situations and Structures* (Oxford: Oxford University Press, 1975), pp. 21-63, and Richetti's *Popular Fiction before Richardson: Narrative Patterns, 1700-1739* (Oxford: Clarendon Press, 1969), pp. 13-18, 92-96.

41. Homer O. Brown's "The Displaced Self in the Novels of Daniel Defoe," *ELH* 38 (1971): 562-90, is particularly useful in calling attention to the contradictions in the novel that arise out of fear.

42. Michael McKeon describes this episode as "the beginning of the move-

ment of narrative 'atonement,' when Character and Narrator come together."
Origins of the English Novel, p. 318. We agree with McKeon and others that
this is a turning point in the novel, but we would like to rephrase the reason
why it is so. When critics focus on events at the level of consciousness, there is
a tendency to overlook the degree to which intellectual labor is responsible for
displacing and subordinating manual labor.

43. In *God's Plot and Man's Stories: Studies in the Fictional Imagination
from Milton to Fielding* (Chicago: University of Chicago Press, 1985), Leopold
Damrosch, Jr., notes that "*Crusoe* reflects the progressive desacralizing of the
world that was implicit in Protestantism and that . . . ended by disenchanting it
altogether" (192). This Weberian concept of Protestantism as progressive secularization overlooks the fact that mystification does not depart with the de-
sacralization of the universe. Indeed, *Robinson Crusoe* demonstrates how the
magical qualities once attributed to God are transferred onto the "self" as God
becomes part of personal life in the form of useful knowledge in the service of
the individual.

44. Keith Thomas, *Man and the Natural World: A History of the Modern
Sensibility* (New York: Pantheon Books, 1983), pp. 121–40, identifies this question as the inevitable consequence of challenging the Christian notion of soul,
which had ensured man's essential difference from animals and set him above
them. With that challenge came the problem of how to preserve the difference
between human nature and bestial nature. The problem was resolved by stressing
the difference between reason and sensation rather than their continuity and
reason's dependency on sensations.

45. For an important discussion of how Defoe's narrative "delineates the
subjective order—the structure of feeling" of a disciplinary institution such as
the penitentiary, see John Bender, *Imagining the Penitentiary: Fiction and the
Architecture of Mind in Eighteenth-Century England* (Chicago: University of
Chicago Press, 1987), pp. 43–83.

46. Karl Marx, *Capital,* trans. Ben Fowkes (New York: Vintage Books, 1977),
1:288–300. See our discussion in chapter 5.

47. Reprinted in *Defoe: The Critical Heritage,* ed. Pat Rogers (London and
Boston: Routledge and Kegan Paul, 1972), p. 53.

48. Marx, *Capital,* pp. 168–73.

49. Maximillian E. Novak, in both "Crusoe the King and the Political Evolution of His Island," *SEL* 2 (1962): 337–50, and *Economics and the Fiction of
Daniel Defoe* (Berkeley: University of California, 1962), has suggested that *Robinson Crusoe* should be read in terms of a theory of property. Although it may
start out in that way, in our estimation *Crusoe* is not so resolved. If, as Novak
has suggested, democracy does offer a solution to the problem posed by this
novel, then we are forced to rethink the conventional notion of democracy,
bringing it much more into line with Foucault's notion of discipline than mainstream literary criticism or historians are generally willing to do. Other critics—
such as G. A. Starr and J. Paul Hunter—have argued that the novel is about the
spiritual rather than the economic. This seems to us a matter of emphasis. Property in *Crusoe* is precisely the sort of issue that distinguishes this text from more
"orthodox" spiritual autobiographies.

50. See Charles F. Bahmueller, *The National Charity Company: Jeremy Ben-*

tham's Silent Revolution (Berkeley: University of California Press, 1981), pp. 58–75.

51. Jean Baudrillard, "Simulacra and Simulations," in *Selected Writings,* ed. Mark Poster (Stanford: Stanford University Press, 1988), pp. 166–84.

52. On this point, see Leonard Tennenhouse, "Simulating History: A Cockfight for Our Times," *The Drama Review* 34 (1990): 137–50.

CHAPTER 8

1. See, for example, David Cressy, *Coming Over: Migration and Communication between England and New England in the Seventeenth Century* (Cambridge: Cambridge University Press, 1987), and his *Literacy and the Social Order: Reading and Writing in Tudor and Stuart England* (Cambridge: Cambridge University Press, 1980); Ian K. Steele, *The English Atlantic, 1675–1740: An Exploration of Communication and Community* (New York: Oxford University Press, 1986); David D. Hall, *World of Wonder, Days of Judgment: Popular Religious Belief in Early New England* (Cambridge: Harvard University Press, 1990); Michael Warner, *The Letters of the Republic: Publication and the Public Sphere in Eighteenth-Century America* (Cambridge: Harvard University Press, 1990); and Richard D. Brown, *Knowledge Is Power: The Diffusion of Information in Early America, 1700–1865* (New York: Oxford University Press, 1989). Hall and Warner are particularly useful for explaining the importance of print in New England, while Brown offers the most detailed discussion of the means by which information was distributed in the colonies.

2. *Imagined Communities: Reflections on the Origin and Spread of Nationalism* (London: Verso, 1983).

3. In *Settler Capitalism: The Dynamics of Dependent Development in the Southern Hemisphere* (New York: Oxford University Press, 1983), Donald Denoon identifies versions of exceptionalism in the historiography of such settler societies as South Africa, Australia, New Zealand, Uruguay, Chile, and Argentina, which indicates that such exceptionalism is not unique to North America or even to British colonies. Ian Tyrrell, in "American Exceptionalism in an Age of International History," *American Historical Review* 96 (1991): 1031–55, notes that "in an era of unprecedented internationalization in historiography, the legacies of nationalism and exceptionalism still haunt the study of American history" (1031). In our estimation, the only way to avoid the problem posed by the alternatives of nationalism and exceptionalism is to historicize nationalism. We have chosen to do so by showing that the discursive phenomena associated with exceptionalism can also be identified with the emergence of a modern middle class and thus with a new brand of nationalism in Europe. We thank Michael Denning for calling the work of Denoon and of Tyrrell to our attention.

4. Lennard Davis, *Factual Fictions: The Origins of the English Novel* (New York: Columbia University Press, 1983), Nancy Armstrong, *Desire and Domestic Fiction: A Political History of the Novel* (New York: Oxford University Press, 1987), Michael McKeon, *The Origins of the English Novel, 1600–1740* (Baltimore: Johns Hopkins University Press, 1987), and J. Paul Hunter, *Before Novels: The Cultural Contexts of Eighteenth-Century Fiction* (New York: W. W. Norton,

1990), are among the most important of recent attempts to fix such an origin for the English novel.

5. Samuel Richardson, *Pamela; or, Virtue Rewarded,* ed. William M. Sale, Jr. (New York: W. W. Norton, 1958).

6. It is reasonable to ask how this heroine differed from the heroines of such Elizabethan plays as Greene's *Friar Bacon and Friar Bungay* or Thomas Heywood's *Fair Maid of the West.* In Greene's play, for example, the inherent desirability of Margaret is meant to challenge the ideology of Petrarchanism that characterized Elizabethan romantic comedies. The prince's son falls in love with Margaret, the keeper's daughter, only to pass her on to the Earl of Lincoln, whom she really adores, and who woos her much as if the royal gaze itself has given her new value. Unlike the heroines of eighteenth-century domestic fiction, Margaret does not bring her values with her into the aristocratic household when she marries. Much the same elevation of a woman to aristocratic status occurs in *The Fair Maid,* where Bess the bar girl undergoes a trial of her chastity and fidelity. In neither play is the commoner allowed to transform aristocratic culture; aristocratic culture transforms the girl. For a discussion of how Jacobean city comedies modified these conventions, and yet in their use of the nonaristocratic female were different from eighteenth-century novels, see Leonard Tennenhouse, *Power on Display: The Politics of Shakespeare's Genres* (New York: Methuen, 1986), pp. 154–71.

7. As in preceding centuries, sleeping arrangements in the early eighteenth century might place two or more unrelated people of different sexes and classes in the same bed. J. M. Beattie describes the case of a clerk accused of "assault with intent to ravish" his master's young daughter "with whom he shared a bed in his master's house. The child had been found 'inflam'd and excoriated' and was discovered to have the clap. [The clerk] had blamed it on a ten-year-old boy who also slept with them, but a doctor testified that it was not possible such a Youth should contract the foul Disease and give it to a child." *Crime and the Courts in England, 1660–1800* (Princeton: Princeton University Press, 1986), pp. 127–28. This was one of the few cases of rape prosecuted during the eighteenth century. The fact of three people sleeping together was not considered unusual. Beattie contends that, during the eighteenth century, such cases were unlikely to be brought to court unless the victim were a child. A study of Old Bailey indictments indicates the same lack of legal attention to rape at the very time when Richardson wanted readers to consider a sexual assault the gravest threat to a woman's identity. Of seventy-three victims on record, "seventy-one were females. . . . More than half were under the age of eleven years; it is not clear," the study concludes, "why cases of alleged rape of adults seldom came to trial." Thomas R. Forbes, *Surgeons at the Bailey: English Forensic Medicine to 1878* (New Haven: Yale University Press, 1985), p. 88. We thank Susan Sage Heinzelman for calling this study to our attention.

8. It should be noted that Pamela's parents have enough education to write good standard English; Richardson included their letters among those being assembled as models for young women to imitate. Equally important, apparently Pamela's father once owned property. He writes to her, "We are, 'tis true, very poor, and find it hard to live; though once, as you know, it was better with us"

(5). This makes Pamela's station as a servant relatively fluid. It does not, however, place her in the social group that, according to Lawrence Stone and Jeanne Fawtier Stone, allowed its members to fall in and out of respectability through marriage and ownership of property. According to their *An Open Elite? England, 1540–1880* (Oxford: Clarendon, 1984), the gentry was an extremely fluid social group from which one could decline by necessity to the status of a merchant, and to which tradesmen could rise, given sufficient prosperity. In 1710, Richard Steele is quoted as claiming, "as did many others before and after him, that 'the best of our peers have often joined themselves to the daughters of very ordinary tradesmen upon . . . valuable considerations' " (20). Pamela is not of this station; but even if she were potential gentry (as Clarissa is), her desirability as a wife to someone decidedly above her would remain essentially the same. Her decline according to one system of values—that associated with the "old" society, and especially with an older middle class—occurs simultaneously with her rise according to another system of values (private virtue, companionship, femininity), associated with the new class and its rise to hegemony.

9. Defoe's *On Religious Courtship* (1722) can be regarded as an exception to this rule. That the text was neither received as fiction nor recuperated by literary criticism later on testifies, we feel, to its lack of the features we are identifying with captivity narratives.

10. In their influential treatise *Practical Education*, Maria and her father Robert Edgeworth recommended *Robinson Crusoe* as more suitable reading for girls than boys. "To girls this species of reading cannot be as dangerous as to boys: girls must soon perceive the impossibility of their rambling about the world in quest of adventure" (111). Their logic has another side. Just as it was assumed young ladies would never imagine imitating Crusoe's economic adventure, so it was understood that the female readers could benefit from the example of a hero who assembled a self-enclosed household where money was not the most important thing.

11. Ian Watt acknowledges his inability to explain why the puritanical Richardson should have made "his entry into the history of literature by a work which gave a more detailed account of a single intrigue than had ever been produced before." If their economic interests are what define them as a group, why indeed should the new business-oriented readership have been so interested in the protracted seduction of a nonaristocratic female? *The Rise of the Novel* (Berkeley: University of California Press, 1957), p. 172.

12. In his study *Before Novels*, Hunter identifies most of the kinds of writing that went into the novel and whose characteristics we locate in captivity narratives—the didactic guide book, the spiritual autobiography, sensational journalism, tales of wonder, and travel books. We would argue that, although all the ingredients for the novel were certainly in English culture before novels, the recipe for combining them had to be developed outside the geographical boundaries of modern England. The novel is, from this perspective, a colonial formation.

13. For the place of domestic fiction in the middle-class hegemony, see Armstrong, *Desire and Domestic Fiction*, pp. 59–95.

14. See R. W. G. Vail, *The Voice of the Old Frontier* (Philadelphia: University of Pennsylvania Press, 1949), pp. 29–61.

15. There is considerable evidence that Jesuit accounts were rarely intended for a general readership. Father Jogues begins his narrative with this explanation as to why he chose to write in Latin rather than French: "Reverend Father in Christ—the Peace of Christ. Wishing, as I do, to write your reverence, I hesitate first in which language to address you, after such long disuse, almost equally forgetful of both, I find equal difficulty in each. Two reasons, however, induce me to use the less common idiom. I shall be better able to use the words of Holy Scripture.... I also wished this letter to be less open to all." "Captivity of Father Isaac Jogues, of the Society of Jesus, Among the Mohawks," in *Held Captive by Indians*, ed. Richard VanDerBeets (Knoxville: University of Tennessee Press, 1973), pp. 4–5.

16. The material of these anti-tales could be found in letters and official documents concerning captives who chose not to return when given the choice, as reported by Alice C. Baker in *True Stories of New England Captives* (Cambridge: E. A. Hall, 1897) and Emma Lewis Coleman in *New England Captives Carried to Canada between 1677 and 1760 during the French and Indian Wars*, 2 vols. (Portland, Maine: Southworth Press, 1925). Such accounts provided the basis for a paragraph in the Treaty of Utrecht (1713) that details the exchange of prisoners. The treaty gave those who converted to Catholicism during their captivity the choice of remaining in Canada.

17. We are summarizing here the information in Kathryn Zabelle Derounian, "The Publication, Promotion, and Distribution of Mary Rowlandson's Indian Captivity Narrative in the Seventeenth Century," *Early American Literature* 23 (1988): 239–61, and in Vail, *Voice of the Old Frontier.*

18. We rely on Vail, *Voice of the Old Frontier,* for these details of the printing history of Rowlandson's account.

19. Cotton Mather, for example, reported the accounts of Mehetable Goodwin, Mary Plaisted, and Mary Ferguson in his sermons, and transcribed that of Hannah Swarton; see Vail, *Voice of the Old Frontier.*

20. Carroll Smith-Rosenberg argues that the same bundle of discursive features that made England fall in love with *Pamela* took the colonial readership by storm within a few years of that novel's success in England. Furthermore, she describes Richardson's narrative in terms that support our model of the captivity narrative and its political effects: "Novels of social realism, *Pamela* and *Clarissa* ... focused on the plight of the woman/individual in the harsh commercial world, be it the world of domestic service or of the eighteenth century's heartless marriage market. In both novels, the virtuous young woman is cut loose from the protection of family and friends. Finally, problematizing both class and the family, these novels privileged the woman as writer and the empowering nature of her words." "Misprisioning *Pamela*: Representations of Gender and Class in Nineteenth-Century America," *Michigan Quarterly Review* 26 (1987): 21.

21. In "The Figure of Captivity: The Cultural Work of the Puritan Captivity Narrative," *American Literary History* 3 (1991): 1–26, Tara Fitzpatrick distinguishes the narratives that featured female captives as those which posed a peculiar problem for Puritan divines: "They vacillated, at once decrying the sinfulness of the generation that had tempted God's fury by straying from the 'hedge' of the covenanted community and then extolling the enlightenment accessible

only to those whom God had chosen to try by fire in the wilderness" (9). This double-edged theological message was apparently all the more problematic because the messenger was a woman (5). We are suggesting that the very qualities posing a theological problem for these divines solved an ideological problem for an emergent colonial culture. Fitzpatrick neglects to account for the fact that in novels that observed the Rowlandson model, these women were "authors" rather than prophetic speakers. They narrated their own histories, histories of themselves not only as Christians in relation to God but also—and perhaps more importantly—as Englishwomen who demonstrated the power of their kind of literacy in the midst of a non-English culture. No matter that they, much like Pamela, were ventriloquized or filtered through the writings of one or another male. They nevertheless existed in print and persisted for readers as the female source of a distinctively British American experience.

22. We feel justified in drawing this equation between Indian captivity and slavery because there is a striking resemblance between these seventeenth- and early-eighteenth-century descriptions of captivity and the language that would later be found in African-American slave narratives. The similarities include references to one's captor as "master," the representation of the captive as someone who no longer owns her or his own body, comparisons between the captive and a beast of burden, and the fact that the writer had been seized under conditions resembling war. These same features identify the slave in the political discourse of the seventeenth century as someone who does not have to be considered a man.

23. The heritage of captivity narratives sheds some light on why the English in India responded to the mutiny of 1857 with tales of rape when there was little evidence of sexual violence. English readiness to characterize a native insurrection against the colonial government as involving the rape and massacre of innocents can be attributed to a tradition of representing English colonialism, not as aggression on the Europeans' part, but as a situation where the native population threatened the lives and virtues of English women and children, putting Englishness itself at risk. This narrative tradition clearly gathered strength after eighteenth-century fiction had turned the threat to the English captive into a sexual threat.

24. Mary Rowlandson was captured by Algonquins. Her master was a Narragansett and the squaw with whom Rowlandson lived was a Pocasset. The narrative, however, does not distinguish among the Algonquins but lumps them together as Indians. In recent years, scholars have tried to avoid this generic category. We have retained it in order to remain faithful to Rowlandson's practice. We refer to her captors as she does, as belonging to a single nation rather than to different tribes. It should be noted that the important difference for her was not racial (red versus white) but national (Indian versus English). For a discussion of this point, see Robert F. Berkhofer, Jr., *The White Man's Indian: Images of the American Indian from Columbus to the Present* (New York: Knopf, 1978), pp. 3–25, and Francis Jennings, *The Ambiguous Iroquois Empire: The Covenant Chain Confederation of Indian Tribes with English Colonies from Its Beginnings to the Lancaster Treaty of 1744* (New York: W. W. Norton, 1984), p. 5.

25. Captivity accounts by Hannah Swarton, Hanna Dustan, Elizabeth Hanson, John Williams, and John Gyles are among those which set the English off against

the Indians, French, and Catholics. After being a slave to two successive Indian masters, Gyles was apparently sold to a French master. His narrative frequently notes differences between the English and the Indians, the English and the "Papists," and the English and the French. When his French mistress hears an English force is likely to attack her region, she asks Gyles not to reveal where valuables are hidden. "Madam," he replies, "it is contrary to the nature of the English to requite evil for good. I shall endeavor to serve you and your interest." "Memoirs of Odd Adventures, Strange Deliverances, etc. in the Captivity of John Gyles," in *Puritans among the Indians: Accounts of Captivity and Redemption, 1676–1724*, ed. Alden T. Vaugh and Edward W. Clark (Cambridge: Harvard University Press, 1981), p. 129. A comment by Williams indicates the degree to which he assumed that retaining one's Englishness during captivity depended on retaining the language: "We have reason to bless God who has wrought deliverance for so many, and yet to pray to God for a door of escape to be opened for the great number yet behind, not much short of an hundred, many of which are children, and of these not a few among the savages and having lost the English tongue, will be lost and turn savages in a little time." "The Redeemed Captive Returning to Zion," in *Puritans among the Indians*, p. 225. On second-generation captivity narratives see Roy Harvey Pearce, "The Significances of the Captivity Narrative," *American Literature* 19 (1949): 1–20 and Tara Fitzpatrick, "The Figure of Captivity," 1–26.

26. The power that traditionally accrued to English colonial discourse when it seemed to issue from the body of a victim is discussed in "Introduction: Representing Violence; or, 'How the West Was Won,' " in *The Violence of Representation: Literature and the History of Violence*, ed. Nancy Armstrong and Leonard Tennenhouse (New York: Routledge, 1989), pp. 1–26.

27. "A Narrative of the Captivity and Restauration of Mrs. Mary Rowlandson," in *So Dreadfull a Judgement: Puritan Responses to King Philip's War, 1676–1677*, ed. Richard Slotkin and James K. Folsom (Middletown: Wesleyan University Press, 1978), p. 335.

28. "A Narrative of Hannah Swarton Containing Wonderful Passages Relating to Her Captivity and Deliverance," in *Puritans among the Indians*, p. 154.

29. This European practice of seeing non-European landscapes as blank was not confined to the Americas. According to J. M. Coetzee, from 1652 to the end of the eighteenth century, European writers frequently found the South African landscape illegible. They did not regard the Hottentots as having any culture, because their way of life lacked European features much as the landscape did. "Idleness in South Africa," in *Violence of Representation*, pp. 119–39.

30. In *The Lay of the Land* (Chapel Hill: University of North Carolina Press, 1975), Annette Kolodny describes the relationship of English subjects to the North American landscape in terms that exactly invert the way gender actually operates in the captivity narratives we have been discussing. Indeed, one might even understand the puritan captivity narrative as rewriting the lush pastoralism that first attracted earlier settlers to Virginia. Where that landscape was represented as a fecund female nature that could be captured and improved by a contrastingly masculine European culture, the New England landscape that Rowlandson describes is either inert and lifeless or else seething with demonic mas-

culinity. When the colonial subject is female, by implication colonial control of such a landscape has to be imagined in terms of labor and domestication rather than capture and rape.

31. Precisely the sort of narrative that bases national identity on a print vernacular rather than on a sacred text would distinguish the New World nation from its Old World counterpart. Benedict Anderson suggests that the difference between the Christian nation and the modern nation is a matter of what one would die for. The newer idea of the nation "is always conceived as a deep horizontal comradeship." *Imagined Communities,* p. 16.

32. In his extensive study, *American Puritanism and the Defense of Mourning: Religion, Grief, and Ethnology in Mary Rowlandson's Captivity Narrative* (Madison: University of Wisconsin Press, 1990), Mitchell Robert Breitwieser argues that Rowlandson's work is realistic because it "is an account of experience that breaks through or outdistances her own and her culture's dominant means of representation, and because it is itself a continuation of that breakthrough rather than a fully composed and tranquilized recollection" (10). By reading Rowlandson as a modern subject, Breitwieser inadvertently supports our contention that Rowlandson's style of narration exceeds the historical limitations of her time because it provided the basis for the English novel and thus for later styles of psychological realism.

33. In a paper entitled "Red, Black, and Female: Constituting the American Subject," presented at the University of California Humanities Institute Research Seminar on Poststructuralism and History (1990), Carroll Smith-Rosenberg argues that the masculine representation of imperialism, in which America is a supine woman, changed decisively in the nineteenth century to one in which America is a captive woman. We wish to thank her for sharing that manuscript with us.

34. David Hall notes that in seventeenth-century New England the word *illiterate* signified an ignorance of Latin: "By this standard, all but a mere handful of the colonists were illiterate. Yet, though ordinary people were excluded from the world of Latin, they were comfortably acquainted with the language of their Bibles. To be sure, many wrote with difficulty, or not at all. But when defined as the skill of reading English, literacy was almost universal." *World of Wonder, Days of Judgment: Popular Religious Belief in Early New England* (Cambridge: Harvard University Press, 1990), p. 32. E. Jennifer Monaghan argues that a substantial percentage of women in Colonial America could read but could not sign their names, in "Literacy Instruction and Gender in Colonial New England," in *Reading in America: Literature and Social History,* ed. Cathy N. Davidson (Baltimore: Johns Hopkins University Press, 1989), pp. 53–80. Margaret Spufford has made a similar argument with regard to England, in *Small Books and Pleasant Histories: Popular Fiction and Its Readership in Seventeenth-Century England* (Cambridge: Cambridge University Press, 1981), pp. 22–35.

35. Elizabeth Hanson, "God's Mercy Surmounting Man's Cruelty," in *Puritans among the Indians,* p. 237.

36. Ellen Lansky first called this resemblance to our attention. We are very much in her debt for this insight.

37. Quoted in Derounian, "Rowlandson's Indian Captivity Narrative in the Seventeenth Century," p. 244.

38. Quoted in ibid., p. 249.

39. In *Shamela*, one of the many lessons Oliver draws from *Pamela* is: "All Chambermaids are strictly enjoyned to look out after their Masters; they are taught to use little Arts to that purpose: And lastly, are countenanced in Impertinence to their Superiors, and in betraying the Secrets of Families." Henry Fielding, *Joseph Andrews, with Shamela and Related Writings*, ed. Homer Goldberg (New York: W. W. Norton, 1987), p. 305. In *The Rise of the Novel: Studies in Defoe, Richardson and Fielding* (Berkeley: University of California Press, 1957), p. 270, Ian Watt discusses Fielding's conservative view—his belief in a "class fixity"—as the basis for a fundamental difference between Richardson's novels and those by Fielding.

40. In *Regeneration through Violence: The Mythology of the American Frontier, 1600–1860* (Middletown: Wesleyan University Press, 1973) Richard Slotkin makes the important observation that "whereas early emigration and Indian war tracts portrayed English colonization metaphorically as Exodus—the journey of Israel from a fallen Egypt to the Promised Land—the captivity narratives portrayed it as a figurative Babylonian captivity, an exile from a lost, conquered, and debased promised land of England" (93). We would simply add that the promised "return" is an essential feature of the biblical prophecies that were directed at the faithful who were carried off into captivity in Egypt, Assyria, or Babylon. See, for example, Amos 9:13–15, Isaiah 10:20–23, and Jeremiah 23:1–6.

41. In "The Figure of Captivity," Fitzpatrick compares Rowlandson's account with the later narrative of John Williams. She notes that where "the atomizing tendencies of the woman's narratives had challenged the theological unity, now a man's narrative would recreate that unity on political and increasingly rationalistic grounds" (18–19). She notes further how "striking [it is] that women were among the leading creators of a mythology that has since had so resonantly masculine a voice" (20). The operations of gender in this narrative cease to cause bewilderment, however, as Armstrong has argued in *Desire and Domestic Fiction*, pp. 1–27, once one is willing to entertain the possibility that the modern subject was not only first and foremost a writing subject but also a woman who could claim no political power save that of literacy alone. Our comparison of Rowlandson with Richardson argues that this was the case in England as well as in North America. Both of these narratives use the woman to dramatize the rise to hegemony of writing over speech.

42. Breitwieser has discussed Rowlandson's inability to reintegrate with the community upon her return as her inability to complete the mourning process. *American Puritanism*, pp. 119–29.

43. Slotkin notes that the popularity of captivity narratives peaked between 1680 and 1716, and that between 1680 and 1720 three out of the four bestsellers in America were captivity narratives (the fourth was *The Pilgrim's Progress*). And, he writes, "even after 1720 the tales of captivity continued to be popular, although they shared the market with other types of narrative; and the first tentative American efforts at short fiction and the 'first American novel' (Brown's *Edgar Huntly*) were very much in the vein of captivity narratives." *Regeneration through Violence*, pp. 95–96.

44. In discussing Richardson's influence on nineteenth-century American fic-

tion and on the reform movement, Smith-Rosenberg notes: "Indeed, the family does not transform Pamela; instead Pamela, as the upwardly mobile individual, transforms the family, making both her parents' family and Mr. B's family middle class. . . . Just as Pamela never goes home again to her parents' poor cottage, a person, transformed into an individual by the new commercial economy, could no longer return to the family—unless she transforms it in turn." "Misprisoning *Pamela*," p. 22.

45. Renato Rosaldo, "Imperialist Nostalgia," in *Culture and Truth: The Remaking of Social Analysis* (Boston: Beacon Press, 1989), pp. 68–87.

46. We are drawing here on Homer Obed Brown's forthcoming book, *Institutions of the English Novel* (Oxford University Press). We thank him for allowing us to read the chapter on the process by which nineteenth-century writers created a place in the canon for Defoe.

47. We were encouraged to pursue our present course of argument by Cathy N. Davidson's statement, "Everyone knows that the first American fiction imitated earlier British originals, but we are not so sure just what that means. Did 'the American novel' imitate 'the British novel' (phrases which assume each national product was monolithic and the influence equally so)? Or did Charles Brockden Brown imitate William Godwin? . . . Yet Godwin in his 1817 Preface to Mandeville acknowledged his debt to Brown, and Brown was also credited with influencing Godwin's daughter, Mary, and her husband, Percy Bysshe Shelley." *Revolution and the Word: The Rise of the Novel in America* (New York: Oxford University Press, 1986), p. 10. However, Davidson focuses on how American writers used the conventions of the English novel as "a political and cultural forum"; she does not ask how conventions of the American novel might have been used by English authors as a political and cultural forum back in England.

48. In *The Development of American Romance: The Sacrifice of Relation* (Chicago: University of Chicago Press, 1980), Michael Davitt Bell encapsulates the dominant view: "The story of British influence on American fiction is fascinating and important, but it is not the whole story. What seems even more fascinating—to me, as . . . to many others—is the story of how British models were transformed, transmuted, or regenerated by American conditions" (4). Jay Fliegelman, *Prodigals and Pilgrims: The American Revolution against Patriarchal Authority, 1750-1800* (Cambridge: Cambridge University Press, 1982), makes a singular effort to bring the captivity narrative to bear on a discussion of the American novel (140–48). In doing so, however, he does not challenge the prevailing belief that the English novel was the literary prototype of the American novel.

Index

Affective individualism, 76
AIDS discourse, 90
American colonies: aristocratic culture promised by, 43–44; distinguished from Old World, 204, 208, 209, 210–12; English culture transformed in, 197, 198–99, 214–16, 268nn.47–48; Old World's link with, 11–12, 20–21, 25, 26, 142, 144, 196, 197, 220n.24; print capitalism, role of in, 21, 22, 24, 142, 145–48, 161–62
American exceptionalism, 197, 260n.3
American landscape, 170–71, 206–7
American literature, 11, 215–16, 220n.22, 268nn.47,48. *See also* Captivity narratives; Fiction
American Renaissance, 11
The Anarchy of a Limited or Mixed Monarchy (Filmer), 168–69
Anderson, Benedict, 20–21, 22, 24, 141–48, 161–62, 163, 196–97, 214, 251n.13
Annaliste historiography, 150–54, 251n.16
Areopagitica (Milton), 66
Ariès, Philippe, 151
Aristocracy, 92, 93, 165–70, 212. *See also* Body: aristocratic
Aristocratic culture, 19, 38, 39–41, 66–67, 91–109 passim, 114–15, 116, 117, 145, 146, 158–59, 164, 165, 200, 210, 213, 215, 241n.36, 267n.39
Armstrong, Nancy, 202
Arnold, Matthew, 157

Artisans, 77, 95–98, 238n.15, 238–39n.16
The author: 1, 2, 4–5, 7, 8, 17, 21–22, 29, 34–35, 36–38, 40, 65, 110–11, 113, 215, 216; Ralph Josselin as, 179; John Milton as, 12, 13, 15, 29–32, 36–37, 47, 113; as mythology, 14–15, 16; Samuel Richardson as, 194–95

Bahro, Rudolf, 137–38, 248–49n.33
Bakhtin, Mikhail, 93
Barthes, Roland, 10, 11–12, 13–14, 27, 56, 57, 86
Baudrillard, Jean, 194
Bauman, Zygmunt, 119–20
Bennington, Geoff, 6–7
Bentham, Jeremy, 192
Bloom, Harold, 33, 34, 222n.12
Boccaccio, Giovanni, 91–92
Body: aristocratic, 92, 93, 99, 107, 109, 171, 178; in captivity narratives, 199–200, 204, 206, 261n.7, 262n.11; individuated, 152, 180, 181–82, 183, 207; laboring, 171; mass, 91–92, 93, 94–95, 105, 107; modern, 45; self-replicating, 177–78
Bourgeoisie. *See* Middle class
Buckingham Presenting the Liberal Arts to Charles and Henrietta (Honthorst), 100
Bunyan, John, 11
"Bureaucratic rivalry," 137–38, 248–49n.33
Bush, Douglas, 27–28, 31, 222nn.3–4

Compositor:	Impressions, A Division of Edwards Brothers, Inc.
Text:	10 / 13 Sabon
Display:	Sabon
Printer:	Maple-Vail Book Mfg. Group
Binder:	Maple-Vail Book Mfg. Group